The Politics of Prohibition

American Governance and the Prohibition Party, 1869–1933

This book introduces the intrepid temperance advocates who formed America's longest-living minor political party – the Prohibition Party – drawing on the party's history to illuminate how American politics came to exclude minor parties from governance. Lisa M. F. Andersen traces the influence of pressure groups and ballot reforms, arguing that these innovations created a threshold for organization and maintenance that required extraordinary financial and personal resources from parties already lacking in both. More than most other minor parties, the Prohibition Party resisted an encroaching Democratic-Republican stranglehold over governance. When Prohibitionists found themselves excluded from elections, they devised a variety of tactics: they occupied saloons, pressed lawsuits, forged utopian communities, and organized dry consumers.

Lisa M. F. Andersen is Assistant Professor of History and Liberal Arts at The Juilliard School in New York.

The Politics of Prohibition

American Governance and the Prohibition Party, 1869–1933

LISA M. F. ANDERSEN

The Juilliard School, New York

CAMBRIDGE
UNIVERSITY PRESS

CAMBRIDGE
UNIVERSITY PRESS

32 Avenue of the Americas, New York NY 10013-2473, USA

Cambridge University Press is part of the University of Cambridge.

It furthers the University's mission by disseminating knowledge in the pursuit of
education, learning and research at the highest international levels of excellence.

www.cambridge.org
Information on this title: www.cambridge.org/9781316615928

© Lisa M. F. Andersen 2013

First published 2013
First paperback edition 2016

A catalogue record for this publication is available from the British Library

Library of Congress Cataloguing in Publication data
Andersen, Lisa M. F.
The politics of prohibition : American governance and the Prohibition Party, 1869–1933 /
Lisa M. F. Andersen, The Juilliard School, New York.
pages cm
Includes bibliographical references and index.
ISBN 978-1-107-02937-8 (hardback)
1. Prohibition Party (U.S.) – History.   2. Prohibitionists – United States.   3. Prohibition –
United States.   4. United States – Politics and government – 1865–1933.   I. Title.
JK2382.A53   2014
324.2732–dc23   2013009964

ISBN 978-1-107-02937-8 Hardback
ISBN 978-1-316-61592-8 Paperback

To my parents,
for making it possible.
To my husband,
for making it bearable.

Contents

Acknowledgments

Books first begin as conversations. I would therefore like to thank the many mentors and friends who talked and debated with me during graduate school at the University of Chicago, where this book began as a dissertation. Kathleen Conzen and Neil Harris never let me leave a meeting without a clearer understanding of what problems had emerged and what to try next. James Sparrow pointed me in the right direction when my sources called for deeper political analysis, especially regarding political institutions. Amy Dru Stanley, my advisor, provided nuanced and insightful feedback and taught me how to ask better questions, abandon unproductive pathways, and engage texts thoughtfully.

For serious critiques mixed with wine and cheese, I would like to thank everyone in the University of Chicago's Social History workshop. Extra thanks to Moira Hinderer, Grant Masden, and Matt Millikan, who read drafts of multiple chapters. Joanna Grisinger added legal thinking to the mix, Aaron Shkuda commiserated, and John Deak reminded me that the United States is not always an exception. Emily Brunner, Tracy Steffes, and Matthew Perry gave substantial recommendations regarding the book's organization. To those three, I offer thanks tinged with apologies for such large infringements on their time.

How could anyone who serves in a Liberal Arts department located within a performing arts institution resist interdisciplinary approaches? For inspiring ideas and chocolate I would like to thank my colleagues: Mitchell Aboulafia, Renée Baron, Greta Berman, Aaron Jaffe, Anthony Lioi, Michael Maione, Anita Mercier, Roger Oliver, Ron Price, Gonzalo Sanchez, Jo Sarzotti, and Harold Slamovitz. Columbia graduate student George Aumoithe did meticulous work as a summer research assistant.

When studying a minor party, one of the great concerns is that archival collections might be eliminated to make more room for victorious groups. I therefore toast the following institutions for their helpful staffs, for their extraordinary collections, and in several cases, for the financial support that permitted me to visit. Thanks to the Brooklyn Historical Society, Center for Research Libraries, Detroit Public Library, Kansas Historical Society, Minnesota Historical Society, National Archives in Washington DC, New York Historical Society, New York Public Library, New York University's Bobst Library, Ohio Historical Society, Tennessee State Library and Archives, The Juilliard School's Wallace Library, University of Michigan's Bentley Historical Library, University of Chicago's Regenstein Library, and Wisconsin Historical Society. The Juilliard School's John Erskine Faculty Prize, the University of Chicago, and the Gilder-Lehrman Institute of American History provided funding for research and writing.

As the dissertation transitioned into a book, several scholars were extremely generous with their time and advice. For reading various chapters, I would like to thank Richard Franklin Bensel, Melanie Gustafson, Mark Wahlgren Summers, and Jon Zimmerman. Even before Jack S. Blocker, Jr., graciously found time to read part of the manuscript, his own work on the Prohibition Party had already helped to demystify these partisans' intricate web of relationships and ideas. Many thanks also to those who chaired conference panels wherein my early research was presented, including William Rorabaugh, Liette Gidlow, Mark Neely, and Kip Kosek. Mr. Wood of Harriman, Tennessee's, historical society shared his love of his community and also pointed me toward some new documents. New York University's History of Education workshop gave helpful feedback on the third chapter.

Two anonymous readers for Cambridge University Press gave meticulous advice, and my editors, first Eric Crahan and then Deborah Gershenowitz, have gracefully guided this book through the publishing process. Parts of this manuscript are reprinted with permission from the *Journal of Women's History* and *Journal of Policy History.*

My parents, Kay Andersen and Don Andersen, have offered unending, patient support. My husband, Matthew Perry, has shared in every challenge and triumph. Cute photos of my children, David and Christopher, sit on my desk to remind me to work efficiently and get home. And sometimes they draw on my drafts.

Introduction

Modern Americans no doubt think of the temperance movement as a rather dry affair. And when considering the Prohibition Era, the images most easily recalled are those of colorful resistance: flappers, gangsters, moonshine, and speakeasies. However, a competing image can be found at the Brooklyn Historical Society, deep within a collection that can only be described as the jumbled contents of a Prohibitionist's desk drawer. A photo taken at a turn-of-the-century Prohibition Party picnic stands out as modern and familiar. About three dozen women and men link arms in small groups and as couples, giving open smiles to the camera. Among the younger picnickers, hats have been cast aside or put at jaunty angles, and most leave their jackets unbuttoned. Only the white temperance ribbons festively attached to sashes and lapels give clue to the issue convening this particular group. One can easily imagine these lively Prohibitionists singing a chorus of Sam Booth and George T. Evans's flirtatious melody "The Lips that Touch Liquor Will Never Touch Mine." Promises of sobriety sealed friendships and romantic relationships alike.

Another surprise is a souvenir photograph of the 1892 Prohibition Party convention held in Cincinnati's Music Hall. The photo is part of the Library of Congress collection, and it showcases the Prohibition Party's formal politics, consisting of nominations, campaigns, and voting. The convention floor is packed with nearly a thousand delegates, and spectators fill many of the balcony seats. Banners with mottos or stars and stripes cover the woodwork, demonstrating a well-organized effort. The 1892 campaign would prove the party's most successful, with more than 270,000 Americans casting ballots in favor of Californian John T. Bidwell. The Prohibition Party aspired to govern, believing that it was necessary to capture offices if it was ever to see anti-liquor laws enforced and, to this end, mimicked the major parties whenever an opportunity arose. If the Democrats became donkeys, and Republicans became elephants, the Prohibitionists insisted that they were camels. About the Illinois Prohibition Party's adoption of this mascot in 1908, one Prohibitionist noted that "the camel is the original water wagon, that it can discern a fresh supply of water further than any quadruped; that it can travel faster than an elephant or a donkey, and that it always has a hump on itself."[1] The race was on.

This book investigates the Prohibition Party – led by temperance advocates, women, and former abolitionists – and how its members harnessed moral aspirations to politics and partisan strategies during the nineteenth and early twentieth centuries. Prohibitionists' lively debates, both internal and with other civic associations, provoked new inquiries into the role of religion in politics, the process of translating vision into policy, and the most reputable reasons for founding a new party. The party's founders sought to build on antebellum Americans' proclamation that the party system would remain an indispensable unit for organizing government and that it would generally be dominated by two major parties.[2]

Yet the Prohibition Party disputed antebellum Americans' assumption that a drive for self-preservation would encourage major parties to fight for voters by capturing new issues and movements. To be sure, in the 1830s, the Anti-Masonic Party had provoked the Whigs to incorporate anti-secret society language into their party platform.[3] On the other hand, it had required the emergence of the Republican Party around the antislavery issue to make urgent policy makers' debates.[4] When Democrats and Republicans seemingly operated on a new basis after the Civil War, guarding against the introduction of new political issues that might divide their

---

[1] "Camel Prohibition Emblem," *New York Times*, 23 September 1908; Advertisement, "Convention and Campaign Souvenirs," *American Advance*, 5 October 1912.

[2] On two-partyism, see Richard L. McCormick, *The Party Period and Public Policy: American Politics from the Age of Jackson to the Progressive Era* (New York: Oxford University Press, 1986), 162–163.

[3] On the Anti-Masonic Party, see J. David Gillespie, *Politics at the Periphery: Third Parties in Two-Party America* (Columbia: University of South Carolina Press, 1993); Paul Goodman, *Towards a Christian Republic: Antimasonry and the Great Transition in New England* (New York: Oxford University Press, 1988).

[4] Morton Keller notes that "the experience of the 1860s supported the view that parties were ephemeral things, rising and falling with the causes that gave them meaning"; *Affairs of State: Public Life in Late Nineteenth Century America* (Cambridge, MA: The Belknap Press of Harvard University Press, 1977), 276.

ranks, Prohibitionists saw an opportunity to become the "new Republicans." They saw in their failure to gain traction a sign that the rules of the game had changed, threatening minor parties' role as a site for building and organizing new constituencies. Prohibitionists feared that they and other minor parties were being relegated to mere protest groups – a fear that was not unfounded.

The Politics of Prohibition has been shaped by scholars' focus on the elected politicians and high-profile political reformers who sought to change the party system, and hence to reconfigure citizens' part in American democracy.[5] Reformers exposed how party bosses and "the interests" abused their power and corrupted parties, and they urged government intervention in a wider array of public issues. Their greatest accomplishments included the secret ballot, the creation of pressure groups, new laws regulating nominating conventions, and the administrative state. Reformers provided democratic leaven to party politics by modifying parties' internal procedures, promoting party realignment, engaging in independent voting, and, at the same time, creating alternative political organizations. They weakened the party system's prestige and, arguably, its power.[6] Still, there were limits to their success that historians have

[5] Much of the best research on how political institutions changed has emerged from the new political history and from American political development, two schools that have brought historians and political scientists into closer dialogue. On changes in political institutions, including political parties, pressure groups, and the administrative state, see Samuel P. Hays, "Political Parties and the Community-Society Continuum," in *The American Party Systems: Stages of Political Development*, ed. William Nisbet Chambers and Walter Dean Burnham, rev. ed. (1967; repr. New York: Oxford University Press, 1975), 152–181; V. O. Key Jr., *Politics, Parties, and Pressure Groups* (New York: Thomas Y. Crowell Company, 1942); Peter H. Argersinger, *Structure, Process, and Party: Essays in American Political History* (Armonk, NY: M.E. Sharpe, 1992); Keller, *Affairs of State*; Morton Keller, *Regulating a New Society: Public Policy and Social Change in America, 1900–1933* (Cambridge, MA: Harvard University Press, 1994); Paul Kleppner, *Continuity and Change in Electoral Politics, 1893–1928* (New York: Greenwood Press, 1987); McCormick, *Party Period;* Sidney M. Milkis, *Political Parties and Constitutional Government: Remaking American Politics* (Baltimore: Johns Hopkins University Press, 1999); Steven Skrowneck, *Building a New American State: The Expansion of National Administrative Capacities, 1877–1920* (New York: Cambridge University Press, 1992); James Sundquist, *Dynamics of the Party System*, rev. ed. (1973; repr. Washington, DC: The Brookings Institution, 1983); Theda Skocpol, *Diminished Democracy: From Membership to Management in American Civic Life* (Norman: University of Oklahoma Press, 2003).

[6] An extensive historiography foregrounds the relationship between political leaders – both professional politicians and influential reformers – and political institutions. On the influence of national party leaders, see Scott C. James, *Presidents, Parties, and the State: A Party System Perspective on Democratic Regulatory Choice, 1884–1936*

underexplored, and by taking a marginalized group of voters as its subject, this book investigates these limits. Most significantly, there is the question of how much and in what ways Democrats' and Republicans' dominance over party politics constrained the capacity of other reforms to disperse political power and ensure representative government.

The chapters that follow trace how the control of the party system by Democrats and Republicans came to be, the development of Prohibitionists' objections to this system, and the diverse responses that Prohibitionists' outcry provoked from other citizens. The starting point is a description of Prohibitionists' convictions, including an investigation of the ideas that distinguished them from other Americans who wrote and spoke about the anti-liquor movement and the party system. Chapter 1 examines antebellum drinking habits and the Prohibition Party's roots in a small but growing temperance movement. Chapter 2 analyzes the sources of Prohibitionists' dissatisfaction with the Republican Party and disgust with the Democrats and considers why reformers were often critical of Prohibitionists' goals. Chapter 3 explores why the Prohibition Party welcomed women – who remained ineligible to vote – and the ways in which women's participation opened Prohibitionists to new understandings of partisanship.

The next section explores Prohibitionists' ideas and experiences in the context of the party system's declining prestige and the reforms meant to purify it. Chapter 4 investigates the violent public response that ensued when Prohibitionists received enough votes to assure the election of a candidate unsupported by a majority of voters. Chapter 5 considers the dramatic political experiment engaged by the Prohibitionist families who built partisan cities in the 1890s. It also explores how utopian city-building shaped party leaders' responses to a new threat: state ballot laws

---

(New York: Cambridge University Press, 2000). On lawyers, corporate actors, professional politicians, and party bosses, see Keller, *Affairs of State*. Gilded Age Mugwumps were generally less successful at purging corruption and installing "good government" than Progressive Era reformers, but their work set a precedent. On Gilded Age reformers, see John G. Sproat, *"The Best Men": Liberal Reformers in the Gilded Age*, rev. ed. (1968; repr. Chicago: University of Chicago Press, 1982); Nancy Cohen, *The Reconstruction of American Liberalism, 1865–1925* (Chapel Hill: University of North Carolina Press, 2002); Michael Schudson, *The Good Citizen: A History of American Civic Life* (New York: The Free Press, 1998). On Progressive Era reformers, see Richard Hofstadter, *The Age of Reform: From Bryan to F.D.R.* (New York: Vintage Books, 1955); Robert Wiebe, *The Search for Order, 1877–1920* (New York: Hill and Wang, 1967); Richard L. McCormick, "The Discovery That Business Corrupts Politics: A Reappraisal of the Origins of Progressivism," *American Historical Review*, 86:2 (April 1981): 247–274.

that tended to disqualify minor parties from elections. Chapter 6 investigates how Prohibitionists reacted to the new political ideal of strenuousness by advocating personal health, manhood, and partisan community.

The final chapter concludes the Prohibition Party's story by depicting partisans' debate with reformers, pressure groups, and anti-prohibitionists about the relative value of nineteenth-century governance through
courts and parties and twentieth-century forms of governance that prioritized professional and centralized leadership. The party's work culminated in a dramatic gesture: the refusal of formal party leadership to
endorse the campaign for a national prohibition amendment.

This book is about minor parties' struggles, the ascendency of a Democratic-Republican stranglehold over party politics, and an ensuing transformation in the meaning of American mass democracy. The Prohibition
Party's attempts to preserve itself and remain politically relevant provoked indignant, violent, and eventually dismissive responses from other
politicians and reformers. By the twentieth century, many Americans had
willingly accommodated to the idea of a Democratic-Republican political duopoly and criticized Prohibitionists' attempts to envision a form of
politics that transcended customary understandings of partisanship and
reached into the world of everyday relations. To Prohibitionists' critics,
gestures such as celebrating women leaders, engaging in direct action
protests, pressing lawsuits, building utopian societies, and organizing
consumers were dangerously deviant and potentially undemocratic. Even
Prohibitionists generally viewed these experiments as short-term solutions. Only because electoral participation was a disappearing option did
they blur distinctions between social and political activism and boundaries between social and political movements. Left with few other means
to attract attention and preserve their constituency, they would continually seek to revitalize their sense of partisan community through oratorical contests, rallies, and picnics like that featured in the Brooklyn
photograph.

Prohibitionists' fears about the implications of Democratic and Republican dominance over the party system failed to rouse many of their fellow
Americans to action; most voters continued to vote for the same parties
that they had supported for decades and therefore did not sense a loss in
their political agency when minor parties struggled. Americans widely dismissed Prohibitionists' anxieties as irrelevant even if true, instead focusing
on how to advance their interests through the established political order.
And perhaps most importantly, they concluded that a fixed two-party system possessed the immeasurable advantage of producing election results

that registered majority consensus rather than the confusing diversity of public opinion. They kept the donkey and the elephant while exiling the camel, leaving it to bleat protests to a dwindling audience. Ultimately, this is the story of how Americans came to embrace the idea of an adequate democracy – functional and steady, if not necessarily pure or ambitious.

PART I

BUILDING A CONSTITUENCY

I

Temperance, Prohibition, and a Party

Drinking liquor was the antebellum status quo, a practice so pervasive that there was little need to defend it. Taverns served as community centers, surplus rye and apples would rot if not distilled or fermented, and besides, Americans enjoyed imbibing. However, from the 1810s onward there flourished a growing temperance movement – that is, a movement encouraging people to limit the quantity and type of liquor they consumed. This movement nagged that the nation's alcohol consumption levels had crossed the threshold of acceptability. Newspapers highlighted incidents wherein drinkers beat their spouses and children, had fatal accidents at work, fell into poverty, and committed crimes. Gossip and fiction gave special emphasis to the specter of urban overindulgence. Tapping into widespread anxiety about the nation's developing market economy, temperance advocates imagined the fates of young migrant workers who drifted away from the surveillance of families, ministers, and neighbors. Lonely and lost in cities, how many youths would find the comforting lure of drink too tempting to resist? At the same time, some of the ambitious farmers and manufacturers who embraced the market economy's promise came to support temperance as an expression of their faith in self-improvement.[1] More and more

---

[1] On the early temperance movement and its connection to a growing market economy, see Joseph R. Gusfield, *Symbolic Crusade: Status Politics and the American Temperance Movement* (Urbana: University of Illinois Press, 1963); Norman H. Clark, *Deliver Us From Evil: An Interpretation of American Prohibition* (New York: W.W. Norton & Co., 1976; William J. Rorabaugh, *The Alcoholic Republic: An American Tradition* (New York: Oxford University Press, 1979); Ian Tyrrell, *Sobering Up: From Temperance to Prohibition in Antebellum America, 1800–1860* (Westport, CT: Greenwood Press, 1979).

people came to argue that liquor consumption was disrespectable and dangerous.

Temperance advocates' calculation of the scale of liquor consumption could be and often was overstated, but also had some foundation in fact. By modern standards nineteenth-century Americans drank copious amounts. In 1830 adult Americans drank somewhere between 4 and 7 gallons of pure alcohol per year as compared to modern Americans' 2.8 gallons per year.[2] Lest the implications of high consumption levels seem abstract, the Washingtonian temperance society encouraged newly sober individuals to share their tragic lives in confessional "experience speeches" throughout the 1840s. One can well imagine the impression made by a former drinker who, as remembered by one witness, "stated that for years he had loafed around the markets and wharves without any regular means of subsistence, sleeping in the markets and on the sidewalks, almost without clothes, or friends, and that all he sought for was rum."[3] Temperance advocates throughout the 1840s and 1850s sought to amplify the effects of *moral suasion* – the use of personal appeals to encourage individuals to refrain from drink – with regulations upon sales to children, Sunday tavern closings, and restrictive liquor licensing. At its most aggressive, the temperance movement secured prohibition laws in thirteen states and territories.

Reflecting upon their history, many Prohibition Party founders would recall how events surrounding the Civil War sealed their disenchantment with moral suasion's limitations. Northern reformers, in particular, were horrified by how war had exacerbated soldiers' drinking habits. No amount of distributing temperance pamphlets, offering lectures, or sponsoring ministers could undo the impression that alcohol consumption was legitimate escapism when the Union government was financing war with a liquor tax, and even granting soldiers a liquor ration.[4] On the other hand, seeing the federal government protect fugitive slaves and

---

[2] Thomas Pegram, *Battling Demon Rum: The Struggle for a Dry America, 1800–1933* (Chicago: Ivan R. Dee, 1998), 7, 31. See also Rorabaugh, *The Alcoholic Republic*, 7–11; Tyrrell, *Sobering Up*, 4.

[3] Benjamin Estes, *Essay on the Necessity of Correcting the Errors Which Have Crept into the Washington Temperance Movement and of Its Bringing to Its Aid the Church of God* (New York: Job Printing Office, 1846), 6, in Tyrrell, *Sobering Up*, 164. See also Katherine A. Chavigny, "American Confessions: Reformed Drunkards and the Origins of Therapeutic Culture" (PhD dissertation, University of Chicago, 1999).

[4] The liquor ration was finally revoked in 1862, although sutlers (civilian merchants) and medics continued to supply the troops.

freedpeople bolstered Northern temperance advocates' faith in the government's capacity to promote radical reform if so committed. National prohibition might be achieved county by county, state by state, or all at once, but it would relentlessly bring liberation to more people. Prohibition would free "self-made slaves" who were dominated by appetites, if not the lash.[5] Agreeing that prohibition's turn in the reform spotlight had come with slavery's conclusion, significant numbers of former abolitionists infused the temperance cause with their skills and prestige.

Most male temperance advocates (including those favoring prohibition) found their postwar home in the Republican Party, which claimed to hold a monopoly upon moral ideas. A few would gain prominence in its ranks during the 1860s, and many would emerge as lesser lights by serving on committees, giving lectures, and coordinating voters on election days. Nonetheless, some prohibition supporters grew frustrated with what they perceived as Republican lethargy in the face of an unprecedented opportunity to dry up the nation. Some of them drew upon the prewar Free Soil and Liberty parties' examples to inspire new allegiances, founding the Prohibition Party in 1869. In so doing, they completed their evolution from temperance advocates into (small "p") prohibitionists into partisan Prohibitionists. The new party would embody the most zealous political tendencies of a passionate social movement. It would bring energetic moral perfectionism into the world of party politics.

* * *

The Civil War era that preceded the Prohibition Party's founding might seem like a "passive interlude" in the temperance movement's history.[6] This lull can largely be explained, however, by the fact that temperance advocates were not single-issue reformers, but rather had multiple loyalties. Typical temperance advocates identified themselves as Christians – often Methodist and sometimes Presbyterian, Congregationalist, or Baptist – who opposed prostitution, gambling, prizefighting, and

[5] Gerrit Smith quoted in "Temperance: Meeting of the National Convention," *Chicago Tribune*, 3 September 1869. The language of slavery and emancipation was used very frequently in dry discourse. On the gendered dimensions of this language, see Elaine Frantz Parsons, *Manhood Lost: Fallen Drunkards and Redeeming Women in the Nineteenth-Century United States* (Baltimore: Johns Hopkins University Press, 2003).

[6] Jack S. Blocker, Jr., *American Temperance Movements: Cycles of Reform* (Boston: Twayne Publishers, 1988), 71; Pegram, *Battling Demon Rum*, 43–45.

Sabbath violations, among other public vices.[7] In California, demands
for reforming the railroad industry sometimes moved to center stage.[8]
Under the duress of war most reformers deemed their obligations to
the Union paramount and the opportunities for advancing abolition to
be the most promising; the same community leaders who might have
organized temperance fraternities or run dry legislative campaigns were
instead coordinating support services through the United States Sanitary Commission or religious conferences. The temperance movement's
self-imposed low profile during wartime might be compared to that of
a closely related cause: the women's rights movement. Women's rights
advocates routinely restrained their activities by canceling conventions or
withholding criticism of politicians during the Civil War.[9]

The individuals who would eventually become prohibition advocates
and join the Prohibition Party would memorialize the Civil War as a
moment of stealthy awakening, one that created enough tension to fuel
the movement for decades. Army life, temperance advocates alleged, had
disengaged soldiers from the influence of women and family, which would
have otherwise offered swift discipline against excessive drinking.[10] Only
a few veterans could – as Prohibitionist John C. Pepper would do in his
postwar pension request – declare, "as to vicious habits I have none.
I did not use intoxicants in the service, or very rarely, eschewing even
quartermaster's whiskey."[11] Press reports regretfully described soldiers'
undisciplined conduct, including that of a Pennsylvanian regiment stationed in Washington, DC. The regiment would "go into a tavern, call
for a drink all round, and then in a very unceremonious manner tell the

---

[7] Jack S. Blocker, Jr., *Retreat from Reform, The Prohibition Movement in the United
States, 1890–1913* (Westport, CT: Greenwood Press, 1976), 10. The best collective
biography of early Prohibitionists is Louis E. Van Norman, ed., *An Album of Repre-
sentative Prohibitionists* (New York: Funk and Wagnalls, 1895); see also Mark Lender,
*Dictionary of American Temperance Biography: From Temperance Reform to Alcohol
Research, the 1600s to the 1880s* (Westport, CT: Greenwood Press, 1984).

[8] Gilman M. Ostrander, *The Prohibition Movement in California, 1848–1933* (Berkeley:
University of California Press, 1957), 39.

[9] Lori D. Ginzberg, *Elizabeth Cady Stanton: An American Life* (New York: Hill and Wang,
2009), 107; Ellen DuBois, *Feminism and Suffrage: The Emergence of an Independent
Women's Movement in America, 1848–1869* (Ithaca, NY: Cornell University Press,
1978), 52.

[10] Blocker, *American Temperance Movements*, 71–72. See also Clifford S. Griffin, *Their
Brothers' Keeper: Moral Stewardship in the United States, 1800–1865* (1960; repr.
Westwood, CT: Greenwood Press, 1983), 242–264.

[11] Letter from John C. Pepper to Hon. William Lochren (Commissioner of Pensions),
10 October 1894, File of John C. Pepper, Civil War and Later Pension Files, National
Archives Building, Washington, DC.

bar-tender to charge the damages to President Lincoln." "The worst of it," proclaimed a fellow soldier in the *New York Times,* was that officers could not be counted on to keep soldiers in check because they too were "frequent participants in these scenes."[12] The *German Reformed Messenger* similarly decried how "the sin of drunkenness prevails to a fearful extent in the army."[13]

Temperance advocates were particularly alarmed by the prevalence of drinking among military-aged men because they expected these individuals to emerge as postwar leaders; even though per capita drinking did not rise tremendously between 1850 and 1865, temperance advocates channeled their disquiet into the matter of who was doing this drinking. In other words, this was not merely a middle-class attempt to control the working class but also an endeavor to save "our boys."[14] During the war, temperance advocates worried that "when the soldiers leave the service, come to the rear, and to their homes," they would be unfit for public and family life.[15] And after the war, temperance advocates would recall that men who were "flushed with victory, and flushed with the newly-formed drinking habit" were indeed granted "the public offices of trust, honor, and profit in the nation they had saved."[16] Institutions that might have been used to hold back the liquor traffic would be placed in the hands of its newest recruits.

Characterizing the liquor industry as intensely predatory, temperance advocates argued that it had exploited wartime anxieties to create a market among frightened young men who had supposedly shown little previous interest in its products. For temperance advocates, the most persuasive evidence of malicious intent lay in how the liquor industry created its first national professional organizations during wartime. In 1862 the United States Brewers Association (USBA) organized German immigrants and a few native-born American brewers situated mostly in Eastern states.

[12] Frederick Robinson, Letter to the editor, "Discipline Among Soldiers," *New York Times,* 27 September 1861.

[13] "Drunkenness in the Army," *(Chambersburg, PA), German Reformed Messenger,* 5 October 1864.

[14] On drinking rates, see Blocker, *American Temperance Movements,* 65. On "our boys" rhetoric, see Gaines M. Foster, *Moral Reconstruction: Christian Lobbyists and the Federal Legislation of Morality, 1865–1920* (Chapel Hill: University of North Carolina Press, 2002), 4.

[15] J.W. Alvord, "Temperance," *(Boston) Zion's Herald and Wesleyan Journal,* 15 February 1865. See also "Selected," *(New York) Christian Advocate and Journal,* 29 August 1861. *Zion's Herald* and the *Christian Advocate* were Methodist publications.

[16] G.H. Jasper, "Temperance in New Hampshire," *Zion's Herald,* 3 August 1876.

The organization's purpose was to support expanded markets and to check the tide of prohibitive legislation.[17] Both the National Temperance Convention, a group consisting of members from many temperance fraternities and associations, and the International Order of Good Templars (IOGT) would later cite the USBA's founding as a catalyst for their increased willingness to explore political activism and eventually make calls for a new anti-liquor party.[18] They would conclude that "while the nation was bowed in sorrow, bathed in tears and steeped in blood," the liquor industry had "planned and plotted for the development of their destroying, debauching and dehumanizing traffic, and entered into partnership with the government to pay a good part of its infernal revenue as internal revenue to the United States treasury."[19]

The Internal Revenue Act of 1862 institutionalized the liquor traffic's "partnership with the government" in a way that worried prohibition advocates more than any other previous dealings because tax revenues might disincentivize liquor traffic regulation.[20] The *Minnesota Radical*, an early and influential Prohibition Party newspaper, would melodramatically recall that the government had "become partners in the infamous business of drunkard making by receiving into the public treasury a portion of the blood money drawn from the pockets of the deluded and insane victims of the accursed traffic."[21] The Internal Revenue Act also lent legitimacy to the trade by exploiting the historical connections between morality and democratic governance; the process of licensing the sale of liquor not only affirmed its legality but lent it the tacit endorsement of the federal government. Those who would later become Prohibition Party members recalled their concern that the federal government was "taxing and thereby sanctioning vice."[22]

---

[17] Amy Mittelman, *Brewing Battles: A History of American Beer* (New York: Algora Publishing, 2008), 28–45. Ad hoc associations had emerged in the 1840s, and there were a few professional and protective organizations in the 1850s. However, the USBA was distinguished by the fact that its efforts were national rather than subject to local conditions. See Kyle Volk, *Moral Minorities and the Making of American Democracy* (forthcoming from Oxford University Press).

[18] D. Leigh Colvin, *Prohibition in the United States: A History of the Prohibition Party and of the Prohibition Movement* (New York: George H. Doran Company, 1926), 62–63.

[19] "Why a Prohibition Party?" *(Chicago) Lever*, 3 February 1898.

[20] The Prohibition Party, *A Condensed History of the Prohibition Party: The 75 Year Struggle for National Prohibition* (Chicago: The National Prohibitionist, 1944?), 1.

[21] "War is Inevitable – Politically," *(Waseca) Minnesota Radical*, 25 April 1877.

[22] G.H. Carrow, "*Do Not Take Temperance into Politics!*" (N.p.: n.p., 1879), 73. See also C.H. Payne, "Shall We Frame Iniquity into a Law by Taxation?" *(Chicago) National Freeman*, May 1881.

Liquor taxes would provide between one-half and two-thirds of federal internal revenue during the next half century.[23] These taxes would make possible the massive expansion in federal government that historians and political scientists widely refer to as *state building*. Prohibitionists were certainly alarmed by the particular source of this revenue, but they also contributed to the impulse to make this war measure into a permanent tax when they demanded the kind of new laws and law enforcement that would make necessary greater government capacity. Complementing the work of lobbying groups such as farmers who wanted agricultural assistance and transportation subsidies, lobbyists for moral causes encouraged the federal government to take on greater regulatory responsibilities and to expand its bureaucratic reach in the process.[24] Never before had such ambitions seemed so desirable or possible. To many burgeoning prohibitionists, moral suasion seemed like a feeble, fading alternative to the vital promise of outlawing alcohol altogether.

However, it would be incorrect to interpret the growing momentum in favor of prohibition as evidence that moral suasion strategies were extinct. Indeed, some temperance advocates continued to exclusively promote moral suasion for religious reasons. They proposed that pamphlet distribution, religious tracts, and ministerial visits targeting the drinking population would avoid the problem of coercing individuals into acting morally and hence denying them the choices that catalyzed a freewill movement toward religious salvation.[25] Only people who confronted the temptation to live an evil life could pursue the salvation granted to those who chose to live well; people who lacked self-determination when they performed good acts moved no closer to God because such acts were not the result of an authentic commitment to God's grace.

Prohibitionists were in no way opposed to what they called *personal work* by temperance evangelists and indeed hoped that such tactics could head off drunkenness among at-risk individuals. Prohibitionists were also generally churchgoers, members of moral suasion organizations, and

---

[23] Blocker, *American Temperance Movements*, 66.

[24] On farmers, see Elizabeth Sanders, *Roots of Reform: Farmers, Workers, and the American State, 1877–1917* (Chicago: University of Chicago Press, 1999). On lobbyists, see Foster, *Moral Reconstruction*; Pegram, *Battling Demon Rum*, xii–xiii; Morton Keller, *Affairs of State*.

[25] This was especially key in Catholic theology. See Tyrrell, *Sobering Up*, 299–300. For the persistence of this argument into the 1880s, see R.S. Bader, *Prohibition in Kansas: A History* (Lawrence: University of Kansas Press, 1986), 54. For an example of the moral suasion argument in the 1890s, see H.M. Brooks, *Common Sense, or Why the Prohibition Party Has Failed* (Paris, IL: Beacon Company, ca. 1890).

abstainers. Still, overwhelmed by the scale of the problem as they saw it, prohibition's supporters argued that drunkards were incapable of making reasoned choices unless they were first made sober. They argued that moral suasion had never been sufficient and never would be, and they sought to better convey why this was the case.[26] The key problem with alcohol as a product – a feature that distinguished its consumption from other vices such as prostitution, gambling, and prizefighting – was that it undermined individuals' abilities to understand their own best interests. Such self-knowledge was a critical precondition not only for salvation but also, many would conclude, for democratic government.

* * *

Postwar temperance advocates were divided and disorganized, but not without hope. After all, this would not be the first time they had built a movement on little more than optimism. In the 1810s and 1820s, the temperance movement had been reluctant to demand any more than that individuals self-regulate the type and quantity of liquor consumed. Temperance advocates such as Lyman Beecher and Theodore Weld had suggested that congregants avoid whiskey and other spirits and instead stick to moderate amounts of wine and beer. Few people had proposed and no organization asserted that Americans should give up alcohol entirely or that government should make the liquor industry illegal. The American Temperance Society, the most popular temperance organization of the 1830s, flooded the country with pamphlets urging relatively modest goals on individuals: Stop consuming distilled liquor, and cut all ties to liquor businesses.[27]

It was only in the 1840s that a trajectory leading to a prohibition movement emerged. *Teetotaling* – the complete abstaining from all forms of liquor, including wine, beer, and cider – emerged as the standard to which dry advocates aspired, and a new organizational form, the temperance fraternity, came to dominate the temperance landscape. More likely to include working-class and middle-class individuals than elites, temperance fraternities such as the Washingtonians, Sons of Temperance, and IOGT quickly established connections between temperance advocates around the country, although their greatest successes were always

---

[26] See, for example, James Black's advice about clarifying the limits of moral suasion in his letter to William Goodell, 2 September 1877, Box 10, Correspondence A–L, Series I: William Goodell Papers, William Goodell Family Papers, Special Collections and Archives, Hutchins Library, Berea College, hosted through the online portal of "Slavery, Abolition, and Social Justice: 1490–2007," (WGFP).

[27] Pegram, *Battling Demon Rum*, 20–23; Tyrrell, *Sobering Up*, 54–79.

in the Midwest and East. The Washingtonians had extraordinary popularity, with 200,000 pledged members in 1841 and more than 1 million two years later.[28] The Sons of Temperance attracted approximately 220,000 members by 1850, committing these members to the organization through elaborate rituals, a clublike atmosphere, and mutual life insurance policies.[29] Although the Washingtonians and Sons of Temperance relegated women to auxiliary organizations, the IOGT ranks swelled in part because they included women who brought husbands and sons to meetings.[30] Temperance fraternities acted as a leadership training ground for future Prohibition Party luminaries such as James Black, John Russell, Martha "Mattie" McClellan Brown, Amanda Way, Gideon T. Stewart, and John T. Bidwell.[31]

It therefore carried great significance when these organizations expressed an increasing preference for alcohol regulation and restriction. It seems likely that native-born Americans' anxieties about German and Irish immigrants' Sunday and public consumption made legal strategies more appealing. After all, moral suasion did not easily cross language and cultural barriers.[32] In seeking out a strategy more aggressive than moral suasion endeavors, some native-born voters joined the American (Know-Nothing) Party, which proposed to regulate the saloons and beer gardens where tenement-dwelling immigrants gathered as part of its program for curtailing immigrants' political rights.[33] Maine's Neal Dow, who ran for governor as a Whig candidate, was likely understood by contemporaries to be a Know-Nothing.[34] No-license campaigns were by far the most popular means of restricting the liquor traffic. Citizens in a

---

[28] Pegram, *Battling Demon Rum*, 27; Tyrrell, *Sobering Up*, 160.

[29] Pegram, *Battling Demon Rum*, 31.

[30] The International Order of Good Templars also included African-American members. See David M. Fahey, *Temperance and Racism: John Bull, Johnny Reb, and the Good Templars* (Lexington: University Press of Kentucky, 1996). On women's relationships to temperance lodges, see Ruth Alexander, "'We Are Engaged as a Band of Sisters': Class and Domesticity in the Washingtonian Temperance Movement, 1840–1850," *Journal of American History*, 75 (December 1988): 763–785; Jed Dannenbaum, "The Origins of Temperance Activism and Militarism among American Women," *Journal of Social History*, 15 (Winter 1981): 235–252; Tyrrell, *Sobering Up*, 179–182.

[31] For a more comprehensive list of Prohibition Party leaders with fraternal affiliations, see Anne-Marie Szymanski, *Pathways to Prohibition: Radicals, Moderates, and Social Movement Outcomes* (Durham, NC: Duke University Press, 2003), 235 n.108.

[32] For a discussion of the strengths and weaknesses of this interpretation, see Tyrrell, *Sobering Up*, 215–216 and 264–269.

[33] Christine Sismondo, *America Walks into a Bar: A Spirited History of Taverns and Saloons, Speakeasies and Grog Shops* (New York: Oxford University Press, 2011), 131–136.

[34] Sismondo, *America Walks into a Bar*, 136.

local community might demand that the government officials in charge of licensing taverns refuse to grant any licenses and hence create de facto prohibition. Enforcing a no-license policy nevertheless proved difficult not only because loophole provisions permitted alcohol to be sold for "medical purposes" but also because local governments pressured into refusing licenses often lacked the resources to prosecute offenders.

In the 1850s, state laws banning liquor sales emerged as a new strategy to improve upon the results of local efforts at moral suasion, restrictions on sales to minors, Sabbatarian laws, and saloon licensing.[35] The first state to ban the manufacture and sale of alcoholic beverages was Maine, which passed its *Maine Law* – a term henceforth synonymous with state prohibition legislation – under Governor Neal Dow in 1851. Between 1852 and 1855 twelve other states and territories enacted similar legislation: Massachusetts, Minnesota, Rhode Island, Vermont, Michigan, Connecticut, New York, Indiana, Delaware, Iowa, Nebraska, and New Hampshire.[36] This list suggests the continuing growth of the prohibition movement in the Midwest and East. In explaining the relative lack of Maine Laws in the South, some historians have suggested that the mounting sectional crisis over slavery cut short white Southern interest in reforms that could be painted as meddling Yankee agitation.[37]

The Maine Laws' influence was undermined when several state courts overturned the statutes' aggressive search provisions and when public interest in enforcement declined. Stories of lawbreaking abounded in the popular press, often presented in humorous ways to convey support for violators. However, most historians attribute the laws' ultimate failures to a decline in intraparty factionalism. In the early 1850s, factionalism within the Whig and Democratic parties had created opportunities for the introduction of new issues, but with the establishment of a new party system, one polarized around the slavery issue, there was no incentive for parties to take up the liquor issue and good reason to fear how it might divide (or re-divide) their constituencies.[38] The small temperance parties

---

[35] Tyrrell, *Sobering Up*, 225–289.

[36] Pegram, *Battling Demon Rum*, 40.

[37] Gusfield, *Symbolic Crusade*, 54. For responses to this interpretation, see Ian Tyrrell, "Drink and Temperance in the Antebellum South: An Overview and Interpretation," *Journal of Southern History*, 48: 4 (November 1982): 485–510; Douglas W. Carlson, "'Drinks He to His Own Undoing': Temperance Ideology in the Deep South," *Journal of the Early Republic*, 18 (Winter 1998): 659–691.

[38] For example, Pegram, *Battling Demon Rum*, 43–44. For theoretical analysis of factions in historical perspective, see Daniel DiSalvo, *Engines of Change: Party Factions in American Politics, 1868–2010* (New York: Oxford University Press, 2012).

that had formed in a few states and cities sputtered in and out of existence, posing little threat to major party governance.[39] Prohibitionists' sources of support evaporated. Only five states would still have Maine Laws by 1865, when the Civil War concluded.[40]

The new party system also had the perhaps unanticipated effect of moving most temperance advocates into the same party: the Republican Party.

If factionalization within the party system led by the new Republican Party (founded in 1854) and the established Democratic Party had precipitated the dissolution of Maine Laws, it also had the perhaps unanticipated effect of moving most temperance advocates into the same party: the Republican Party. The best explanation for this is not because the Republican Party advocated temperance or prohibition policies, but because more urgent political problems intervened. The Republican Party was firmly antislavery, and most temperance advocates held antislavery sympathies. Likewise, the Republican Party was pro-Union, and the most fervent temperance advocates were residents of the North. By the 1860s intervening political conditions unrelated to Americans' alcohol consumption resulted in most temperance advocates being placed in the same party – a party that had made few open promises to do anything to advance prohibitory legislation. Postwar, such a situation was likely to create new rivalries within the Republican Party. These tensions would be amplified by the Reconstruction quagmire.

* * *

Almost as soon as the Civil War was over, a series of explosive debates over critical issues illuminated disagreement among the Northern

---

[39] On these early (and often briefly lived) temperance parties, see Ostrander, *Prohibition Movement in California*, 17–20, featuring California's People's party; "Religious Summary," *Zion's Herald and Wesleyan Journal*, 8 October 1851, featuring Cincinnati; "Political Intelligence," *National Era* (Washington, DC), 21 December 1854, and "Municipal Election," *The Liberator*, 17 December 1858, featuring Boston; "Domestic," *New York Observer and Chronicle*, 11 January 1855, featuring Brooklyn's election of a temperance party mayor; Norman H. Clark, *The Dry Years: Prohibition and Social Change in Washington* (Seattle: University of Washington Press, 1965), 21 on Maine Law Whigs in Oregon; Colvin, *Prohibition in the United States*, 51. Attempts to connect the people directing these early endeavors to the later Prohibition Party must remain a bit speculative. However, it seems suggestive that temperance fraternities often called the founding convention of temperance parties, just as they would for the Prohibition Party, and that many future Prohibitionists were involved in the Free Soil Party at a time when it often supported temperance party fusion tickets.

[40] Pegram, *Battling Demon Rum*, 45.

reformers coalesced within the Republican Party. Citizens and politicians divided over the matters of how Confederates should be punished, Southern states' standings should be restored, and freedpeople should be protected. The last issue was particularly volatile. Abolitionists who had united on the principle of ending slavery now showed no such consensus regarding the question of their obligations to impoverished and undereducated freedpeople. Some argued that key organizations such as the American Anti-Slavery Society (AASS) should be disbanded, whereas others argued that the work of such groups had barely begun.[41]

Previously latent divisions also became apparent among that broad group of reformers who had favored both abolition and women's rights. The women's suffrage movement split almost as soon as it organized, with some advocates' plan to harness women's suffrage to the Fifteenth Amendment thwarted by others who were anxious to introduce black male suffrage as quickly as possible.[42] The National Woman Suffrage Association and the American Woman Suffrage Association would institutionalize this rivalry, remaining separate until 1890.

In the midst of these widely reverberating controversies, prohibition advocates clamored for party leaders' attention. Prohibitionists' frequent tantrums decried how Republican moderates defined theirs as the party of moral reform while refusing to introduce alcohol restriction as an important campaign issue. For these Republicans, "moral" issues were being framed more along the lines of debt repayment, making prohibitionists an unwelcome distraction, even an annoyance.[43] Together with dissatisfied labor reformers and social purity (that is, anti-prostitution) promoters, prohibition advocates suggested that the Republican Party's embrace of a free market economy – aggressively promoted as part of an effort to extend free labor's blessings to the South – left dangerously unrestricted not only the rights of employers to make exploitative contracts with labor but also the rights of producers to sell any and all things as commodities.[44] The Prohibition Party's founders would capitalize on the Republican Party's idea that politics could be about moral issues and

---

[41] William Lloyd Garrison retired from the AASS in 1865, whereas Wendell Phillips led the movement to assure its continuation. The AASS eventually disbanded in 1870.

[42] DuBois, *Feminism and Suffrage*, 162–202; Ginzberg, *Elizabeth Cady Stanton*, 103–132.

[43] On debt repayment as a moral issue, see Gretchen Ritter, *Greenbacks and Goldbugs: The Antimonopoly Tradition and the Politics of Finance in America* (New York: Cambridge University Press, 1997), 36.

[44] On debates over Reconstruction labor relations, see Amy Dru Stanley, *From Bondage to Contract: Wage Labor, Marriage, and the Market in the Age of Slave Emancipation* (New York: Cambridge University Press, 1998).

also on the failure of the Republican Party to fully extrapolate all of the implications of the antislavery movement.

To the extent that Republican Party leaders acknowledged the discontent of frustrated prohibition advocates, they urged this relatively small faction to remain within party ranks and to work diligently for the nomination of dry candidates. Prohibitionists might support candidates who favored no-license policies or else strict enforcement of Sunday tavern closings. Over the course of several campaigns, prohibitionists might persuade more and more fellow partisans of the efficacy of their cause, and convince this larger constituency to endorse candidates with still more aggressive political demands. But to expect politicians to move beyond the level of reform that the majority of their constituency sought, argued Republican leaders, was unrealistic and, if engaged, would likely result in the party's dissolution and thereby Democratic victory.

During heated moments, the Republican establishment was very frank in its assessment, arguing that "the party cannot afford to be made responsible for irrelevant issues, or to be saddled with the odium which attaches to all the theories of crotchets of scalous [sic] but intolerant minorities." They included liquor law advocates within the "intolerant minority" ranks.[45] Surely "the great work of restoring the Union and guaranteeing permanence to the results achieved by the war" was of larger importance, and "the period is not one in which [Republicans] can afford to assume the responsibility of every cry which individuals raise in the Republican name."[46] With reluctance, casual converts to prohibition agreed to stay the course with the Republican Party, responding to a call that "every temperance man use his best endeavors to see that so righteous a measure as the Excise Law . . . shall not be made a pretext for the defeat of the only political party which can be safely trusted with the government." Lay low, urged Republicans, or else risk inadvertently aiding the Democrats' "bad breath vote."[47]

Deeply committed prohibitionists, including those who would found the Prohibition Party, were likely to dismiss as self-serving those assertions by Republicans that all accomplishments of the Civil War were at stake with the perpetuation of Republican power. And even if Reconstruction was at risk, many of these prohibitionists had begun to question the importance of Reconstruction relative to other political issues. They thereby dovetailed with a broader shift in Northern political culture. A

---

[45] "The Moral of the Elections," *New York Times*, 11 September 1867.
[46] "The Republican Party – Its Greatest Peril," *New York Times*, 21 September 1867.
[47] "The Call to Battle," *(Oskaloosa, KS) Independent*, 31 October 1867.

widespread desire to end Reconstruction – sometimes sustained by the overly optimistic conviction that the work of restoring union and protecting freedpeople was already complete – encouraged the advancement of political issues unrelated to the maintenance of troops in Southern states. Prohibitionist dissidents embodied one side of an impassioned debate that would divide the Republican Party's reform element. With both sides using the abolitionist past as a touchstone, Republican reformers debated whether the most authentic postwar expression of antislavery principles lay in protecting freedpeople who had once been chattel slaves or in extending the battle against unfreedom to new groups of oppressed people.

Several thinkers who would shape Prohibition Party political philosophy had been Free Soil or Liberty Party members before joining the Republican Party. Gerrit Smith, Samuel Hastings, Myron H. Clark (a former Whig governor of New York), Methodist minister J.G. Evans, Horace Waters, and William Goodell, for example, argued that their antislavery convictions had inevitably propelled them to the conclusion that social ills must be confronted in the order of their greatest threat to personal freedom. Smith and Goodell had been particularly prominent in the Free Soil movement.[48]

When confronted with a political party that perpetuated unfreedom, Free Soilers had concluded that reformers must leave that party – but not necessarily politics – to avoid becoming complicit in unfreedom's perpetuation. Gideon T. Stewart would describe how

the logic of Chase, Sumner and the other leaders of the anti-slavery reform proclaimed that chattel slavery was a crime against God and man; that the Whig and Democratic parties embodied that crime; that all the slaveholding criminals were in those parties; and morally and politically identified with their crime. Hence they appealed especially to all Christian voters, to come out of the crime parties, to wash their hands from the blood of the slave.

Assuming that slavery and the liquor traffic were comparable problems, Stewart argued that prohibition advocates leaving the Republican Party acted in the spirit of antislavery minor parties.

---

[48] On the Free Soil Party, see Frederick J. Blue, *The Free Soilers: Third Party Politics, 1848–1854* (Urbana: University of Illinois Press, 1973); John Mayfield, *Rehearsal for Republicanism: Free Soil and the Politics of Antislavery* (Port Washington, NY: Kennikat Press, 1980). For an example of a much lower-profile Liberty Party member turned Prohibitionist, see P. Knight, "What is Wanted is Real Prohibition with No Strings Attached," *National Enquirer*, 12 April 1917.

In the light of anti-slavery logic, and of God's truth, every Christian citizen and every man who stands in either of these two great crime parties [Democratic or Republican] is morally and politically identified with the Liquor Crime; he is personally responsible and guilty before God and man for that crime, and all the blood and tears and bitter woes and curses of that crime, rest on his soul and in his hand, while he votes the crime tickets.[49]

The goal of a minor party was both to liberate the voter from responsibility for immoral governance and to build and organize a constituency of sufficient numbers to threaten ongoing political arrangements. Maine Law Whigs, Free Soilers, Know-Nothings, and Maine Law Democrats had anticipated just this antislavery minor party ideology when they sometimes united under "temperance party" tickets. Cleveland in 1851 and Maine in 1854 had followed this course.[50] Maine Law Whigs, Maine Law Democrats, and Republicans had also nominated a temperance ticket in New York in 1854, electing several candidates.[51]

Many people who did not have a personal history with the Free Soil Party or temperance party voting nonetheless shared with former abolitionists the tendency to view abolitionist parties as models for political development. Throughout the 1870s, Prohibitionists would routinely explain their own continuity with abolitionist traditions by describing drunkards – a constructed category that preceded both the idea and the language of an "alcoholic" – as being in "bondage" because they had been "made slaves" by the liquor industry and now required "emancipation."[52] In the course of explaining why his new Prohibition

---

[49] Gideon T. Stewart, "Total Separation from and Prohibition of the Liquor Crime, its Parties and Politicians" in *The Prohibition Party Against the Rum Power with its Crime Ruled Political Parties and Crime Consenting Churches, From the Public Addresses of Gideon T. Stewart* (N.p.: n.p., 1889), 143. The speech was initially delivered in 1879. Ensuing generations of Prohibitionists would include the children and grandchildren of abolitionists. For example, John Woolley poignantly recalled how he "watched my mother come and go noiselessly with food and clothing for the black man and woman in the corner, eating silently, while my father was out stealing his own horse out of his own barn to drive the fugitives"; John Woolley, "The Prohibition Party," *The Independent*, 27 September 1900.

[50] "Religious Summary," *Zion's Herald and Wesleyan Journal*, 8 October 1851. Prohibitionists who began in other minor party movements include John T. Bidwell, who was nominated for governor by California's anti-railroad Dolly Varden party in 1874 and rejected a fusion nomination with the Prohibition Party in the same year; Ostrander, *Prohibition Movement in California*, 40 and 57. Bidwell would eventually become the Prohibition Party presidential candidate in 1892.

[51] Colvin, *Prohibition in the United States*, 44.

[52] For example, see H.A. Thompson, "Prohibition County Convention: Address of President H.A. Thompson," *Delaware (Ohio) Signal*, 23 December 1873; "The Battle,"

journal was titled *The National Freeman*, John Russell would summarize that "bad as African slavery was in its time, it did not curse humanity so deeply as does the infinitely more degrading vice of bondage to the demon of strong drink."[53] Although contracts became the key lens through which Americans understood independence and obligations, the language of slavery remained salient as a reference point. Moreover, it was far more fluid and transferable than modern Americans might imagine and was broadly applied by reformers who fully understood the horrors undergone by Southern slaves.[54] If contract required that a person possess self-ownership, then drunkards were self-enslaved.

Women involved in the women's rights movement, of course, often asserted that they too were among the unfree. This logic made them particularly open to the argument for political integrity set forth by Prohibition Party founders, as did the fact that their ineligibility to vote limited their preexisting loyalty to the Republican Party. Whereas men with prohibitionist leanings might have been tempted to remain with a party that offered them camaraderie during election season and opportunities for office, women who had honed their skills in the abolitionist and women's rights movements had been left outside of the Republican embrace. Only loosely tethered to the Republican Party, they might well shift attention to the new party. Women, moreover, had for years served as active agents within the temperance cause, particularly within the temperance fraternities that had gained influence in the 1850s. Temperance fraternities, in turn, had a critical role in making the official call for a Prohibition Party. A session of the Right Worthy Grand Lodge of Good Templars at Oswego, New York, first demanded a national convention to found a new party.[55] The first three names signed to the ensuing published call were heads of the Sons of Temperance, IOGT, and Temple of Honor.[56]

Delaware Signal, 2 June 1874; "The National Prohibition Party," *Delaware Signal*, 16 February 1876. *Drunkards* was used by contemporaries to describe people who drank too much – however defined or quantified – in an era without the medical concept of addiction or a truly therapeutic response. To be a drunkard was to have a moral failing. Throughout this book, the term drunkard will be used when it was this real or imagined category of people to whom reformers referred; a simple replacement of the term drunkard with the modern term *alcoholic* would suggest that historical thinkers understood addiction much better than they actually did and perhaps that they judged it less harshly than they did.

53 Untitled, *National Freeman*, January 1881.
54 On the language of slavery and contract, see Stanley, *From Bondage to Contract*.
55 Colvin, *Prohibition in the United States*, 63.
56 Colvin, *Prohibition in the United States*, 65.

Nowhere were the intellectual and institutional roots of the Prohibition Party more on display than at the Prohibition Party's founding convention on September 3rd, 1869, when Gerrit Smith directed his keynote address to a sympathetic audience of reformers. Smith spoke not only with his own significant authority as a reformer, but as a cousin of renowned suffragist Elizabeth Cady Stanton and as the well-known financier of John Brown's raid on Harper's Ferry, Virginia. And he was unsatisfied that "slavery is gone, but drunkenness stays."[57] Granting comparable distinction to the antislavery and anti-liquor causes, Smith suggested that the movement to eliminate liquor was more urgent because

the lot of the literal slave, of him whom others have enslaved, is indeed a hard one: nevertheless it is a paradise compared with the lot of him who has enslaved himself – especially of him who has enslaved himself to alcohol. The noblest of souls may dwell beneath chains which others have imposed, but self-imposed chains strike debasement through and through the soul. Happy, too, may the literal slave be, if only he has left his inner man – his essential self – unconquered, but no outward advantage can bring happiness to the victim of alcohol – to him who has killed his own soul. Then, too, the literal slave does harm to no one, while the self-made slave, of whom we speak, is a curse to his kindred, a burden upon us all, and in no small share of the cases, a terror to all.

Smith's reflection on images of paradise and the soul, moreover, resonated with the shared religious foundations of abolitionists and dry advocates. At the first convention, delegates expressed Christian principles by singing hymns, starting sessions with prayers, interrupting proceedings so that they could attend prayer meetings, and welcoming a large number of ministers to their ranks. In a particularly provocative example, permanent chair James Black blocked the introduction of an unpopular resolution by recognizing a singer from the floor, who broke into the hymn "The Promised Land To Morrow." When a second attempt was made to introduce the resolution after the hymn concluded, it was only brought forward over "much laughter and cries of 'song' to call the singer to again interrupt" with another hymn. These Christians were rambunctious. Within the Prohibition Party, Smith and his fellow delegates suggested, they would energetically draw on religious traditions to purify the political arena just as antislavery proponents had done a decade before.[58]

---

[57] Gerrit Smith quoted in "Temperance: Meeting of the National Convention," *Chicago Tribune*, 3 September 1869.

[58] "Temperance: Meeting of the National Convention," *Chicago Tribune*, 3 September 1869.

Smith expressed a conference consensus when he argued that no American could sincerely claim ignorance of the liquor problem. Drunkards' failings were brought to the attention of a wider society when degraded individuals became "incendiaries, madmen, and murderers" who threatened people and property. Fundamentally, the conflict over liquor restriction was a political inquiry into the conditions of democratic citizenship. Democratic society, Smith reminded his audience, bound the Christian to important moral obligations; every citizen who could vote against impediments to the salvation and safety of his peers must do so. This, in turn, required party organization because democratic government "will not respond to the call to suppress the dram shop unless it comes from a great political party." Attempting to work within the Democratic or Republican parties was out of the question because "both of our existing political parties are in such homage to the interests and policies which cluster around and uphold the dram shop that neither of them will ever consent to demand its suppression."[59] Unrepresented by the major parties, dry advocates would need to organize as a new political party to advance their vision for society.

Eager Prohibitionists created the Declaration of Principles as their first official statement, a concise articulation of party intentions that could be distributed and quoted by the press. Sections one and two pledged fidelity to civil and religious liberty and predictably asserted that "the traffic in intoxicating beverages is a dishonor to Christian civilization, inimical to the best interest of society." Prohibitionists carefully positioned themselves as advocates for freedom who wanted to restore drunkards to citizenship, rather than as a coercive organization. The third section called for the establishment of a new political party and attributed blame for the liquor traffic to "the existing political parties" that "either oppose or ignore this great and paramount question."[60]

The fourth resolution in the Declaration of Principles discouraged the party from giving prominence to issues other than the liquor traffic. The convention quickly agreed to support the fifth resolution to form a central committee with one representative from each state and territory. Final resolutions proposed from the floor were also quickly adopted, including a resolution against Sabbath desecration and in recognition of God. The

[59] "Temperance: Meeting of the National Convention," *Chicago Tribune*, 3 September 1869.

[60] "Temperance: Meeting of the National Convention," *Chicago Tribune*, 3 September 1869.

former point alluded to a popular explanation for why prohibition was not an innovative attempt to limit Americans' personal liberties: The right of the government to restrict citizens' behaviors on one day implied a right to restrict it more often.[61]

The Declaration of Principles's resolution to organize as a party would distinguish Prohibitionists from all other anti-liquor advocates, including many who supported prohibition, and from the distinct work of Republican and Democratic temperance advocates. John Russell, a Michigan temperance editor and minister, argued that the failure of Democrats and Republicans to place a prohibition resolution in their platforms, their tendency to nominate men who were not known for prohibition principles, and the failure of Democratic and Republican newspapers to endorse prohibition principles demonstrated not simply indifference, but a self-conscious refusal to embrace the anti-liquor issue. Delegate Amanda Way added that when Republican-dominated governments did pass regulations on the liquor traffic, they frequently repealed them after only a few years.[62]

Prohibitionists would never question their assumption that most Americans wanted to end the liquor traffic and hence never view their project as coercive. Instead, they would position themselves as advocates for democracy, providing the American people with an alternative when the major parties' indebtedness to liquor interests and fear of alienating the wet voting minority made them reluctant to engage the liquor problem.

* * *

The transition from a modest temperance movement to an absolutist prohibition movement to the creation of a Prohibition Party took more than fifty years and was never fully embraced by most people favoring liquor restriction. Nonpolitical methods continued to be popular, and few prohibition advocates were willing to grant the liquor issue the same importance accorded to Reconstruction. For these reasons and others, abandoning the Republican Party would prove a harrowing decision for many Prohibition Party members. And it would carry personal as well as political consequences. In an era in which a good man was largely

[61] "Temperance: Meeting of the National Convention," *Chicago Tribune*, 3 September 1869.
[62] "Temperance! Second and Last Day's Session of the National Convention," *Chicago Times*, 3 September 1869.

defined by the consistency of his voting record, leaving one party for another could undermine one's civic reputation.[63] For many Prohibitionists who had spent the last decade upbuilding the Republican Party, it would prove frustrating to lose the opportunities for pleasant camaraderie, office holding, and government employment that loyal partisanship had promised. Without immediate electoral success to sustain it, the Prohibition Party would struggle to keep its constituency. Early Prohibitionists would have little more than a vibrant moral and political ideology to sustain them.

[63] Michael E. McGerr, *The Decline of Popular Politics: The American North, 1865–1928* (New York: Oxford University Press, 1986), 14.

2

Disorderly Conduct in the Emancipation Era

Prohibitionists' own sense of their importance aside, the Republican *Chicago Tribune* cruelly described the Prohibition Party's 1869 founding convention as a meeting of "well-meaning busybodies" who resembled no one so much as consumptive elderly ladies.[1] The *Chicago Times*, a paper with Democratic sympathies, categorized the Prohibition Party as "the new fanaticism."[2] Even temperance luminaries such as Neal Dow, a former Whig governor who had ushered in state prohibition in Maine, and circus entrepreneur P.T. Barnum expressed opposition to the party idea for being too peculiar.[3]

Most Americans agreed that voting for candidates from multiple parties or being a political independent was morally suspicious behavior and that new parties were probably filled with crackpots. Family and ethnoreligious identity had historically bound individuals to their party, and everyday social patterns of work and leisure reinforced these ties.[4] The recent Civil War, moreover, had imbued partisanship with incredible intensity. Northern states had generally voted Republican, and Southern states had overwhelmingly cast Democratic ballots, and every ensuing

---

[1] "The Temperance Party," *Chicago Tribune*, 2 September 1869; Untitled, *Chicago Tribune*, 4 September 1869.

[2] "The New Fanaticism," *Chicago Times*, 3 September 1869.

[3] "The Inevitable Step," *Zion's Herald*, 21 October 1869; "Temperance and Politics," *New York Times*, 25 April 1870, depicts a discussion between Gerrit Smith and P.T. Barnum at the Cooper Institute in New York.

[4] Paula Baker, *The Moral Frameworks of Public Life: Gender, Politics, and the State in Rural New York, 1870–1930* (New York: Oxford University Press, 1991); Joel H. Silbey, *The Partisan Imperative: The Dynamics of American Politics before the Civil War* (New York: Oxford University Press, 1985).

campaign was therefore intensified with "bloody shirt" waving. Internal factionalism within the Democratic and Republican parties did little to lessen the rank and file's party loyalty, although it did leave party leadership unsettled. At the time that Prohibition Party founders – people who, more often than not, had been Republican "lesser lights" – decided to start a new party, their accusation that the current party system was broken was anathema to most other citizens, who were deeply invested within it.

The Prohibition Party's first generation of theorists was a small cadre that emphasized national politics and that exchanged ideas through national conventions, committee meetings, and a small number of newspapers including the *Penninsular Herald*, the *Delaware Signal*, and the *Minnesota Radical*.[5] They quickly agreed on an ultimate goal: to disrupt the liquor industry's political influence by grafting anti-liquor Democrats and Republicans together in the same party, and thereby forcing pro-liquor leftovers in the Democratic and Republican parties to fuse into a new anti-Prohibition Party. This transition had been prevented thus far, Prohibitionists asserted, only because the liquor traffic had unfairly infiltrated both the Democratic and Republican parties by offering bribes and threatening to withdraw votes. In so doing, the liquor industry had artificially kept both major parties alive despite the fact that the slavery issue had been resolved. As an unfortunate corollary, Prohibitionists asserted, the liquor industry's product made a voter too inebriated to recognize how the Democratic-Republican system undermined his interests.

Leading Republicans insisted that it was the Prohibition Party, not the Democratic-Republican system, that threatened democracy. Prohibitionists would detract from the somewhat dry Republican Party without achieving electoral victory and would hence leave the temperate majority of Americans totally unrepresented. The very wet Democratic party, which did not represent the majority, would seize control of government. At the Prohibition Party's first convention, one attendee had concluded that "wherever the friends of temperance have entered on distinct party organization they have ruined their cause." A second asked, "Is it wise for the gentlemen to sever their connection with the other parties, and adhere to this one with but a single plank? Can we draw from the other

---

[5] The earliest national committee records available for historians' review begin in 1888. However, there is information about national conferences, nominations, and executive committee meetings through a few pamphlets of proceedings and through newspaper reporting.

parties enough to give us the ascendancy? I have my doubts." Alternatively, he was "in favor of instructing these [major] parties. If the dominant party nominates a whisky man let the temperance men refuse to vote for him, and thereby defeat him."[6] Democratic governance, party opponents argued, was meant to express the will of the majority, which could not be effectively conveyed if there were more than two parties in the field.

When a small number of convention attendees, including the future first president of the Anti-Saloon League, voted against the forming of a new party, the convention's most passionate advocates lost patience.[7] Opponents were "loudly hissed by some of the members, despite the fact that there were several ladies voting in the negative."[8] For one moment in one space, Prohibitionists had the upper hand when it came to ridiculing their antagonists.

Prohibitionists grudgingly acknowledged that "there are many objectors to our party, who fear that we shall draw recruits so much more largely from one than from the other, as to make it work death to the Republican party, and give a stronger life to the Democratic party." Provocatively, they nonetheless declared "Happy and honored Republican party, if this shall be its end!"[9] The *Peninsular Herald* acknowledged to its 5,000 readers that "it is said that the formation of the new party will so weaken the Republican ranks as to throw the democrats into power. Well, what then? Certainly, so far as temperance and morality are concerned, we could not be worse off."[10]

During the infamous 1876 election, Democrats and Republicans engaged in their fiercest debates about the future of Reconstruction and with it the future of freedpeople throughout the South. The very real possibility that the nation would elect its first Democratic president since before the Civil War amplified tensions between parties and sections to a fever pitch. It was a striking measure of their devotion when Prohibitionists remained with their party rather than realigning with the Republicans. They refused to make the transition that major parties pressed on

---

[6] "Temperance! Second and Last Day's Session of the National Convention," *Chicago Times*, 3 September 1869.

[7] On Hiram Price's stand, see Jack S. Blocker, *Retreat from Reform*, 156.

[8] "Temperance! Second and Last Day's Session of the National Convention," *Chicago Times*, 3 September 1869.

[9] "Address of the New York State Anti-Dramshop Convention, Held in Syracuse, Dec. 22nd, 1869," *(Detroit, MI) Peninsular Herald*, 19 January 1870.

[10] D.C. Wright, "Splinters," *Peninsular Herald*, 8 September 1869. The lowercase "democrats" is part of the original document.

them – namely, to define themselves not as a constituency-building organization but as a mere protest group. The role of minor parties, Prohibitionists insisted, was to slowly but surely become major parties.

* * *

From the beginning, the odds were stacked against the Prohibition Party.
When the founding generation of Prohibitionists acknowledged that "our
movement must be one of gradual and moderate growth for a time," it
was because they could hardly do otherwise.[11] On the positive side, this
concession that immediate victory was unlikely meant that the potentially
competing impulses to preserve ethical purity and to please a constituency
could thrive alongside each other. Certain that compromise would no
sooner help them make a dry America than strict adherence to founding
ideals, Prohibitionists vigilantly protected the moral, absolutist integrity
of their agenda. At the national level, their formal political strategy never
included cultivating fusion with Democrats or Republicans or attempting
to influence the decisions made within these parties, although desperate state parties or individual partisans occasionally made such gestures.
Throughout the early 1870s hardworking Prohibitionists gathered up
the fledgling state parties in Illinois, Michigan, and Ohio and connected
them to the national party.[12] They coordinated other state parties formed
after the first national convention, including those of New York (1869),
New Hampshire (1870), Massachusetts (1870), Pennsylvania (1871), and
Connecticut (1872), and brought them into conversation with each other.
They started newspapers and identified the best speakers in their ranks.

The party's early principles developed quickly among a small group
of thinkers who communicated in a limited number of arenas. Theorists
began from the point of consensus that all regulatory strategies should
be rejected, despite these strategies' popularity with other individuals in
the anti-liquor movement. Most temperance advocates were Northern
Republicans who embraced local option, wherein states permitted communities to vote on whether or not to offer liquor licenses, to charge
either a high or low fee for these licenses, and to thereby regulate the

---

[11] "The National Convention," *Peninsular Herald*, 4 January 1872. The *Zion's Herald*
estimated that the Prohibition Party would come to power within 30 years; Untitled,
Zion's Herald, 1 December 1870.
[12] Although histories written by Prohibition Party members do not typically reference it, a
Temperance Party also existed in Maine contemporary to the national Prohibition party's
founding. See Untitled, *Maine Farmer*, 10 July 1869, for an account of a convention and
platform.

number of liquor-selling establishments in their vicinity. Local option advocates argued that this policy epitomized democratic principles because it brought the liquor question directly before the people.[13] Democrats, whose constituency largely consisted of Northern urban immigrants and white Southerners, often counterargued that such regulations violated personal property rights. Prohibitionists, in turn, argued that local option actually subverted more democratic principles than it protected. Local option stripped the rights of citizens in neighboring no-license communities to prevent the entry of liquor into their territory from license areas. Drunkards and the violence and crime they perpetuated, the drain of public support for their families, and liquor itself all moved freely into areas where local option had rendered liquor sales illegal.

An influential pamphlet by "Father of the Prohibition Party" John Russell decried that "'local option' is local nonsense, as those who try it are destined to prove in the end."[14] Russell's *Peninsular Herald* would "advise our friends to reject all compromises. Remember we are aiming at a grand and final result, to secure which we have chosen a direct line of action, and any deviation from it will hinder rather than help our cause. Principle is our main capital."[15] In any case, Prohibitionists' moral indictment of local option chipped away at this strategy's legitimacy even before court decisions in the late 1870s and 1880s disputed the right of state legislatures to allocate their constitutionally derived authority to municipalities.

There were early signs that Prohibitionists' peppiness was not completely delusional. Flouting the widely held contention that Prohibitionists would "amount to little" because they were building "castles up in the air," Prohibitionists recruited celebrity abolitionist Wendell Phillips as their candidate for governor of Massachusetts in 1870; Phillips was also nominated by the Labor Party four days later.[16] Six states ran

---

[13] On this argument during the early Republic and antebellum eras, see Kyle Volk, "The Perils of 'Pure Democracy': Minority Rights, Liquor Politics, and Popular Sovereignty in Antebellum America," *Journal of the Early Republic* 29 (Winter 2009): 641–679.

[14] John Russell, *An Adequate Remedy for a National Evil; or a Vindication of the National Prohibition Party* (Detroit: New World Book and Job Print, 1872), 12. D. Leigh Colvin notes that approximately 100,000 copies of this pamphlet were distributed during the 1872 election; Colvin, *Prohibition in the United States*, 99–100.

[15] "A Dangerous Dodge," *Peninsular Herald*, 31 March 1869.

[16] "Temperance Men in Council – A Third Party," *Christian Advocate*, 9 September 1869; Theodore L. Cuyler, "A Plain Word with Temperance Friends," *The Independent*, 7 October 1869. On the Phillips campaign, see "The Elections in Other States," *New York Times*, 9 November 1870. Published accounts featuring Phillips at Prohibition

Prohibition tickets in 1870, with a combined vote of 20,012.[17] The election of George H. Vibbert, a widely known temperance lecturer who worked with Phillips and William Lloyd Garrison, to the Massachusetts legislature in 1871 was a remarkable victory.[18]

To the annoyance of Republicans, early Prohibitionists also routinely committed candidates and party resources to elections where there was no possibility of victory, but only of disrupting the equilibrium between the major parties. Eager Prohibitionists in Detroit, for example, "were fully aware that they had not the perfect organization and the daily paper necessary for a fierce fight, and therefore contented themselves by acting consistent; nominating a ticket, voting it and asking other people to do the same."[19] This new party was somewhat more than the "party on paper" mocked by many Republican temperance reformers but something less than a powerful political force.[20] Prohibitionists' conviction that representing the principles of their party was virtuous regardless of electoral success, and their hope that these activities would publicize their search for a constituency, sustained them throughout their first several years. They measured their small accomplishments in the context of the "great obstacles, such as want of thorough organization and money, the misrepresentation of old party papers and politicians, the luke warmness of professed temperance men, and the prejudices naturally antagonistic to any innovation."[21] When Prohibitionists carefully monitored the polls, insisting that every vote for their party be counted despite the unlikelihood of victory, they demonstrated profound dedication.

Although imperfectly organized, Prohibitionists at the 1872 national convention nominated party founders James Black and John Russell as their presidential and vice-presidential candidates. Black had worked as an organizer for the Washingtonians, Sons of Temperance, and IOGT and had been a key figure in promoting the National Temperance Society

Party conventions appear until at least 1876. He also pursued antimonopoly politics throughout the 1870s; Ritter, *Greenbackers and Goldbugs*, 65–66.

[17] Colvin, *Prohibition in the United States*, 87.

[18] "Personal," *Zion's Herald*, 13 April 1871; Colvin, *Prohibition in the United States*, 87–88; "Dr. George H. Vibbert Dies in Chicago," *(Westerville, OH) American Issue*, 8 May 1915.

[19] "The City Election," *Peninsular Herald*, 10 November 1869.

[20] Theodore L. Cuyler, "A Plain Word with Temperance Friends," *Independent*, 7 October 1869. Cuyler would still oppose the party method years later. For example, Theodore L. Cuyler, "The Temperance Reform: What Next?" *Independent*, 15 April 1897.

[21] "The Beginning," *Peninsular Herald*, 23 February 1871, reprinted from *(Cleveland, Ohio) Prohibition Era*.

and Publication House, founded in 1865. The Methodist attorney from
Pennsylvania had also served as chair of the Prohibitionists' first national
convention. Russell was a Methodist minister, prominent IOGT leader,
editor of the *Peninsular Herald*, and the party's national chair.

Black and Russell did not completely meet the requirements of those
Prohibitionists who wanted to nominate candidates not only "by reputation, honesty, political sagacity" but also by "*administrative experience.*"[22] Neither had ever been elected to a political office, leading one
political commentator to conclude that "of these gentlemen we cannot
say any thing – for we know nothing of them, never having heard of
them before."[23] However, politically pragmatic Prohibitionists acknowledged that even individuals with more popular reputations were unlikely
to achieve victory. Why nominate an individual in 1872 who might be
a viable candidate in a future election wherein Prohibitionists could
make a more sincere effort at victory? In the meantime, Prohibitionists could make an important symbolic gesture that clearly articulated
the party's principles to the voting public. The party's most pragmatic
thinkers acknowledged the delicate balancing act that was involved in
selecting candidates – namely, "we must select candidates of such conceded fitness for the place that the objection to the candidates may
not be the strongest argument against the success of the party." The
only condition was that "the candidates ought not to be new converts
to the Prohibition doctrine."[24] The nomination of candidates was further complicated by the fact that some high-profile founders such as
Gerrit Smith had already returned to the Republican party; between elections, Prohibitionists would struggle to recruit more voters than they
lost.[25]

Prohibitionists were content to slowly gain an organizational foothold
in Midwest and Northeastern states and were pleasantly surprised to find
a loyal if small constituency in the South and West. They persevered even
when many other Americans wondered "whether these gentlemen intend
to keep up the farce of running for office until the election closes."[26]
Unfortunately, the low number of reported votes for the Prohibition
Party presidential candidate challenged even partisans' modest hopes for

[22] W.W.B., "The Work of the National Convention," *Peninsular Herald*, 25 January 1872.
Italics are author's.
[23] "New Parties," *(Boston) Youth's Companion*, 21 May 1872.
[24] W.W.B., "The Work of the National Convention," *Peninsular Herald*, 25 January 1872.
[25] Smith would die in 1874.
[26] Untitled, *Chicago Tribune*, 24 February 1872.

the 1872 election; about 5,500 votes were tallied in 6 states. The local and state results ran ahead of the presidential ticket, but Prohibitionists primarily conceived of themselves as reformers with a national agenda and thus assessed their standing by these meager national returns.[27] Most votes were cast in Michigan, Ohio, and Pennsylvania. Only a few hundred voters supported Prohibition candidates in Connecticut, New Hampshire, and New York.

Some of the low returns could be attributed to sabotage from political rivals. Undercounting, inaccurate counts, and intercepted ballots were persistent problems for Prohibitionists, as was the case for most political candidates.[28] Some of the lackluster returns could be explained by the prolonged nature of Reconstruction, which preoccupied many reformers and scared former abolitionists into continuing to vote Republican. Compounding all of these problems, the Prohibition Party's national committee had provided the campaign with no funds, leaving this work to struggling state parties. State parties had been underprepared for this responsibility. In Michigan the state party employed a single state organizer at a fixed salary and set aside only $200 to pay for campaign literature.[29]

Far more troubling, Prohibitionists had to come to terms with the fact that the party's anticipated constituency of middle-class reformers, anti-liquor advocates, and Protestants did not choose to express themselves through a single-issue party. Perhaps they were put off by the platform's advocacy of women's suffrage or by the fact that church organizations lacked any formal control of the party apparatus.[30] Regardless of the reason, their party had less popularity than the cause it advocated. Party historian D. Leigh Colvin understatedly summarized the extent of partisans' frustration with their failures, noting that "after the disappointing

---

[27] This difference between combined state returns and national returns would persist throughout the party's history. For example, in 1875, 9 states polled a total of 42,185 votes, a number that would not be surpassed by any national ticket until 1884; Colvin, *Prohibition in the United States*, 109.

[28] On election fraud, see Tracy Campbell, *Deliver the Vote: A History of Election Fraud, An American Political Tradition – 1742–2004* (New York: Carroll & Graf Publishers, 2005); Mark Wahlgren Summers, *The Era of Good Stealings* (New York: Oxford University Press, 1993).

[29] Minutes of the State Central Committee of the Prohibition Party of Michigan, 2 February 1872, Folder: Prohibition Party, National Committee; Minutes, 1872, of the State Central Committee of the Prohibition Party of Michigan, Box: 7, Prohibition Party National Committee Records, Bentley Historical Library, Ann Arbor, Michigan.

[30] Blocker, *American Temperance Movements*, 100; Blocker, *Retreat from Reform*, 166.

vote in 1872 a number who in the beginning had looked favorably upon separate party action became discouraged and quit."[31] However, one might also wonder that the hemorrhaging was not even greater. Those who did stay within the party would become its core constituency, recommitting themselves to producing moral and political analyses of parties and the party system and to developing stronger institutions to spread party ideology. Two fundamental premises would guide party doctrine: The party system itself was the most appropriate conduit for bringing public opinion to policy makers, and the liquor industry had temporarily cheated this system when it organized drinkers as a balance of power between the two major parties.

For Prohibitionists, the appeal of minor party organization lay in its capacity to extricate the voter morally and politically from participation in civic decline while still permitting him to participate in the polity. Continuing to draw on the legacy of antislavery third parties, Prohibitionists argued that joining with their party provided citizens the only means to relieve themselves of complicity in the liquor trade.[32] Both the Democratic and Republican parties approved of licensing liquor-selling establishments – Democrats because it kept the trade open and Republicans because it restrained it. This flew in the face of Prohibitionists' belief that licensing for any reason provided a government sanction. Until Americans abandoned the major parties that supported this problematic practice, "it may be justly charged, that we are a nation of drunkard-makers" because the "indifferent looker-on" allowed parties to permit drunkard making on his behalf.[33] The *Minnesota Radical*, edited by future Prohibition gubernatorial candidate and state chair James E. Child, urged "shame on the professed temperance man who votes to license others to do what he has not the courage to do himself, and then has the impudence to denounce

---

[31] Colvin, *Prohibition in the United States*, 106. See also "Balance of Power," *Delaware Signal*, 3 November 1875.

[32] For example, Dr. Barrows, "Temperance Political Organization," *Zion's Herald*, 18 November 1869. For an example of the argument against this interpretation of minor parties, see William Lloyd Garrison, "Moral and Political Action," *The Independent*, 24 November 1870.

[33] John Russell, *An Adequate Remedy for a National Evil*, 3–4. Russell's analysis frankly asserted an idea earlier put forth by Reverend Barrows in 1869, namely, that "to adhere to our parties when they are supporting the rum traffic, and crushing the Temperance cause, is to partake of all their guilt"; Dr. Barrows, "Temperance Political Organization," *Zion's Herald*, 18 November 1869. Barrows explicitly connected voters' current attempts to absolve themselves from responsibility for the drunkard problem to the work of the Liberty, Free Soil, and Republican parties that had wanted to distance themselves from culpability for slavery.

others because they consistently oppose the whole iniquity!"[34] Support for flawed "solutions" would not relieve the voter from culpability for the individuals left unsaved. So as to be morally consistent, "the only relation between [the Prohibition Party] and each of the other parties, is that of eternal and uncompromising hostility, for both are the mere wings of the great enemy against which we are at war."[35]

Prohibitionists' most important critique fused worries about citizen culpability to an analysis of established parties' inherent inability to introduce new issues.[36] John Russell asserted that "Prohibitionists do not assume that their party is necessary simply because others are corrupt, but because they are *organically disqualified* to handle the political issues which we make."[37] Here Prohibitionists suggested how the inadequacy of Democrats and Republicans was rooted in the historical circumstances of their formations. These parties had been created to dispute issues other than prohibition and "the [prohibition] question not having been adopted by either party at the time of its organization, the antagonistic elements cannot now be harmonized."[38] James Black, who spoke with the authority of one who had helped organize the Republican Party in 1854, described how the major parties "having been organized for other purposes, are divided on the liquor question, each having members who favor and others who oppose liquor suppression and hence neither can take decided steps in that direction."[39] This was a problem because "while temperance men are scattered through both the other parties, other party issues will control them, and render a concentration of effort on this [prohibition] question impossible."[40]

Prohibitionists believed that the experience of prohibition advocates was similar to the early abolitionists' split between Whigs and Democrats because when "the old parties were divided on the slavery

---

[34] "Rochester People and Falsehood," *Minnesota Radical*, 16 February 1876.

[35] "The Next Campaign," *Delaware Signal*, 15 November 1876.

[36] For additional information about the decline in issues in post-Civil War party politics, see Elizabeth S. Clemens, *The People's Lobby: Organizational Innovation and the Rise of Interest Group Politics in the United States, 1890–1920* (Chicago: University of Chicago Press, 1997), 22.

[37] John Russell, *An Adequate Remedy for a National Evil*, 9–10. Italics are author's.

[38] John Russell, *An Adequate Remedy for a National Evil*, 6. See also J.F. Hume, "The Old Parties Unreliable," *National Freeman*, May 1881.

[39] James Black, "Is There a Necessity for a Prohibition Party?" *Delaware Signal*, 11 October 1876. Black published a pamphlet with the same title in the same year.

[40] State Central Committee of the Temperance Party of Michigan, "Address," *Peninsular Herald*, 3 March 1869.

question . . . nothing was done toward removing it."[41] They might just as persuasively have alluded to the ongoing critiques of Greenbackers. These antimonopolists noted that the Democratic Party's alliance of Western-ers who supported the use of greenback currency and Easterners who demanded a return to the gold standard undermined that party's abil-ity to coordinate a coherent national position. Republicans were like-wise divided between constituents favoring inflation or the gold stan-dard, and thus both major parties refrained from acting, or else acted in a contradictory fashion.[42] The currency issue would only become a national campaign matter in the 1890s, despite having simmered for two decades.

In a two-party system, a major party's mixed character meant that it could not endorse prohibition without driving the pro-liquor part of its constituency to the other party. John Russell and national committee chair Simeon B. Chase, a former state legislator who had helped organize the Republican Party in Pennsylvania, anticipated that immediately after "the incorporation of prohibition into the platform of either the Democratic or Republican party" there would be "an abandonment of that party by all in favor of the continuance of the liquor trade."[43] This would give the opposition party an enormous and immediate advantage. The liquor industry preyed upon major parties' fear of such an event to better manipulate them. To defend their business, "they warn politicians, that if either party shall take issue against their business they will leave them."[44] Prohibitionists concluded that endorsing prohibition would undermine the survival of the major party that made this bold commitment, that major parties fully understood this fact, and that they had deliberately decided to keep prohibition off the political agenda and be negligent in enforcement. John Russell concluded that it was "the policy of the two old parties . . . to ignore this [prohibition] question as far as possible – to give temperance people just legislation enough to pacify them, and to keep liquor dealers quiet by *not executing* the imperfect statutes enacted against their business."[45]

---

[41] H.A. Thompson, "What is Your Duty?" *Delaware Signal*, 1 November 1876.

[42] Ritter, *Greenbacks and Goldbugs*, 34–47.

[43] Simeon B. Chase (chair) and John Russell (secretary), "Address of the National Com-mittee of the Prohibition Party," *Delaware Signal*, 15 July 1874. See also "Michigan: Meeting of the Temperance Party in State Convention," *New York Times*, 13 June 1872.

[44] State Central Committee of the Temperance Party of Michigan, "Address," *Peninsular Herald*, 3 March 1869.

[45] John Russell, *An Adequate Remedy for a National Evil*, 6. Italics are author's.

It was in response to the problem of major parties' incapacity for radical reform that Gideon T. Stewart, the former head of the Sons of Temperance and IOGT in Ohio, urged that a minor party "may pass between [the major parties], and by drawing the temperance voters from both, unite them in the Prohibition party, and thus practically divide the Liquor Crime strength and conquer it."[46] From its home in the college town surrounding Ohio Wesleyan University, the *Delaware Signal* agreed that "there is a vast amount of temperance sentiment tied up, latent in the old parties, and especially in the Republican party, which it is a part of the work of this new party to disengage, set free, organize, and make effective."[47] Just as "a very large and valuable element of the Republican party was drawn from the Democratic ranks during the first years of its organization," Prohibitionists would detach anti-liquor advocates from their pro-liquor parties to form a new major party.[48] This new party would include the majority of Americans, a majority who wanted prohibition.[49] Prohibitionists further theorized that the liquor-favoring Democrats and Republicans remaining in those parties would then fuse together to form a new pro-liquor party.

Prohibitionists' imperfect organization nonetheless left Republicans with ample fodder for mockery. The mainstream press publicized numerous accounts of Prohibitionists nominating candidates who humiliated the party by refusing to run on its ticket.[50] About a state convention in Ohio – a hotbed of temperance sentiment – the *New York Times* rather snidely noted that "attendance was small, and but little enthusiasm was

---

[46] Gideon T. Stewart, "The Prohibition Party of Moral Action and Civil Liberty Against the Liquor Crime" in *The Prohibition Party Against the Rum Power*, 24. This speech was originally given in 1871. See also "The Maine Law and Political Parties," *Delaware Signal*, 31 May 1876.

[47] "Need of a Prohibition Party," *Delaware Signal*, 10 February 1875. The *Delaware Signal* was edited by L. Barnes, J.W. Sharpe, and Joseph Woods Lindsey until 1876, at which point the treasurer, Thomas Evans, Jr., took over the entire enterprise.

[48] "'The Republican Party – The Next Contest,'" *Delaware Signal*, 4 November 1874.

[49] On Prohibitionists' beliefs that most Americans wanted prohibition, see James E. Child (state chair), "Prohibition Address: To the Voters of Minnesota: Adopted by the State Prohibition Convention held at Minnesota Sept. 3d 1878," *Minnesota Radical*, 4 September 1878; *National Prohibition Reform Party: Its Candidates, Platform, Address, and Some Reasons Why it is Pre-eminently Deserving the Support of the People of the United States* (Detroit: William A. Scripps, 1876), 14; James Black, "The Rise and Progress of the Policy of Prohibition Legislation in America: Remarks made by James Black at the Opening of the National Prohibition Conference, held in New York City Sept. 25th and 26th, 1877," *Delaware Signal*, 30 January 1878.

[50] For example, "The Prohibitionists," *New York Times*, 25 October 1874; "The Spring Elections," *New York Times*, 2 April 1875.

manifested," thereby ridiculing not only Prohibitionists' numbers but also their spirit.[51] Prohibitionists were "intemperate in their talk" but otherwise "helping their cause in no sense."[52]

More often than not, the Prohibition Party found itself caught between major party rivals each seeking to advance their own interests. The *New York Tribune* summarized Republican newspapers' reports that Prohibitionist gatherings were insignificant "and that the ticket nominated will make scarcely a ripple on the surface of the political waters." In contrast, some Democratic organs hoped to spark Prohibitionists' kindling – and hence draw voters away from the Republicans – by communicating that they were "profoundly impressed with the character and number" of Prohibitionist gatherings.[53] Both sides readily conceded that any new Prohibitionists would likely come out from Republican rather than Democratic ranks.

To those temperance advocates reminding would-be Prohibitionists that the Republican Party was making intermediate steps toward prohibition, Prohibitionists responded in 1874 that "for fourteen years the National Government has been in the hands of Republicans, and for a much longer time had the [Ohio] State Government been fashioned in accordance with their ideas, and at no time has there been even an attempt made to insert a temperance plank in the National or State platform."[54] Republicans' lock on political authority for over a decade should have assured even greater achievements if they had really been desired. H.A. Thompson, a university president from Ohio who would be a future party candidate for governor and vice president, insisted that "not a single original prohibitory law has ever been enacted by [the Republican party] since its origin."[55] In New York, Prohibitionists denied any predisposition toward the Republican Party when recalling that "the only law we have on the subject of liquor selling is a license law; and this was in part the work of a Republican Legislature and in part a Democratic

[51] "The Prohibition State Convention," *New York Times*, 27 February 1874.

[52] "The Connecticut Election," *New York Times*, 3 April 1874.

[53] "Political Notes," *New York Tribune*, 26 June 1874. Republican-oriented publications had noted from the beginning that the Democratic Party's interests would be served if it became a "foster parent" to the young Prohibition Party. For example, "The Temperance Party," *(Cincinnati, OH) Western Christian Advocate*, 8 September 1869. This was meant to indict Prohibitionists rather than sincerely advise Democrats.

[54] J.S.R.H., "The Prohibition Party," *Delaware Signal*, 19 August 1874.

[55] H.A. Thompson, "What is Your Duty?" *Delaware Signal*, 1 November 1876. Thompson was the president of Otterbein University, affiliated with the United Brethren Church.

one." Moreover, "a license law is not 'temperance legislation.'"[56] Prohibitionists observed that "even the Republican [party], filled as it is with good temperance men, is so concerned with the beer element that separation would be political death. The leaders know it, and do not wish to die."[57]

Republicans, in turn, continued to argue that Prohibitionists were a "disorganizing element" that disrupted elections.[58] For example, when Prohibitionists polled 10,000 votes in the Ohio election of 1873, they assured a very wet Democratic candidate's victory, thus impeding the enactment of majority sentiment, which supported liquor restriction.[59] Prohibitionists subverted the majority only to advance an impure and irresponsible minority to power. The case of Connecticut, wherein the 1874 vote doubled that of 1873 and approached 5 percent of the total returns, suggested the possibility that such a sequence of events might repeat.[60]

Ira D. Brown, who characterized himself as a Republican temperance advocate, framed this political problem in moral terms, arguing that

all men are morally accountable for their exercise of the elective franchise, and whosoever so casts this vote as to certainly produce certain results, is responsible before God and man for those results; and if yourself, and the other members of the "Independent Prohibition Party," with your eyes open to the consequences, hand over New York to the foul embraces of Tammany Democracy, you are verily guilty of all the consequences that flow from it to the end of time!

"To vote the Prohibition ticket," Brown continued, "is to contribute toward the achievement of a Democratic victory with all its consequent evils."[61] From here it was but a short step for Republicans to speculate that Prohibitionists' campaigns were funded by Democrats. In Connecticut, the *New York Times* charged the Prohibition Party with being capable only of work that was "encouraged by the Democratic leaders."[62] In New York, "Democratic managers are willing to pay liberally to keep

---

[56] Walter Farrington, Untitled letter to the editor, *New York Times*, 25 November 1875.
[57] "What About the Crusaders Now?" *Delaware Signal*, 9 June 1874.
[58] "Political Affairs," *New York Times*, 5 September 1873.
[59] "The Prohibition State Convention," *New York Times*, 27 February 1874. Republicans braced for a similar problem in New Hampshire in 1874; "New-Hampshire Politics," *New York Times*, 7 March 1874.
[60] Colvin, *Prohibition in the United States*, 108.
[61] "The Prohibitionists," *New York Times*, 25 October 1874, reprinted from *Syracuse (New York) Journal*.
[62] "The Connecticut Election," *New York Times*, 3 April 1874.

a Prohibition ticket in the field."[63] Prohibitionists feebly protested that their empty coffers proved their integrity.[64]

Prohibitionists grudgingly conceded that successful recruitment from the Republican Party would likely result in some Democratic electoral victories before the Prohibitionists could win consistently. This, they claimed, was an acceptable collateral consequence. As reformers and former abolitionists, Prohibitionists acknowledged that "we deplore the temporary success of the Democracy as much as anyone," but also asserted that

we would not allow such a possible triumph to deter us from a persistent and consistent line of duty; and besides, whatever of Democratic success may result from this course of action is clearly chargeable to those who, by refusing to advocate prohibitory measures, or by nominating and supporting license men, have made such action on our part a positive duty.[65]

There might even be an advantage to having control of government pass to the Democrats. This party was an "open enemy" to liquor restriction, quite different from the Republicans who used "concealed weapons of death and cowardly pretence of friendship for our principles."[66] This rhetoric did not endear Prohibitionists to Democrats, but Prohibitionists and Democrats were not destined to look on each other favorably in any case.

To those reformers who would nonetheless defend Republicans as more dry and moral than Democrats, Prohibitionists objected that both the Democratic and Republican parties encumbered democratic government when they relinquished their responsibility to be sites for vigorous political deliberation. Political parties should be perfected versions of the broader polity's meeting-place democracy, but Democrats and Republicans had instead been complicit in a conspiracy to suppress discussion of the liquor problem.[67] In 1873, Gideon T. Stewart decried how the "disappearance of former issues from the political field" had left "nothing

---

[63] "A Word to the Prohibitionists," *New York Tribune*, 4 November 1876.

[64] "The State Canvas," *New York Tribune*, 11 October 1876.

[65] "'Helping the Democracy and Injuring the Cause,'" *Delaware Signal*, 25 October 1876. See also J.T. Yarrington, *The Great Question* (Pennsylvania: 1873), 6.

[66] "Victory! Victory!!" *Delaware Signal*, 8 November 1876.

[67] Mary Ryan uses the phrase "meeting-place democracy" to explain the nature of face-to-face, interactive politics in *Civic Wars: Democracy and Public Life in the American City during the Nineteenth Century* (Berkeley: University of California Press, 1997). She argues that this style of democracy was superseded by a "politics of publicity" at the end of the century.

for the two great parties to draw a separating line upon, with or without the difference 'twixt tweedle dum and tweedle dee.'"[68] To form alliances with such parties, even on the basis of prohibition-friendly candidates, offered few apparent benefits.

* * *

Prohibitionists' conviction that major parties would eventually die out and be succeeded would not prove popular, but it had roots in historical experience. Although America had almost always had just two national major parties, the identity of these two parties had changed as frequently as had the key issue in American policy. In the first eight decades of the United States, the Federalists, anti-Federalists, Democratic-Republicans, National Republicans, Know-Nothings, and Whigs all had turns as national major parties. Most Americans living in the post-emancipation era could recall the rise of the Republican Party in the 1850s from the ashes of the Whig Party.[69] Reviewing this long historical tradition, Prohibitionists concluded that the Fifteenth Amendment, which was being ratified by the states as the Prohibition Party's founding convention met, meant that the Republican Party's work was done and that an issue other than freedpeople's protection should be at the core of party politics. Freedmen would have suffrage and could defend themselves with the vote.

Prohibitionists' logic was therefore not completely ridiculous. However, the anxious and harsh overreaction of some Democrats and many Republicans in the face of Prohibitionists' minute funding and lack of substantial electoral success therefore begs further explanation; Prohibitionists were hardly an immediate threat. Arguably, both Prohibitionists' endeavor to topple the Democratic-Republican system and the overreactions of the major parties to this challenge can be best understood in the context of the Democrats' and Republicans' internal conflicts. To the editors and politicians who coordinated postwar Democratic and Republican activities, and to the Prohibitionists who hoped to capitalize upon these parties' weaknesses, factionalism and renegade resistance to Democratic and Republican party discipline were ever apparent in the years from 1865 to 1876. Debates between Prohibitionists and major party leaders provided Democrats and Republicans with the opportunity to

---

[68] Gideon T. Stewart, "True Public Service Reform" in *The Prohibition Party Against the Rum Power*, 71. This speech was originally delivered in 1873.

[69] For an example of public recollection, see "The Parting of the Ways," *Zion's Herald*, 24 September 1868.

discuss disquiets about splintering that they might otherwise be reluctant to publicly engage, for fear of amplifying the problem within their party ranks.[70]

Postwar factionalism might well have been expected within the Democratic Party, which was attempting to reunite Northern and Southern constituents. Fighting on opposite sides of a war was not the kind of dispute that could be set aside without hard feelings. Southern Democrats could not overlook how Northern Legitimist Democrats had distanced themselves from Confederates by favoring candidates such as Union General George B. McClellan and passing numerous resolutions of appreciation for soldiers. One historian has summed up the Northern Democratic perspective, in turn, as viewing the Southern wing as "something of an albatross."[71] True, the Democratic Party derived political legitimacy from being the only national party – the Southern Republican Party was virtually nonexistent previous to war and was inadequately organized throughout Reconstruction – but with the benefits of national party-dom came great difficulty keeping diverse constituents united.

To keep everyone happy, Democrats typically defined their party in terms of what it opposed: interventionist federal government, taxation, and government regulation of social relations and behaviors. Ideological favor for personal liberty was an adaptable discourse. To white Southerners, it meant that the federal government should not interfere with contracts between white employers and black labor. To immigrants in the urban North, it meant that government should not restrict the number of saloons, which often served as an ethnic community's bank, meeting hall, and recreation center. On the basis of protecting personal liberty, Democrats from both sections could organize together against the Northeastern and Midwest-based Republican Party, which defined itself as an advocate for activist government and internal improvements, and the catchalls of morality, patriotism, and prosperity.[72]

---

[70] On the history of Reconstruction and Reconstruction politics, see Eric Foner, *Reconstruction: America's Unfinished Revolution, 1863–1877* (New York: Harper & Row, 1988); Michael W. Fitzgerald, *Splendid Failure: Postwar Reconstruction in the American South* (Chicago: Ivan R. Dee, 2007).

[71] William Gillette, *Retreat from Reconstruction: 1869–1879* (Baton Rouge: Louisiana State University Press, 1979), 58.

[72] One of the most coherent and concise surveys of post-Civil War national party politics is Robert W. Cherny, *American Politics in the Gilded Age, 1868–1900* (Wheeling, IL: Harlan Davidson, Inc., 1997), 22–45.

Notwithstanding agreements among Democrats, there were problems inherent to organizing a national party around the issues of local and personal freedoms. For rights-focused Democrats, the very nature of American political institutions – particularly the fact that any citizen could print ballots to distribute at polls on election day – created easy ways to circumvent already-lax national party discipline. Local party bosses might print variations of the ballot they had been instructed to print, replace official candidates' names with new choices, or simply propose alternative tickets after the regular party nominations were closed. Individual voters who accepted ballots on the day of the election might not even know that they had cast a ballot that diverged from the list of candidates sanctioned by nominating conventions. Their ballot might read "Democratic Party" on the top; given the number of offices it would be difficult to recognize deviations. And voters might not have cared even if they did notice. Nineteenth-century polling sites were chaotic environments that one political scientist has described as having an unseemly "auctioneering atmosphere" in which voters expected to be compensated with money, liquor, or both.[73]

Democrats' allegiance to the principle of local determination, moreover, inhibited coalition-building when the locality was divided. In particular, irreconcilable responses to freedmen's expanding suffrage threatened to splinter the Southern branch of the party because these responses demanded incompatible strategies. On one side, Democratic-Conservatives – largely elites and former Whigs, and initially the most powerful faction of Southern Democrats – planned to ratify new state constitutions, thus accepting African-American suffrage. They argued that accepting African-American suffrage was a necessary prerequisite for cultivating fusion candidates with Republicans, which in turn was necessary because the disfranchisement of former Confederates would make it nearly impossible to elect Democrats until amnesty increased the number of white voters.

Democratic-Conservatives hoped to swing votes toward the more conservative group of Republicans whenever two groups of Republicans nominated separate tickets, something that frequently occurred in state-level elections. And if they could also capture African-American votes by

---

[73] Jerrold G. Rusk, "The Effect of the Australian Ballot Reform on Split Ticket Voting: 1876–1908," *American Political Science Review*, 64:4 (December 1970), 1221. See also Richard Franklin Bensel, *The American Ballot Box in the Mid-Nineteenth Century* (New York: Cambridge University Press, 2004).

virtue of bringing white employers' pressure to bear on black labor, so much the better.

Bourbon Democrats, in contrast, believed that the best way to salvage the Democratic Party in the South was to refuse to recognize the political and constitutional changes of Reconstruction, including African-American suffrage. In so doing, the party would retain the integrity of its principles and assure the existence of a home to which gradually re-enfranchised former Confederates could return.[74] As the re-enfranchisement of former Confederates expanded and as white violence and restrictive taxes forced African Americans away from the polls, many Southern states became essentially one-party domains, further stimulating factionalism that could only be resolved by primary elections.[75] Primary elections conducted by the Democratic Party emerged in the South not only to create a space for mass participation within what was otherwise one-party rule but also to diffuse dissent within the party.[76]

With a large plurality in Congress, Stalwart and Half-Breed Republicans were cooperating better than Conservative-Democrats and Bourbon Democrats. All the same, there was a looming conflict between President Andrew Johnson and Congress. The legislature and executive were unable to agree upon who should be in charge of Reconstruction, what should characterize the terms for Southern states' restored status, and how much protection should be extended to freedpeople. So apparent was the tension within Republican leadership that Northern Democratic Legitimists tried to persuade fellow partisans that support for Andrew Johnson could encourage him to break from the Republican Party while simultaneously dispersing any accusations that Democrats were innately traitorous.[77] And indeed, in 1866 Johnson expressed his vision for a dramatically different Republican Party, one that might even possess a new name, and that would exclude Southern proslavery and secessionist leaders, Northern Democrats who had opposed the war, and Radical Republicans.[78]

---

[74] Michael Perman, *The Road to Redemption: Southern Politics, 1869–1879* (Chapel Hill: University of North Carolina Press, 1984), 60.

[75] George H. Mayer, *The Republican Party, 1854–1966*, 2nd ed. (New York: Oxford University Press, 1967), 171–220.

[76] L. Sandy Maisel, *Parties and Elections in America: The Electoral Process*, 2nd ed. (New York: McGraw-Hill, Inc., 1993), 149; V.O. Key, Jr., *Southern Politics in State and Nation* (New York: Alfred A. Knopf, 1949), 444–450.

[77] Joel H. Silbey, *A Respectable Minority: The Democratic Party in the Civil War Era, 1860–1868* (New York: W.W. Norton & Company, 1977), 177–184.

[78] Richard Abbott, *The Republican Party and the South, 1855–1877 – The First Southern Strategy* (Chapel Hill: University of North Carolina Press, 1986), 46.

Little came of this threat, and he was largely discredited by impeachment in 1868, but even the whiff of a bolting president illuminates the extraordinary intraparty conflict at hand.

Regional tensions were also made acute by the Northern Republican Party's neglect of Southern party development. Republicans had won and could continue to win national elections without the support of Southern states because the Northern states had a much greater population and hence more votes in the electoral college. In the end, Northern Republicans in Congress were unable to muster enthusiasm for Southern speaking tours, fund-raising, or even carefully considered patronage. These gestures would have been necessary for the party to remain competitive after Democratic-leaning former Confederates were re-enfranchised.[79]

When crafting a Reconstruction policy, the Republican Party consistently emphasized the protection of Northern electoral support over the opportunity to build a Southern constituency. Republicans did eventually support suffrage for African Americans, who were likely to vote Republican in memory of emancipation. However, when a Republican-dominated Congress advanced the Fifteenth Amendment, it did so largely because an amendment was more likely to appeal to Northern voters than would experiments with property redistribution. Freedpeople's demands for land, civil rights, and social services, in turn, were widely used by Northern Republicans as a rationale for abandoning African Americans to the questionable mercies of former Confederates.[80]

The feeble Republican Party in the South struggled over strategy design, always with the specter of more and more re-enfranchised former Confederates looming on the horizon. So-called Centrist Republicans – typically men with political experience who focused on material improvements and had no particular interest in African-American civil rights – accepted white re-enfranchisement as inevitable and therefore sought to court these would-be voters in advance. A second group of Regular Republicans – often Northern migrants who represented African-American voters and relied on the distribution of federal patronage – simultaneously sought to restrict white former Confederate voters and to disband Conservative-dominated state governments. These strategies were contradictory and incompatible because one could not easily appeal

---

[79] Abbott, *Republican Party and the South*, especially 58–69.
[80] Heather Cox Richardson, *The Death of Reconstruction: Race, Labor, and Politics in the Post-Civil War North, 1865–1901* (Cambridge: Harvard University Press, 2001), xiv, 47, 98–111, 121.

to and disfranchise the same group of would-be constituents – that is, former Confederates.[81] African-American voters, Republicans recognized, could be held in the party with minimal concessions, but without some white support, Republicans could not be elected to state offices in a post-amnesty political world.

By the early 1870s, most Northern Republicans were exasperated that a free labor economy in the South remained elusive. The idea that the party owed special protection to African Americans was losing whatever favor it had once held, and the Northern media increasingly (and unfairly) characterized freedpeople as having plundered state governments for handouts because they were too lazy or immoral to work. From this conviction emerged the Liberal Republican revolt, which called for a rapid conclusion of Reconstruction and the re-enfranchisement of white former Confederates. Former rebels could presumably restore order to Southern state governments while, not inconsequentially, being so grateful to Republicans for reinstatement that they might consider switching parties.[82] Liberal Republicans – "best men" of education and standing who expressed alarm over the growth of federal power and corporations – first bolted in the 1870 Missouri election, running tickets opposed to Regular Republicans and winning their campaign.[83]

In 1872, the Liberal Republicans decided to bolt the national Republican Party ticket after the nomination of Ulysses S. Grant, who they considered irretrievably corrupt. Meeting in Cincinnati, the Liberal Republicans were surprised to find their ranks infiltrated by other reformers and anti-Grant factionalists, who then nominated the *New York Tribune*'s editor, Horace Greeley, as the party's candidate. David Davis, who already held the Labor Reform Party nomination, had hoped to receive the Liberal Republican endorsement and run as a fusion candidate; his loss to Greeley discouraged him enough that he dropped out of the race entirely, leaving the Labor Reform Party with no candidate and, soon, no party.[84]

For his part, Greeley had not previously been involved with the Liberal Republican movement. Yet Greeley was a palatable candidate to many Democratic leaders, and Liberal Republicans and their new adherents

---

[81] Perman, *Road to Redemption*, 22–56.

[82] Richardson, *Death of Reconstruction*, 89–100; Charles W. Calhoun, *Conceiving a New Republic: The Republican Party and the Southern Question, 1869–1900* (Lawrence: University Press of Kansas, 2006), 35.

[83] On the Liberal Republicans, see John G. Sproat, *"The Best Men"*; McGerr, *Decline of Popular Politics*, 42–68.

[84] Ritter, *Greenbacks and Goldbugs*, 48.

hoped that he would emerge as the *fusion candidate* – that is, become
a candidate nominated by both Liberal Republicans and Democrats for
the same office. Democrats were intrigued by the idea of such a coalition
because Southern Democrats, in particular, had been fusing with local and
state-level Republican splinter groups for several years. These Southern
Democrats would nominate Greeley as their candidate on the basis of a
shared interest in amnesty for former Confederates. Because endorsing
Greeley would demonstrate Southern support for a Northern candidate,
this nomination would theoretically free up Southern Democrats from
seeming like a sectional, traitorous party, while still giving them a chance
to oppose Grant.

The problem was that rank and file Southern Democrats did not cast
ballots for Greeley, even if they were unexcited by Grant's continuing
presidency.[85] Grant won the 1872 election by a large margin, with the
exhausted and humiliated Horace Greeley dying shortly after ballots were
counted. The meaning of the election of 1872 and the Liberal Republicans' organized bolt nonetheless remained open for interpretation by
political leaders looking toward the 1876 campaign. Had the Liberal
Republicans been successful at bolting and establishing a new alignment
in national politics, or had they been failures at electing their candidate?
The Prohibition Party clamored for the end of Democratic-Republican
control of party politics at the precise moment when war-weary leaders
were struggling to consolidate the support of splintered elites and harness
this support to populist campaigns.

* * *

No gesture more powerfully conveyed Prohibitionists' commitment
to single-issue party politics than their actions during the 1876 election, wherein freedpeople's continued protection and the survival of the
Republican Party in the South was in the balance. Prohibitionists declined
to fuse with Republicans and instead nominated their own candidates:
Green Clay Smith, a Civil War general who was a former Democrat and
elected representative from Kentucky, and Gideon T. Stewart, who was
serving a term as national secretary. In contrast, the Liberal Republicans
agreed to support Rutherford B. Hayes's candidacy despite what they perceived as a mediocre record.[86] Prohibition Party historian D. Leigh Colvin
would later recall how the congressional election of 1874 had carried

[85] Perman, *Road to Redemption*, 125.
[86] Sproat, *"The Best Men,"* 93–100.

the House of Representatives for the Democrats, intensifying Americans' belief that Republicans' dominance in national politics was uncertain and that 1876 was a truly critical election for the nation.[87] The Republicans' candidate, Rutherford B. Hayes, and the Democrats' candidate, Samuel J. Tilden, engaged in a bitter and very competitive campaign throughout 1876, despite their many similarities as conservatives who favored moderate civil service reform. In addition to Reconstruction, Hayes and Tilden's campaign debated fiscal policies, the value of organized labor and responsibilities of capital, and Civil War memorialization.

Most Prohibitionists had been antislavery Republicans and might well have returned to their previous party to express alarm about freedpeople's future in Southern states. They could have used their antislavery ties as an excuse to abandon a not totally successful endeavor, keeping their dignity intact. However, most Prohibitionists explored a very different way of understanding their obligations. They argued that Reconstruction was a failing policy that made the blessing of emancipation into something potentially as dangerous as slavery. Unrestrained liquor consumption was the source of the extraordinary and continuing unrest in the American South, they claimed. "We think it must be admitted that intemperance presents a fearful peril to the colored population of this country," noted Prohibitionists at the 1876 national convention. "That four millions of people so lately emancipated from the low condition of chattel slavery should be a comparatively easy prey to strong drink, is a most natural supposition, and a fact which should excite the fears and engage the attention of those entrusted with the administration of public affairs."[88] Prohibitionists' admiration for the abolitionists' legacy did not divorce them from white America's apprehension that a free African-American population would engage in debauchery and anarchy. Rather, their assumption that liquor held an extraordinary capacity to seduce individuals augmented this anxiety.

Republican Party managers placed enormous pressure on traditional Republican voters and encouraged Prohibition Party candidates to withdraw. They argued that the Prohibition Party was undemocratic because, by attracting temperate Republicans to a party bound to be defeated, Prohibitionists would be aiding a party that did not actually represent

---

[87] Colvin, *Prohibition in the United States*, 113. Joel H. Silbey describes the small margins by which national campaigns were won and lost between 1876 and 1892; *The American Political Nation, 1838–1893* (Stanford: Stanford University Press, 1991), 219.

[88] *National Prohibition Reform Party*, 10.

the will of the majority into power: the Democrats. The Prohibition Party would both subvert the nation's preference for continued Republican rule and obscure the true measure of national support for anti-liquor restriction. Prohibitionists defensively questioned, "When will that time come that our right to exist as a party will be confessed? When shall we not be arrogantly charged with designedly acting as allies of the party against whose leading sentiment we chiefly labor?"[89] They rejected "the great, the ever present charge against us...that we are helping the democracy" by asserting that "we are simply advocating down-right prohibition of the liquor traffic."[90] In Southern state elections Prohibitionists would be similarly accused of aiding the Republicans to undermine the Democrats.[91]

Unmoved by Republican indictments and pleas, Prohibitionists hyperbolically denied any preference between the Republican Party to which most members had formerly belonged and the Democratic Party they reviled. At Prohibitionists' 1876 national convention, they insisted that

so far... from having any special care as to whether Democrats or Republicans administer the government during the next four years, the wise course for every one opposed to dram-shop rule is to vote a ticket which represents his own principles, and thereby help to render it "morally certain" that neither of them shall ever elect again, and even prevent such a misfortune at this time if possible.[92]

At the same time, the development of a *pairing off* strategy belied Prohibitionists' greater affinity for Republicans. Prohibitionists urged Republican temperance advocates to "seek a neighbor Democrat, and... agree to pair off and each vote the Prohibition ticket."[93] Such a voter could be assured that he would not influence the outcome of the election against Republicans unless by so doing he and his partner ushered a Prohibitionist into office.

For Prohibitionists, the returns of the 1876 election were again disappointing; Smith and Stewart received only 9,737 votes in 18 states. The largest state vote was cast for John J. Baker, who was nominated as

[89] The Republican press' tendency to dismiss the Prohibition Party as a Democratic ruse is discussed in "Helping the Democrats," *Delaware Signal*, 8 March 1876, and Untitled, *Delaware Signal*, 11 October 1876, as well as many, many other articles.

[90] Untitled, *Delaware Signal*, 4 October 1876. In the original text, the quote beginning with "the great..." appears in all capital letters for emphasis. By "the democracy," Prohibitionists here referred to the Democratic Party.

[91] James D. Ivy, *No Saloon in the Valley: The Southern Strategy of Texas Prohibitionists in the 1880s* (Waco, TX: Baylor University Press, 2003), especially 36–38.

[92] *National Prohibition Reform Party*, 12.

[93] "How to Test Them," *Delaware Signal*, 25 October 1876.

a fusion candidate by Massachusetts Prohibitionists and Greenbackers, with Baker receiving 12,127 votes. State returns were unsatisfactory, but they were better than national returns.[94] Loyal Prohibitionists like H.A. Thompson reprimanded deserters, chiding that "those who went into this great moral warfare, expecting it to be a sharp cavalry charge, and then a quick and glorious victory, did not carefully count the cost."[95] Thompson also attempted to raise spirits by asserting that "new men are coming to our ranks daily. True, others are dropping off, but only for a time. They have grown disheartened, and have thought to try once more for success in the old parties. The chains that bound them can never be reunited as they once were."[96]

To this end, Prohibitionists creatively interpreted the desertion of timid partisans as a critical first step toward eventual success. Questioning "Are we as a party really weaker now than heretofore?" some Prohibitionists resolved that "I believe we are not, but much stronger" because the dispersal of party voters inspired remaining voters to commit themselves as permanent members, not as people who were temporarily discontent with the major parties and hoping for a "protest vote."[97] In a *Minnesota Radical* article descriptively entitled "Not a Failure," one Prohibitionist declared that "the Prohibitionists are every day gaining in confidence, organization, esprit de corps, and moral force, as well as in numbers. They have needed just the experience they have passed through to give them backbone."[98] With particular pride, Prohibitionists asserted that their party was disproportionately composed of young voters, suggesting its bright future.[99]

Distinguishing their ranks as something different than a "protest vote" was particularly important for Prohibitionists given the Greenback and Greenback-Labor parties' concurrent development.[100] Most historians

---

94 Colvin, *Prohibition in the United States*, 114. Paul Kleppner argues that the Greenback and Prohibition parties both socialized voters to abandon party loyalty and expressed discontent with industrialization, thus explaining the movement of many voters between the two minor parties; "The Greenback and Prohibition Parties," in *History of U.S. Political Parties*, 1550, 1559.

95 H.A. Thompson, "Address of H.A. Thompson," *Delaware Signal*, 7 March 1877.

96 H.A. Thompson, "Need of Patience," *Delaware Signal*, 13 December 1876.

97 J.A. Mouser, Untitled letter to the editor, *Delaware Signal*, 20 December 1876.

98 "What of the Future?" *Minnesota Radical*, 27 June 1877, reprinted from *(Albany, New York) Living Issue*.

99 "Not a Failure," *Minnesota Radical*, 19 September 1877.

100 Gretchen Ritter has identified the antimonopoly movement as consisting of the Labor Reform Party, the Greenback and Greenback Labor parties, the Antimonopolist Party,

have suggested that Greenbackers fundamentally viewed themselves as a protest group. Created in the wake of the 1873 depression, the Greenback party built on the foundations of worker and farmer organizations to express antimonopoly sentiment and, more specifically, a condemnation of the National Banking System and the return to a gold standard for currency. It expressed sincere unease about significant problems. Nonetheless, the Greenback Party and its successor, the Greenback-Labor Party, tended to perform best in midterm elections and very poorly in presidential election years. This was a problem these parties shared with many citizens' tickets organized during the 1870s. Whereas in 1876, the Greenback candidate for president received less than 1 percent of the national vote, the Greenback-Labor Party of 1878 would elect 15 congressmen, including future Populist Party presidential candidate James Baird Weaver. Mark Wahlgreen Summers has interpreted this as evidence that voters "looked to state offices for substantive change," were often organized around interests with only regional appeal, and most importantly, did not want to permanently alter the identity of the two governing parties. "They were sending a message about governance" and "voting for congressmen was a less dangerous way for party loyalists to express anger."[101] During a highly competitive party system, protest voting worked, assuming that its goal was to provoke changes in major parties rather than to overturn them.

Unlike the Free Soil or Prohibition parties, the Greenback Party seems to have been both led and populated by citizens who anticipated a return to the major parties rather than either remaining independent or coalescing with other minor parties to form a new party. In the American South, for example, most Greenback or Greenback-Labor voters identified as disgruntled Democrats, frustrated by elite "rings" but also reluctant to align with African Americans.[102] North Carolinian antimonopolists only needed to suggest that they might form a separate Greenback Party to encourage Democrats to channel antimonopoly sentiment into their platforms, in the process ensuring the party's dominance in the state.[103] In

the Union Labor Party, the People's Party, and the National Democratic Party, as well as "scores of state-level parties." Ritter, *Greenbacks and Goldbugs*, 1, 2 n. 2.

[101] Mark Wahlgren Summers, *Party Games: Getting, Keeping, and Using Power in Gilded Age Politics* (Chapel Hill: University of North Carolina Press, 2004), 202–203.

[102] Matthew Hild, *Greenbackers, Knights of Labor, and Populists: Farmer-Labor Insurgency in the Late-Nineteenth-Century South* (Athens: University of Georgia Press, 2007), 9–44.

[103] Ritter, *Greenbacks and Goldbugs*, 111, 113–123.

the North, "outcasts and exiles remembered their old party homes and in their minds wove fantasies about how a return might be possible."[104] As an example of the sort of suicidal gesture that only a protest party would make, political scientist Gretchen Ritter has noted that the nomination of Peter Cooper, the New York industrialist who had founded Cooper Union, could not be interpreted as a serious nomination given that Cooper was over eighty years old when selected by his party.[105]

Both leaders and voters in the Greenback movement viewed their actions as provoking policy change from Democrats and Republicans, rather than as building a constituency. This distinguished Greenbackers from the Prohibition Party, wherein leadership and a fair portion of voters had pledged themselves to continually vote with their party. Prohibitionist leaders claimed that functioning as a protest party was never their intent, even as they grudgingly conceded that their party had sometimes been little more than "a party of protest, not, as now, an organization of power."[106]

As for Democrats and Republicans, the outcome of the 1876 election was initially unclear. Tilden carried the South and several Northern cities with a popular margin of 300,000 votes over Hayes. However, disputed returns from Louisiana, South Carolina, Florida, and Oregon could challenge Tilden's supremacy in the electoral college if all of these states cast for Hayes. When Congress reconvened in January, it created a special electoral commission that awarded Hayes the disputed votes and the presidency. Congress agreed to approve this resolution after agreeing on its own set of political bargains, later referred to as the Compromise of 1877. Democrats agreed to support Hayes after Republicans pledged to appoint at least one Southern Democrat to the president's cabinet, to grant control of federal patronage in Democratic regions to the Democratic Party, to provide federal aid for Southern states, and to withdraw federal troops from states occupied under Reconstruction. This last condition, supported by the other mechanisms, would discontinue assistance that had led to improvements in the economic and social status of freedpeople and would facilitate the reestablishment of rigid racial hierarchy. As such, it represented a significant step back from the Republican Party's initial ambitions.

[104] Summers, *Party Games*, 203.
[105] Ritter, *Greenbacks and Goldbugs*, 52.
[106] Alphonso A. Hopkins, "Prohibition vs. Regulation: Speech Delivered by Prof. Alphonso A. Hopkins at Syracuse, N.Y.," *New York Pioneer*, October 1885.

Prohibitionists were horrified not only by the abandonment of freed-people but also by the fact that this abandonment required Republicans to rescind campaign pledges. For the sake of expediency, Republicans had subverted the platform supported by voters. Even the president's cabinet epitomized the relinquishing of prewar Republicans' ideals by including "a traitor on one side and a loyalist on the other" for political ends.[107] With their worst opinions of Republicans confirmed, Prohibitionists believed that the ethical superiority of their own political strategy was vindicated.

After the 1876 election, Prohibitionist leadership called for members to simply intensify their efforts along the paths that were already established, rather than encouraging a change in strategy that might either concede ideological ground to angry Republicans or require resources that Prohibitionists lacked. One Prohibitionist epitomized this impulse when he declared that "We must organize! Something has been done during the past few years, but we have greatly lacked organization . . . we can and must do better now."[108] Prohibitionists called for more county organizations, mass meetings, town caucuses, and conventions. They asserted that "the Prohibition party must be organized and conducted the same as other parties in this country, leaving out the frauds and corrupt practices of the whisky brawlers of the old parties."[109] This meant "local activity in the towns, piling up intelligence around the people and organizing them into strength against this great ruin" – all done with authentic commitment rather than the half-hearted gestures that still seemed too common among some partisans.[110]

What distinguished the party after 1876 was not a bold departure, which might have been expected in the wake of the Reconstruction crisis, but rather startling conformity with its previous guiding philosophy. The 1876 election was a significant turning point for Prohibitionists because, by neither bowing to Republican pressures to drop out nor disclosing alarm about the end of freedpeople's protection, Prohibitionists severed the last and most meaningful connections binding them to the Republican Party.

---

[107] Judge Pitman quoted in "The Prohibition Party," *New York Times*, 12 September 1877.
[108] G.F. Wells (vice president for first congressional Prohibition Alliance), "To the Prohibitionists of the First Congressional District," *Minnesota Radical*, 19 May 1880.
[109] "How to Organize," *Minnesota Radical*, 4 December 1878.
[110] A. Willey, "Hints to Temperance Men," *Minnesota Radical*, 5 May 1880.

Prohibitionists adamantly insisted that the liquor problem, and not Reconstruction, was the most critical issue in American politics. Its potential for destructiveness was simply too great to be ignored. H.A. Thompson argued that alcohol consumption created a litany of problems that were "political" in scope:

the traffic in intoxicating liquors has always been...the source of crime, pauperism, disturbances of the peace, insecurity of life and property, breaking up of homes and separation of families, hindrances to education, bankruptcies and losses in trade, causing one-half and more of our burdensome taxation, corruption in politics and legislation, degeneration of the moral and physical powers of citizens, loss of health and wealth, promotion of idleness and vice, and many more public injuries to the body politic, threatening the perpetuity of our free Government.

He concluded that "if these matters do not come within the province of government, then it has no province."[111] If prohibition could relieve some of this burden on government, the state would run more efficiently and be able to put funds toward the arts, education, and industry. The elimination of the drink traffic would help American democracy operate the way that it should. A.A. Miner, a Universalist minister and former president of Tufts College, mourned that "we know very well that there is misjudgment everywhere, in politics, in corporate enterprises, in individual enterprises – misjudgment that springs from a clouded mind that alcoholic beverages have helped to disturb."[112] Whereas critics might argue that prohibition limited people's access to free choice, Prohibitionists argued that their favored policy would make "a nation of sober people, *capable* of self-government."[113]

Republican politicians continued to woo Prohibitionists and head off temperance advocates leaving their party by promising that high license fees would sufficiently limit the number of saloons while lowering taxes for the average citizen. Prohibitionists expressed their contrasting conviction that individuals who favored license implicated themselves in the

[111] H.A. Thompson, "What is Your Duty?" *Delaware Signal*, 1 November 1876.

[112] A.A. Miner quoted in *Proceedings of the Fourth National Convention of the Prohibition Reform Party, Held at Cleveland, Ohio June 17, 1880* (New York: National Committee of the Prohibition Reform Party, 1880), 19–20. Alonzo Ames Miner was the president of Tufts College from 1862–1864 and served on the Massachusetts State Board of Education in 1869 and as president of the state temperance alliance. He was the Prohibition Party candidate for governor in 1878; "The Rev. Dr. A.A. Minor," *New York Times*, 15 June 1895.

[113] "The Tyranny of Majorities," *Minnesota Radical*, 17 April 1878. Italics are author's.

liquor traffic both when they voted and when they accepted a share of the profits; any tax relief derived from licensing vice was a bribe for the American taxpayer's permission. Such licensing "made the saloonists our partners and *agents* in the business."[114] Whereas Democratic or Republican abstainers and temperance advocates might consider themselves better than their partisan peers, Prohibitionists asserted that such men were as bad if not worse. Gideon T. Stewart scolded that

here is a Christian Temperance citizen who says "I do not drink a drop of the poison and yet I regularly vote the ticket of one of these two parties." That is true, but at your side is a voter of the same party, who drinks up his fifty gallons and your fifty gallons too, every year, and you vote the same ticket with him. In other words, you help him to vote the hundred gallons. You both vote with the Liquor Criminals and for the Liquor Crime.[115]

The abstainer was as guilty as the brewer because "those who enact such [license] laws are as guilty in the sight of God and good men as they would be were they themselves to deal out the poisonous liquid, and send the miserable victims reeling into a drunkard's hell."[116] Well-meaning temperance advocates within the major parties had mortgaged their integrity to party machines that could not advance the movement for national prohibition.

With particular viciousness, the *Delaware Signal* declared that "if we are to wait for prohibition until [Republicans] give it to us, we will wait a long time. This is only a trick of Satan, *alias* the Republican party. It is astonishing how this temperance (?) party, as it pretends to be, dodges and writhes to keep men from voting for what is temperance."[117] The greatest dodge lay in how both the Democratic and Republican parties "will *almost* pass the [prohibition] bill year after year" to suggest that temperance advocates could "stick to the proud old party another year and success will be certain."[118] Voters were complicit in this process

[114] "The Slanders of Our Enemies," *Minnesota Radical*, 25 September 1878. Italics are author's.

[115] Gideon T. Stewart, "The Ballot Test of Temperance for Party Prohibition against the Liquor Crime" in *The Prohibition Party Against the Rum Power*, 53. This speech was originally delivered in 1879.

[116] "Let Us Reason Together," *Minnesota Radical*, 9 January 1878.

[117] C.W. Kohr, Untitled letter to Brother (Thomas) Evans (Jr., the editor and publisher), *Delaware Signal*, 1 January 1879. The question mark is the author's and is intended to convey the ridiculousness of any claim that the Republican Party was truly a temperance party.

[118] "Another Year Has Passed," *Minnesota Radical*, 28 February 1877. Italics are author's.

because years of timidity had "degraded temperance men to the condition of mere pawns moved around upon the political chess-board at the will of the players for the defense of King Alcohol."[119] Even leading Prohibitionists occasionally strayed from party doctrine and became "pawns"; Amanda Way and Frank Sibley would work with major party politicians to advance state prohibition in Kansas in 1880.[120] As an alternative to such alliances, Prohibitionists might instead consider broadening the platform. The possibilities of such a strategy were suggested by what happened in 1878, when the Greenback Party reached out to labor and then polled over one million votes, electing fifteen congressmen.[121]

After considering various possibilities, Prohibitionists committed to just one significant change in political method for the 1880 election: a celebrity candidate.[122] Former governor Neal Dow was widely credited with the Maine Law, but had until recently been an opponent of the dry party idea. Now he seemed convinced. At the 1880 national convention, James Black nominated Dow with the expectation that he would be the first of many individuals with "national representative names... names which would at once receive the acclaim of those who have been long in the temperance work."[123] This was a symbolically laden passing of the torch from a man epitomizing ideological purity to one representing pragmatic party builders' greatest hopes. A shadow was cast only by concerned Prohibitionists who believed that Dow's true loyalties remained with the Republican Party. These Prohibitionists speculated that Dow's personal charisma had bolstered the otherwise faltering legitimacy of the Republican Party as a temperance party in his state and, as a by-product, had prevented the growth of Maine's Prohibition Party.[124] Dow's refusal to actively campaign added some credibility to these claims about his split loyalties.

Neal Dow received a mere 10,364 votes in the 1880 election, leaving Prohibitionists to renegotiate their strategy in the context of a decade of

---

[119] G.H. Carrow, "Do Not Take Temperance into Politics!" 80.

[120] Bader, *Prohibition in Kansas*, 51 and 67.

[121] Kleppner, "The Greenback and Prohibition Parties," 1561.

[122] For an example of Dow's reputation among Prohibitionists, see A. Willey, "National Prohibition Ticket," *Minnesota Radical*, 11 July 1880.

[123] James Black quoted in *Proceedings of the National Convention... 1880*, 35.

[124] "General Neal Dow and the Prohibition Party of Maine," *Delaware Signal*, 22 October 1880; N.F. Woodbury, "Maine Prohibitionists," *National Freeman*, January 1881. Woodbury was Maine's first Prohibition Party state chair. The *National Freeman* was edited by John Russell; the article was solicited by Thomas W. Organ. The cited article was published in the paper's first issue.

electoral failure rather than the anticipation of success. The nature of this transforming environment was summarized by the proud Prohibitionist who optimistically asserted that "there is something sublime in the character of the handful of Prohibitionist voters who remain true to their principles year after year in defiance of persuasion and ridicule, and the overwhelming numbers of their opponents." Nonetheless, even this partisan conceded that it was foolish to talk of future victory without making any changes in how the party was conducting its affairs. He resolved that "signs of the times seem to indicate that the Prohibition party, as now organized, cannot attain political supremacy in the nation."[125]

Republicans continued to criticize Prohibitionists for reckless constituency building in the context of looming Democratic victories, arguing that this activity was an "abrogation of the broader duties of citizenship for the accomplishment of a single purpose, not always either broad or important."[126] The vote could never simply be about exercising a right to individual expression. Because Prohibitionists drew most of their supporters from the Republican Party, Prohibitionists weakened the one political institution powerful enough to battle the Democrats, who most vocally supported the liquor industry's continuation.[127]

"The third-party Prohibition agitators are the habit of comparing themselves to the early Abolitionists," noted a Kansas newspaper, but they had forgotten that "there was a class of Abolitionists who were cranks and fanatics. They were of both sexes, the women wearing short hair and the men wearing long hair. But they were mere annoyances, not helpers in the real anti-slavery movement. They had an offensive and exasperating manner. They made men mad, instead of convincing or persuading them." The disgust of abolitionist peers with these radicals was only increased when "there was a 'third party' formed by these cranks, which actually defeated the Whig party at times when an important advantage over slavery might have been obtained by a Whig victory at the polls."[128] Prohibitionists did not really vote for a principle,

---

[125] Francis M. Cummings, "Our Duty," *Delaware Signal*, 1 December 1880.

[126] "Prohibition and Politics," *New York Times*, 7 August 1881. See also "Prohibition of Good Government," *New York Times*, 26 October 1883.

[127] "What Shall We Do to Check the Use of Intoxicants?" *(Philadelphia) Friends' Intelligencer*, 15 April 1882.

[128] "The Abolitionists and the Prohibitionists," *(Topeka?) Commonwealth*, 28 October 1884, Kansas Prohibition Scrapbook #2, pages 241–242, Kansas State Historical Society, Topeka, KS. See also Gail Hamilton, "Prohibition in Politics," *North American Review*, June 1885.

Republicans argued, because Prohibitionists did not vote in a way that advanced that principle.[129]

* * *

Prohibitionist editors, organizers, and other doctrine makers sought to transform their minor party into a major party and recognized that as a consequence of their growth either or both of the Democratic and Republican parties would disappear from the party system. Many contemporaries dismissed this plan as idealistic bluster. Nevertheless some leading Republicans aggressively countered Prohibitionists' proposal, even labeling the party a Democratic subterfuge. In the highly competitive postwar political environment, this accusation was tantamount to accusing Prohibitionists of inciting Southern rebellion, abandoning freedpeople, and encouraging liquor consumption.

Without a massive network of office holders and newspapers through which to propagandize, and unable to purchase votes because they were moralists with few funds, Prohibitionists sought out a new way to meet the Republicans' challenge. They enthusiastically embraced an innovative strategy that had been present (although not always emphasized) since the party's founding. At the local, state, and national levels, Prohibitionists welcomed women as their partisan peers. Women had been speakers and organizers in the antislavery movement but were excluded from its institutionalization in the Republican Party, left politically adrift or at least undeveloped. The Prohibition Party would provide an unprecedented opportunity for women to bring the skills they had acquired in civic organizations to politics and political parties.

[129] N.W. Jordan, "The Third Party," *Zion's Herald*, 19 December 1883.

3

Women's Peculiar Partisanship

When the 1869 founding convention of the Prohibition Party seated thirty women delegates, it became the first political party to include women – citizens ineligible to vote – as party members and, even more notably, shapers of the party agenda. Women spoke from the floor, entered debates, introduced resolutions, and voted on the platform. Amanda Way and fellow delegate Fanny Woodbury were featured speakers, and Mrs. Balton was spontaneously called to address the convention and take a seat on the platform.[1] One woman delegate from Minnesota concluded that "women wanted to work with the Temperance party, and it was too magnanimous to refuse them the privilege."[2] However, her deliberately understated comments, and the audience's rapt attention, actually underscored the importance of what had transpired.

The Prohibition Party chose to welcome women as "peers in every respect" because women's inclusion in party ranks reconciled a key tension in party philosophy.[3] Namely, women's involvement expressed Prohibitionists' desire to both emulate major parties' success and be fundamentally different from them. Not for Prohibitionists was that "vast and corrupt party machinery by which the old parties are operated," and thus they turned to women workers and women leaders as an

---

[1] Amanda Way volunteered to withdraw as a speaker so that the convention could further discuss Gerrit Smith's address and how it might be modified for publication, and was rescheduled to speak at the second night's evening session. She gave a second speech on women's rights at a postconvention session.

[2] "Temperance: Meeting of the National Convention," *Chicago Tribune*, 3 September 1869.

[3] *Proceedings of the Fourth National Convention... 1880*, 31.

alternative labor source whose contributions could help a fledgling party meet the electoral system's demands.[4] In turn, women who joined the Prohibition Party were not without their own expectations. Drawing on recent experiences as part of Civil War-era civilian associations, they perceived themselves to be skilled leaders capable of managing complex bureaucracies and making substantial contributions.[5] They also insisted that temperance, as a matter of family economy and personal morality, was an issue in which women were distinctly invested as wives and mothers.

This matter of making women "peers in every respect" was as complicated as it was unprecedented in the world of party politics. Women Prohibitionists' activism was routinely scrutinized by the women themselves, by male partisans, and by outsiders, and these individuals analyzed it through both gendered and partisan lenses. Even when working side by side with men, women members acting under party mandate inevitably ascribed new gendered meanings to their work.

Gender conventions could create extraordinary opportunities; Prohibitionist men and women observed that widely held assumptions about women's moral purity and men's obligation to protect them could be harnessed to new types of party work such as lawsuits and direct action. And nowhere more than in the case of the Women's Crusade, a movement wherein respectable women entered saloons to demand concessions from bartenders and owners, could Prohibitionists see the dramatic potential of women's politics. In the post-Crusade era, women Prohibitionists would emerge as high profile party leaders, and the party would formalize its relationship with Crusading women through an alliance with the Woman's Christian Temperance Union in 1882. Remarkably, this alliance made the majority of the Prohibition Party's constituency female. Although the question of women's suffrage would prove the key backdrop against which a consensus regarding women's partisanship was worked out, women's Prohibition Party activities and the discourse surrounding these activities also galvanized an idea of *partisanship* that pushed beyond

---

[4] Rebecca Edwards, *Angels in the Machinery: Gender in American Party Politics from the Civil War to the Progressive Era* (New York: Oxford University Press, 1997), 41. My analysis departs from Edwards' work by describing the intense nature of women's involvement in the 1870s while identifying the mid-1880s as a period of declining involvement and by drawing more extensively from Prohibition Party sources rather than WCTU sources.

[5] See Lori D. Ginzberg, *Women and the Work of Benevolence: Morality, Politics, and Class in the Nineteenth-Century United States* (New Haven: Yale University Press, 1990).

voting and elections. With a new idea of partisanship, the very essences of *politics* and *democracy* were seemingly opened for debate.

* * *

To understand the radicalism of Prohibitionists' decision to include women members, one must first grasp the extent to which Gilded Age Americans considered partisanship to be not only common for men and unusual for women but also honorable for men and ethically problematic for women. So entrenched was what Elisabeth Clemens calls the "logic of appropriateness" connecting "actors and organizational form" that even some women's rights advocates hesitated at the threshold of partisan politics for fear that political parties, which were longtime male sanctuaries, would make women corrupt.[6] Amanda Way, a delegate to the first national convention, alluded to these concerns when she explained that "it has been told me often that if I dabbled in the dirty pool of politics, I would be so thoroughly contaminated that I would be unfit to go home . . . but I believe I do not feel much the worse for being here."[7] Way argued against conventional claims that self-interested men could use partisanship to direct their competitive impulses into useful corridors, whereas party discipline might render women unable to direct political housekeeping. For most Americans, party politics by definition involved constant, lubricating compromises that threatened to undermine women's moral character. Party politics also involved swearing and bickering that respectable women could not bear.[8]

This is not to say that women were without partisan sympathies. Prohibitionist "Mother" Eliza Stewart, for example, referred to this tendency when she asserted that political contests had consistently swept "both men and women off their feet into the seething whirlpool, for

---

[6] Clemens, *People's Lobby*, 203. Some historians assert that the idea of women's moral superiority also fueled post-Civil War women's politics. Linda Gordon, *Heroes of Their Own Lives: The Politics and History of Family Violence* (New York: Viking Press, 1988); Peggy Pascoe, *Relations of Rescue: The Search for Female Moral Authority in the American West, 1874–1939* (New York: Oxford University Press, 1990).

[7] "Temperance!" *Chicago Times*, 3 September 1869.

[8] On the distasteful connotations of partisanship, see Glenn Altschuler and Stuart Blumin, *Rude Republic: Americans and Their Politics in the Nineteenth Century* (Princeton: Princeton University Press, 2000); Mark Voss-Hubbard, *Beyond Party: Cultures of Antipartisanship in Northern Politics before the Civil War* (Baltimore: Johns Hopkins University Press, 2002); Richard Hofstadter, *The Idea of a Party System: The Rise of Legitimate Opposition in the United States, 1780–1840* (Berkeley: University of California Press, 1970).

the time blinding them to every other object but the success of 'my party.'"[9] However, major parties generally limited women's participation to symbolically expressive occasions – a daylight costume parade, a gathering of women in the convention hall's balcony, a presentation of craftwork gifts to a candidate – when their limited sojourn into a political arena would demonstrate the particular significance of a campaign.[10] Even radical abolitionist and Socialist parties had restricted women to either the limited domain of educational work or separate auxiliaries.[11]

Neither major party would seriously consider soliciting women's assistance in designing platforms or policy for decades. To highlight their own progressiveness, Prohibitionists eagerly reported that when Henry Blackwell, the nationally prominent reformer, proposed in 1876 that "women who are known to be Republicans in principle" be invited to the Republican Party's primary meetings, he was hissed by fellow partisans.[12] Women citizens likewise had a limited role in routine party work. Only in the late 1880s would Republicans lethargically organize women in auxiliaries under the guidance of J. Ellen Foster, waiting until 1892 before two women first served as alternates for delegates to the Republican National Convention. The Democrats would lag even further behind, providing no financial backing to the women who organized fledgling support clubs in the 1890s. No women served in an official capacity at the Democratic National Convention until 1900.[13]

Prohibitionists believed that they had found a compelling basis for disrupting the male/partisan, female/apartisan paradigm. They argued that their party's dedication to a moral agenda would ensure that policy making and advocacy could be consistent with the highest values of their

---

[9] Mother Stewart, Untitled, *Delaware Signal*, 10 November 1880. See also Edwards, *Angels in the Machinery*; Jo Freeman, *A Room at a Time: How Women Entered Party Politics* (New York: Rowman & Littlefield Publishers, Inc., 2000); Melanie Gustafson, *Women and the Republican Party, 1854–1924* (Urbana: University of Illinois Press, 2001).

[10] Mary Ryan, *Women in Public: Between Banners and Bullets, 1825–1880* (Baltimore: Johns Hopkins University Press, 1990).

[11] Michael Pierson, *Free Hearts and Free Men: Gender and American Antislavery Politics* (Chapel Hill: University of North Carolina Press, 2003); Mary Jo Buhle, *Women and American Socialism, 1870–1920* (Urbana: University of Illinois Press, 1981). For an example of a Liberty Party nominating convention in which women did participate, see Lori D. Ginzberg, *Untidy Origins: A Sotry of Woman's Rights in Antebellum New York* (Chapel Hill: University of North Carolina Press, 2005), 124–125.

[12] An account of the incident and a pithy response by Prohibitionists is featured in "Are They Women?" *Delaware Signal*, 18 October 1876.

[13] Freeman, *A Room at a Time*, 41; Gustafson, *Women and the Republican Party*, 77.

gender. The party's straightforward platform against the liquor traffic and the absence of any history of scandals suggested to women that their purity would not be exploited to make the immoral appear legitimate. In turn, women's participation would "assist materially in giving the movement character and standing" because "if a woman's way is soft, it is a kind of softness with a power in it."[14] For a party routinely accused of being a sneaky Democratic ruse to sabotage Republicans, such means to secure public respect for its integrity was important. And for some women, the unlikelihood of imminent electoral success made Prohibition partisanship appealing because defeat removed the temptation of spoils and, hence, appearance of corruption. C. Augusta Morse diplomatically suggested that women were "enthusiastic [members] because our prayers and our efforts win to our ranks all who love purity more than popularity."[15]

Prohibitionists would find it impolitic to ever suggest that women joined their party to advance their gendered interests; making promises of reward or horse trading would be counterproductive because it would erode the public esteem granted to women and hence the value of their endorsement. Prohibitionists did argue, however, that women wanted suffrage so that they could advance moral causes in a way that was consistent with their own pursuit of dignity. Prohibitionists asked, "Can not the temperance party then, ought it not, in fact, make an effort to give so important an ally, the right to help in its political work?"[16]

At least one delegate to the first national convention desperately tried to persuade fellow delegates that "by adopting [a woman suffrage plank] they would enlist many women on their side, advocates of female suffrage whom they could not afford to ignore. They must not place any bar to the admission of women to the party."[17] When the party nonetheless hesitated at the threshold of a women's suffrage plank, outside critics such as prominent women's rights reformer Mary Livermore scolded the Prohibition Party.[18] John Russell mounted a defense that was an offense. Scolding Livermore for scolding Prohibitionists, Russell declared that

---

[14] The Women of Minnesota," *Minnesota Radical*, 6 March 1878; A.G.S., "Proving Things and Doing Things," *Minnesota Radical*, 11 July 1877.

[15] C. Augusta Morse, "Why Are We Enthusiastic?" *Delaware Signal*, 8 December 1880.

[16] C., "Notes from the Interior," *Peninsular Herald*, 23 February 1870.

[17] "Temperance: Meeting of the National Convention," *Chicago Tribune*, 3 September 1869.

[18] Livermore would join the Prohibition Party in 1887; Untitled, *Weekly Censor*, 10 November 1887.

"the women of the Nation did not do their duty in the matter at all. They were generally invited to be there... they should have been there for the interest they are supposed to take in the temperance reform."[19] By both embracing women who attended the first convention and chiding those women who did not, Prohibitionists like Russell voiced their expectation that women were not simply tolerated, but rather *obligated* to participate in future proceedings. It was therefore cast as a testament to women's confidence in the party – rather than as a gesture catering to otherwise uninterested women – when every national party platform starting in 1872 included a suffrage plank.

The party took still greater delight in finding that men could also be attracted to a party for its universal suffrage position. J.H. Coulter, chair of the Ohio party, expressed the depth of his dedication to women's suffrage when he reflected that "I united with the Prohibition party about two years ago [in 1873] simply because they boldly adopted in their platform the principle of equal and exact justice to all citizens, women as well as men."[20] Women's vote, Coulter and others assumed, would inevitably mean more moral elections.

Just as Prohibitionists avoided the appearance of luring women to the Prohibition Party through suffrage support for fear of undermining a valuable ally's reputation, so did they assiduously avoid the suggestion that women's welcome was contingent upon their willingness to labor. Such an admission would have reeked of undignified desperation because the Democratic and Republican parties seemingly had no trouble finding enough male leaders to speak to crowds of people, assemble and deliver pamphlets with information about candidates, and usher voters to the polls. However, it was true that Prohibitionists lacked enough male personnel to run campaigns in the extraordinary style of major parties without women's assistance.[21] They were further disadvantaged because they could not distribute alcohol to attract partisans to vibrant candlelight parades or to reward partisans for coming to the polls. Nor could their

---

[19] "The Chicago Agitator on the Prohibition Convention," *Peninsular Herald*, 22 September 1869.

[20] J.H. Coulter, "The Curiosities of Misrepresentation," *Delaware Signal*, 21 April 1875.

[21] On the awesome scale, diversity, and pace of political participation in nineteenth-century campaigns, see Bensel, *American Ballot Box in the Mid-Nineteenth Century*; McGerr, *Decline of Popular Politics*; Summers, *Party Games*; R. Hal Williams, "The Politics of the Gilded Age," in *American Political History: Essays on the State of the Discipline*, eds. John F. Marszalek and Wilson D. Miscamble (Notre Dame: University of Notre Dame Press, 1997), 108–142; Silbey, *American Political Nation*.

candidates buy a round to guarantee popularity with regulars at local drinking establishments. As late as 1877, one Prohibitionist periodical would understatedly suggest that "every Prohibitionist should consider himself a specially authorized committee of one" because "the present state of our organization seems to make this method necessary."[22] What was true in 1877 was so much more true in the party's first few years.

Women's recruitment, in turn, would ensure that women had an opportunity to refine the meaning of women's partisanship. Often former abolitionists, early women Prohibitionists were overwhelmingly white and middle class, belonged to temperance fraternities, and were frequently Methodist, Baptist, Presbyterian, or Congregationalist. Only rarely were they Southern – Sallie Chapin was the only Southern woman from among the nine women who served on the national committee between the party's founding and 1884 – and there is little evidence of African-American women's membership despite the fact that there was an active temperance community among such women and that African-American men occasionally served as party leaders.[23] Leading women

---

[22] C.W.B., "Practical Thoughts for Prohibitionists," *Delaware Signal*, 17 January 1877.

[23] Mattie McClellan Brown (1876–1896); Adella R. Worden (1876–1880); Fannie W. McCormack (1876–1880); Mrs. C.W. Pinkham (1880–1882); Sallie F. Chapin (1882–1888); Mary Woodbridge (1882–1884); Frances Willard (1882–1888); Mrs. E.M.H. Richards (1884–1888); Emily Pitt Stevens (1884–1888). The national committee raised funds, allocated them to state parties, determined what documents would be published at party expense, and appointed temporary officers for national conventions; it was the first sieve in determining party protocols. For more information about Sallie Chapin, see Frances Willard, *Woman and Temperance, or The Work and Workers of the Woman's Christian Temperance Union*, 3rd ed. (Hartford, CT: Park Publishing Co., 1883), 540–555. In the 1890s Chapin, a nurse and novelist, would also serve as the president of South Carolina's WCTU and as an endorser for Electropoise, "a panacea for nervousness, brain fatigue, and general debility"; Advertisement, *Voice* (New York), 5 July 1894. She died in 1896.

The Prohibition Party's African-American membership is illuminated through scattered examples. In 1876, two of the five attendees at Kentucky's convention were African American; "First Gun from Dixie," *New Voice*, 18 April 1888. In the mid-1880s, Mississippi Prohibitionists included both white and African-American partisans in their ranks; "General Temperance News," *Center*, 29 July 1886. The Prohibition Party nominated Frank M. Thurman, an African American, for coroner of Jackson County, Michigan, in 1886, and Thurman was then endorsed by the Republicans and won the election; "Field Notes," *Center*, 9 December 1886. Bishop Henry M. Turner, a prominent African-American nationalist, promoted the Prohibition Party as an alternative to the Republican Party. Turner spoke at state conventions (including that of his home state of Georgia) and addressed the 1887 national meeting and the 1888 national convention; "National Prohibitionists," *Center*, 8 December 1887; "State Prohibition Committee," *Kansas Prohibitionist*, 8 April 1886; "National Convention," *Center*, 7 June 1888. In Michigan, Rev. D.A. Graham advocated for the Prohibition Party; "Where Shall We Go?" *Center*,

Prohibitionists included editor, lecturer, and IOGT leader Martha "Mattie" McClellan Brown; United States Sanitary Commission leader "Mother" Eliza Stewart; and founding committee member of the American Woman Suffrage Association and former abolitionist Amanda Way.[24]

23 August 1888. In North Carolina, Rev. C.N. Grandison did similar service; "What a Colored Minister Says," *Lever*, 18 November 1885. A "Prof. Price" from North Carolina – perhaps Joseph C. Price – was also identified as a "distinguished Prohibitionist"; "Alabama Wants Tanner for Vice-President," *New Voice*, 23 February 1888. J.J. Smallwood of Virginia was a professional orator who formally joined the party in 1888; "The Prohibition Park," *New Voice*, 12 July 1888; "Where Stands J.J. Smallwood?" *New Voice*, 27 September 1888. John A. Duling was described as "the future Moses of the Negroes" in "The Colored Vote of Ohio," *Voice*, 23 July 1885, and Rev. H.E. Brown described black and white Prohibitionists sitting together at state conventions in "Prohibition Wiping Out the Color Line," *Voice*, 30 July 1885. The *Lever* had an ongoing campaign to send its publication to African-American ministers in the South throughout the 1880s.

There are numerous references to African-American men serving as delegates and offering resolutions at national conventions or engaging in partisan oratory competitions, but I have not located any African American elevated to the national committee. The national convention of 1888 "threatened to leave its hotel in support of black delegates to whom the management had refused the use of the dining facilities"; Blocker, *Retreat from Reform*, 60. Reports of this incident included the only allusion to an African-American woman delegate that I have encountered. A similar gesture toward boycott was made by partisans who discovered that lecturer J.H. Hector had extraordinary difficulty finding accommodations during a stop in Chicago; "Hector in Chicago," *New Voice*, 5 September 1888. Colored Men's Prohibition Clubs occasionally made appearances during campaigns; "Colored Prohibitionists," *New Voice*, 18 October, 1888. African-American students, presumably of both genders, were solicited by Intercollegiate Prohibition Association organizers, who helped students establish clubs at historically black colleges during the 1890s and 1900s.

Reverend J.H. Hector was the party's "Black Knight," an orator who spoke to crowds of African Americans and white Americans, with his wife and daughter in supporting roles. I have located more references to Hector than can be here included, and they begin as early as the 1880s, meaning that he was already a seasoned speaker when he addressed the national convention in 1904. Intriguingly, the party's national chair (perhaps disparagingly) intimated that Hector was a better fundraiser than organizer. Prohibition State Executive Committee (MN) Minutes, 20 February 1905, PSECM.

[24] Born in 1838, Mattie McClellan Brown developed her public speaking skills by lecturing on patriotic topics during the Civil War. She had a significant role in the founding of the IOGT – she joined in 1861 and was made grand chief Templar of Ohio in 1872. Brown had helped to found the Ohio Prohibition Party in early 1869 before contributing to the founding of the national party, and she intensified her efforts for the Prohibition Party after leaving the IOGT in 1876 when it refused to admit African Americans as members. A frequent contributor to Prohibitionist newspapers, she also edited the *Alliance Monitor*, a party paper founded in 1878, and *Temple Visitor*, a publication for Good Templars. Brown served on the national platform committee in 1876 and helped initiate communication about union with the WCTU in 1877. She served as vice president of the Ohio Prohibition Executive Committee in 1874 and 1875 and then sat on the national committee of the Prohibition Party from 1876 to 1896.

Women would be systematically depended on as a group, and so it was extremely helpful that so many early women Prohibitionists had experience building and maintaining reform organizations.[25]

Despite all the pledges to make women "peers in every respect," Prohibitionists quickly found that women partisans could never be just like men because they and their observers constantly ascribed gendered meanings to women's work. The act of getting newspaper subscriptions to party papers, for example, was construed as a rebellious female response to the ostensibly male-only problem of drunkenness.[26] When John Russell's *Peninsular Herald* asked "who would be the first lady to take stock in this good enterprise" in 1870, it urged, "ladies, we want your help. Every woman who wishes to destroy the greatest curse of her sex, will help to destroy the wicked liquor traffic."[27] Such an invitation structured in such a manner had particular importance given the *Peninsular Herald*'s position as the only party periodical with a national circulation during the organization's first few years. In an 1871 contest sponsored by the *Peninsular Herald*, the paper's selection of inducements for agents selling subscriptions – an organ and a sewing machine – again implied that these agents would generally be women. The *Peninsular Herald* reinforced this by noting that "any lady wishing a Piano can do good while earning half its cost."[28] By 1872, the *Peninsular Herald*'s editorial staff

---

In 1869, Amanda Way was a forty-one-year-old, single woman and the elected leader of a temperance lodge for women and men. She had lent her considerable support to abolition before the Civil War, even offering her home to refugees on the Underground Railroad, as well as serving as a nurse for the Union army. Way also helped organize Indiana's first women's rights convention in 1851 and later the American Woman Suffrage Association and would serve as a minister and lecturer until the Methodist Episcopal general conference discontinued granting licenses to women.

Eliza Stewart was born in 1816 and was raised as a Methodist. She entered public life through participation in the United States Sanitary Commission during the Civil War, a war in which both her husband and sons enlisted. She was also a member of the IOGT. In 1875, Stewart was placed on the Committee on Resolutions at the Ohio Prohibition Convention. She was nationally sought as a party speaker because of her maternal and charismatic appeal and frequently served as a delegate to national conventions and conferences. One of the best sources of information on Stewart is an obituary: "Mother Stewart Goes Home," *(Chicago) National Prohibitionist*, 13 August 1908.

[25] This composite portrait is drawn from women party leaders' obituaries and from collective biographies including Frances Willard and Mary Livermore, *A Woman of the Century* (Buffalo, NY: Charles Wells Moulton, 1893) and Lender, *Dictionary of American Temperance Biography*. On the characteristics of male and female Prohibitionists, see Blocker, *Retreat from Reform*, 8–38.

[26] On the masculine gendering of drunkenness, see Parsons, *Manhood Lost*.

[27] "To the Ladies," *Peninsular Herald*, 12 January 1870.

[28] Advertisement, "Premiums! Large and Small, and Suitable to all Tastes and Circumstances!" *Peninsular Herald*, 27 April 1871.

emphasized its relationship with women readers by including women's columns featuring both the suffrage movement and housekeeping tips.

Women's activism, in turn, could be used as a means to shame men into greater participation. Citing "too little manliness of the men, or, too much indifference or cowardice, to do this just and righteous work," Prohibitionists encouraged women to consider how much more they could protect their homes by using political strategies to combat political problems.[29] When a group of Michigan Prohibitionists became discouraged and considered giving up monthly meetings, "the suggestion was resisted at once" because "the ladies especially seemed urgent that the meetings be continued."[30] Women's abilities to extract greater service from men by leveraging their position as pitiable dependents also placed them at the core of new local and state organizations, where personal relationships were key to maintaining fledging parties. Exemplifying this trend, New York Prohibitionists pointedly encouraged both "the men and women of our State, who are weary of the madness and murder, the wretchedness and ruin which comes from dram selling, to do all in their power and as speedily as possible towards organizing in their respective localities political action against this worst enemy of the American people."[31]

Women's political strategies were praised for being partisan even when they were dissimilar from the traditional work of political parties, and occasionally *because* they were dissimilar. Some prominent Prohibitionists were early supporters of married women's civil damage suits against bartenders and their landlords; wives who depended on their husbands for financial support, these Prohibitionists asserted, should press claims against the liquor sellers who made husbands into inebriates.[32]

[29] "Work to Be Done," *Peninsular Herald*, 1 February 1872.

[30] L.P.S., "From Portland [Michigan]," *Peninsular Herald*, 29 June 1871.

[31] "A New Political Party Formed in New York," *Peninsular Herald*, 5 January 1870.

[32] On civil damage suits, see Parsons, *Manhood Lost*, 36–50. Apparently the first civil damage law, an early Wisconsin law (1849) permitted not only wives but also town boards to sue liquor vendors for recovery of damages created by purchasers of alcohol. I have encountered only one example of enforcement: Joseph Schafer, "Prohibition in Early Wisconsin," *Wisconsin Magazine of History* 8:3 (March 1925): 283, 288, and 299. Civil damage law was also enacted by Kansas' 1859 legislature but apparently never produced any legal action: Bader, *Prohibition in Kansas*, 21. In Illinois and Massachusetts, dramshop acts legislated in the early 1870s were interpreted by the courts to give not only consumers' families but also property holders whose possessions were damaged by minors and drunkards the ability to sue liquor dealers: Perry Duis, *The Saloon: Public Drinking in Chicago and Boston, 1880–1920* (Urbana: University of Illinois Press, 1983), 97–98. In at least one instance, the Prohibition Party proposed that a spouse should be permitted to sue dealers for damages related to any ensuing divorce

In 1872 the prosecuting attorney in an Ohio civil damage case encouraged Prohibitionist Eliza Stewart to present opening remarks to the jury; Stewart obliged and the case was won. Several other women then approached Stewart for assistance, and in 1873 Stewart addressed a jury while supported by community women who prayed in the back of the courtroom.[33] Successes encouraged even conservative Prohibitionists to overcome initial hesitancy about the appropriateness of lawsuits as a political tactic. And by 1879 the *New York Times* would credit Prohibitionists with the creation of new civil damages legislation in Massachusetts, asserting that Prohibitionists had "in the campaign last Fall, exerted themselves to secure a strong representation in the Legislature, while the attention of the leaders of the other parties was concentrated on the Governor fight."[34]

The events of the Women's Crusade of 1873–1874 further expanded notions about what women's partisanship should be and do by encouraging Prohibitionists to consider if direct action protests could be a viable means of attracting publicity to the cause and the party most supporting its advancement. After some early apprehension regarding the propriety of such actions, which were not traditionally part of parties' repertoire, Prohibitionists eventually came to applaud Crusading women throughout the Midwest. Respectable, white, middle-class women gathered together in churches before occupying barrooms, pharmacies, doctors' offices, and other sites where liquor was sold. They arranged themselves in large processions to control the space, "calling the gray haired mothers to the front, placing the singers in the middle, and the younger women in the rear."[35] Then they prayed, sang, and refused to leave until the proprietor agreed to stop liquor sales. Whereas such activism by men might have been construed as inhibiting the seller's property rights, Prohibitionists observed that the era's widespread social assumption that women were motivated only by their moral compass, that they did not want to be in an immoral place or act in an aggressive manner, and that they should never

---

if liquor sales rendered the other spouse immoral: "Protect the American Home from Divorce," *American Advance*, 22 July 1911. For examples of enforcement in Michigan in the 1880s, see "Michigan News," *Center*, 2 February 1888; "More Tax, Please," *Center*, 23 February 1888.

33 Willard, *Woman and Temperance*, 83–85.

34 "Temperance in Massachusetts," *New York Times*, 26 April 1879. Limited documentation makes it difficult to confirm this claim's accuracy, but it suggests public knowledge of Prohibitionists' agenda.

35 "The Women's Temperance Crusade in Delaware," *Delaware Signal*, 3 March 1874.

be assaulted by men because of their physical delicacy provided women with a peculiar leverage. Women were seldom categorized as "mobs" and generally avoided police removal.[36] Thus, women's direct action was provocative while simultaneously offering opponents a limited range of responses: Liquor vendors could either give up their trade or else arrest the women, with either choice drawing more attention to the anti-liquor cause.

Both civil damage lawsuits and direct action protests excited women because they highlighted how wives' legal dependency upon husbands gave them special insight into the liquor traffic's evils. Writing in a party newspaper under a descriptive pseudonym, "Justice" claimed a uniquely feminine authority as the widow and mourning mother of drunkards. Arguing that women well understood the liquor problem's political roots, she dismissed as naïve those preachers and temperance advocates who asserted that "we need no law but the law of love to suppress this crime of drunkard-making." She challenged opponents of prohibition to "ask the drunkard's wife, and as you look upon her emaciated form she will point with one hand to the hovel that shelters her starving children, and with the other toward the palatial mansion of the rum-seller, who has despoiled her of her home, beggared her children, and made her husband a maniac – all under this law of love." Justice threatened to perpetuate the tactics of the Crusade, this time by urging the party to "form all of the innocent sufferers of the rum traffic in Mt. Vernon [Ohio] into a procession" and "march them in review."[37] Likewise urging the wider adaptation of Crusade tactics, other Prohibitionists declared that women should "visit saloons in the evening with their husbands and sons" so as to create awkward social situations dramatizing the gap between legality and respectability.[38]

The Prohibition Party's response to civil damage lawsuits and the Women's Crusade's direct action protests set a precedent wherein party women were encouraged to innovate. However, perhaps even greater attention was devoted to pulling the wider women's anti-liquor movement under the party mantle. Prominent women Prohibitionists participating in the Crusade attempted to connect the movement more firmly

---

[36] Such was not necessarily the case during the antebellum era, wherein liquor sellers occasionally pressed lawsuits against female vigilantes for destruction of property; Szymanski, *Pathways to Prohibition*, 83–84.

[37] Justice, Untitled, *Delaware Signal*, 18 July 1877.

[38] Loti Walker, "Let the Women Visit the Saloons," *(Columbus) Kansas Prohibitionist*, 23 January 1884.

to the Prohibition Party by sending regular reports to the party press and by speaking with their Crusading peers about how to institutionalize the movement's achievements.

Together, men and women Prohibitionists publicized an interpretation of the Crusade as evidence that "the women have come out, and are standing by the side of us" and that "they have adopted our platform, and are fighting upon it."[39] Such bold pronouncements of Women's Crusade and Prohibition Party alliance were not created whole cloth; for example, the Crusades started in Ohio under the guidance of Mother Stewart, and Amanda Way led several crusades in Kansas.[40] Nonetheless, the party press underreported incidents wherein Crusade leaders explicitly denied party affiliation. When Stewart, speaking as both a Prohibitionist and Crusade leader, claimed that "Crusaders are Prohibitionists every one of them," the *Delaware Signal* was quick to report her assessment as fact despite many movement leaders' explicit nonpartisanship.[41] Presumably editor and publisher Thomas Evans Jr. spoke with some inside knowledge, as his wife was prominent in Delaware, Ohio's Crusade.[42] Selective silence similarly prevailed when a group of Crusading women put forth a dry slate in an Iowa town, and Prohibitionists praised them for having "put up a temperance ticket recently, and worked for it like beavers. They not only electioneered, but on election day they haunted the polls, hired a brass band to make music, peddled tickets, etc., and their ticket was elected by fifty majority."[43] The *Delaware Signal* neglected to mention whether these women were organized as the local Prohibition Party, implying without stating a connection to the party. However, given the proliferation of temperance tickets and temperance parties during the 1850s, it was quite possible that these women had organized independently.

Prohibitionists' boldly attempted to co-opt the Women's Crusade during the party's 1874 Ohio convention, which was held in a small city with a very active Crusade movement. Crusading women were reported to have given Prohibitionists a "cold shoulder" after being patronizingly

---

[39] "Where Do We Stand," *Delaware Signal*, 10 March 1874.

[40] On the Women's Crusade, see Jack Blocker, *"Give to the Wind Thy Fears": The Women's Temperance Crusade, 1873–1874* (Westport, CT: Greenwood, 1985). "The Deacon's Saloon, or Amanda Way's First Crusade," *(Indianapolis) Patriot Phalanx*, 7 January 1904.

[41] "The Crusade and the Republican Party," *Delaware Signal*, 21 October 1874.

[42] Mother (Eliza Daniel) Stewart, *Memories of the Crusade*, 3rd ed. (Chicago: H.J. Smith & Co., 1890), 340.

[43] Untitled, *Delaware Signal*, 31 March 1874.

advised to harness their moral suasion to legal prohibition. The *New York Tribune* chastised that "but for the unseemly haste of the Prohibitionists" to appropriate the Women's Crusade energy, "they might easily reap a great harvest of votes as the result of the women's movement." In contrast, "if they insist upon claiming a share in the inauguration of the movement and a hand in its direction, they will gain fewer votes and have the ill-will of both men and women who believe that this movement is of God and that love, not law, is the instrument directly ordained to secure the closing of dram-shops." Such critiques had merit. Local Crusaders resolved not to attend John Russell's public lecture and only grudgingly permitted him to address their meeting. And even this was too much for some deliberately apolitical women to bear. One woman at the Crusaders' meeting "sprang to her feet, and excited but in good temper insisted that this movement was of God and blessed of God, and assured hear hearers that the only advisors of the women were their honored pastors and a discrete advisory committee; that no outside counsel was needed."[44]

At the same time, Prohibitionists were making similar accusations regarding other temperance leaders. Prohibitionist William Goodell believed that the major parties saw in Dio Lewis, the minister whose temperance sermon had inspired the first uprising, a means "to guide that movement in a less dangerous direction" so that Crusaders would not dare to "excite a strong sentiment against the licensing of the liquor traffic, to the manifest danger of the political parties, whose subserving to the license system constituted the chief item in the political capital." Goodell and other Prohibitionists assumed that merging with the Prohibition Party would otherwise be the Women's Crusaders' natural course. How ignorant was Lewis, complained Goodell, to assume that "women were incompetent to do any thing without his supervision."[45]

Women Crusaders' energizing influence upon the anti-liquor movement was formally organized as the Woman's Christian Temperance Union (WCTU) in 1874. Struggles to articulate the new organization's relationship to the Prohibition Party immediately ensued. Reporting on the first WCTU national convention, the *Delaware Signal* discerned tension between attendees regarding what the relationship between the

---

[44] "War on Whiskey," *New York Tribune*, 7 March 1874. See also Blocker, "*Give to the Winds Thy Fears,*" 70–71.

[45] William Goodell, Drafted letter, Box 2, 2–11, WGFP. Goodell was also a frequent contributor to the *Delaware Signal*.

women's organization and the Prohibition Party should be, tension that was expressed through a series of minor disputes. An initial controversy was about whether the assembly should permit Eliza Stewart to record her name as Mother Stewart, rather than as *Mrs.* Stewart. Some delegates argued that Stewart's emphasis upon her maternal authority slighted everyone else. However, their resolution was lost, and Stewart entered her name as she saw fit, thereby establishing her authority as a mother among mothers.

Martha "Mattie" McClellan Brown was the subject of a second controversy when her qualification to run for WCTU presidency was challenged because she was not a regular state-appointed delegate. The *Delaware Signal* expressed its agreement with convention rumors that "the fight against Mrs. Brown was a fight against the political prohibitionists," concluding that "if so, the political prohibitionists carried the day in the decision of this one question at least." Despite these victories in technical matters, neither Stewart nor Brown was elected to the presidency, which fell to Annie Wittenmyer, who opposed lending the Prohibition Party WCTU support. For the moment, Prohibitionists grudgingly concluded that the WCTU was probably "evenly mixed" between party Prohibitionists and women without such sympathies. They rather snidely suggested that Republican husbands had too much influence on women who were as yet underprepared for politics.[46]

* * *

The inclusion of women and the frequent expressions of enthusiasm for women's distinct partisanship might have been a mere stopgap solution to fixing a maligned reputation and labor shortage. However, in the post-Crusade era women entrenched themselves in the formal policy-making apparatus, gaining a more secure foothold for themselves even as the party's male membership increased and stabilized. Prohibitionist women served on the high profile committees that wrote national platforms – platforms for which they remained ineligible to vote. They represented their home states on the select national committee. And at the state and local levels, women's participation was a constant feature of party life.

Ohio's Prohibitionists, for example, pointedly invited "all the voters of Franklin county, and all those who *ought to be voters*, and believe in the legal suppression of the dram-selling business, and the enfranchisement of

---

[46] "The Woman's Temperance Convention," *Delaware Signal*, 25 November 1874; "National Convention of Temperance Women," *Delaware Signal*, 23 December 1874.

women."[47] Lists of attendees and minutes suggest that women frequently attended state meetings everywhere from Missouri to Massachusetts. And at the 1878 Ohio convention, partisans noted that "the presence of so many women was very cheering, especially such noble, persistent workers for God and humanity, as Mother Stewart, of Springfield, Mrs. Janney, of Columbus, and Mrs. Dyer, of this county. Their talk in the Convention" – although left intriguingly unquoted by the party press – "was admired by all, being full of matured thought and wise instructions."[48] Likewise, in Minnesota in 1878 the state convention placed two women on the four-person committee on resolutions and platform, and Mrs. A.T. Anderson was a principal speaker. C. Augusta Morse, leading the charge for greater women's leadership within the Prohibition Party, memorialized that the Crusade was "the dawn of a new era in women's relation to reform. Never again can women be silenced by the ghost of the old dogma that her voice is not to be heard in public, or that social propriety or feminine delicacy will exclude her from open conflict with the rum demon."[49] As early as 1875, Prohibitionists would boldly assert that "the day is past when any question can be raised as to the propriety of women attending a political convention. Women now go wherever they want to go, and wherever duty calls them, and few if any question its propriety."[50]

Most importantly, county and state parties validated women's standing as full party members through quotas. The 1872 Michigan convention had anticipated this trend when it appointed five women to an executive committee to complement the work of the men's state committee.[51] After 1874, examples proliferated. Ohio's Huron County divided leadership between men and women when it placed Mrs. A.E. Danfort and Mrs. Mc.C. Murray on the five-person county central committee. This committee reported to an advisory committee "consisting of a lady and gentleman from each township as far as practical."[52] In another Ohio county, Prohibitionists organized an executive committee of five, which would contain "three voters and two ladies."[53]

---

[47] "Franklin County Prohibition Convention," *Delaware Signal*, 18 July 1877. Italics are author's.
[48] Untitled, *Delaware Signal*, 27 February 1878.
[49] C. Augusta Morse, "Women's Relation to the Temperance Reform," *Delaware Signal*, 10 November 1880.
[50] Crusader, Untitled, *Delaware Signal*, 17 February 1875.
[51] "Michigan: Meeting of the Temperance Party in State Convention," *New York Times*, 13 June 1872.
[52] "The Movement," *Delaware Signal*, 9 September 1874.
[53] E.S. Churchman, Untitled letter to the editor, *Delaware Signal*, 19 September 1883.

Wisconsin provided the most dramatic case. The ninety Prohibitionists who organized the state party specified that each town or voting
precinct should have a council of ten electors balanced by a council of
ten women; the electors would be chosen by the mass convention, and
the women's council would be chosen by temperance women. Wisconsin Prohibitionists wanted to formalize the inclusion of women leaders
because women had already been so successful at "stimulating the people
to independent organization for Prohibition."[54] The state organization
declared that the women's council's "status and duties – except in matters political – shall correspond to those of the former council" and that
"these two councils . . . shall be the permanent representative bodies of the
local party."[55] At the state level, organizations of thirty-three men and
thirty-three women would similarly share authority. Here, Prohibitionists struggled with language and meaning as they attempted to transform
traditional forms of partisanship to resonate with new constituencies.
Wisconsin's Prohibitionists failed to clarify who was in the mass convention and whether women should be given a double vote if they were part
of the mass. They provided women with a new kind of authority, even as
they continued to struggle to achieve consensus about whether men and
women should have complementary or identical roles.

Despite the fact that Prohibitionists' plans for the nature of women's
inclusion were occasionally vague or contradictory, Wisconsin's explicit
commitment to making women part of the party nonetheless struck some
Prohibitionists as amazing. One male Prohibitionist who was delighted
with "the influence of working and praying women" exclaimed about
Wisconsin's organization that "a plan of organization was added providing for committees with equal numbers of voting citizens and women to
propose nominations for public offices! What is this world coming to?"
He expressed his confidence that the leadership of women would mean
that "Wisconsin is not much longer to be classed among the beer-and-
whiskey governed States."[56]

---

[54] James Goodell, "From Wisconsin," *(Cleveland, OH) Prohibition Era*, reprinted from
    an uncited periodical, originally published 1 June 1874. This clipping was found
    within Samuel D. Hastings' Scrapbook titled "The Prohibition Question: 1867–1868–
    1869–1870," 123, Wisconsin Historical Society Rare Books Collection, Madison, WI
    (SDHS).
[55] "New Organization: The Temperance People to Act Independently of Other Parties,"
    from an uncited periodical, [1872–1874?], 120, SDHS.
[56] James Goodell, "From Wisconsin," reprinted in *(Cleveland, OH) Prohibition Era* from
    an uncited periodical, originally published 1 June 1874, 123, SDHS.

In embracing women and women's political style, however, Prohibitionists did not necessarily erode the centrality of the vote in how Americans understood their political world. Prohibitionists instead sought to elevate the standing of their women allies and women partisans – and hence their own party's prestige – by aggressively advocating suffrage. They often dismissed anti-suffrage as a hypocritical position of the liquor trade. One newspaper editor mocked those opponents of women's suffrage who argued that "it is perfectly appropriate (?) for girls and women to go to a beer hall and drink and dance all night, with men, but for an intelligent, sensible woman, of mature years, to go to the polls and cast a ballot would be taking the 'highway to prostitution!' Such is the logic of saloon oratory."[57]

Prohibitionists frequently asserted that their party would benefit disproportionately from the expansion of suffrage because women were generally in favor of prohibitory legislation.[58] Women's suffrage emerged as a high profile party issue, as suggested when Kansas' Prohibition Party declared for the "civil and political equality of all men and women" in its first resolution in the 1874 platform, even before describing its position on prohibition.[59] Ohio's state committee chair likewise summarized that the party platform should "express our deep hostility, not only to the fearful traffic in intoxicating drinks, but to that deep injustice that fails to acknowledge woman as the political equal of man."[60] Prohibitionists took a bolder and more consistent position on women's suffrage than they did on civil service reform, tariff reform, or the numerous other issues in which they expressed interest.

And as the party grew, it more explicitly acknowledged a reliance on women's labor to create the sustainable institutions that would make the party competitive with Democrats and Republicans. In Illinois, twenty of

---

[57] "Beer Logic," *Delaware Signal*, 20 June 1877.

[58] For example, "Political Convention: The New York Prohibitionist State Convention," *New York Times*, 24 June 1874; "Woman Suffrage and Prohibition," *Chicago Daily Tribune*, 25 August 1882.

[59] "Platform of the Temperance Party of Kansas, adopted at its State Convention, at Leavenworth, September 10th, 1874," Prohibition Party Miscellaneous Items, Kansas Historical Society, Topeka, KS. Kansas' state Prohibition Party was named the "Temperance party." State parties frequently had different names than the national party, as also evident in the "Anti-Dramshop party" in New York and the "Union party" in Michigan.

[60] "Opening Address of Chairman of State Central Committee," *Delaware Signal*, 11 March 1875.

the seventy-five individuals who met to form the state party and make nominations were women.[61] State party organ the *Minnesota Radical* similarly encouraged both "men and women" in the city of Albert Lea to "organize a temperance party which shall extend through out the county."[62] In 1879 the president and secretary of the Minnesota State Committee asked women to help organize local parties by lending their special abilities. They noted that "it is of the highest importance to organize and unite our strength in prohibition clubs in all the towns where there are three men and as many women who are in earnest. Their regular meetings can be made of great value by discussion, addresses, written articles, extracts, facts, music by the women, etc."[63] Even when Prohibitionists sometimes slipped into assuming the male gender of their group, women were included as an important presence; the *Delaware Signal* argued that "in every locality where there are enough Prohibitionists with their wives, sons, and daughters, to form a Prohibition Society, regular meetings should be held weekly, either at some hall, or at each other's houses."[64] Ohio began extensive organization after the 1874 elections to institutionalize the support of new voters; local Prohibition clubs embraced "all who are in favor of the Prohibition Party, including ladies."[65] Some of the often-named ladies were vocal, such as Mrs. A.T. Anderson of Minneapolis, a public speaker with significant standing in the state party, who used her attendance at a local meeting to denounce churchgoing Republicans as hypocrites.[66] Vocal or not, the presence of women figured prominently in Prohibitionists' descriptions of their everyday gatherings.

Prohibitionist women also worked within existent local party organizations to distribute tickets and watch the polls. The women of Albert Lea, Minnesota, drew upon widely held assumptions that women were more virtuous than men when they became "determined to be present at the polls, and supply hot coffee and refreshment for those who were working for the temperance cause, in order that they might all remain through the day." Apparently concerned that eager women Prohibitionists would

[61] Untitled, *Chicago Daily Tribune*, 1 July 1874.

[62] "The Fight at Albert Lea," *Minnesota Radical*, 22 March 1876.

[63] R.P. Lupton (chair of the Minnesota committee) and A. Willey (secretary), "Prohibition Reform Party," *Minnesota Radical*, 17 December 1879.

[64] "The Next Campaign," *Delaware Signal*, 15 November 1876.

[65] Gideon T. Stewart, "Ohio Prohibition Society," *Delaware Signal*, 23 December 1874.

[66] "Prohibition City Convention in Minneapolis," *Minnesota Radical*, 7 April 1880.

influence male voters, opposition parties "sprinkled the floor, benches, and stoves, with red pepper" to chase the women away from the polls, but "the ladies choked and coughed" and "stood to their post nobly." Prohibitionists insisted that women's tenacity positively influenced electoral outcomes because "their presence contributed greatly to the encouragement of their friends."[67] The poor behavior of the men tormenting these women provoked chivalry from male voters because it dramatized the moral problems inherent to the pro-liquor position and called for good men to protect respectable women. Ohio's state organizer validated such activism by declaring:

I will venture to make one suggestion to the noble ladies of our State, who are helping so nobly in this glorious cause, and that is that they, as far as possible, go to the places of holding election, on election day, and there by their presence, their prayers, and influence, assist in winning this great battle for God, and the right. I for one am sorry they cannot aid the cause by their votes.[68]

Women Prohibitionists in some Ohio cities responded by renting homes near polling places and decorating them with banners.[69]

There are also scattered examples of women who served as party candidates. Jennie Willing, a professor in Ohio Wesleyan's Department of English, was the Illinois party candidate for state school commissioner in 1874.[70] Mrs. Gage suggested that a woman should be placed on the New York state ticket in 1874; although her proposal was not accepted by the convention, delegates did place her on the resolutions committee to demonstrate a continued commitment to encouraging women's participation.[71] Fannie Randolph was Kansas Prohibitionists'

---

[67] "Albert Lea Vindicated," *Minnesota Radical*, 28 March 1877, reprinted from the *(Moorhead, MN) Enterprise*. Prohibitionists might have similarly described the activities and public response to women who electioneered at the California polls. The women suffered catcalls and were barricaded inside their luncheon tent. Anti-prohibition crowds held a mock funeral for at least one temperance orator; Ostrander, *Prohibition Movement in California*, 49–51. For a similar example in 1880s Michigan, see "Luther Insults Ladies," *Center*, 23 February 1888.

[68] E.S. Churchman, Untitled letter to the editor, *Delaware Signal*, 19 September 1883.

[69] Mark Wahlgren Summers, *Rum, Romanism, and Rebellion: The Making of a President, 1884* (Chapel Hill: University of North Carolina Press, 2000), 89.

[70] "Prohibitionists," *Delaware Signal*, 16 September 1874. The Illinois WCTU officially thanked the party for "the honor it has conferred upon us by nominating a woman" in "Coming to their Senses," *Delaware Signal*, 25 November 1874. See also "The Prohibition Party," *Chicago Daily Tribune*, 4 September 1874.

[71] "State Convention of Prohibitionists at Auburn, N.Y.," *Chicago Daily Tribune*, 25 June 1874.

choice for Superintendent of Public Instruction in 1884.[72] Women's candidacy might be interpreted as evidence of either the party's openness to women's advocacy or the party's practical inability to fill nominations with men, but likely women's nominations expressed a dovetailing of idealism and self-interest.

When significant and persistent financial problems impeded the Prohibitionist struggle to build up state and local parties, Prohibitionists encouraged women to help overcome "the poverty of the treasury," wherein "these wants are so self-evident to every intelligent man and woman that the mere mention of them is sufficient."[73] In Ohio, three women responded to the call for funds by taking a place among the fourteen initial "life members" of the state Prohibition Society, founded in 1876 to act as the fund-raising arm of the party.[74] Explicitly appealing to "temperance men and women," the Minnesota State Committee similarly appealed to all Prohibitionists to contribute to the campaign expense fund in 1879.[75] Women should join men in subsidizing the costs of campaigns and operating expenses because "we need their [women's] financial aid in order to meet our necessary expenses," perhaps even more than the "prayers and encouragement" also being sought.[76]

Over time, the distinctly gendered meanings ascribed to women's party work became so widely understood that they could be taken for granted. A subscriber to the *Delaware Signal* expressed a broadly held belief that women were the best people to coordinate funding and distributed campaign issues when he urged, "let a few temperance workers, ladies will be more successful, go around and canvas the township for funds to procure the extras to be distributed in the township."[77] Tantalizingly, he left unsaid whether women were desirable as agents because they had more time for mundane tasks, because their gender made the solicitation of funds less unseemly than it would be for men, or because it would be awkward for potential subscribers to refuse an attractive or determined woman. C.O. Keeler, a Kansas Prohibitionist, was similarly vague about

---

[72] S.P. Morse, "Reform Notes," *(New York) American Reformer*, 13 September 1884. I have not found any evidence that Amanda Way was a candidate for office until 1900, when she was nominated by the Idaho Prohibition Party for Representative in Congress; "Political," *New York Observer and Chronicle*, 12 April 1900.

[73] "Political Organization," *Minnesota Radical*, 12 June 1878.

[74] "Life Members of the Ohio Prohibition Society," *Delaware Signal*, 28 June 1876.

[75] "Money in It," *Minnesota Radical*, 7 May 1879.

[76] C. Augusta Morse, "Women's Relation to the Temperance Reform," *Delaware Signal*, 10 November 1880.

[77] A Subscriber, "That Extra," *Delaware Signal*, 22 December 1880.

why women were superior agents but agreed on this point. Keeler wrote the editor of the *Kansas Prohibitionist* that he had intended to distribute a stack of newspapers in Baltimore but instead found that a woman temperance worker "could distribute them to better advantage than I could." Both "amused and pleased," Keeler proudly concluded that "I have never met a more determined set of women than these temperance women of Baltimore."[78] M.V.B. Bennett, a struggling editor as well as a member of the Prohibition Party's national committee, responded by specifically soliciting women's assistance in increasing the *Kansas Prohibitionist's* circulation beyond its meager 4,000 subscribers. Three times in one brief article, Bennett called for female rather than male agents: "We want one hundred ladies to enter their names as special agents, and canvass for us."[79] The overlapping purposes of selling newspaper subscriptions – as a way to contribute to party finances and to persuade new voters to join the party – meant that women newspaper agents were supporting the party in multiple, important ways. As agents for these newspapers, women were the nodes of a network that sustained the entire party.

More often than not, when women acted it was men who interpreted the meaning of these actions for the wider public. This trend might have been sustained by lingering customs whereby women seldom spoke in public, or because Prohibitionist editors were reluctant to grant women a platform, or for the reasons suggested by a would-be correspondent from Duluth named Sarah B. Stearns. Stearns responded to the call for women's action with the hope that she could "be able to render some assistance in getting subscribers for your Campaign Paper" before concluding that "I wish I had time to write a few articles for it."[80] Certainly, women's busy schedules as wives and mothers explain part of their relative silence. All the same, it is of interest that, when they did make public proclamations about their commitment to party work, early women Prohibitionists rarely articulated a vision of themselves as a distinct group within the party and instead defined themselves as embedded within its mainstream. The comments of Mattie McClellan Brown, who founded and edited the *Alliance Monitor* to support the Prohibition Party, are

---

[78] J.D. Lewis, Untitled letter to the editor, *Kansas Prohibitionist*, 25 April 1883.
[79] "One Hundred," *Kansas Prohibitionist*, 6 June 1883. M.V.B. Bennett's name is only recorded as "M.V.B." in every Prohibition Party periodical and record I have encountered, probably because – as noted in a Republican Party publication – his full name was Martin Van Buren Bennett.
[80] Sarah Stearns, "A Woman's Views," *Minnesota Radical*, 4 September 1878.

fairly representative. She explained her purpose to the 1875 Ohio State Convention:

I shall make the paper just as good as I can... and as soon as you shall put up the ticket that the convention has nominated, I shall support the men in the hearing, and in the eyes of those who are voters. This I can do. I cannot vote for them, but I can advocate their cause with the voters, perhaps with some degree of influence.[81]

Although perhaps not so impressive by modern standards, it was at the time remarkable that at the 1880 national convention, 10 of the 142 official delegates were women – hardly a majority, but nonetheless a notable presence. Women made up approximately 6 percent of the 1869 convention; they made up 7 percent of the 1880 convention but more frequently accepted leadership positions. Mary A. Woodbridge, president of the Ohio WCTU, shared the responsibilities of temporary secretary with Mattie McClellan Brown.[82] Once the convention was organized, women served on important committees from which they had been excluded in 1869. Mrs. A.C. Hillard of Wisconsin and Mrs. E.J. Gordon of Massachusetts served on the Committee on Permanent Organization and Rules, and Mrs. Foote of Wisconsin was included on the platform committee. In addition, four women were selected as either vice presidents or secretaries for the sixteen-person permanent convention committee. Although no women were nominated for national office, Mattie McClellan Brown did have the honor of nominating the vice-presidential candidate, H.A. Thompson. Prohibitionists asserted that "it is now woman's proper mission to succeed in this matter, by centering in the domestic relation every interest of life. Then let her dare... to cast a ballot; dare to speak, and dare to sing temperance... Then who shall say woman can do nothing? Boasting man, be silent!"[83]

The Prohibition Party's formal embrace of women's suffrage through party platforms continued to legitimize and validate the presence of women within the party. At the 1880 national convention, for example, Prohibitionists discussed why women's suffrage should be supported and in so doing illuminated two distinct rationales for women's partisan involvement: because they were innately entitled to represent themselves and because their contributions or potential contributions made them desirable voters. One group favored woman suffrage on the grounds that

---

[81] "The State Convention," *Delaware Signal*, 11 March 1875.
[82] *Proceedings of the National Convention... 1880*, 15.
[83] A.G.S., "Proving Things and Doing Things," *Minnesota Radical*, 11 July 1877.

women had a right and capacity for it, as evidenced by their engagement at the national nominating convention. A delegate emphasized that "what we want is to declare that she be placed upon a perfect equality with man, irrespective of this or that particular interest."[84] A second group, in turn, suggested that Prohibitionists needed to favor women's suffrage as Prohibitionists – that is, they should favor it simply because women would be likely to vote for the policy that the party advocated. These individuals favored a plank that would demand women's suffrage "as a rightful means for a proper settlement of the liquor question."[85] Intriguingly, any assertion that women might not belong in parties or at conventions was absent from the record.

Even as she affirmed that it was unlikely that more women would join the party in appreciation for its endorsement of women's suffrage than would join for their love of prohibition alone, the tone of Mattie McClellan Brown's speech at the 1880 convention nonetheless belied both her satisfaction that the party held such a progressive position on women's suffrage and her sense that it was an appropriate gesture of respect for women members. Rousing the crowd, Brown expressed appreciation to "my brethren of the prohibition movement, [who] have invited the multitudes of women to come with all the forces and powers they are able to bring to bear in defense of your principles."[86] The Prohibition Party's endorsement of women's suffrage acknowledged women's political capacity and made a long-term commitment to fulfilling a vision of women's political equality. Moreover, by categorizing women as potential voters, Prohibitionists could reinforce their assertion that their party was serious about electoral victory even as it sought out participation from nonvoters.

Mattie McClellan Brown was heartily applauded by fellow delegates when she expressed surprise "that so many of the ladies of this country have so long been devoted to those parties which have been content to throw out the merest crumbs of recognition, the merest flowers of courtesy or flattery, while they have refused obstinately to give them a place on the floor, much less on the platform, with them." Returning to the inextricable interests of men and women, she then expressed her hope that Prohibitionists' examples would inspire a new practice of politics

---

[84] *Proceedings of the National Convention... 1880*, 31.
[85] *Proceedings of the National Convention... 1880*, 29.
[86] Mattie McClellan Brown quoted in *Proceedings of the National Convention... 1880*, 17.

wherein "we will not have men's conventions on the one side and women's conventions on the other, but men and women in equal status, in equal privilege, in equal right, working together in the great process of building a grand Humanity for God."[87]

* * *

By the 1880s, the anti-liquor movement was truly thriving, largely because the Woman's Christian Temperance Union had energized it. The WCTU had become the largest federation of women in the country, and it embraced a wide variety of reforms, advocating kindergartens, police matrons, and social purity in addition to temperance.[88] Still, the achievement of prohibition through political measures was of greatest interest for both the WCTU and the Prohibition Party, and both organizations asserted that such measures were best accomplished through political parties. As early as 1874, Prohibition Party founder John Russell had explained the essential compatibility of the two organizations: "The difference between us and some of the workers in the Woman's Christian Temperance Union is simply that we go further than they do."[89] In 1878, Prohibitionists had suggested that the WCTU was moving toward a recognition of these common interests, and potentially shared organization, concluding that "we congratulate the sisters on their disposition . . . They acknowledge the stand we have taken to be the only correct one, that no other party has taken it, that it must be taken, and finally that there are at least Prohibition *papers* taking on the right 'political aspect.' Come on, sisters." Explicitly inviting WCTU members to fuse with Prohibition Party membership, the *Delaware Signal* suggested that "You will find the *party* pretty soon, for you will fail to find the 'broad political plank' in either of the others."[90]

Although classic historical accounts such as Ruth Bordin's *Woman and Temperance* emphasize Frances Willard's role in eventually unifying the Prohibition Party and WCTU constituencies in the 1880s, this trajectory was also grounded in the labors of women Prohibitionists in the 1870s. For example, Amanda Way, Eliza Stewart, Mattie McClellan Brown, and

---

[87] Mattie McClellan Brown quoted in *Proceedings of the National Convention . . . 1880*, 17–18.

[88] The most comprehensive study of the WCTU is Ruth Bordin, *Woman and Temperance: The Quest for Power and Liberty* (Philadelphia: Temple University Press, 1981).

[89] Untitled, *Delaware Signal*, 12 August 1874.

[90] "The New Reporter, Organ of the W.C.T.U., on Prohibition," *Delaware Signal*, 25 October 1876. Italics are author's.

Harriet Goff held important party positions and guided WCTU development in the years previous to Willard's presidency. Connecticut's women
Prohibitionists likewise suggested the alliance's deep historical roots when
they founded a state WCTU in 1874 while attending a party convention.[91]

When WCTU members considered the prospect of alignment with
Prohibitionists it was because they hoped it would help them fulfill new
WCTU president Frances Willard's political philosophy: *Home Protec-
tionism*. Willard had first expressed her belief that women needed to begin
voting and working in parties to protect their homes in an 1878 address
before the national WCTU convention.[92] She asserted that "a mother's
love" was a deep-rooted instinct, as entrenched as the desire for self-
preservation. Regarding mothers as "a class" whose ability to care for a
family and ability to restrain hunger and brutality was contingent upon
the regulation of liquor, Willard called for "good men and brave" to
"match force with force, to set over against the liquor-dealer's avarice
our instinct of self-preservation; and to match the drinker's love of liquor
with our love of him!"

If women were provided with suffrage, Willard argued, they could use
that suffrage to render the liquor traffic as "doomed as was the slave
power when you gave the ballot to the slaves." Willard concluded that
"by the changeless instincts of her nature and through the most sacred
relationships of which that nature has been rendered capable, God has
indicated woman, who is the born conservator of home, to be the Nemesis
of home's arch enemy, King Alcohol." Willard frankly retorted to critics
of woman suffrage that

nothing worse can ever happen to women at the polls than has been endured by
the hour on the part of conservative women of the churches in this land, as they, in
scores of towns, have plead with rough, half-drunken men to vote the temperance
tickets they have handed them, and which, with vastly more propriety and fitness,
they might have dropped into the box themselves. They could have done this in
a moment and returned to their homes, instead of spending the whole day in the
often futile endeavor to beg from men like these the votes which should preserve
their homes from the whisky serpent's breath for one uncertain year.

Without undermining the arguments of the American Woman Suffrage
Association and National Woman Suffrage Association that women

---

[91] "The National Convention," *Lever*, 31 July 1884.
[92] Frances Willard, *Glimpses of Fifty Years: The Autobiography of an American Woman*,
3rd ed. (New York: Women's Temperance Publication Association, 1889), 374–381.

ought to have suffrage simply because it was a right of citizenship, Willard nonetheless asserted that "for my own sake, I had not courage" to ask for the ballot, whereas "I have for thy sake, dear native land, for thy necessity is as much greater than mine." Women needed the ballot to better protect their homes, hence the "home-protection ballot."[93]

Willard's interest in using the Prohibition Party to secure a home protection ballot grew more widely known after she became WCTU president in 1879 and began to speak about women's suffrage and partisan politics in her annual addresses. Prohibitionists, in turn, enthusiastically responded to her expressed interest because Willard's institutional authority and personal charisma would encourage many other women to similarly support the party and provide it with the credibility that a national reform figure could bestow.[94]

In her autobiographical *Glimpses of Fifty Years*, Willard explained that her conversion to partisan Prohibitionism was made possible by a satisfying journey through the American South. The trip helped Willard set aside lingering fears that a powerful minor party would cripple Republicans dedicated to freedpeoples' protection, leaving freedpeople to Democratic exploitation. Her apprehensions were assuaged by numerous conversations with Southern women who assured her that white Southerners had no desire to rebel a second time. Willard engaged South Carolinian Sallie Chapin to speak at the 1881 WCTU national convention; Chapin assured listeners that the South fully accepted its loss and that parties other than the Republican Party could therefore safely share in national power.

It seems possible that Willard's frustration that the General Conference of the Methodist Episcopal Church did not accept women delegates also encouraged Willard to consider alternative sites for advancing the WCTU agenda. Willard herself was named a lay delegate in 1888 only to be refused a seat; no woman would be granted a seat until 1896.[95] Creating independent institutions provided different and sometimes better sorts of opportunities. Willard began preparing for an official WCTU

---

[93] The text of Willard's first "Home Protection" address appears in Willard, *Woman and Temperance*, 452–459.

[94] Frances Willard's personal charisma and the enthusiasm of WCTU admirers is well-documented in Ruth Bordin's *Frances Willard: A Biography* (Chapel Hill: University of North Carolina Press, 1986).

[95] For an interesting exchange, see George W. Woodruff, ed., *Journal of the General Conference of the Methodist Episcopal Church Held in Cincinnati, Ohio, May 1–28, 1880* (New York: Phillips & Hunt, 1880), 255–257. See also Bordin, *Woman and Temperance*, 113–114.

declaration in favor of Prohibitionism by establishing openly political home-protection clubs because these clubs would provide WCTU members with leverage within the Prohibition Party once the two groups united.[96] Willard's own willingness to abandon Republican Party interests and her friendliness toward the Prohibition Party began to take root among many members such as Mrs. A. who concluded that "Nobody need grumble to me about 'third party' as though it was something dreadful. I'd like to know if Illinois isn't governed by one to-day. A 'third party' is throttling the best life of our communities, and its name is 'whiskyite.'"[97]

In her boldest step yet, Willard spoke with Prohibition Party leaders John B. Finch and George W. Bain at an 1881 meeting in Lake Bluff. They all agreed to more fully commit to unification.[98] At the Prohibition Party's 1882 national convention following the Lake Bluff meeting, Prohibitionists reconstituted themselves as the Prohibition Home Protection Party. This reorganization demonstrated the degree of Prohibitionists' commitment to the recruitment of women and their confidence in the effectiveness of these women as political agents. Rev. Plum, a delegate from Missouri, encouraged women to "take muskets in their hands and destroy the saloons."[99] One woman delegate proudly asserted that "'the smartest men in this Convention are women,'" leading a fellow attendee to respond that

indeed, it would be a remarkable convention which could produce many men as skillful in management, as eloquent in speech, as ready with pen, and as powerful to lead and influence other minds, as Frances Willard, Mrs. Foster of Iowa, Mrs. Lathrop of Michigan, Mrs. J.A. Brown and Mrs. Mary B. Willard of Chicago, and the successful lawyer, Miss Phoebe W. Cozzins, of St. Louis. The women were not the power behind the throne, they were on it, and they wielded the scepter with grace and self-possession.[100]

---

[96] Ruth Bordin describes the political intentions of WCTU president Frances Willard: "She was committed to a legislative solution on the federal level for the temperance problem; she was convinced national prohibition could be achieved only by political action in which women fully joined because they had succeeded in getting the ballot; she saw the Prohibition party as the only vehicle through which constitutional prohibition could be achieved and which would accept women as equals in working for that goal" in *Woman and Temperance*, 117. On home-protection clubs, see Bordin, *Woman and Temperance*, 124.

[97] Mrs. A. quoted in Willard, *Woman and Temperance*, 460.

[98] Bordin, *Woman and Temperance*, 124.

[99] "Prohibitionists in Council," *New York Times*, 24 August 1882.

[100] A.C. George, "Prohibition Movements," *Zion's Herald*, 13 September 1882. There was a bit of a stir about adding the names of so many women to the national committee and committee on resolutions. See "Prohibitionists in Council," *New York Times*, 24 August 1882; "The Prohibitionists," *Washington Post*, 24 August 1882. J. Ellen

Combining with the WCTU gave women the majority voice within the party, even though these same women were generally ineligible to vote.

Frances Willard supported and often guided the unification process, noting that this was a desirable combination for the Prohibitionists because it added individuals who already possessed experience in the creation of a national organization and national campaigns; who knew how to integrate local, state, and national tiers of leadership; and who had name recognition and political contacts. In turn, Willard would describe the Prohibition Home Protection Party as "woman's answered prayer."[101] The WCTU's 1882 national convention adopted a resolution that their organization would "commit themselves to that party, by whatever name called, that shall give to them the best embodiment of prohibition principles, and will most surely protect our homes."[102] Implicitly, this could only mean support for the Prohibition Party because the major parties continued to prefer regulation to restriction. Gideon T. Stewart remained chairman of the national committee of the newly named party, but Frances Willard and Sallie Chapin were named to the national executive committee. The creation of the Prohibition Home Protection Party mapped the most pervasive type of men's political organization in nineteenth-century America, the party, onto the WCTU's numbers, structures, and leadership.

Prohibitionists were less successful at building sustained alliances with women who advocated suffrage as their primary issue. Recalling the long campaign to recruit women, Mattie McClellan Brown attributed the party's failure to suffragists' obliviousness. Brown asserted that

I am surprised, I say, that so many of the very intelligent women of this country who advocate suffrage and equal status of women everywhere should come repeatedly, year after year, quadrennial after quadrennial, into those great conventions of men and ask favors of them, when here, in this grandest party that we ever organized on this continent is open to her such great privilege – equal in status with men on the floor.[103]

Nonetheless, Prohibitionists made two significant choices that might account for their limited success at systematically recruiting larger numbers of suffragists. First, Prohibitionists occasionally downplayed their

Foster was a loyal Republican and left the Prohibition Party soon after the convention, if she had ever really belonged in the first place.

[101] Willard, *Glimpses of Fifty Years*, 382. See also. Woman's Christian Temperance Union, *The Reason Why* (Chicago: Woman's Temperance Publishing Association, 1884).

[102] Willard, *Glimpses of Fifty Years*, 383.

[103] Mattie McClellan Brown quoted in *Proceedings of the National Convention . . . 1880*, 17.

interest in women's rights to leave open future opportunities for recruiting in the American South, a region in which they believed women's suffrage was unpopular. For example, Thomas Evans, Jr.'s *Delaware Signal* reminded Southern Prohibitionists that "it be understood that while we adopt Woman Suffrage – simply because we think it just – we do not look upon it as the great idea, to which Prohibition is a mere appendage."[104] Such a comment seemed misleading at best given the rest of the party's unequivocally pro-suffrage record but could have nonetheless been discouraging to suffragists.

Second, Prohibitionists failed to fully engage the organized woman suffrage movement, either the National Woman Suffrage Association or the American Woman Suffrage Association. They courted very few leaders of the women's suffrage movement in the columns of the party press and granted still fewer suffragist leader invitations to conventions. Nor did Prohibitionists send affiliated delegates to suffrage conventions.[105] It was an exception rather than the rule when Mrs. Janney of Columbus, Ohio, moved among her peers at a Prohibition Party mass meeting to solicit memberships in a women's suffrage organization.[106]

In 1883 and 1884, Prohibitionists' conventions and newspapers roused partisans for a major campaign, the party's first truly national campaign that was intended to authoritatively convey popular support for prohibition. And yet even with the focus on the electoral arena as never before, Prohibitionists continued to give priority to the involvement of nonvoting women.[107] Thomas W. Organ was the campaign manager in New York for the 1883 campaign, and his work included ensuring the circulation of pledge books for voters and the distribution of countless ballots around the state. It was therefore especially telling when he exclaimed that "our movement has behind it the power of the mothers, wives, and sisters of the State, and it is going ahead with rapidity."[108] C.C. Leigh, Prohibitionists'

[104] "The Curiosities of Misrepresentation," *Delaware Signal*, 21 April 1875.

[105] A notable exception occurred in Kansas, wherein Anna C. Wait, a member of the Prohibition Party and the WCTU, organized Kansas' Equal Suffrage Association and coordinated its activities with the WCTU. There was an extensive overlapping membership. Bader, *Prohibition in Kansas*, 102.

[106] "Mass Meeting," *New Era*, 3 July 1885.

[107] In his work on the 1884 election, Mark Wahlgren Summers asserts that "of all parties, [the Prohibition party] was the only one that could count on active support from women, and especially from the churchgoing ladies of the Woman's Christian Temperance Union"; *Rum, Romanism, and Rebellion*, 2.

[108] "Hopes of the Prohibitionists," *New York Times*, 2 November 1883. Organ was also an editor for the National Prohibition Alliance. He would continue to be prominent in New York City's Prohibition Party even after he became a speaker for the Socialist

candidate for mayor of New York in the same year, explained how women partisans were an important part of his campaign strategy. He described:

in the [campaign] circular I shall appeal to the mothers and sisters of the city, who sometimes do more effective work than the men themselves at the polls. I shall tell them that, while every mother of the African race, as she lulls her babe to sleep, can bless God that it can never be a slave, neither she nor other mothers can be assured, under our present laws, that their children will not become slaves to the dram-shop.[109]

At the Pennsylvania state Prohibition Party convention in Pittsburgh, the convention at large enthusiastically embraced a set of resolutions created by women delegates who had met separately previous to the convention. These women resolved

that we urge women everywhere, and especially the women of the W.C.T.U., to avail themselves of the power, under the Providence of God put into their hands by the Prohibition party, and clasp the hands held out to us in hearty sympathy and desiring our aid, by attending municipal, county, district, and state conventions, and by working systematically to gain votes before the election and at the polls.[110]

Women Prohibitionists were ready to work for their party, and the Prohibition Party was happy to have them.

Mattie McClellen Brown further argued that women's ability to discern "noble principles" obligated them to lead men in politics, even partisan politics. Those other women who attempted to remain out of politics or implicitly supported the Republican Party compromised themselves; they had aligned with "a crime protecting party" in the vague hope "to prevent [the] imaginary or suppositious evil" of a temporary Democratic victory. Brown scolded women that "we are not to choose between two evils, but to choose right only."[111] Brown argued that just as she had read *Uncle Tom's Cabin* and promptly abandoned the Democratic Party, so should other women with major party interests cease supporting parties that had rejected women's suffrage and protected the drink trade through licensing. Brown insisted upon women's superior ability to discern moral

Labor Party; Blocker, *Retreat from Reform*, 89; Thomas W. Organ to T.C. Richmond, 31 March 1893, T(homas). C. Richmond Correspondence, Wisconsin Historical Society Special Collections. Madison, WI (TCRC).

109 "The Brooklyn Prohibitionists," *New York Times*, 25 October 1883.
110 "The Women at Pittsburgh," *Lever*, 11 September 1884.
111 M[attie] McClellan Brown, "A Letter from Cincinnati to Mrs. Mary A. Livermore," *Delaware Signal*, 12 November 1884.

moral (men?)

principles, their obligation to act in a morally pure manner, and their duty to extend moral consistency into the partisan realm.

Perhaps the most elegant testimony to women's central place in the party came from Frederick Gates, New York's 1884 campaign coordinator. Gates reminded fellow partisans schooled in "old party" political culture that the Prohibition Party thrived with the participation of women members. In the *Lever's* columns, Gates recommended: "Don't forget to invite the ladies and the ministers. They are both deeply interested in the movement." By categorizing women with ministers, Gates expressed his respect for women's moral authority, and by affirming their desire to participate, he appropriated this moral authority for the party that they supported. Gates expected women Prohibitionists to contribute to the New York campaign by signing a pledge promising to support the party's candidates, distributing campaign literature in public places and among friends, and soliciting ever more pledge signatures. Gates also encouraged women to hold office within their local campaign clubs and suggested that women officers could even be preferable because "the officers should all be in hearty sympathy with the work, and able to give some time and thought to it." Thus, "ladies," who presumably had more flexible schedules, "can fill some of these places best." Gates again reminded Prohibitionists of the need to consider women members when creating a suitable club meeting place: "Keep it neat and clean, and cheerful (give the ladies a chance). Smoking, tobacco spitting, etc., are out of place."[112] Gates' guidelines did not protect women from the realities of party life, but rather reconceptualized party life in a way that accounted for them.

* * *

Women's activism encouraged Prohibitionists to acknowledge a wide range of activities beyond voting as legitimate partisan strategies. In the course of working to bring publicity to their struggling party, Prohibitionist women demanded clarification of laws by pressing civil damage cases in court, engaged in direct action by occupying saloons, spoke in public to raise popular support for temperance, and created grassroots organizations so that groups of citizens whose opinions were not solicited by policy makers could nonetheless make their voices heard. So entrenched did women's strategies become that male Prohibitionists would also adopt them in coming decades.

---

[112] Frederick Gates, "St. John and Daniels Clubs," *Lever*, 11 September 1884.

At the same time, women's inclusion in party politics would suggest the limitations of partisanship and even suffrage as a means of influencing policy makers. When Prohibitionists granted women access to nominating conventions and opportunities to design platforms, they illuminated the problem of how very few individuals controlled the choice of who would appear on the ballot. As early as 1872, John Russell had asserted that the relative power of Prohibitionist women at conventions highlighted the lack of power held by men who belonged to major parties but did not attend conventions. Russell summarized that

as the nomination of candidates for the various civil offices, and the adoption of party platforms, are not unfrequently [sic] as influential for good or evil as the more direct act of casting the ballot, certainly the denial of the legal right to vote constitutes no valid reason for adding to the injury the further proscription of women from caucuses and conventions.[113]

Oddly for a group that strove to protect institutions rather than uproot them, Prohibitionists had harkened back to Henry David Thoreau's critique of conventions "made up chiefly of editors, and men who are politicians by profession" from wherein "the respectable man . . . adopts one of the candidates thus selected as the only *available* one, thus proving that he is himself *available* for any purpose of the demagogue."[114]

In a system wherein most individuals did not have access to the nominating process, Prohibitionists concluded that "elections have become simply ratifications" wherein citizens allowed "our most favored men to select themselves to the best positions."[115] This observation provoked a new set of questions about democracy and governance for Prohibitionists to explore, bringing them far beyond the liquor question. What were the implications of letting political parties monopolize the process of selecting candidates? How authentic was American democracy when citizens only voted between preselected candidates chosen by an elite group within these parties? How could Americans discipline elected officials for poor policy making when they were nominated by parties rather than voters? Such questions would take on increasing significance in the late 1880s

[113] John Russell, "An Important Question in Two Parts," *Peninsular Herald*, 25 January 1872.
[114] Henry David Thoreau, "Civil Disobedience" in *Civil Disobedience: Solitude and Life Without Prejudice*, rev. ed. (1849; repr. Amherst, NY: Prometheus Books, 1998), 21–22. Italics are author's.
[115] "Is It a Political Question?" *Kansas Prohibitionist*, 4 April 1883.

and 1890s, in the wake of unfolding political rivalries and new political reforms.

In 1884, however, Prohibitionists' understanding of the implications of women's partisanship mostly extended to an appreciation for women's productivity and a hope that women would someday be eligible to vote for the policies they sought. Prohibitionist women and men prepared for the upcoming presidential election by debating policy at conventions and working together in local clubs. Perhaps the legacy of women's partici-pation would be electoral success, if not in 1884, then soon after.

PART II

THE MINOR PARTY PROBLEM

4

"Collateral Consequences" of the 1884 Election

For many American political thinkers, it was the dramatic and unexpected outcome of the 1884 presidential contest that first made the role of minor parties a problem warranting significant discussion. The Prohibition Party unwittingly played a considerable part in this transformation when its presidential ticket polled 150,000 votes, 15 times more than the party's 1880 returns. Here Prohibitionists benefited from both the unusual unfitness of the Democratic and Republican candidates and middle-class, white, native-born citizens' ever-increasing anxieties about urban disorder. The unexpected increase in Prohibitionist returns was important because it influenced the outcome of the election, albeit by taking enough votes from New York Republicans to tip the Electoral College to the Democratic candidate, Grover Cleveland. Prohibitionists, who were mostly former Republicans with deep-rooted hostility toward Democrats, were as surprised and dismayed by this outcome as anyone. Prominent party orator George W. Bain unhappily described Cleveland's election as the "collateral consequences" of Prohibitionists' improved returns, the unfortunate by-product of an otherwise satisfying campaign.[1]

Angry Republican voters, political theorists, and popular journalists had another opinion. They widely argued that votes cast for a minor party had precipitated a result – namely, Cleveland's election – that was undesired by a majority of voters and was hence dangerously undemocratic. As an alternative to forming minor parties, these critics

---

[1] St. John would retort that "the other fellows got the collateral and I took the consequences"; "St. John's Repartee," *Lever*, 25 March 1885. See also A.J. Jutkins, *Hand-book of Prohibition* (Chicago: Lever Print, 1885), 5.

posited an innovation in American political institutions: the nonpartisan pressure group. The development of nonpartisan pressure groups and a Republican Anti-Saloon movement, both of which attempted to recruit from the same pool of anti-liquor advocates as the Prohibition Party, encouraged Prohibition Party leaders to more clearly articulate how minor parties enhanced the party system's efficacy. Minor parties did not impede democracy, argued Prohibitionists. Minor parties assured that elections were democratic processes because they guaranteed that all citizens' voices were heard. Pressure groups, moreover, were inherently problematic because they relied on the same major parties whose authority they claimed to challenge. Legislators alone were capable of introducing prohibition, and legislators were partisan.

Even while under attack by postelection Republican mobs and a more restrained nonpartisan movement, the possibility that their relatively high returns indicated a rising tide of support raised Prohibitionists' spirits. How could once-only Prohibition Party voters be converted into regular partisans? One possibility was to become more inclusive; in particular, Prohibitionist leadership focused on building their party organization in the South. However, in the course of pursuing new constituents some Prohibitionists also voiced substantial concerns about how women's standing in the party limited the Prohibition Party's popularity with people who could actually vote. Given Southerners' ostensible opposition to suffrage, Prohibitionists wondered if the women's suffrage issue should be set aside.

Eventually the Prohibition Party concluded that women were more than dead weight, renewing the women's suffrage plank at the 1888 national convention. Suffrage plank advocates – dignified, churchgoing people – riotously shook noisemakers and declared themselves to be "cranks," appropriating a term that others had used to slur them. At the risk of undermining their attempts to build a constituency, Prohibitionists committed to an irregular strategy that would limit mass appeal at a pivotal moment. It was thus in the midst of taunting Republican critics that Prohibitionists first moved toward a new understanding that their political enemies had long held: the assumption that minor parties were not necessarily constituency-building organizations, but rather protest groups.

* * *

Many of America's elite thinkers – especially those who had been Liberal Republicans – saw the 1884 election as a low point in American political culture.[2] Writing to Charles Milnes Gaskell from his farm near Boston, Henry Adams adopted a cynic's tone to describe how

the public is angry and abusive. Everyone takes part. We are all doing our best, and swearing at each other like demons. But the amusing thing is that no one talks about real interests. By common consent they agree to let these alone. We are afraid to discuss them. Instead of this, the press is engaged in a most amusing dispute about whether Mr Cleveland had an illegitimate child, and did or did not live with more than one mistress; whether Mr Blaine got paid in railway bonds for services as Speaker; and whether Mrs Blaine had a baby three months after her marriage.

Never inclined to think particularly well of popular political discourse, Adams claimed that the 1884 campaign was significantly worse than any other in his memory. He concluded that

[n]othing funnier than some of these subjects has been treated in my time. I have laughed myself red with amusement over the letters, affidavits, leading articles and speeches which are flying through the air. Society is torn to pieces. Parties are wrecked from top to bottom. A great political revolution seems impending. Yet, when I am not angry, I can do nothing but laugh.[3]

Adams's depiction of the election hostilities was echoed in the experience of William Dean Howells. Even in Howells' refined, traditionally Republican social circles he found himself ostracized for his allegiance to the Republican candidate. He became "a very drab-colored sheep at best in the eyes of people whom I tell I should vote for him."[4]

These descriptions of heightened campaign passions are not meant to trivialize the important political issues at hand. Questions about the tariff, wartime memories, injustices against African Americans in the South, and pensions remained unresolved. New issues were also entering the political discourse. Most exciting to reformers, civil service reform

---

[2] Sproat, *"The Best Men,"* 111–141.

[3] Henry Adams to Charles Milnes Gaskell, 21 September 1884, in *The Letters of Henry Adams*, ed. J.C. Levenson et al., vol. 2 (Cambridge, MA: Belknap Press of Harvard University Press, 1982), 551.

[4] William Dean Howells to John Hay, 17 September 1884, in *John Hay-Howells Letters: The Correspondence of John Milton Hay and William Dean Howells, 1861–1905*, ed. George Monteiro and Brenda Murphy (Boston: Twayne Publishers, 1980), 84. On the Liberal Republican critique, see Sproat, *"The Best Men"*; Cohen, *Reconstruction of American Liberalism*. Sproat's text features an intriguing account of Mark Twain's chastisement of Howells, urging that Howells simply refrain from voting rather than voting for Blaine (128).

took center stage, with Americans reinspired after the 1883 Pendleton Act exempted 15,000 jobs from politicians' appointments.[5] On the political horizon, anti-liquor advocates argued that politicians should pay closer attention to their concerns. Consistent with each party's history and philosophy, Republicans expressed some sympathy for how temperance could improve public morals, whereas Democrats firmly argued that personal habits should not be subject to state regulation.

Nor should the comments of men like Adams and Howells be taken as incontrovertible proof that the 1884 election was more impassioned than the campaigns of 1876 and 1880. For Adams and Adams, their worry that the ribald enthusiasm of election time had overflowed into a complete demise of decorum was colored by the fact that they themselves were caught between loyalties rather than enveloped within a comforting affiliation. Nonetheless, the 1884 campaign did have a distinct character engendered by the viciousness of the scandals associated with it. Scandals that were the lifeblood of political interest swirled around each major party candidate, and it was scandals to which men like Adams and Howells ascribed blame for America's dismal political scene.

Republican James Blaine had provoked scrutiny of his affairs when newspapers discovered he married his wife twice in two different states. Such behavior was definitely odd and, according to many newspapers, suggested premarital intimacy. The Blaine campaign was most damaged by accusations that the candidate had used his position as speaker of the house for personal gain. Even dedicated Republican Theodore Roosevelt privately acknowledged that Blaine was "objectionable" because "his personal honesty, as well as his faithfulness as a public servant, are both open to question."[6] Blaine was also widely accused of having taken money from corporations and government job seekers. As the consummate party insider, Blaine could not escape association with the Grant administration's embarrassments, including the Whiskey Ring, Salary Grab, and Crédit Mobilier fiascos. For much of the public, tariff-favoring and private-legislation-sponsoring Blaine embodied the worst abuses of a party already too inclined toward controlling the money supply, offering

---

[5] On civil service reform, see Steven Skowronek, *Building a New American State: The Expansion of National Administration* (New York: Cambridge University Press, 1992), 47–84. The most comprehensive discussion of the political events and ideas contextualizing the 1884 election is Summers' *Rum, Romanism, and Rebellion.*

[6] Theodore Roosevelt to Anna Roosevelt, 8 June 1884, in *The Letters of Theodore Roosevelt,* ed. Elting E. Morison, vol. 1 (Cambridge, MA: Harvard University Press, 1951), 70–71.

subsidies, protecting trusts, and engaging in downright illegal practices.[7] The Greenbackers had registered these fears in the 1870s, and the Populists would make similar antimonopoly arguments in the 1890s; in the 1880s questions about Republicans' business ethics were more diffuse but at least as profound.

Republican newspapers and politicians defended their candidate by drawing the public's attention to the fact that the Democratic candidate, Grover Cleveland, acknowledged that he had not married the mother of his son. The former New York governor had a satisfactory reputation as a proponent of important civil service reforms, but his personal conduct made many Americans who supported good government uncomfortable. Other Northern voters refrained from voting for a Democratic candidate out of fear that doing so would encourage Southern rebellion. As the campaign thrived upon unflattering accusations against two candidates of questionable merit, most of the public remained gleefully unengaged by substantial political issues. Political independents largely agreed with Prohibitionists that the campaign between Republicans and Democrats had devolved into a "filth-flight" over the dismal question of whether *"private sin or public corruption* was the lesser bar to political preferment." The *Michigan Prohibitionist* summarized that "decent people" were "no longer able to conceal their mortification."[8]

Republican Party leaders, busy trying to defeat the Democrats, resented the ankle biting of Prohibitionists. They repeatedly asked Prohibitionists to remove their candidate, the former governor of Kansas, John P. St. John. Republicans insisted that their support for local liquor regulation made them significantly drier than the very wet Democrats and thereby deserving of Prohibitionists' endorsement. After all, St. John himself had been a Republican until only very recently.[9] Under the auspices of the

---

[7] For a characterization of the Republican Party during the Gilded Age, see Lewis L. Gould, *Grand Old Party: A History of the Republicans* (New York: Random House, 2003), 86–90.

[8] "It is Finished," *Lever*, 13 November 1884. Italics are author's. "Most Humiliating," *Michigan Prohibitionist*, 9 October 1884. On the unsettled nature of how "good character" was defined in different areas of Gilded Age life, see Richard White, "Information, Markets, and Corruption: Transcontinental Railroads in the Gilded Age," *Journal of American History* 90 (June 2003): 20 and 24.

[9] There is only sparse evidence that St. John had communicated with the Prohibition Party previous to his nomination, and he joined the party only immediately before his nomination. For an example of brief correspondence with the party, see Samuel M. Dickie to John P. St. John, 25 February 1879, Folder 5, Box 19, John P. St. John Collection, Kansas Historical Society, Topeka, Kansas (JSJC). St. John sat on the board of managers

newly created New York State Temperance Assembly eleven temperance Republicans boldly used the *New York Tribune*'s columns to beg St. John to excuse himself.[10] Fredrick Douglass similarly encouraged St. John to step aside.[11]

Republican Party staff members eventually resorted to an unsuccessful and ill-conceived attempt to bribe St. John, asking the candidate to pepper his speeches with pro-Republican sentiment and stay away from states where Republicans' lead was precarious. Willingly implicating themselves in the controversy, Republicans argued that St. John's failure to reply merely proved that he intended to accept a better bribe from the Democrats.[12] It seems at least as likely that St. John did not know that others were trying to bribe him; negotiations were conducted by his campaign manager.[13]

As the 1884 election drew closer, steadfast Prohibitionists forged a tenuous alliance with political independents. Mugwumps, reform-minded individuals who were frustrated by Republican policies and corruption, advocated a new form of citizenship that rested upon a voter's self-education on political issues and that individual's willingness to move between parties to support specific policies. Faced with an unsatisfactory Republican candidate, these voters shifted their loyalty to Cleveland or St. John. Mugwumps were less likely to support antimonopolists or Greenbackers, possibly because these parties were poorly organized

of the National Christian Temperance Union with Ferdinand Schumacher, one of the future founders of Harriman, a few years before St. John's presidential campaign. See the letterhead from O.J. Benham to John P. St. John, Folder 8, Box 19, JSJC. The extent to which St. John's willingness to be selected as the party's nominee in advance of the national convention was still very questionable is discernable in the recollections of A.A. Hopkins; A.A. Hopkins to John P. St. John, 22 March 1913, Scrapbook 7, Box 3, JSJC; "The Logical Candidate," *Patriot Phalanx*, 23 June 1904.

[10] Prohibitionists first addressed this new organization in "St. John's Reply" and "The History of the Scheme," *Lever*, 23 October 1884. See also Untitled, *Christian Union*, 16 October 1884.

[11] Frederick Douglass, *New York Tribune*, 10 October 1884, in Scrapbook "1884 Tribune" in the George B. Hillard Papers, New York Public Library Special Collections, New York (GBHP).

[12] John B. Finch, "The Clarkson – St. John Controversy," *(Columbus, KS) Times*, 26 February 1885; A.J. Jutkins, *Hand-book of Prohibition* (1885), 110; Untitled, *Lever*, 27 November 1884; "Clarkson's Latest," *Lever*, 14 January 1885; John P. St. John, "What Governor St. John Knows about Bribes," *Voice*, 1 January 1885; "St. John's Defense," *Times*, 27 November 1884; "St. John," *Times*, 22 January 1885; "St. John's Sell Out," *Chicago Daily Tribune*, 14 November 1884; "St. John's Complete Vindication," *Washington Post*, 24 January 1885. The *New York Times* included a mocking article suggesting that St. John had actually meant to sell out to Equal Rights Party candidate Belva Lockwood in exchange for her hand in marriage, rum, and cigars.

[13] Summers, *Rum, Romanism, and Rebellion*, 230–237.

and possibly because their platforms did not morally rebuke Republicans from a disinterested position. Economic recovery also stole some of the antimonopolists' momentum.[14] And although Prohibitionists and Mugwumps understood the role of minor parties differently, their visions were not mutually exclusive; there was sufficient common ground to work together. Critically, both visions were contingent upon the expectation that votes cast for the Prohibition Party were unlikely to shape the results of the election, and both groups believed that they shared a common commitment to the ethical practice of politics. In a campaign otherwise bereft of much moral value or meaningful political discussion, voting for the Prohibitionists' candidate offered political independents an opportunity to register both their continuing involvement in politics and their disgust with it.

Mugwumps who voted for Prohibition Party candidates did not necessarily believe that the liquor traffic was America's most important political issue or that prohibition was the solution to the liquor problem. For example, eminent reformer Washington Gladden did not yet favor prohibition policy but enthusiastically supported John St. John in 1884. He did so because he believed that "the supreme issue in this campaign is one of character, and that every man who believes that morality is the supreme thing, ought to vote for the only candidate who is known to be a clean and upright man." Expressing his disgust with Republicans who teased that his vote would be thrown away, Gladden questioned, "Have you never heard that there is a God who loves righteousness and hates iniquity? Do you think that a man who votes against a flagrant wrong ever loses his vote? I tell you nay."[15]

Prohibitionists would have preferred it if Gladden had openly endorsed their issue as well as their party. However, Gladden's endorsement, as well as those of WCTU President Frances Willard and prominent clergy members such as Presbyterian Howard Crosby and Baptist Jesse B. Thomas, encouraged them to hope that mainstream reformers would elevate their party's status in American politics.[16] Even staunch Republican Henry Ward Beecher publicly flirted with the idea of supporting the party before concluding that he would vote for Cleveland.[17] Without having to make any significant concessions in its platform in terms of accepting license or

---

[14] On the Greenbackers and Anti-Monopolists at this moment, especially their critique of major party policies that created more favorable economic opportunities for creditors than producers, see Gretchen Ritter, *Goldbugs and Greenbacks*.

[15] A.J. Jutkins, *Hand-book of Prohibition* (1885), 78.

[16] On Howard Crosby, see "Howard Crosby for St. John," *Voice*, 2 October 1884.

[17] "New York City," *Chicago Daily Tribune*, 21 October 1884.

taxation, the Prohibition Party attracted support from a "mixed multitude" of voting Americans frustrated by the quality of major party candidates. Prohibitionists had won over Americans who wanted to "count as a protest."[18]

Democrats and Republicans recognized that the presidential election would be close and that even small incidents could influence its outcome. Party leaders encouraged their candidates to pay particular attention to New York and Ohio, contested states whose large contributions to the Electoral College were seemingly up for grabs. Republicans, attempting to pick off more Democrats than the Democrats had stolen Mugwumps, actively courted the Irish-American vote, which had traditionally supported the Democratic Party. Thus, when a Republican minister denounced Democrats as the party of "rum, Romanism, and rebellion" at a New York campaign event held just days before the election, it was a public relations disaster. Blaine's reluctance to respond to the remark made the situation even worse. The comment seemed to many Irish Americans to epitomize an insulting pitch of Republicanism; there would be no mass movement into the Republican Party this year, even though Blaine would do better in Irish neighborhoods than any previous Republican candidate.

Without a mass movement of Irish voters, Blaine could not do well enough to compensate for the hemorrhaging of Mugwumps and temperance Republicans into the Prohibition Party. In the critical state of New York, Blaine lost, Cleveland won, and this victory secured Democratic control of the Electoral College. A change of only a few hundred votes would have made all the difference. However, as the returns stood, Cleveland would take office as the first Democrat-elected president since the Civil War. If Reconstruction had not ended in 1877, it was surely dead in 1884.

Angry riots ensued. Republicans blamed "Prohibition cranks" for Cleveland's election, even Republicans in areas where temperance principles might have otherwise made people more sympathetic to

---

[18] Henry Graham, *Will a Prohibition Party Help the Cause of Prohibition?* (Boston: The National League [Non-Partisan and Non-Sectarian] for the Suppression of the Liquor Traffic, 1885), 22. For the religious press, see Untitled, *Zion's Herald*, 30 June 1884; "The Prohibition Convention," *Christian Union*, 31 July 1884. On the protest vote, see "Political Issues," *Christian Union*, 9 October 1884; "Political Issues," *Christian Union*, 23 October 1884. The *Christian Union* regularly urged that a large vote for St. John would provoke the creation of a new political party, with a broader platform than the Prohibition Party but similar attention to matters of moral principles.

Prohibitionists' endeavor.[19] In the historically dry town of Colorado Springs, riotous Republicans burned St. John in effigy to intimidate the town's sixty-two Prohibition voters.[20] Although located within a prohibition state – and St. John's home state – Topeka's Republicans similarly made an effigy of their former governor and lynched it.[21] Republicans assaulted and threw eggs at Prohibition voters, editors, and leaders. They vandalized houses, boycotted businesses, and fired Prohibitionist employees. Conventional respect for feminine delicacy was no protection; an effigy of Amanda Way, president of the Kansas WCTU and founding Prohibition Party member, was burned in her home state, and the Naperville, Illinois, WCTU president was egged on her way home from a St. John meeting.[22] In Oberlin, Ohio, a place where the most radical abolitionists had found some solace, a Prohibitionist minister was attacked by a Republican mob.[23]

The violence was widespread enough for the *Washington Post* to describe effigy burners as "making prodigious asses of themselves."[24] Prohibitionists recalled with anger how Republicans "have burned men in effigy and rotten-egged women. They have gone to those who hold

---

[19] Calling Prohibitionists cranks was the most common way to deride the party. For example, see "New Jersey: Cranks Responsible for Republican Defeat," *Chicago Daily Tribune*, 10 November 1884; "St. John in Wisconsin," *Chicago Daily Tribune*, 15 November 1884. The violence against Prohibitionists by Republicans suggests the extent to which a new, less partisan style of politics favored by upper-class reformers did not yet resonate with how other groups of Americans continued to practice politics. For a description of the tension between vibrant political culture and liberal political style, see McGerr, *The Decline of Popular Politics*.

[20] L.D. Ratliff, Untitled letter to the editor, *Lever*, 13 November 1884. For an example in Pennsylvania, see Untitled, *(Detroit) Michigan Prohibitionist*, 13 November 1884. Bader asserts that there were over 100 effigies burned or hanged across the country; Bader, *Prohibition in Kansas*, 76–77.

[21] "Harmless Amusements," *Lever*, 13 November 1884. Violence and the threat of violence during and after elections was not without precedent; Bensel, *The American Ballot Box in the Mid-Nineteenth Century*. St. John would reflect in 1888 that "I have not been burnt in effigy since the 3rd day of July . . . They used to burn me every day; then twice a week; then once a week; then in quarterly installments; then half yearly installments; and now they are becoming annual"; Untitled, *Weekly Censor*, 16 February 1888, reprinted from *Home Life*.

[22] For example, see J.W. Haggard, Untitled letter to the editor, *Lever*, 20 November 1884; W.H. Boole, "Showing the Cloven-Hoof," *Lever*, 20 November 1884; Untitled, *Lever*, 4 December 1884; "Is it Wise?" *Voice*, 1 January 1885; "Dastardly and Defiant," *Voice*, 6 August 1885; A.B. Leonard, "Doctor A.B. Leonard's Great Speech," *Lever*, 8 July 1885.

[23] "Parsons and Politics," *(New York) Nation*, 4 December 1884.

[24] "What Did It?" *Washington Post*, 17 November 1884.

opinions of their own, and said, 'If you vote your convictions of right at the ballot box we will work against you, and we will ruin or injure your business. You shall be called a 'crank,' a swindler, a villain."[25] Calling Prohibitionists cranks became common usage, a way to condemn both the dangerousness and ridiculousness of Prohibitionists' methods.

It was Republicans' assumption about the role of minor parties that best explains the bitterness that they directed against Prohibitionists. Republicans fundamentally viewed the Prohibition Party as a faction – a difficult-to-discipline group of insurgents within the Republican Party – rather than as an independent organization. Drawing on their own experience with the Liberal Republican departure in 1872, they assumed that minor parties did not function independently of their relationship to one or both major parties.[26] Their rhetoric therefore conflated the position of Mugwumps and Prohibitionists in relation to the Republican Party. St. John was a "renegade Republican" rather than a Prohibitionist.[27]

To control this "faction," Republicans had historically promised just enough to dry voters to help religious individuals rationalize avoiding the stigmatism of minor party membership. This was especially true in states with close elections or during eras wherein Democrats and Republicans were evenly matched for the presidency. Such had been the case in Iowa in the late 1870s, for example. After the Prohibition Party's 1877 gubernatorial candidate received 4.3 percent of the vote, Iowa's Republicans reconsidered their position. The Republican platform of 1879 declared support for submitting a dry referendum to the voters, and the Republican gubernatorial candidate regained a large number of the previous

---

[25] Olin J. Ross, "A New Issue in Politics," *Voice*, 1 October 1885. For another nice summarizing statement, see "Republican Post-Election Vindictiveness," *Nation*, 4 December 1884. For an early example of Prohibitionists attempting to reappropriate this slur, see Untitled, *Center*, 24 March 1886.

[26] For example, "What the People Say," *Chicago Daily Tribune*, 2 August 1884; "Small, Compact Parties," *Nation*, 4 December 1884; Gail Hamilton, "Prohibition in Politics," *North American Review*, June 1885. On factions and their history, see DiSalvo, *Engines of Change*. The ethics of a minor party's attempt to exert influence on a major party were explored in Cuthbert Mills, "The Permanence of Political Forces," *North American Review*, January 1880. About the Greenback Party, Mills concludes that "the degree of influence which the Greenback or National organization may exert on the two chief parties" was identical to "the damage it may thereby inflict on the country" (91). This assumption about the goals of minor parties has also been favored by historians. Paul Kleppner notes the prevalence of this interpretation in "The Greenback and Prohibition Parties," in *History of U.S. Political Parties*, 1550.

[27] "St. John in Wisconsin," *Chicago Daily Tribune*, 15 November 1884.

election's Prohibition Party voters, who really were just an angry faction.[28] These voters embodied political scientist Daniel DiSalvo's observation that factions often move their parties into innovative ideological and policy territory, shifting them to the left or right and thereby becoming "the spirit that animates the partisan body."[29]

However, nationwide, a large segment of the Prohibition Party had proven reluctant to cooperate, caucus, or fuse with Republicans, even after being warned that the election of a wet Democrat in 1884 was likely and after Republicans had made some gestures toward the antiliquor movement. These Prohibitionists declared themselves to be part of a minor party intellectual tradition that understood voting for a minor party as a means of constituency building behind a particular issue, rather than as a mere protest vote.[30] For Prohibitionists, the most relevant example was that set by the Free Soilers, some of whom had joined the Prohibition Party. The Prohibition Party asserted that a minor party's increasing returns were the best way to make it attractive to new recruits, even when such an increase did not lead to immediate electoral victory. Prohibitionists urged that "we as a party are but planting our votes year after year, to increase and multiply."[31] Horace Waters, a passionate Baptist who owned a major piano sales room on Broadway, had argued in his 1882 pamphlet, A Third Party Needed, that "public opinion can be made more readily by ballots than in any other way"; elections were opportunities to build public opinion, not simply reflect it.[32]

---

[28] Szymanski, Pathways to Prohibition, 136.

[29] DiSalvo, Engines of Change, 32–59, 179. DiSalvo also notes that splinter parties – minor parties that have immediately moved out from major parties – are generally ineffective at changing the agenda of their party of origin, if such a goal was their intention; 87–95.

[30] For example, "Here We Stand, Here We Stay," Voice, 6 November 1884.

[31] Isaac Newton Pierce, Prohibition: Is it Right? How to be Obtained? Is a Party Necessary? (N.p.: n.p., 1884), 3. Garden metaphors abounded when Prohibitionists discussed party development. The Lever's editorial staff noted that "every vote cast for Prohibition is good seed well sown, and will eventually bid a crop of which we may all feed proud" in "The Ohio Campaign," Lever, 9 September 1885. See also Samuel Ives Curtiss, "Important Issues," Chicago Daily Tribune, 30 October 1884.

[32] Horace Waters, A Third Party Needed (New York: Prohibition Lecture Bureau, n.d.), 1. The date of publication does not appear on this pamphlet, but the New York Public Library and Brown University Library, which possess the only two remaining copies of this pamphlet, list its publication at 1882 and 1886, respectively. The text of the pamphlet refers to how the election of a Democrat in 1884 "will convince" the Republicans to disorganize; the future tense noted here suggests that the pamphlet was indeed written in 1882 and not significantly revised for 1886 publication. However, the Brown pamphlet also includes a brief analysis of the 1884 Prohibition Party vote for St. John on

Prohibitionists' immersion in a society where most people were Democrats or Republicans made them better attuned to the arguments of Republicans than the Republicans were to them. The Prohibition Party had formulated election strategies well aware of both their continuity with a minor party tradition of constituency building and their divergence from major party expectations that they were a mere protest group. Primarily through the *Voice*, the party's first periodical with a truly national circulation, leading party theorists had urged rank and file partisans to coordinate an ever-more aggressive version of the campaigns they had previously waged.

To expand their constituency in 1884, the national committee had scheduled St. John to tour through Illinois, Indiana, Ohio, Michigan, Pennsylvania, Maryland, New York, Connecticut, Massachusetts, and New Jersey. These areas were traditional Republican strongholds, selected from among the thirty-four states where Prohibitionists would cast ballots for the party, but they were also areas where temperance sympathies were strongest. At the same time, Prohibitionists' route generally avoided states where independent or antimonopoly parties were already established and where the public's appetite for protesting the major parties was therefore already being met.[33] Prohibitionists explaining their strategy assured fellow partisans that they meant to recruit without consideration of how it might influence Democrats or Republicans, respectively. They would only consider how to maximize their own returns.

In contrast, angry Republicans pointedly argued that minor parties were a "public misfortune" because they could too easily "bring about the election of a President who will not be the choice of a majority of the whole people of the United States." They concluded that Americans should "prevent or discourage the formation of third parties" because they were a threat to the ideal of majoritarian government.[34] Minor parties' capacity for obscuring the intent of the electorate was made still

its last page, suggesting that some new information was added even if the older content was not revised.

[33] For more information on antimonopoly parties, see Ritter, *Greenbacks and Goldbugs*, 51. Prohibitionists, Greenbackers, and labor parties overlapped in Indiana and Illinois.

[34] George Ticknor Curtis, "How Shall We Elect Our Presidents?" *(New York) Century*, November 1884. These arguments built on the ideas formulated in Jacksonian America by partisans who argued that without parties, presidential elections would be routinely thrown to the House of Representatives. See Gerald Leonard, *The Invention of Party Politics: Federalism, Popular Sovereignty, and Constitutional Development in Jacksonian Illinois* (Chapel Hill: University of North Carolina Press, 2002), 13–14.

more undemocratic by the fact that minor parties necessarily appropriated most of their voters from the party they most resembled. In the 1884 election, Republicans asserted, the Prohibitionists had drawn more anti-liquor voters away from the moderately temperate Republican Party than from the wet Democratic Party. Partisans were horrified when asked "whether we were sure that the [Prohibition Party] Pittsburgh convention of 1884 was not largely composed of saloon-keepers and their attorneys, who organized the Prohibition party for the express purpose of defeating the Republican party."[35] A church officer in Jamestown, Ohio, expressed outrage at female congregants who were "part of a political party that is a Democratic side-show." He vented his anger until Mrs. Monroe, one of the Prohibitionist congregants, "answered the gentleman in a way he did not expect. She made him feel small."[36]

Mrs. Monroe's efforts aside, the assumption that Prohibitionists were focused upon Republican destruction continued. Republicans asserted that it was most apparent when the Prohibition Party refrained from organizing in the American South, a region that was overwhelmingly Democratic. Democrats, more agitated about the political attractiveness of emerging agrarian and labor parties, offered Republicans unexpected support. They expressed concern about how Greenback and labor voters would unwittingly undermine the only political party strong enough to combat Republican fiscal policies: the Democrats.[37] As the center of anti-monopoly sentiment began to shift from the West to the South, it encroached more and more on Democratic territory. Labor tickets brought together farmers and workers, with at least 189 such tickets emerging in 1886 alone. Democrats used a variety of strategies in response. They appropriated minor party agendas, and engaged in violence and ballot fraud.[38]

In the wake of the 1884 election Prohibitionist leaders were clearly shaken by both the extent of the violence and vitriol directed against partisans and the possibility that this circumstance would unnerve their

---

[35] "The Pittsburgh Convention," *New Era*, 12 June 1885. See also Untitled, *New Era*, 15 May 1885.

[36] R.H.Y., "Jamestown, Ohio," *New Era*, 7 August 1885. Her words were intriguingly unquoted.

[37] For example, (Senator) Joseph E. McDonald quoted in "The Result and the Cause," *Washington Post*, 7 November 1886.

[38] Leon Fink, *Workingmen's Democracy: The Knights of Labor and American Politics* (Urbana: University of Illinois Press, 1983), 26; Hild, *Greenbackers, Knights of Labor, and Populists*, 45–121.

rank and file. They concluded that "there is something dangerous about
this. It is antagonistic to the very spirit of our institutions" when men
attempted to intimidate other men for how they voted.[39] Bitter and
angry, Republicans rejected Prohibitionists' contention that democracy
was a process of individuals expressing themselves, not an outcome. In
the columns of the *North American Review*, a Prohibitionist adamantly
defended the principle that "every voter has an unquestioned right to
register his convictions at the ballot box." Voting for a minor party was
a perfectly democratic action for people who "would rather be right with
their conscience in a feeble minority, than wrong with the majority."[40]
Those who antagonized minor party movements attempted to "deny the
right of free speech and a free ballot" at the foundation of rule by the
people, even as they accused Prohibitionists of subverting democracy.[41] It
seems likely that Prohibitionists' ongoing work with Republican-voting
reformers who convened through fraternities, religious conventions, mis-
sionary societies, peace societies, and boards of education heightened
their sense of injury about being misunderstood.

In "The Philosophy of Third Parties" (1885), minister Alfred Wheeler
made the Prohibition Party's boldest argument for the inextricability of
moral issues, minor parties, and democratic government. Wheeler claimed
that the demand for minor parties was rooted in citizens' "duty to combine when the execution of a worthy purpose calls them to action."
Wheeler rather verbosely continued that

so far from third parties being contra-indicated in a free state, the conservation of
public morality, without which the freest commonwealth cannot abide, calls from
them as arbiters, and just in proportion as facility is given for their organization,
and their functions are duly recognized, will the safety of those institutions and
the solidity of governments that stand in the choice and live by the will of the
people.

In other words, minor parties introduced the moral issues that protected
the integrity of the electorate and thereby made democracy ethically sustainable. Wheeler concluded that it was folly to

talk about power being necessarily distributed between two parties and there
being no place of a third in a popular government! As states become larger,

[39] Olin J. Ross, "A New Issue in Politics," *Voice*, 1 October 1885.
[40] P.S. Goodman, Untitled letter to the editor, *North American Review*, August 1885.
[41] A.B. Leonard, "Doctor A.B. Leonard's Great Speech," *Lever*, 8 July 1885. Leonard was
      a Methodist minister with extensive involvement in overseeing foreign missions. His son
      became a leader in New York's Anti-Saloon League.

their interests more diversified and complex, the tendency to the organization of parties to advance these interests grows stronger. Without free, unfettered scope for the development of this tendency, high public morality must remain a dream.[42]

Democrats, Republicans, and even some independent voters challenged Prohibitionists by contending that conformity could actually advance democratic governance. By helping Americans assemble a position that adequately reflected the majority of citizen interests, the major parties prevented an unmediated vote for an infinite number of candidates and thereby warded off electoral victory by meaningless margins. In contrast, elections won by a small number of votes were a "positive public danger" because they undermined public confidence in the integrity of elections, and thereby the stability of democratic governance. Thus, noted the *Independent*, "it is ... every man's duty to make his vote tell in this direction to the utmost of his ability, by voting for a candidate who has some chance of being elected, so as to make the majority of such candidate, if he gets a majority, as large as possible, and thus put the result beyond doubt."[43]

This was a particularly salient critique given recent political history, wherein Democrats and Republicans had routinely accused each other of deal making and corruption throughout the close presidential elections in 1876 and 1880. Voters who did not take advantage of the opportunity to join with fellow citizens of similar mind to defeat those with a dramatically different opinion were "morally responsible for the known natural results of their acts," especially the likelihood that their most dissimilar rival would gain from their neglect.[44] Likewise, "people who satisfy some whimsy by not voting, or vote for some fancy candidate who is not in the running, help to bring about the close contests between the two real candidates, of which we have just been witnessing an example, and which ought to fill every man and woman in the country with alarm."[45]

* * *

The 1884 election had opened up a discussion about the party system's benefits and limits that fueled exploration into a new type of political

---

[42] Alfred Wheeler, "The Philosophy of Third Parties," *Voice*, 13 August 1885.

[43] "The Independent Organization," *Nation*, 20 November 1884.

[44] Albert Griffin, *Powerless for Good, but Powerful for Evil* (New York: L.W. Lawrence, 1887), 23.

[45] "The Independent Organization," *Nation*, 20 November 1884.

organization: the nonpartisan pressure group.[46] Formerly, the phrase *nonpartisan* had been sparsely used and, when used, had been loosely applied to organizations that engaged in activities outside the parameters of formal politics. Literary clubs, law and order leagues, religious congregations, and fraternities exemplified nonpartisan anti-liquor groups in the mid-nineteenth century. The work of these organizations was often conducive to the inclusion of individuals with different party allegiances simply because partisanship was irrelevant when using techniques like moral suasion, outreach, and mutual support; cross-party alliances were a byproduct of the strategy, not the strategy itself. It was only after the founding of the National League for the Suppression of the Liquor Traffic, which defined itself as "non-partisan and non-sectarian" in all of its literature, that the phrase *nonpartisan* came to denote an organized political lobby. In particular, the term came to describe a body of citizens that engaged in the pursuit of legislation and the support of candidates and that drew from and appealed to both major parties without being a party itself.[47]

What would be the charm of organizing apart from party politics during this most partisan age? The stakes were fundamentally moral, nonpartisans argued. Nominating candidates meant the pursuit of self-interest and thus the subordination of moral values to the competitive demands of the electoral marketplace. Nonpartisans declared that "the

---

[46] A small nonpartisan organization in Ohio, founded in 1882, anticipated a wave of such groups. "Non-Partisan Temperance Men," *Chicago Daily Tribune*, 21 July 1885; Untitled, *(Detroit, MI) Center*, 9 July 1885. On the Ohio Voter's Union, organized from 1883–1885, see Colvin, *Prohibition in the United States*, 385; "Non-Partisan Temperance Men," *Chicago Daily Tribune*, 21 July 1885. Ohio nonpartisans had organized together to persuade the Republican Party to take a relatively temperate stance, threatening to vote for Democratic candidates if the Republican Party did not oblige. The Republican Party leadership did obey, however, and Ohio's Prohibition Party had polled significantly fewer votes than it had in other states with similarly strong temperance traditions; temperate Republican candidates had largely won office. Thus, there was moral governance without political mayhem. Michael McGerr suggests that the origins of nonpartisan pressure groups lie in the extra-party organizations of Liberal Republicans in the 1860s; *The Decline of Popular Politics*, 58–62.

[47] The term *nonpartisan* would take on additional meaning in the twentieth century. Historian Mark Kornbluh distinguishes nineteenth-century special interest groups, which "mediated their concerns through partisan politics," from those of the twentieth century, which "were increasingly independent and began to usurp many of the functions previously performed by the parties" in *Why America Stopped Voting: The Decline of Participatory Democracy and the Emergence of Modern American Politics* (New York: New York University Press, 2000), 116.

party that gives promise of success at the polls will attract and befoul itself, unavoidably, with the filthy scum always floating on the surface of the political tide."[48] Nonpartisans therefore hoped to attract virtuous people by refusing to engage "the people under the props of party, with office-seekers in its trail." They claimed that reform through political parties was unlikely to be received favorably by the religious public because "political parties in this country have acquired the reputation of using methods for their successes which render active service in them incompatible with the profession of the Gospel minister, if not also with the high standing of any Christian worker."[49] The idea that any party could embody moral ideas, as Republicans had once claimed to do, was in decline.

In contrast to the innately sordid character of political parties, National League founder and Methodist minister Daniel Dorchester defined "non-partisan temperance" as a movement that pursued legislation against the liquor traffic, but that nonetheless avoided "partisan issues and struggles."[50] Dorchester sought to organize "a strong antipathy against partisan temperance action, and an unwillingness to be, in any way, com-promised by such action, or to be drawn into a *quasi* support to partisan temperance."[51] His ideas here resonated with a strong antebellum tradi-tion in which religious leaders sought to keep partisanship out of religious life and congregations disciplined ministers who moved into partisan cir-cles; the abolition movement had made the division between religion and politics more porous, but it did not completely overcome the perception that religion's purity required isolation from politics. National League members would support local interparty (citizen) tickets and attend pri-mary meetings to pursue the nomination of dry candidates. They would form law and order leagues to enforce existing statutes and to pro-mote constitutional prohibition. Members would then be left to act as their own individual conscience suggested.[52] They would not nominate

[48] Hiram King, "Non-Political Prohibition," *Reformed Quarterly Review*, October 1885.

[49] S.M. Merrill, *Outline Thoughts on Prohibition: People or Party – Which?* (Cincinnati: Crantson & Stowe, 1886), 40, 49.

[50] Daniel Dorchester, *Non-Partisan Temperance Effort Defined, Advocated, and Vindi-cated* (Boston: The National League [Non-Partisan and Non-Sectarian] for the Suppres-sion of the Liquor Traffic, 1885), 7.

[51] Dorchester, *Non-Partisan Temperance Effort Defined, Advocated, and Vindicated*, 5. Dorchester's comment epitomizes what Elisabeth Clemens has described as "linking pressure group tactics to a deep strain of popular antipartisanship"; *The People's Lobby*, 18.

[52] Dorchester, *Non-Partisan Temperance Effort Defined, Advocated, and Vindicated*, 9.

candidates themselves, nor coordinate campaigns for particular candidates, but merely give their votes to candidates who had anti-liquor records and who made temperate promises.

The Prohibition Party was convinced that the National League was really a Republican organization, and the presence of so many prominent Republicans on the executive board did little to challenge this conviction. Daniel Dorchester was joined by J. Ellen Foster, E.E. Hale, Julius H. Seelye, and John Long.[53] Although the National League's level of funding and number of members is difficult to assess, the organization's legacy is at least partly revealed in the number of state nonpartisan leagues emerging in its wake, including the Delaware State Temperance Alliance, the Union Prohibitory League of Pennsylvania, and Tennessee's Temperance Alliance.[54] By mid-1885, virtually all newspapers of record and many religious and social reform movements excitedly discussed nonpartisanship's strengths as a form of political organization; even if these were mere paper organizations, the discourse was certainly popular. At least one minister enthusiastically embraced the National League for coordinating "non-political sentiment," seeing no conflict between this purpose and the fact that it "appears to have for one of its objects the suppression of the Prohibition party."[55] Nonpartisanship could be consistent with Republican interests.

The thrust toward nonpartisan political organizations in American politics was nowhere more evident than during the constitutional amendment campaigns that roused Midwest and Eastern states in the 1880s. The achievement of amendments, nonpartisans claimed, would fully establish the capacity of nonpartisan political organizations to lead the anti-liquor movement. Prohibition campaigns occurred in nineteen states (thirteen after 1884), overwhelmingly through the submission of nonpartisan referenda on constitutional amendments. And when voters in twelve states rejected prohibition most anti-liquor advocates claimed that the

---

[53]   Harry J. Hersey, "Correspondence: The National Anti-Liquor League," *Christian Union*, 12 November 1885. For insight into the roles of J. Ellen Foster and Daniel Dorchester, see K. Austin Kerr, *Organized for Prohibition: A New History of the Anti-Saloon League* (New Haven: Yale University Press, 1985), 59–60.

[54]   On the Delaware State Temperance Alliance, see "Delaware in Line," *Lever*, 22 February 1888. On the Union Prohibitory League of Pennsylvania, see "Non-Partisan Prohibitionists," *Washington Post*, 27 September 1889. On the Tennessee Temperance Alliance, see "Mrs. Wells Checks Them," *Voice*, 3 March 1887 and "The Tennessee Nonnies," *Voice*, 24 November 1887. There were, of course, some state-level alliances formed before the National League, including the Kansas State Temperance Union.

[55]   Hiram King, "Non-Political Prohibition," *Reformed Quarterly Review*, October 1885.

very opportunity to stage campaigns for state amendments had been a victory.[56]

As eager temperance advocates, Prohibitionists were initially inclined to support any legislative crusade for prohibition conducted with enthusiasm. Prohibitionists H.W. Conant, Alphonso Alva (A.A.) Hopkins, John B. Finch, John P. St. John, Frances Willard, Mary Lathrop, Anna Gordon, George R. Scott, and Walter Thomas Mills all worked for the Rhode Island amendment campaign in 1886.[57] They campaigned for Edwin Metcalf for Rhode Island state attorney general and rejoiced when the amendment passed.[58] For Prohibitionists, who had a very small record of electoral successes, participation in a movement with tangible triumphs gave them a sense of accomplishment that assuaged their apprehensions. They set aside concerns that constitutional amendments might not have a meaningful impact on reducing the liquor traffic and that amendment victories might strengthen a potential rival.

Prohibitionists later recalled having supported the National League because "we had hopes for it. There is work that nothing but a nonpartisan society can do."[59] Partisan Prohibitionists did not necessarily see their work as nonpartisans did; nonpartisans viewed Prohibitionists as workers following their leadership, whereas Prohibitionists believed that their work ultimately advanced party goals because it politicized potential party recruits. In 1887, John B. Finch summarized the party's position through the previous decade, suggesting that "the education of the people in amendment campaigns will be helpful, but if it were not for that I should consider it time and money wasted to ever go into such a campaign again."[60] The difference in perception about the purpose of state amendment campaigns largely accounts for the early harmony between organizations.

Ultimately it was the type of victories achieved by nonpartisans on constitutional amendment campaigns that pushed the party's leading theoreticians into admitting that the nonpartisan and partisan strategies

---

[56] Szymanski, *Pathways to Prohibition*, 139.

[57] "The Motives of Prohibitionists," *Voice*, 3 June 1886. Ever the broker, Finch was simultaneously trying to organize a reunification of the Good Templar Order, which had divided in 1876 over the question of admitting African-American members. He would succeed in 1887.

[58] "The Rhode Island Victory," *Lever*, 14 April 1886.

[59] "Dr. Dorchester's Manifesto," *Voice*, 21 May 1885.

[60] John Finch quoted in Colvin, *Prohibition in the United States*, 208. On the pervasiveness of this point of view among "the best thought of the party" in the 1870s and 1880s, see "No Apology for Progress," *Vindicator*, 4 February 1916.

were fundamentally incompatible. Murmurs of discontent emerged as partisans began to review the results of Kansas and Iowa, which had gone dry in 1880 and 1882, respectively. Poor enforcement in Kansas suggested that "the prohibition law is not and never will be enforced in Kansas under the Republican party."[61] Iowa's lax prohibition enforcement demonstrated not the impracticality of the policy but only the fact that "as long as the success of the law depends on the zeal of officials elected on other issues, the law is in continual jeopardy."[62] Overall, the situations in Kansas and Iowa proved that even if nonpartisans were able to incite politicians to pass a prohibitory law, that law "is orphaned at the beginning. No party will stand behind it. Nobody is responsible for it. If it is disregarded by public officials, there is no penalty to pay."[63]

Some Prohibitionists even went so far as to declare that they wanted no more prohibitory laws until sufficient means of enforcement could guarantee their near-absolute success. In Michigan, the Prohibition Party concluded that an 1887 statute had required "time, energy, and money" – ten Prohibition Party members had sat on the thirty-person State Amendment Committee – however, it was ultimately a futile endeavor because of its dubious legality, which compounded the problem of how it distracted from constituency building.[64] Georgia's evangelist and future gubernatorial candidate Sam Small likewise asserted that, if given a choice, he would prefer open sales and consumption to the charade of high license that nonpartisans recommended.[65] Prohibitionists came to define a "nonpartisan" as "a darned fool who expects to get prohibition without voting for it."[66]

Were poor enforcement not enough, Prohibitionists also took offense when nonpartisans treated their partisanship as an obstacle. In Missouri, "non-partisan partisan gudgeons" sold out Prohibitionist candidates and supported the Republicans despite that party's refusal to submit a

---

[61] "The Prohibitory Law is Not Enforced in Kansas as it Should Be," *Kansas Prohibitionist*, 15 April 1886. See also Cole McGrea, Untitled letter to the editor, *Kansas Prohibitionist*, 3 June 1886.

[62] "What Iowa Teaches," *Voice*, 23 July 1885.

[63] (Reverend) D.E. Platter, "Why I Voted the Prohibition Ticket," *Lever*, 28 July 1887.

[64] "Pedigree and Pocket Book: The Prohibition Party, in Convention Assembled, Scores the Republicans," *Detroit Free Press*, 28 June 1888, quoted in Szymanski, *Pathways to Prohibition*, 258 n.118. Szymanski, *Pathways to Prohibition*, 155.

[65] Joe Coker, *Liquor in the Land of the Lost Cause: Southern White Evangelicals and the Prohibition Movement* (Lexington: University Press of Kentucky, 2007), 61. Small was also affiliated with the Populist Party at various points.

[66] Untitled, *Lever*, 9 September 1885.

constitutional amendment to the people after promising to do so.[67] Prohibitionists would bitterly recount how, after they had assisted in a nonpartisan campaign for a prohibitory amendment in Michigan in 1887, nonpartisans and Republicans had demanded that Prohibitionists "withdraw their party ticket as an inducement for the Republicans to go for the Amendment. Otherwise they, the Republicans, would defeat the Amendment."[68] Los Angeles's *Weekly Censor* would assert that "a non-partisan election nowadays means one in which Republicans and Democrats maintain their distinctive political relations intact, but the Prohibitionists are invited to drop their party principles and help the old machines to shear the sheep."[69] As for the National League, it struggled to maintain local organizations and collapsed after only a year, having done little more than distribute anti-Prohibition Party tracts. Political scientist Ann-Marie Szymanski suggests that the problem was top-heavy leadership, with many prestigious people uncommitted to the everyday work of local organizing and campaigning.[70]

State elections in 1886 inspired many Prohibitionists to conclude that the party did not need to make demeaning compromises with non-partisanship; Prohibitionist candidates received almost 300,000 votes nationwide.[71] Party chair John B. Finch concluded that "we act on the basis of those to whom prohibitory law is comparatively nothing and Prohibition everything" when explaining the party's withdrawal from nonpartisan campaigns and programs.[72] Thus, "we will not compromise or temporize with either of the old parties to get them to take up this issue." Unlike the nonpartisans, "we don't want them to take it up! Because if either of them should take it up, it would do so only because they were whipped into doing it; and if the time should come to sell us out, it would sell us out as cheap as it had bought us."[73] In 1887, the *Lever*'s editorial staff "bid non-partisanship good-bye forever."[74]

[67] "Along the Lines: Missouri Letter: Prohibitionists Sold Out," *Lever*, 12 January 1887.
[68] L.C. Pitner, "Michigan," *Lever*, 20 April 1887.
[69] Untitled, *Weekly Censor*, 10 May 1888.
[70] Szymanski, *Pathways to Prohibition*, 54–56; August F. Fehlandt, *A Century of Drink Reform in the United States* (Cincinnati: Jennings and Graham, 1904), 271. See also "National League for the Suppression of the Liquor Traffic," in *Standard Encyclopedia of the Alcohol Problem*, ed. Ernest Hurst Cherrington (Westerville, OH: American Issue Publishing Company, 1928), 1858–1859.
[71] Szymanski, *Pathways to Prohibition*, 134.
[72] "The Motives of Prohibitionists," *Voice*, 3 June 1886.
[73] John B. Finch, "Aspects of our Lives," *Voice*, 27 May 1886.
[74] "Good-bye, Non-Partisanship," *Lever*, 6 April 1887.

However, remaining aloof from the crescendo of nonpartisan state amendment campaigns proved to be an impossible standard of doctrinal purity for individual partisans. It became unusual for Prohibition Party newspapers to report partisans' nonpartisan activism, but the WCTU's *Union Signal* and the religious, reform, and independent presses registered many examples. Clinton B. Fisk joined a nonpartisan campaign to encourage Tennessee's African-American population to vote for the state amendment proposed in 1887.[75] John B. Finch, for all of his misgivings, would be memorialized as having been "as active as any one in participating in the campaigns for state constitutional prohibition up until his death in 1887."[76] In Texas, newspaper editor James B. Cranfill worked with a diverse group of anti-liquor advocates to support an 1887 state prohibition campaign; he considered public scrutiny of an alliance with Northerners more dangerous to the prohibition cause than an alliance with nonpartisans.[77] Party orators from around the nation went to South Dakota to stump for prohibition in 1889.[78] In Pennsylvania and Washington, state Prohibitionists considered nonpartisan alliances and called national speakers such as Walter Thomas Mills to their aid.[79] The rank and file hemorrhaged time and funds into nonpartisan endeavors, especially amendment campaigns. In a remarkable example, the *Voice* claimed to have raised a $34,000-campaign fund for state prohibition in Nebraska in 1890.[80] Prohibitionists protested and patronizingly dismissed nonpartisan campaigns that put legislative achievements before the election

---

[75] Paul E. Isaac, *Prohibition and Politics: Turbulent Decades in Tennessee, 1885–1920* (Knoxville: University of Tennessee Press, 1965), 36. This activism was likely promoted after the Supreme Court case of *Kansas v. Mugler* (1887), which affirmed the legality of state prohibition amendments. On *Mugler*, see Richard S. Hamm, *Shaping the Eighteenth Amendment: Temperance Reform, Legal Culture, and the Policy, 1880–1920* (Chapel Hill: University of North Carolina Press, 1995), 51–55.

[76] Colvin, *Prohibition in the United States*, 226. About this campaign, the *Prohibition Journal* would note that "it took only one campaign for him to throw the high license fallacy to the winds and, if we remember correctly, he declared against constitutional amendment campaigns before his untimely death"; "Finch and Amendments," *Prohibition Journal*, 15 January 1914.

[77] Ivy, *No Saloon in this Valley*, 45–69.

[78] Szymanski, *Pathways to Prohibition*, 157.

[79] Blocker, *Retreat from Reform*, 47; Samuel D. Hastings to T.C. Richmond, 28 February 1889, TCRC.

[80] Colvin, *Prohibition in the United States*, 210. I am a bit doubtful that partisans were actually able to muster this kind of fund-raising clout for no other reason than they were normally so pressed for funds. For example, national chair Charles Jones commented that the national committee had less than $5,000 in its treasury at the start of 1905, and in 1908 the national party reported that it had $500 in its treasury; Minutes of the

of Prohibition Party candidates, but individual partisans and sometimes even local and state parties would be drawn into these movements for decades.

Perhaps some of these amendment-chasing Prohibitionists were responding to the party's extraordinary failure to mobilize Northern evangelical churches.[81] Although largely evangelical Christians themselves, Prohibitionists remained unable to convince other evangelical Christians to become Prohibitionist. This problem persisted despite the fact that some Prohibitionists had prominent roles within church governing bodies. For example, John Russell, Silas C. Swallow, and Clinton B. Fisk were all delegates to the 1880 General Conference of the Methodist Episcopal Church. In 1884 and 1888, Clinton B. Fisk would repeat as a delegate, but it was Daniel Dorchester, president of the flailing National League, who would chair the conference's Committee on Temperance and the Prohibition of the Liquor Traffic.

In some ways, the 1888 Committee on Temperance and Prohibition suggested accommodation between partisans and nonpartisans, such as when it cited the common ground that even "milder liquors, and in however moderate quantities" were problematic, as "confirmed by the impartial demonstration of life-insurance experts." Nonetheless the conference would also table a fairly restrained resolution urging that "while we do not presume to dictate to our people as to their political affiliations we do express the opinion that they should not permit themselves to be controlled by party organizations that are managed in the interests of the liquor traffic."[82] Even a halfway commitment still seemed like too much, and more conventional resolutions predominated. Reviewing its record in 1894, the Connecticut Baptist Convention's Temperance Committee would concede that a "division of opinion as regards the wisest methods"

Prohibition National Committee, 20 November 1907, and Meeting of the National Committee, 14 July 1908, Folder: Prohibition National Committee Minute Book 1907–1908, Charles Jones Papers, Bentley Historical Library, Ann Arbor, MI (CJP). In 1888, only $15,000 was pledged for the national campaign, and only $20,000 in 1892; "Bidwell and Cranfill," *Voice*, 7 July 1892. Szymanski also notes that the Nebraska Prohibition Party allied with the state WCTU and IOGT to provide volunteers for the campaign; *Pathways to Prohibition*, 44.

[81] Szymanski cites these churches' concerns that the factions among coreligionists created by partisanship would make congregation growth and revivals impossible; *Pathways to Prohibition*, 50.

[82] David S. Monroe, ed., *Journal of the General Conference of the Methodist Episcopal Church Held in New York, May 1–31, 1888* (New York: Phillips & Hunt, 1888), 457, 327–328.

had been "allowed to close our lips" and "restrain our activities" during the previous years.[83]

The full measure of Prohibitionists' lost opportunity to organize Protestants was suggested by the tremendous gap between electoral support for state constitutional amendments and for Prohibition Party candidates, even in states where the amendments were not achieved. The combined state amendment referendum campaigns of Maine, Ohio, Iowa, and Kansas in 1884 had yielded 620,000 votes, whereas the Prohibition Party had received just 45,000 votes for St. John in these same states.[84] Some of the amendment-favoring voters might have advocated prohibition for reasons of health or economy, but the overall religious nature of the anti-liquor movement at this historical moment suggests that most of these voters were probably churchgoers not yet persuaded of the efficacy of minor party voting.

When liberated from the decorum of a religious convention, nonpartisans retorted that it was not only the sense that parties were inherently corrupt, but the "utter impracticality" of minor party organization that had led nonpartisans to reject this method.[85] They taunted that "history does not record the success of a single victory against the liquor traffic, achieved by the influence and vote of a Prohibitory political party."[86] In contrast, nonpartisans proudly pointed to their own record of legislative achievements and relatively temperate office holders – the same achievements to which Prohibition Party speakers, campaign organizers, and donors had contributed. If enforcement was imperfect, at least there were laws ready to be enforced. Nonpartisans further contended that legislation by a single party actually had less chance of being enforced than a multiparty or nonpartisan effort because a single party's support necessarily meant that its rival political party was opposed to it and would continue to agitate against it. Constitutional prohibition, introduced by the people and secured through the majority, would become the settled policy of government, Methodist Bishop S.M. Merrill argued.[87] "If the

---

[83] P.S. Evans, ed., *Seventy-First Annual Report of the Connecticut Baptist Convention Held with the Central Church of Norwich, October 16th and 17th, 1894* (New Haven, CT: Hoggson & Robinson, 1894), 42.

[84] Gail Hamilton, "Prohibition in Politics," *North American Review*, June 1885; Hiram King, "Non-Political Prohibition," *Reformed Quarterly Review*, October 1885.

[85] *The Third Party: As Seen by the New York Independent, the Leading Religious Journal* (New York: S.W. Benedict, 1886), 2.

[86] *Third-Party Temperance Efforts: Facts Which Should Be Thoroughly Digested* (N.p.: n.p., 1886), 2.

[87] Merrill, *Outline Thoughts on Prohibition: People or Party – Which?*, 35–36.

moral conviction of the people demands prohibition, and States enact it by unpartisan legislation, finding support for it on its merits above party questions," then "the probability that it will be enforced is much greater than if it depended upon party."[88]

When Republican anti-liquor advocates founded the Anti-Saloon Republican movement in 1886, there was much about it that vindicated angry Prohibitionists' suspicions that the National League had been a Republican group in nonpartisan disguise. The Anti-Saloon Republican National Committee was formed for the purpose of advocating a bolder anti-liquor platform in the Republican Party, and it shared several of the same leaders as the nonpartisan National League, including Rufus S. Frost, Henry W. Blair, and Hiram Price. Price, who had voted against forming a party at the Prohibitionists' first national convention, would later become president of the Anti-Saloon League. J. Ellen Foster was a leading speaker for the National League and Anti-Saloon Republicans, in addition to launching the Non-Partisan Women's Christian Temperance Union. Other prominent leaders included Kansas' Albert Griffin, who more than anyone was the voice of the movement, and Noah Davis, who served on the New York Supreme Court and had ruled over William "Boss" Tweed's trial in 1873.[89] These temperance Republicans worked with fellow Republicans whose anti-liquor records were less aggressive. For example, Henry Blackwell attended the founding state convention of the Massachusetts Anti-Saloon Republicans, although there is little to suggest continued involvement.[90] Theodore Roosevelt was appointed to the executive committee and spoke on the movement's behalf, although Roosevelt's personal correspondence suggests that he too thought of the organization as an innocuous alternative means to prevent further Mugwump-like revolts; Anti-Saloon Republicans were "harmless enough," and

---

[88] Merrill, *Outline Thoughts on Prohibition: People or Party – Which?*, 71.

[89] Robert Smith Bader attributes the movement's founding to Kansas Republicans; *Prohibition in Kansas*, 78. A brief communication between Griffin and St. John preserved in the St. John Collection suggests the tight and overlapping political networks within which most anti-liquor public figures worked. Griffin, at that time the editor of an anti-liquor newspaper, arranged for St. John to speak at a local anti-liquor event. See Albert Griffin to John P. St. John, 5 April 1879, Folder 5, Box 19 (JSJC). The two men served as president and vice president, respectively, of the Kansas State Temperance Union at the time of its founding in 1879; Bader, *Prohibition in Kansas*, 36–37. Their relationship was sometimes tumultuous; Bader, *Prohibition in Kansas*, 56. On Kansas Prohibitionists' poor opinion of Griffin in the 1880s, see Untitled, *Times*, 16 April 1885. Griffin would become an advocate for moral suasion, rather than legal action, by the 1890s.

[90] "War Against the Saloons," *New York Times*, 13 July 1886.

Roosevelt was willing to lend support through a "*short* address" now and again.[91] Affiliated leagues were organized in sixteen states by 1886, mostly in the Northeast and Midwest, with Nevada, Georgia, and Texas also possessing small organizations.[92]

Despite support from a few illustrious figures, the Anti-Saloon Republican movement failed to raise enthusiasm from many prominent Republican leaders or temperance advocates in the party's rank and file. The *Zion's Herald* categorized the Anti-Saloon Republican movement as a "half-hearted and half-way appeal to moral and political duty."[93] The group claimed to have enrolled about 20,000 members.[94] However, even in New York, where the Republican Party rededicated itself to perfecting its organization, no more than 100 Republicans attended any Anti-Saloon Republican state convention in 1886. The *Washington Post* described the few attendees at a September conference as "nobodies without weight or influence."[95]

From the beginning, the Anti-Saloon Republican movement was shackled by the public's suspicion that it was not a good faith effort to spread anti-liquor legislation. It was widely speculated that the Anti-Saloon Republicans were a ruse to capture Prohibitionists and then, once these individuals were pledged to support Republican candidates, to do nothing to actually advance the cause.[96] Sometimes the Anti-Saloon Republicans' hostility toward the Prohibition Party boiled over, as was the case when General Conway of Brooklyn submitted a resolution to the Binghamton Anti-Saloon Convention that began by denouncing the Prohibition Party. "The convention," noted the *Christian Union*, "very sensibly decided that it was not assembled to attack the Prohibitionist." Readers could decide for themselves whether an attack was avoided because

---

[91] Theodore Roosevelt to Henry Cabot Lodge, 15 May 1887, in *Letters of Theodore Roosevelt*, 127.

[92] Given the establishment of the National League of Republican Clubs in 1887, it is possible that there was a connection between the Anti-Saloon Republicans and this broader organization. On the National League of Republican Clubs, see McGerr, *The Decline of Popular Politics*, 80–81. McGerr interprets the National League of Republican Clubs as an effort to more fully introduce the Liberal Republican style into regular Republican politics. On the Anti-Saloon Republicans more generally, see Fehlandt, *A Century of Drink Reform*, 271–276.

[93] "A Grave Mistake," *Zion's Herald*, 28 July 1886.

[94] "Temperance Notes," *Christian Advocate*, 9 December 1886.

[95] Untitled, *Washington Post*, 9 September 1886; "Temperance Notes," *Christian Advocate*, 9 December 1886; Untitled, *Christian Union*, 16 September 1886.

[96] For example, Untitled, *Christian Union*, 19 September 1886.

such opposition really was not the convention's intention or because such a blatant attack would be counterproductive.[97]

Prohibitionists were quick to point out an additional problem in Anti-Saloon Republican premises: Movement members organized as Republicans and thus willingly surrendered the right to depart from their party as a means of building leverage within it. In the end, there was little that Anti-Saloon Republicans were prepared to do as a national organization that members could not do as delegates to Republican conventions. The *Christian Union* concluded that the movement's national convention, which organized with about 300 delegates in Chicago, was a gesture by good men with timid commitment because "no practical method of action was proposed by which to insure that the Republican party should carry out the views of the Convention."[98]

By December 1886, New York's Anti-Saloon Republicans would have to give up the main hall of the Metropolitan Opera House, which they had previously reserved, because only 13 delegates showed up from among the expected 1,200.[99] This hardly bode well for future organizational development, making it challenging to argue that the Anti-Saloon Republicans were even a faction in the technical sense.[100] If not a faction, however, the Anti-Saloon Republicans' organization can partially explain why the 1886 Republican platforms of ten states endorsed referenda on the prohibition question – if not prohibition itself. Or perhaps this innovation might be better explained in terms of fear that the Prohibition Party might again woo Republican voters. Indeed, one Ohio partisan would note that the Prohibition vote increased in "off years" and declined in "important years" because "men are urged to vote the Prohibition ticket, not with the purpose of ultimately electing it, but in order to influence their own parties," which "they had never really left."[101]

Even as the National League and Anti-Saloon Republicans declined, nonpartisan strategy's credibility held fast. "Let it be understood that the temperance vote is a moveable quantity, that it will go where its principles are supported," nonpartisans argued, and "both parties will be eager to get that vote. That is the way the saloon acts, and we can learn from

---

[97] Untitled, *Christian Union*, 16 September 1886.
[98] Untitled, *Christian Union*, 23 September 1886.
[99] "The Anti-Rum Politicians," *New York Times*, 2 December 1886.
[100] On factions, see DiSalvo, *Engines of Change*, 3–6.
[101] "Where We Differ," *New Era and Delaware Signal*, 7 December 1888. On the 1886 platforms, see Hamm, *Shaping the Eighteenth Amendment*, 30.

the enemy."[102] Nonpartisan organizations could effectively coordinate voters to work as a group while still arguing that they were "not, in any proper sense, a political party" because they did "not propose a continued organization to control all the offices or all the policy of the government."[103]

It was the Prohibition Party, a group of voters that had functioned as a balance of power in the previous presidential election, that most feverishly indicted such balance-of-power strategy as "plausible, but not honorable or honest" because it subverted the ideal of majority rule. Anti-liquor advocates needed a method that was ethically consistent with the morality of their issue. They could not emulate "an unscrupulous minority of saloonists, which hold[s] the balance of power."[104] "No honest man," declared the *Lever*, "can go into a [major party] caucus expecting the members of that caucus to support his man if nominated, but determined to scratch the other man, if that other man beats his own man in the caucus." Such work was "a system of political bush-whacking or guerilla warfare."[105] It was a reckless challenge to the regular meaning of party and to politics ordered by political parties, whereby it was commonly understood that belonging to a party required consistent acceptance of the candidate nominated by that party.[106] In contrast, Prohibitionists stuck to their assertion that, unlike pressure groups or saloons, "we want to dictate no laws to an unwilling majority. We want a fair fight on this question, and if the majority say keep the grog-shop, we say keep the grog shop.... We want no un-American methods of ruling if we are in a minority."[107] The Prohibition Party had never intended to be a balance of power – its ambition was to win elections outright – and this intention made the party ethically superior to its nonpartisan counterpart.

In 1887, A.A. Hopkins announced to a mass meeting of Brook-lyn's Prohibition Party members that "there is no longer a question

---

[102] "The Collapse of the Third Party," *Independent*, 23 September 1886.
[103] Merrill, *Outline Thoughts on Prohibition: People or Party – Which?*, 61.
[104] "Plausible, but not Honorable or Honest," *Lever*, 17 February 1886; L.C. Pitner, "The Coming Party," *Lever*, 10 March 1886. See also "The Mugwump Theory of Politics," *Voice*, 3 December 1885; Herrick Johnson, "Prohibition in Politics," *Kansas Prohibitionist*, 27 May 1886. Advocates of nonpartisanship, on the other hand, would encourage the imitation of liquor traffic balance-of-power tactics while casting party politics as inherently contaminating. For example, Hiram King, "Non-Political Prohibition," *Reformed Quarterly Review*, October 1885.
[105] "Plausible, but not Honorable or Honest," *Lever*, 17 February 1886. To *scratch* is to cross out on a ballot.
[106] Silbey, *American Political Nation*, 65–71.
[107] "The Mugwump Theory of Politics," *Voice*, 3 December 1885.

whether Prohibitionists shall take part in non-partisan campaigns. Those campaigns are over." Fellow speaker Josiah Strong disagreed, arguing that such campaigns had an educative value and that "when a man commits himself publicly, by his vote, to the principle of Prohibition... he goes a long way towards the Prohibition party."[108] Although the momentum was toward Hopkins' side of the debate, not all partisans or all state parties made the same resolution at the same time. Even as Hopkins and Strong deliberated, party organizer E.B. Sutton prepared to organize the Washington State Temperance Alliance to support dry candidates, without any conditions regarding the nomination of Prohibition Party candidates. Working in a state with a total population of only 350,000 and wherein the transcontinental railroad had just arrived, Prohibitionists like Sutton sought alliances wherever they could. However, by 1892 even Sutton's Washington peers would reject nonpartisanship, running a full party ticket in the state election.[109] Partisans resolved to wait until they had enough popular support to fully capture government and carry out their moral agenda in its perfect entirety. Of course, resolutions are made to be broken.

Legislating Morality — Purpose of Government?

* * *

Energized by public attention – both positive in terms of their 1884 election results and negative in terms of effigy burning and nonpartisan competition – Prohibitionists considered whether the publicity that ensued from St. John's campaign provided them with a unique opportunity to gain widespread support and become a major party. Could changes to party policy persuade a large constituency of dry voters to join their ranks immediately? Prohibitionists saw the greatest potential for party growth in the South, a region they assumed was full of temperance supporters seeking an alternative to the Democratic Party. *Religion!!*

By virtue of having organized as a political party, Prohibitionists could not help but reinforce the widespread Southern assumption that prohibitionism "suggested disloyalty to the Democratic Party" and hence "to white political supremacy."[110] They could not unmake themselves as a

---

108 "Measures and Methods: The Conference and Mass Meeting of the Prohibition Party Workers in Brooklyn," *Voice*, 6 October 1887. Brooklyn would not be consolidated with New York City until 1897.

109 The Washington State Temperance Alliance constituency would grow "fanatical" – that is, to favor the Prohibition Party – in the 1890s. On E.B. Hutton and the WSTA see Clark, *The Dry Years*, 41–53.

110 Coker, *Liquor in the Land of the Lost Cause*, 79, 101–103. Such concerns would be articulated most frequently in local and state campaigns wherein dry Populist candidates performed well, but certainly applied to Prohibitionists. Proclamations could

party. On the issue of women's suffrage, however, the Prohibition Party could more easily equivocate. Soon some party strategists proposed an idea that once would have been anathema: mitigating the language of their women's suffrage planks. This strategy was lent credibility by Southerners within the party, such as Texas Baptist James B. Cranfill, a future vice-presidential candidate. Cranfill urged opposition to a suffrage plank not because he opposed suffrage but because the plank would alienate fellow Southerners.[111] The thinking went that attracting constituents in the American South – a region where women's suffrage was an unpopular proposition – was more important than rewarding the loyalty of women who were not eligible to vote.[112]

Exemplifying this trend in party thought, the 1885 state convention in New York hedged its endorsement of women's suffrage by "unreservedly declaring that it should not in any sense be made a test of party fealty."[113] Prohibitionists could appear more moderate, and hence more palatable, by simply restraining themselves from engagement with secondary issues. Former New York gubernatorial candidate and *Voice* correspondent A.A. Hopkins enthusiastically praised a plank approved by the 1885 Pennsylvania convention that promised to support women in "whatever measures and to whatever degree" they worked for the protection of the home from alcohol, including "civil equality under the law";

---

also be coded with the accusation that temperance forces had "political designs." For an example in Tennessee, see Isaac, *Prohibition and Politics*, 45–47. Two decades later, the Anti-Saloon League would similarly solicit counterattacks whenever they appeared to threaten Democratic hegemony; Thomas R. Pegram, "Temperance Politics and Regional Political Culture: The Anti-Saloon League in Maryland and the South, 1907–1915," *Journal of Southern History* 63 (February 1997): 66–67. According to Pegram, the disenfranchisement of black voters was a precondition for most white Southern voters' acceptance of state prohibition. C.C. Pearson and J. Edwin Hendricks, *Liquor and Anti-Liquor in Virginia, 1619–1919* (Durham, NC: Duke University Press, 1967) mentions the concern that the Prohibition Party was a Republican ruse, only briefly referencing that such a ruse was problematic because the Democratic Party "was the white man's party," 220. The threat conveyed by such a "ruse" was registered in extraordinary violence against Prohibitionists, 217–218.

[111] Blocker, *Retreat from Reform*, 24–25. On Cranfill's continued allegiance to this strategy, see J.B. Cranfill to T.C. Richmond, 21 July 1894, TCRC.

[112] For example, see S.M. Hammond, "Ought the National Prohibition Platform to Declare for Woman Suffrage?" *(Chicago) Statesman*, May 1888; John Olin, *The Prohibition Party and Woman Suffrage: A Plea for an Honest Platform* (Madison: The Wisconsin Prohibitionist, 1888). For an example of Southern anti-liquor disinterest in women's suffrage, see Szymanski, *Pathways to Prohibition*, 134. For a direct response to Olin's pamphlet, see Untitled, *Weekly Censor*, 19 April 1888.

[113] "The Convention in Detail," *Voice*, 17 September 1885.

this was a step back from promising full suffrage. Even as he expressed his own delight, however, Hopkins captured the reaction of some women delegates: "A little complaint was made about this, by one or two lady delegates, and one said in my hearing, 'We have been sold out.'"[114]

The discussion over the suffrage plank in New York, Pennsylvania, Kentucky, and other states quickly expanded into a broader conversation about the party's philosophy. Did the party's mandate to promote prohibition make compromises on other policies ethically justified? Many Prohibitionists were horrified that this question was even posed. They argued that moral issues (including women's suffrage) were defined by the fact that compromise was never acceptable. J.G. Evans, a Methodist minister who was the former and future president of Hedding College in Illinois and who would later chair the Methodist Episcopal Church's Permanent Committee on Temperance and Prohibition, was the *Lever* correspondent who crafted most of this influential newspaper's statements on suffrage. He questioned, "Suppose it should be true that our growth will be slower if we retain this plank? What of it?" Evans continued,

Are we to abandon an important truth and dodge a great living issue in order to get votes?...It is true that we want votes and must have votes to succeed in our great undertaking. But there are two methods of reaching that end. One is to trail our banner of truth in the mud, compromise our principles and get votes by declining to antagonize errors and vicious policies in government....The other method is the one of true statesmanship, which plants itself upon the right.[115]

Prominent orator George W. Bain, former Montana governor and Civil War hero Green Clay Smith, Mother Eliza Stewart, and Frances Willard resolved that they would not "play the coward and the ward politician in dropping the woman suffrage plank so as to secure some dubious votes."[116] Civil War veteran and Illinois Temperance Union president John C. Pepper insisted that "you are not in a proper state of mind...if you are going to ignore morals in your organization."[117] And silence on the matter of women's suffrage would be no more ethical than opposition. Noted Los Angeles's *Weekly Censor*, "to those who tell us we must hedge and keep mum on the woman suffrage or any other question for policy sake, let us say no – rather proclaim our position on that and any other

---

[114] A.A. Hopkins "The Field at Large," *Lever*, 1 September 1886.
[115] J.G. Evans, "Woman Suffrage," *Lever*, 14 March 1888.
[116] "Notes," *Weekly Censor*, 5 April 1888.
[117] John C. Pepper, "John C. Pepper on Suffrage," *Lever*, 22 February 1888.

question on six feet placards than keep anything secret that we intend to do."[118]

Advocates for a women's suffrage plank further discredited the plank's opponents by comparing them to nonpartisans. J.G. Evans challenged the rationale of T.C. Richmond, a Wisconsin attorney who was the plank's foremost opponent, in the months immediately preceding the 1888 convention. Evans summarized that

> it is claimed that the suffrage plank will have the effect of dividing our forces and that all Prohibitionists cannot be combined in one organization. Bishop Merrill [of the National League] and others have made exactly the same arguments against the Prohibition party. They say in the language of Bishop Merrill, "The combination must be on the broadest possible ground and *restricted to this one purpose*. The combination to be effective must be simple enough to include all classes that will accept prohibition... *Republicans or Democrats, Greenbackers or Labor Reformers*." If we condemn the logic of Bishop Merrill we cannot accept the logic of Mr. Richmond. The same sophistry underlies the conclusion of each, though the cases are in some respects dissimilar.[119]

Prohibitionist strategy building was a slipknot because gestures that might attract more individuals to the party and thereby advance electoral victory were also compromises that could potentially make such victories less meaningful.

The ongoing debate about women's suffrage and the values underlying party policy was further complicated by the matter of what this debate communicated to women in party ranks. Especially after making promises to WCTU women with the development of the Prohibition Home Protection Party in 1882, plank advocates argued that "in 1888 you can't dissolve the compact arbitrarily, without a serious antagonism of the laws of fair dealing, integrity, and honor."[120] One Prohibitionist indignantly demanded of fellow partisans, "Drop suffrage out of our platform, will you?... You can only drop it by dropping her, and you must drop her out first."[121] The consequences wrought by anti-suffrage-plank resolutions were already becoming apparent. Few new women leaders emerged in the late 1880s who had not been welcomed in earlier years. And even though articles in party publications continued to validate the presence of women at meetings, new clubs were also praised when they included

---

[118] "One Idea," *Weekly Censor*, 30 September 1886. See also "[Illegible] to Women," *Weekly Censor*, 6 October 1887.

[119] J.G. Evans, "Woman Suffrage," *Lever*, 14 March 1888. Richmond would leave the Prohibition Party in 1896.

[120] John C. Pepper, "An Open Letter," *Lever*, 4 April 1888.

[121] W.T. Owen," The Party of One Idea," *Delaware Signal and New Era*, 15 March 1889.

more "voters" than "ladies."[122] Women were invited to contribute financially and through work, but they had a less secure position as policy makers.

Attacking the *Voice*, which opposed a suffrage plank, the *Lever* connected the issues of women's suffrage and women's representation, depicting the slippery slope between them:

> If *The Voice* is right in thinking that the suffrage plank ought to be left out of the platform, then *The Voice* must believe that women ought to be excluded from the convention entirely, for certainly if women ought not to vote they ought not to help make platforms to control the action of voters and nominate candidates for men to vote for.[123]

Similarly, the president of the Kansas WCTU expressed her concern that if the upcoming 1888 national convention removed the suffrage plank from the national platform "in the presence of women delegates," they would thereby "take action which will declare these delegates out of place and bar them out hereafter!"[124] Such a concern was not paranoia, as indicated by the comments of one Ohio Prohibitionist who urged that "it will be proper for ladies to go to our conventions as delegates when they have been accorded or shall have secured the ballot," and not before. He explained that he would not be opposed to women as delegates if it were not for the fact that such a policy "carries with it obligations which our party cannot afford to pay, viz., the indorsement [sic] of equal suffrage as a principle."[125] What would happen to the party if women Prohibitionists were alienated by the removal of the suffrage plank, but this removal then made the party no more attractive to anti-suffragists, Southern or otherwise? J.G. Evans pithily concluded that "now I do not mean to be understood that the ungodly should not be permitted, or even encouraged to vote with us, but I object to setting the sisters aside as an inducement for these to number themselves with us."[126]

The mounting friction between Prohibitionists who wanted to remove the suffrage plank and those who wanted to keep it culminated spectacularly at the 1888 national convention. Initial advantage went to the

---

[122] Untitled, *Lever*, 5 May 1886; A.A. Hopkins, "The Field at Large," *Lever*, 25 August 1886; Untitled, *Lever*, 16 May 1888. On the usage of *ladies* and *voters*, see also J.B. Tenner, Untitled letter to the editor, *New Era*, 14 August 1885.

[123] "Worthy of Almost Any Compliment," *Lever*, 9 May 1888.

[124] Fanny H. Rastall (president Kansas WCTU), "Woman Suffrage and the Party," *Voice*, 29 March 1888.

[125] Uriah McKee, "A Voters' Convention," *(Springfield, OH) New Era and Delaware Signal*, 8 February 1898.

[126] (Rev.) G.W. Parry, "The Suffrage Discussion," *Lever*, 16 February 1888.

pro-suffrage plank side when the committee on rules decided against an anti-suffrage plank proposal. When suffrage plank opponents had proposed to hold four hours of discussion on the suffrage question before any resolution, the "wildest confusion ensued for a half hour" as Prohibitionists argued with neighboring delegates and those recognized by the chair.[127] An initial platform was drafted under the leadership of party founder James Black and a committee that included thirty-five men and four women, both advocates for and opponents of the plank. Anna Shaw, president of the National Woman Suffrage Association, gave a brief presentation. The debate between committee members regarding the proposed women's suffrage plank included the presentation of eighteen different versions of the plank and lasted for eight hours; exhausted, the committee appointed a small subcommittee to finalize the text.[128]

The subcommittee eventually decided that the plank would be kept, but that it would argue for the submission of a women's suffrage amendment to voters rather than for the amendment itself. This agreement seemed acceptable to individuals who had not favored a plank because the democratic gesture of submitting an amendment to the people promised allegiance to national principles that were more universal than support for women's rights.[129] This was something that they could explain to the still elusive but desperately sought Southern voter.

At the presentation of the platform committee's resolutions to the full convention, only the suffrage plank was subjected to sustained discussion. A minority report opposing the suffrage plank was supported by national committee member James Tate, prominent land developer Walter Thomas Mills, and 1880 presidential candidate Neal Dow, who opposed even the modified suffrage plank on the grounds that it distracted from the principal issue of prohibition. Grindingly over the course of an entire afternoon, the anti-plank Prohibitionists were overwhelmed by speakers with virtually unmatched party authority, including Mother Eliza Stewart, J.G. Evans, John Russell, editor M.V.B. Bennett, and Frances Willard. The

---

[127] "National Convention," *Center*, 7 June 1888.

[128] The best description of the committee's discussion appears in "How the Platform was Built," *Voice*, 7 June 1888.

[129] Not everyone was pleased with this compromise. The *Statesman* asserted that the committee and convention had "struggled for hours to find words and frame them into a sentence which should express the fact that the Convention favored woman suffrage and yet would not excite the opposition of those who do not believe in woman suffrage. The result was fully equal to the thousands of efforts of the same sort made by other parties in the past – a thing to be explained, apologized for, and ashamed of"; "Editorials," *Statesman*, July 1888.

convention's majority resolved that it cared little that "a large majority of the voters [were] ready to step over and vote for prohibition who are not ready upon the question of woman suffrage" because to them, the platform need only represent the interests of the existing party, even if this necessarily represented only a minority of the population.[130] Opponents to a suffrage plank were not only voted down but shouted down.[131] From among the 1,200 delegates, less than 70 voted in favor of the minority report.

Fundamentally, the women's suffrage plank debate was about the relative merits of two visions of what a minor party should be and do: Some partisans continued to believe that the party should intensify its constituency-building work so that it could become a major party, whereas a second group of partisans with growing influence saw the party as a movement protesting a lack of avenues for communication with policy makers. The convention eventually resolved that it was impossible to disentangle the moral impetus of women's suffrage from the question of whether or not this movement should be endorsed in the platform. They agreed with suffrage plank advocate J.G. Evans that opponents' "willingness... to discard the principle by blotting it out of the platform evinces a weakness of faith, and is at least a half-way concession that the objections to this measure have weight."[132]

For most Prohibitionists, endorsement of women's suffrage expressed a worldview wherein democracy was about both how politics was organized and who participated in it. John Russell asserted that "one question only determines whether women should be allowed to vote or not: are they among the governed?"[133] Such sentiments found ready support from Elizabeth Cady Stanton, who declared that the Prohibition Party had the most promising platform and that "no woman with a proper self-respect can any longer kneel at the feet of the Republican party."[134] The explanation crafted by Prohibitionists to explain to major party critics the necessity of minor parties – that minor parties protected the right of all citizens

---

[130] "The Great Convention," *Lever*, 6 June 1888.
[131] The tone of this discussion carried over from conventions into the party press. When the *Statesman* described recent gestures by the WCTU encouraging an election free from "scandalous personalities," the paper's editorial board noted as an aside that such a reminder would also be useful for distribution "to some of our Prohibition papers engaged in the Suffrage controversy." See "Editorials," *Statesman*, April 1888.
[132] J.E. Evans, "Woman Suffrage Objections Answered," *Lever*, 16 February 1888.
[133] John Russell, "Woman's Suffrage," *Lever*, 2 February 1887.
[134] Elizabeth Cady Stanton, "Parties and Platforms," *Voice*, 20 September 1888.

to vote in a way that clearly expressed their interests – was essentially contingent upon the idea that each citizen had different interests, and no voter could both represent himself and someone else. To no small extent, Prohibitionists' explanation for their minor partyism anticipated what Stanton would declare during the "Solitude of Self" address she would deliver to the National American Woman Suffrage Association in 1892. Namely, the uniqueness and complexity of selfhood meant that no one else should "take on for himself the rights, the duties, the responsibilities of another human soul."

Prohibitionists made the connection between the suffrage plank and a new emphasis on individual politics most explicit when the national convention's delegates drew upon a once reviled epithet to catalyze their support. At the convention, a large group of pro-suffrage plank partisans decided to appropriate the crank label that rivals had once used to dismiss the party as "useless, impracticable, visionary . . . on the verge of insanity."[135] Pro-suffrage plank partisans playfully declared themselves "cranks," giggling over the joke that cranks, after all, were useful at turning things. Manufactures sold S-shaped crank pins, noisemakers, and watch charms to meet partisans' demand for the image in party festivities. The *Voice* reported that "the crank pin is seen upon almost everybody."[136] And delegates repeatedly broke into a song authored by the party's own Silver Lake Quartette:

> Oh, he is a crank, ha! ha!
> And he is a crank, ho! ho!
> We are all of us cranks,
> Won't you come to our ranks
> And laugh as we merrily go?[137]

At the nomination of Clinton B. Fisk, a Civil War hero and the name behind Fisk University, for the presidency, the waving of hats and handkerchiefs was accompanied by "the irrepressible man with a crank" whose "wooden clapper machine added its hideous din."[138] Crank noisemakers likewise echoed throughout the hall when the suffrage plank was finally

---

[135] "The Crank Pin," *Weekly Censor*, 10 November 1887.
[136] "The Day Before the Convention," *Voice*, 7 June 1888.
[137] On crank pins, see an exemplary advertisement in *Voice*, 16 February 1888. The song's lyrics are featured in "An Active Home Field," *Voice*, 23 February 1888. I can only assume that the melody of "He is a Crank" was catchier than the lyrics.
[138] "National Convention, Continued," *Lever*, 6 June 1888.

adopted. Prohibitionists had embraced the crank – independent, even cantankerous, rather than loyal and complicit – as the ideal citizen and argued that their party should express this ideal.

However, the party's new emphasis on defending individual political agency also introduced a novel problem: Individualism was a precarious foundation for party coherence and discipline, to say the least. How much individualism could a political party bear before it lost all solidarity? After the convention, Prohibitionists explored the relationship of voter and party platform more intensely than ever. Must a voter agree with each element in the party platform to vote for it without being a hypocrite? Was a platform a set of critical principles, or was it merely an expression of the party's majority sentiment?[139] Were individuals who dissented from one or multiple planks in a platform – especially planks about moral issues on which there could be no compromise – obligated by democratic principles to separate themselves and form still another new party? In 1888, the *Voice* developed a list of the "questions about which public sentiment is cloudy and chaotic" regarding the methods of popular governance as they related to parties: "What can be done by a party, and what cannot be done; how far a voter should go with a party, and when he should bolt; what exigencies justify the formation of a new party, and when a new party is positively hurtful."[140] Theoretically, Prohibitionists had mounted a challenge that could make citizenship an atomized experience.

Prohibitionists' impassioned discussions eventually narrowed to a concern shared by Democrats, Republicans, and independents: the matter of how and when it was appropriate for an individual to leave his party. Individuals associated with major parties largely maintained the position they had established in 1884. Reflecting upon Cleveland's accidental election, National League secretary J. Ellen Foster had formulated a critique of those individuals who refused to remain within major parties. In *Political Monasticism* (1888) Foster concluded that "under majority rule a citizen may not realize his ideal in government" but "with the ideal always before him, the citizen should vote for the men and the measures most nearly approaching that ideal, provided always he has reason to believe

---

[139] "Woman Suffrage and the National Platform," *Voice*, 17 May 1888, explores the relationship between dominant issues in the party platform and the voters' endorsement of that platform. See also "The Party Fealty Question," *Lever*, 1 September 1887; "The Suffrage Question," *Lever*, 26 January 1888; J.G. Evans, "Woman Suffrage and the Prohibition Party," *Lever*, 9 February 1888; "Give Us Fair Play," *Lever*, 7 March 1888.
[140] "The Relation of Parties to Popular Government," *Voice*, 9 February 1888.

that a majority of the voters of his community or State or of the nation will support the same at the ballot-box."[141] Albert Griffin, president of the short-lived Anti-Saloon Republicans, argued that if a citizen

always attends caucuses, urges the selection of the right kind of candidates, supports the man who is nominated, even if personally distasteful to him, unless he really believes his election would be detrimental to the public weal, and, in such cases, unflinchingly and actively opposes him, at the polls, the [party] managers may become very angry, but they will thereafter take increasing care to secure his support.[142]

Major party advocates maintained that the right to bolt must be limited by a citizen's obligation to ensure the broader democratic character of the election. According to Griffin, individual submission to group discipline was necessary to counterorganize against the far greater evil of the liquor traffic: "The liquor power is now so thoroughly organized, politically, and used so aggressively, that it can be speedily overthrown only by meeting it with a larger political force equally well disciplined."[143] Thus, "we do not advocate, defend or excuse secession from the party" even when the desire to redirect the party's course was justified.[144] Noah Davis, formerly of the Anti-Saloon Republicans, concurred that the individual man's "right to do what he conceives to be good" should be restricted "when evil may follow."[145]

Independents such as H.K. Carroll, a member of the *Independent*'s editorial staff who had also worked with the National League, likewise urged that democratic government was

staked upon the assumption that the larger number of voters will agree on some particular candidate and some particular policy. There is no divine right in parties; the voter may ignore them all, if he chooses; but the absolute independence of the voter, if strictly asserted, would make Republican or popular government impossible. If each voter were to insist upon his right to vote for a different candidate and a different policy from those of every other voter the result would be no choice, no election; no president, no governor, no legislator, no government. Am I wrong, then, in insisting that every voter is under obligation so to vote as that the Government shall proceed in harmony with its fundamental law?[146]

---

[141] J. Ellen Foster, "Political Monasticism," *Zion's Herald*, 5 September 1888.
[142] Griffin, *Powerless for Good, but Powerful for Evil*, 37.
[143] Griffin, *Powerless for Good, but Powerful for Evil*, 7. Whether or not the liquor industry was actually so organized is debatable.
[144] "The Anti-Saloon Appeal to the Chicago Convention," *Independent*, 28 June 1888.
[145] "Against the Saloon," *New York Times*, 21 October 1888.
[146] H.K. Carroll, "How Temperance Men Should Vote," *Independent*, 1 November 1888.

To some Americans, floating voters and groups of voters unhinged from parties seemed like political chaos. During the 1880s, citizens' tickets targeting local issues emerged in innumerable municipalities, and labor tickets appeared in 38 states and 189 localities, undoubtedly heightening the sense of disorder.[147] In this context, even nonpartisans limited the citizen's absolute freedom to disentangle himself from the party system. Building upon the National League's assertion that "non-discipline is weakness, scattering, and waste of power," civil service reformer Dorman Eaton suggested that citizens must remain with their party "when great issues are involved," reserving his right to abandon his party for extraordinary situations rather than simple differences of opinion.[148] In general terms, compromise was morally acceptable.

It was partisan Prohibitionists, not nonpartisans, who made the boldest claims for citizens' rights to depart from their party at will. The *Lever* argued that

if there is anything more contemptible in politics than the doctrine that the party *owns* its members, and that it is dishonorable for a member of a party to leave his party and form other political affinities, we do not know what it is. This spirit would brand as a traitor every man who, under convictions of right and expediency, changes his political associations.

For that matter, Republicans should see themselves as similarly indebted to the individual willing to leave his party because "the Republican party thirty years ago" had been "made up of men who came from other parties."[149] Prohibitionists ridiculed citizens for whom "bondage to party...controls them."[150] They concluded that "parties should be used as instruments for the accomplishment of wise and noble ends in government. But when the citizen becomes so enamored of party that he acts more with reference to party success than righteousness in government, partyism becomes the bane of civilization."[151] "Partisanship," added the *Voice*, "is crowding both judgment and conscience out of American politics."[152]

[147] Ritter, *Greenbackers and Goldbugs*, 53.
[148] Daniel Dorchester, *Non-Partisan Temperance League* (Boston: National League for the Suppression of the Liquor Traffic, 1885), 35; Dorman Eaton, "Parties and Independents," *North American Review*, June 1887.
[149] "The Two Governors," *Lever*, 21 July 1887.
[150] James Baker, "Judge Baker on Suffrage," *Lever*, 7 March 1888.
[151] "Party Supremacy Versus Statesmanship," *Lever*, 5 December 1888.
[152] "What Next?" *Voice*, 8 November 1888.

Anti-liquor advocates outside the Prohibition Party questioned if perhaps Prohibitionists were a bit too proud of their ostensibly principled position. Prohibitionists snubbed most political questions, made planks on issues in which there was virtually no opposition (such as polygamy), or else left their positions ambiguous. For example, the 1888 Prohibition Party platform would resolve that "arbitration is the Christian, wise and economical method of settling national differences, and the same method should, by judicious legislation, be applied to the settlement of disputes between large bodies of employees and their employers."[153] This statement was designed to offend neither group, and so it really meant nothing.[154] Anti-Saloon Republican Albert Griffin noted how the Prohibition Party's demands meant that "all other political aims and ideas must be entirely ignored, or kept in the background, until the drink traffic shall have been suppressed, no matter how long a time that may take."[155] Even the women's suffrage question had nearly been excluded from their platform for fear of dissent among prohibition advocates. This was alienating to the majority of Protestants, who were troubled by polygamy, divorce, Sabbatarian violations, and lotteries; they had interests as producers, financiers, and consumers; and they saw themselves as Northerners and Southerners. They voted accordingly.[156]

Most voters cast their votes in 1888 with one of the major parties. Again, the critical issue between Democrats and Republicans was the tariff, with President Cleveland arguing for a dramatically lowered tariff and Republican candidate Benjamin Harrison arguing against this proposition. Republicans became even more connected to big corporations in the public mind, not only because of their policies but also because of "a systematic effort to raise money from big corporations." Democrats attempted to claim their own terrain as the party of small business and economic freedom.[157] Again, the outcome of the election was strange, and its democratic character could be easily contested; Harrison secured more votes from the electoral college, whereas Cleveland polled more popular votes. Again, New York was the critical state, where a shift in

---

[153] This platform can be found in Colvin, *Prohibition in the United States*, 190–191, among numerous other sources.

[154] John T. Duffield, "Ought Temperance Men to Vote with the Third Party?" *Independent*, 20 September 1888.

[155] Griffin, *Powerless for Good, but Powerful for Evil*, 13.

[156] On Christian lobbyists' agenda, see Foster, *Moral Reconstruction*.

[157] Gould, *The Grand Old Party*, 104–5.

7,000 ballots could have returned Cleveland's administration.[158] New York Prohibitionists cast 30,231 ballots in support of their party. These returns were not enough to solely explain Cleveland's defeat in that state – as they had been in 1884 – because if cast for the Republicans, they would have simply made Cleveland's defeat greater. They were, however, just barely enough to preserve the idea that Prohibitionists were politically potent.

Prohibitionists had taken a bold new position as cranks who embraced their individualism even when it ensured political marginality and social ostracism in perpetuity. They asserted that "cranks are the chosen people of all the ages."[159] Even as they increasingly disavowed interest in the immediate results of their party building, however, they held out hope that the momentum from the 1884 election and the publicity generated through nonpartisan amendment campaigns might buoy their returns. Prohibitionists had hoped for 500,000 or 1,000,000 votes; in the weeks following the election, they projected that they had received at least 300,000.[160] When the tally was actually closer to 250,000 the *Lever* continued to optimistically assert that "the Prohibition party has not received a setback." Prohibitionists rhetorically questioned, "Prohibitionists discouraged? Not at all... Had our vote decreased we would have gone forward all the same."[161] The *New York Weekly Witness*, a non-denominational Protestant periodical with Prohibitionist sympathies, more bluntly suggested that "it cannot be denied that the ardent hopes of a speedy triumph have been blighted."[162]

In February 1889, 700 Prohibitionists met at a national convention in Louisville to evaluate the meaning of the election results and to determine a course of future action. Green Clay Smith, 1876 presidential candidate, began discussion with an opening address claiming that the Prohibition Party "still lives, and grows and strengthens. There is no cause for

---

[158] Cleveland needed New York to win but might have lost the election in any case without a victory in Indiana.

[159] E.G. Columbus quoted in "Reasons Why I'm a Prohibitionist," *Lever*, 7 November 1888.

[160] "General Fisk is Satisfied," *Lever*, 21 November 1888; "The Outlook," *Lever*, 28 November 1888; Helen M. Gougar, "Congratulations to Mrs. Gougar," *Lever*, 5 December 1888; "St. John's Vote Doubled," *Voice*, 8 November 1888; "Up and at 'Em Once More," *Lever*, 22 November 1888; Samuel Dickie, "Address to Prohibitionists," *New Era and Delaware Signal*, 23 November 1888.

[161] "The Prohibition Vote," *Voice*, 18 December 1888.

[162] "In Better Condition than Ever," *Lever*, 13 December 1888.

discouragement, but much to encourage and inspire the faithful with hope."[163] Conversely, some earnest Prohibitionists called for their peers to set aside optimism and more strenuously consider why voters who favored prohibition nonetheless voted for other parties.

Walter Thomas Mills, a leader who believed that the crank identity and the party's embrace of women's suffrage were both extremely problematic, led a constituency of Prohibitionists who argued that the party was not moving in the right direction. Mills offered a plea for party reorganization that would include new members who could push the party toward electoral victory.[164] He declared that "had the Prohibition party secured half a million votes in November last, we would have been able to double before 1892 ... had we secured the half million, I would not have been asked to prepare this article. The 'What Next?' would have been clear enough and that without discussion."[165] Mills suggested a plan for the national committee to call for 500,000 voters from all parties to sign a call for a national convention indicating their commitment to vote for the party endorsing prohibition if such a number could be organized. At the ensuing convention, the Prohibition Party would be dissolved and reconstituted to include these new members on equal footing with the old. With the support of so many signers, a given voter could be assured that he would be part of a mass movement, not merely a protest.

Mills's plan was vehemently rejected by the majority of the convention on the grounds that it excluded nonvoting women from signing the call and that it "makes the assumption that the last election was a failure so far as the Prohibition party was concerned." Cranks such as George R. Scott, a delegate from Nebraska, took Mills to task by arguing that

you come here to tell us that unless we do something of this sort we are in danger of petering out. I say we don't need these new methods. I don't believe it is the thing for us as a party to go around whining, calling for reorganization of our grand party and our glorious idea and beseeching other folks to come in, holding out to them the prospect that they can come in and have their own way.[166]

The *Lever* described Mills as an "obstructionist" and "stupid" and placed upon him and his "little clique of agitators" the "responsibility for the

[163] "The Great Conference," *Voice*, 21 February 1889.
[164] "The Great Conference," *Voice*, 21 February 1889. On Mills's rejection of the crank identity, see Walter Thomas Mills, "Foraker's Forum Fallacies," *Weekly Censor*, 10 November 1887.
[165] "Strictly Confidential," *Lever*, 20 February 1889.
[166] George Scott of Nebraska quoted in "The Great Conference," *Voice*, 21 February 1889.

failure of the Conference to mature some practical plan of work for efficient propagandism."[167]

The *Voice*, although sympathetic to Mills' suggestions, noted that they had brought forth "unnecessarily harsh and even stinging words... by the disputants on both sides. With the first pang of disappointment the more passionate advocates of new methods felt a sense of rebelliousness" checked only by the gentle intervention of Frances Willard.[168] Cranks were in charge of the party and had little remaining patience for party members who attempted to redirect the party's focus to constituency building at the cost of commitment to moral issues. They would leave to nonpartisan organizations the task of catering to the diluted principles of the masses.

* * *

The 1884 election's collateral consequences encouraged some non-Prohibitionist anti-liquor advocates to organize modern pressure groups. For them, the appeal of nonpartisan organization lay in how it rhetorically distanced them from passionate late nineteenth-century party affiliations while letting them maintain those same affiliations. At risk were not matters of self-interest – most advocates were abstainers, in any case – but citizens' abilities to fulfill religious obligations by saving souls. Religious pressures encouraged departures and innovations among a population that might otherwise prefer to avoid politics entirely. The development of pressure groups, in turn, shaped how Americans understood the role of minor parties. When frustrated Prohibitionists defined themselves as cranks, they contributed to a gradual transition wherein minor parties would come to explode commonly held assumptions about the institutions and rituals of political behavior.

In describing the "mischiefs and evils" practiced by political parties, poet and historian A.G. Riddle noted that "great as these are, no one has yet devised agencies to take the place of parties. Nor is it apparent how the proprietary powers can so well otherwise be exercised."[169] The Anti-Saloon League, founded in 1893, would capitalize upon the National League's early successes to build the most pervasive pressure group in the country and to eventually lead the movement for a national

---

[167] "The Springfield Conference," *Lever*, 27 February 1889.
[168] "The Great Conference," *Voice*, 21 February 1889.
[169] A.G. Riddle, "Some Observations Upon the History and Laws of Political Parties in the United States," *Magazine of Western History*, November 1886.

prohibition amendment. In the meantime, Walter Thomas Mills succinctly summarized the nature of the debate between partisans and non-partisans: "The problem is not now how the few can best exercise authority. Authority is no longer vested in the few. Nor is the problem how it may be extended to the many. The many are already our masters. The question is, how shall these many rulers be enabled both to rule and to rule wisely and well?"[170]

Prohibitionists were running out of time and resources. They had likely missed their opportunity to capitalize on publicity generated during the 1884 election, and factions favoring divergent and incompatible strategies became still more difficult to reconcile after the 1888 disappointment. Despite the authority over policy that cranks had seemingly established, a small group of rivals for party leadership seized an unorthodox opportunity to regroup beyond the conventional boundaries of party organization. Such men saw themselves as "men of brains, courage, and practicality" who could "balance out the cranks ... who are so self-assertive."[171] They turned toward an innovative form of political activism, one in which they could participate as party members in a private enterprise. Rather than leaving the party, these Prohibitionists would independently investigate, finance, and control their own plan to attract new voters: the building of Prohibitionist utopian cities.

---

[170] Walter Thomas Mills, "The American School of Politics," *Statesman*, October 1887.
[171] William R. Dobbyn (editor of the *Progressive Age*) to T.C. Richmond, 23 July 1890, TCRC.

5

Writing Prohibition into the Soil

In 1890, Prohibitionists committed to an unprecedented project for a political party when they built a city. The evolving meaning of this peculiar experiment unfolded gradually, and it cannot be fully understood without an examination of the volatile political environment in which it developed. Of particular importance, Prohibitionists drew on Harriman, Tennessee, as a touchstone when confronted with a problem of hitherto unthinkable proportions. The party's newest tribulations were rooted in a procedural change – the government-printed ballot – that was coupled to a seemingly pro-democracy reform: the secret ballot.[1] By granting to legislatures and election boards the prerogative to decide which parties could and could not appear on ballots, state governments facilitated minor parties' exclusion from elections. Between 1888, when Massachusetts passed its ballot law, and the mid-1890s, when ballot reform was nearly universal, Prohibitionists' level of panic spiked. They considered whether the unconventional style of politics embodied by Harriman's modest success might suggest an alternative course for party development.

For cranks, the answer would be no. These Prohibitionists – now widely referred to as "broad gaugers" – argued that if only the party could jettison frivolous activities such as city building and instead incorporate the key ideas of farmers, workers, and suffragists into the party platform, the Prohibition Party could quickly meet the minimum vote

---

[1] For a list history of various states' ballot access laws, see Richard Winger, "Early Ballot Access Laws for New and Minor Parties," in *Others: 'Fighting Bob' La Follette and the Progressive Movement: Third-Party Politics in the 1920s*, Darcy G. Richardson (New York: iUniverse, Inc., 2008), 359–388.

tallies required to get on ballots. But another faction -- called "narrow gaugers" – suggested that Harriman exemplified how non-electoral, non-legislative activism could help the party retain its organizational integrity while weathering a period of ballot exclusion.

Six short years after the Great Land Sale that initiated Harriman, the differences between factions seemed irreconcilable, and the party split at the 1896 national convention. Advocates for a single-issue platform had wrestled party control back from their rivals. However, in the process of advancing what was seemingly a very conservative agenda – one without the radicalism implied by affiliation with antimonopolists, labor organizers, and women's rights advocates – these Prohibitionists proclaimed the legitimacy of a highly unorthodox definition of *partisanship* and hence *politics*. They reached far beyond campaigns and elections and into the sphere of everyday life.

* * *

Prohibitionists were initially optimistic about the secret ballot, which was of necessity government printed and administered. They could never get their party's ballots to every single polling site, the expense of these ballots was a budgetary strain, and partisans suspected that fear of public ridicule kept many would-be Prohibitionist voters from aligning with them. As late as 1890, Prohibitionists celebrated that government ballot printing "will be worth thousands of dollars in every campaign of the Prohibition party. In a city like New York, with over 1,000 districts, the printing, folding, and distributing of ballots has been the most expensive and most laborious part of the campaign."[2] This excited embrace of ballot reform dissipated only when the Prohibition Party confronted a problem rooted in the unprecedented power granted to legislators and election boards; these authorities set and interpreted the eligibility standards by which parties might become ballot qualified.[3] Prohibitionists sensed a conspiracy between Democrats and Republicans when legislators placed ballot eligibility standards just beyond minor parties' reach, generally at 2 to 3 percent of the returns in the previous election.

In some cases the requirements were quite high. In Nevada, for example, Prohibitionists needed to receive at least 10 percent of the vote from

[2] "The Ballot Reform Bill Signed," *Voice*, 8 May 1890.
[3] Restricting candidates from the ballot was often urged on the basis of avoiding "unwieldy" ballots, rather than being explicitly described as a way to disfranchise minor parties. See Michael Lewis-Beck and Peverill Squire, "The Politics of Institutional Choice: Presidential Ballot Access for Third Parties in the United States," *British Journal of Political Science* 25:3 (October 1995): 419.

the previous election (which was very unlikely). In New Jersey, 5 percent of the voting population needed to sign a minor party's petition before a commissioner of deeds, paying a fee for the honor. As an ancillary problem, this process made the "secret" ballot a matter of public record.[4] In other states, the problem was that each party seeking to qualify on the basis of its past electoral record needed to nominate candidates for every general election – something that small parties often struggled to do. For example, Illinois' Prohibitionists jeopardized their standing when they failed to make nominations for a June 1891 judicial election.[5] And no longer could Prohibitionists draw on their own printing and distribution resources to create an alternative ballot for voters.

Reasonably enough, incredulous political scientists have investigated the legitimacy of minor parties' complaints about petition requirements, wondering whether "complaints about legal requirements are either attempted shields for inadequacy or evidence of unwillingness to think realistically."[6] Was it really devastating when, for example, a Pennsylvania law passed in 1891 required local candidates to obtain signatures from voters numbering a modest 3 percent of the local district's past voting population, even when the legislation included the dramatic caveat that organizers could be fined or sent to prison if any of their petition signers turned out to be unqualified?[7]

Nonpartisans seemed capable of continually mobilizing for campaigns. Early twentieth-century Pennsylvania WCTU branches, for example, repeatedly led remonstrance campaigns that not only stifled the granting of liquor licenses but also politicized the women involved; state WCTU membership numbers increased with the movement's success.[8] Around the nation, grass roots anti-liquor movements banned saloons

---

[4] "Prohibitionists Practically Disfranchised in Nevada," *Voice*, 1 November 1894; "A Most Cowardly Act," *Voice*, 2 October 1890. This problem was exacerbated by the difficulty of finding such a commissioner in rural locations, wherein many Prohibition voters lived. The fee was usually about $1 per voter. A similar bill was advanced in New York – one that would have required parties polling less than 5 percent of the previous election's vote to get 3,000 voters to both sign a petition and take an oath before a notary. In Ohio, the state legislature enacted a 1898 law that compelled petition signers to similarly pledge to vote for the candidate of that party.

[5] "Put Up a Prohibition Ticket," *Lever*, 24 March 1892.

[6] For example, "Legal Obstacles to Minor Party Success," *Yale Law Journal* 57:7 (June 1948): 1289.

[7] L.E. Fredman, *The Australian Ballot System: The Story of an American Reform* (Lansing: Michigan State University, 1968), 48.

[8] Szymanski, *Pathways to Prohibition*, 168–169. See also 77–78. Ivy also describes how participation in a local option campaign revived a flagging WCTU chapter in Texas; *No Saloon in this Valley*, 31.

from towns and counties, renewing no license legislation on a regular basis. Prohibitionists themselves noted the opportunity that petition campaigns provided for informing public sentiment, with Chicago partisans concluding in 1891 that their canvasing "brought our ticket prominently before the people. They asked questions, and . . . a discussion was started that resulted in people's thinking."[9] Although no new states would add prohibitory amendments during the 1890s, there were other forms of restriction that suggested that the anti-liquor movement was actually growing, albeit in ways the Prohibition Party failed to capture. Local option campaigns, in particular, made striking inroads. Perhaps Prohibitionists did not fully exploit the opportunity that petitioning requirements thrust on them. Some partisans admitted that embarrassment made them reluctant to participate, and the perception that partisan canvasing violated middle-class propriety seems to have grown more acute over time.[10]

The greatest problem, however, was that petitioning exacerbated the already significant disadvantages of being a new or small party, creating hardships that major parties did not share. Although the work of cultivating popular support for a cause and the work of building a permanent party organization overlap, they are not totally identical. Nineteenth-century parties needed newspapers, buildings, endowments, and means to identify and develop candidates; these are long-term investments that are not always immediately profitable and indeed might be set aside in the interests of mobilizing for a particular campaign. Prohibitionists bemoaned the extent to which their party newspapers were the few and often failing products of private enterprise; while a struggling Democratic or Republican publisher could count on government and party contracts, Prohibitionist publishers could rely on neither. The party had limited office space, finances were constantly a problem, and under-investigated candidates routinely refused to accept nominations.[11]

---

9   "The Baker Ballot Law," *Lever*, 28 January 1892. See also Untitled, *Voice*, 26 November 1891.
10 For examples of resentment tinged with embarrassment, see J.H. Young, "A Minister Justly 'Riled,'" *Voice*, 8 September 1892; "A Most Cowardly Act," *Voice*, 2 October 1890.
11 On the under- or unsubsidized nature of party papers see, for example, Minutes of the National Executive Committee, 23 June 1888, and Minutes of the National Executive Committee, 8 July 1896, Minutes of the Prohibition Party, Bentley Historical Library, Ann Arbor, MI. These records are most conveniently viewed through Randall C. Jimerson et al., eds., *Temperance and Prohibition Papers*, Series II (TPP). See also

There is little to suggest that the Prohibition Party dropped off many official state ballots before the mid-1890s, but Prohibitionist planners identified how, in the long term, the expenditures required to be on ballots would soon pose a challenging distraction. If a party's returns fell below the level for ballot qualification, then a petition campaign meant "a big expense and a great deal of needless labor."[12] Because most laws required that petition signatures be from citizens in various parts of the state, mailing expenses alone could be prohibitive. For example, the Illinois state committee spent over $200 in 1898, trying to get congressional and senatorial nominees on the official ballot.[13] State Prohibition parties might use up their resources trying to get on the ballot and then have nothing left for the ensuing electoral campaign, and the national Prohibition Party was not financially secure enough to bail them out.[14] Relieved when his municipal party finally received the 2 percent needed to gain a place on the official ballot in the coming year, Joseph P. Tracy, a Chicago Prohibitionist, summarized that "nominating by petition is expensive."[15]

New eligibility standards for the government-printed ballot plagued the Populists, a minor party that mobilized Western and Southern antimonopolists, for slightly different reasons than they did the Prohibitionists. Populists had strong momentum from 1892 campaign successes, and this momentum might have been harnessed to a petition campaign that increased grass-roots enthusiasm. However, they had frequently used fusion, the support of a single set of candidates with another party or parties, to secure electoral victory. They had even fused with state Prohibition parties in several instances.[16] New and ever more procedures that used previous election results to determine ballot eligibility delegitimized this practice, instead declaring that the Populists had

"Temperance Papers," *Weekly Censor*, 20 October 1887, which lists the names of eight Prohibition papers in California that emerged and went under in quick succession, in some instances even with some financial support from local Prohibition parties.

[12] "Vote Your Ticket Straight," *Lever*, 27 October 1892.

[13] "Illinois is Alert," *Lever*, 18 August 1898; Untitled, *Lever*, 25 August 1898.

[14] As a point of reference, in 1907 the national party had less than $2,000 in its treasury; Minutes of the Prohibition National Committee, 20 November 1907, TPP.

[15] Joseph P. Tracy, "The Concrete Facts of Practical Politics," *New Voice*, 23 July 1903.

[16] Blocker, *Retreat from Reform*, 50, 78. Fusion in Minnesota in 1890 led to the election of one of only two successful Prohibitionist candidates for Congress. On the history of Prohibitionists' general reluctance to fuse, see "Theater Crowd Cheers Prohibition," *American Advance*, 21 June 1913; Finley C. Hendrickson, "Has the Party Found Itself?" *National Enquirer*, 1 March 1917.

no recognizable previous election tally in such circumstances.[17] For Populists, using fusion – traditionally their most reliable tactic for advancing the party's agenda – would mean losing their legal right to appear on future ballots. Internal debates raged over whether or not fusion could continue to be part of the party's repertoire. In comparison, Prohibitionists seem to have abandoned the strategy without much debate and thus avoided its ballot-excluding consequences.

The trials of Prohibitionists and Populists, however, are not meant to suggest that minor parties were alone in suffering from the effects of a government-printed ballot. Within the major parties, local political bosses such as those of Tammany Hall noted that the government's new authority to decide who would be recognized as the official voice of the party promoted the primacy of national and state party leaders.[18] The regulations guiding government printing that recognized the authority of state and national party committees over candidate selection thereby consolidated the control of party elites over renegade local partisans. In the past such partisans had occasionally printed variations of the ballot they had been instructed to print or had pasted over official candidates' names with new choices; trading and pasting votes guaranteed some offices (and hence spoils).[19] Moreover, the uniform ballot ensured that there was no straightforward way in which alternative tickets could be proposed after official party nominations were closed. Even if partisans were discontent with the Democratic or Republican nominee or if new information about the candidate came to light in the days between nomination and election,

---

[17] Argersinger, *Structure, Process, and Party*, 57. See also Argersinger, "'A Place on the Ballot': Fusion Politics and Antifusion Laws," *American Historical Review* 85 (April 1980): 287–306.

[18] Kornbluh, *Why America Stopped Voting*, 124–125. Urban political machines were simultaneously under attack by anti-party reformers, including Mugwumps. See Kenneth Finegold, *Experts and Politicians: Reform Challenges to Machine Politics in New York, Cleveland, and Chicago* (Princeton: Princeton University Press, 1995); Peter McCaffery, *When Bosses Ruled Philadelphia: The Emergence of the Republican Machine, 1867–1933* (University Park: Pennsylvania State University Press, 1993).

[19] *Knifing* and *pasting* were similar techniques. In *knifing*, a ballot printer would deliberately leave party nominees off that party's ballot, often replacing them with other candidates from other parties. In *pasting*, a voter would attach a slip of paper to cover the name of an undesired candidate with an alternative. Alan Ware, "Anti-Partisan and Party Control of Political Reform in the United States: The Case of the Australian Ballot," *British Journal of Political Science* 30:1 (January 2000): 13–16; Eldon Cobb Evans, *A History of the Australian Ballot System in the United States* (Chicago: University of Chicago Press, 1917), 22–23. On Tammany Hall's use of knifing techniques in 1888, see Fredman, *The Australian Ballot*, 29. Fredman argues that the egregious use of knifing best explains the timing of the movement for a secret ballot.

there was no further opportunity to place an alternative party candidate on the official ballot.[20]

The fact that even municipal bosses, renegade partisans, and major party factions – people not generally noted for discretion – did not more vigorously protest changes in the ballot can be interpreted as a sign of their conviction that staging any resistance to this process of power consolidation was unlikely to result in victory and might leave them alienated from commanding state and national leaders. They were in the awkward position of being invested in the very same institutions that coerced them. Choosing a different tactic, Prohibitionists would boldly protest when party officials in government restricted voters' ticket options. In New York, Prohibitionists proclaimed that ballot reform was a conspiracy; it was "another attempt to . . . turn the State over to a perpetual division of spoils between the bosses of the two old parties."[21] In Massachusetts, it was "designed to . . . disfranchise all voters who refuse to support the Republican and Democratic parties."[22] In Pennsylvania, ballot reform was actually "legislation to throttle reform."[23] For the all the ways that Prohibitionists, Populists, and local major party leaders similarly experienced exclusion from the ballot as a result of government's control of printing and distribution, it was Prohibitionists who most vigorously conveyed their displeasure.

As ballot-qualification status was threatened in more and more states, an ensuing decline in the party vote in presidential elections suggested to Prohibitionists that they were in a life-or-death struggle. The highest state-combined vote had been in 1886, and the Prohibition Party's presidential candidate would never receive more than 2 percent of the national vote after 1892. At this point the Prohibition Party's disappearance from ballots began in earnest because its candidates did not appear in South Dakota or Arkansas.[24] In the same year Prohibitionists in

---

[20] Evans notes that some states permitted the nomination of candidates by petition after the date by which candidates nominated by convention needed to be submitted to the government printer in *History of the Australian Ballot*, 32. However, it seems to have initially been the case that the time span between the date parties needed to submit to the printer and the date that the ballots were printed was inconveniently close.

[21] "Another Plan to Deform the Ballot Laws," *Voice*, 8 February 1894. See also "An Evil Plot," *Voice*, 31 January 1895.

[22] Untitled, *Voice*, 1 March 1894. See also Massachusetts Prohibition State Committee, "To the People of Massachusetts," (N.p.: n.p., 1892?), Folder: Massachusetts Prohibition State Committee, Box: 4, GBHP.

[23] "Pennsylvania Ballot Law," *Lever*, 9 July 1891.

[24] "Attempt at Disfranchisement," *Voice*, 20 October 1892; "No Official Ballot for South Dakota Prohibitionists," *Voice*, 3 November 1892; "South Dakota," *Lever*,

some Illinois districts were unable to place the names of their candidates for the House of Representatives on the official ballot.[25] Prohibitionists in North Dakota and Pennsylvania got their candidates' names on the ticket, but the party name did not appear at the head of the ticket.[26] Nevada's Prohibitionists were too discouraged to nominate candidates in 1894, feeling "practically disfranchised" by extraordinary ballot qualification requirements.[27] In Washington, "failure to register with the State secretary in time" kept candidates off the official ballot in the 1894 election.[28] Utah failed to include the Prohibition Party in its first presidential election in 1896 and Mississippi's state ballot dropped the party in the same year. Illinois lost its place on the state ticket and nearly all district tickets in 1896.[29] Maryland lost its place on the ballot in 1903 because it failed to meet technical requirements for submitting paperwork and struggled to regain a position in the wake of an interrupted voting returns record.[30] There was no state ticket in Tennessee in 1904.[31]

Perhaps the best illustration of Prohibitionists' gradual displacement – and the extent to which this exclusion could be misinterpreted as simple "unpopularity" if historians merely consult election returns – lies in the history of Montana's state party. Montana had enacted the secret ballot in 1889, and the Prohibition Party did not appear on the ballot in 1896. In 1900 no Prohibition Party candidates other than the

---

10 November 1892; "Have They Been Disfranchised?" *Voice*, 17 November 1892; Mrs. N.C. Smith, "The Way They Do in Arkansas," *Voice*, 5 January 1893; Untitled, *Lever*, 24 November 1892. Only two of Arkansas's Prohibition nominees appeared on the official ballot in 1894, with the other party nominations needing to be cast as write-in votes.; "Advancing Lines," *Voice*, 23 August 1894. The year 1892 was the first year in which South Dakota participated in a federal election as a state. The state participated in the 1896 election in some fashion, as indicated by a national executive committee gift of $150 for help with campaign expenses; Minutes of the National Executive Committee, 8 July 1896, TPP.

The process of compiling a comprehensive list of which parties were excluded from official state ballots in any given year is extremely difficult. Consultation with most state historical societies and many secretary of state offices suggests that the maintenance of such historical records is not common practice; copies of ballots, to the extent preserved, are widely uncataloged.

25 "To Illinois Prohibitionists," *Voice*, 3 November 1892.
26 Torger F. How, "Prohibitionists and the Ballot Law in North Dakota," *Voice*, 21 July 1892; H.D. Patton, "Important to Pennsylvania," *Voice*, 22 September 1892.
27 "Prohibitionists Practically Disfranchised in Nevada," *Voice*, 1 November 1894.
28 "Not on the Official Ballot," *Voice*, 8 November 1894.
29 "Chairman Stewart's Appeal," *Lever*, 22 September 1898.
30 "Maryland Prohibitionists, Attention," *New Voice*, 22 October 1903.
31 "The Party's Greatest Vote," *(Harriman, TN) Citizen*, 16 November 1904.

presidential candidate appeared, in 1904 the party did not appear on ballots, in 1908 Prohibitionists might have participated in a broad union of third-party candidates, and in 1912 the party was put to rest.[32] The Montana Prohibition party's on-again, off-again standing on ballots, however, remains largely obscured in the historical record because some enthusiastic partisans continued to write in votes for the Prohibition Party presidential candidates in each of these election years. Yet excluded they were.

Ultimately, the Prohibition Party's disappearance from official ballots was a disadvantage for which write-in votes could not completely compensate. Write-in voting required knowing the names of candidates, and American states' ballots at this time included many offices, sometimes into the hundreds.[33] In South Dakota in 1892, party leadership conceded that although "a small number will write the names of the electors on the blank space of the other tickets," it remained the case that "it has not been generally known who the electors are."[34] Some Prohibitionists attempted to combat the inherent difficulties of asking voters to correctly remember and spell candidate names by using *pasters* – small slips of paper bearing nominees' names – but without much success. For example, when the Arkansas Prohibitionists' ticket was excluded from the official ballot in 1892, the state party attempted to create returns by sending workers with pasters to polling sites. Unfortunately for Prohibitionists, election judges later ruled that the candidates' names were illegally attached.[35]

Prohibitionists found this trend especially exasperating given the achievement of women's suffrage in Colorado, Idaho, and Utah between 1893 and 1896, which theoretically should have enhanced the party's national vote. This is not to say that Prohibitionists were pointedly banned from participation or that strenuous petition campaigns were the only factors in Prohibitionists' declining returns. Moderate and non-partisan, anti-liquor advocates' recent successes with state amendment, local option, and no license campaigns made it difficult to cultivate a sense of urgency for partisan prohibition. In addition, the rise of liquor industry organizations such as the National Retail Liquor Dealers' Association (1893) and the National Wholesale Liquor Dealers' Association (1896) led to vigorous lobbying for better industry practices as

---

[32] Consultation with staff, Montana Historical Society, June 2010.
[33] On short ballot reform, see Schudson, *The Good Citizen*, 171–173.
[34] "South Dakota," *Lever*, 10 November 1892.
[35] Mrs. N.C. Smith, "The Way They Do in Arkansas," *Voice*, 5 January 1893.

an alternative to anti-liquor legislation, the party's efforts to connect with Southern voters pathetically flailed, and there was extraordinary organizational infighting. Many temperance advocates continued to find Prohibitionists abrasive or annoying. However, new ballot qualification requirements certainly played an important role in limiting the Prohibition Party's strategic options.[36] The Prohibition Party could anticipate that with each passing year the secret ballot – the government printed and administered ballot – would take greater hold. And with the exclusion of Prohibitionists and other minor parties from ballots would come the dominance of elite Democratic and Republican leadership over the party system.

* * *

Prohibitionists confronting the stench of failure inherent to ballot exclusion might have sighed with relief that they had already started a project suggesting some hope for the future. Founded in 1890 just 127 miles east of Nashville, the new town of Harriman, Tennessee, integrated work, leisure, property rights, and partisanship, and "delight[ed] the true Prohibitionist: his neighbors are Prohibitionists: the people he meets on the streets are Prohibitionists: he finds Prohibitionists in the shops and stores: he sees Prohibitionists on every hand: he hears Prohibition wherever he goes."[37] Harriman was a comfort, and it was also "an example, so that all may see what Prohibition with warm friends and willing enforcers can do in building a city which shall command the attention of this entire country."[38]

From the beginning, city promoters had proclaimed that Harriman embodied the party's strong moral character, resilience, and hope for the future. During the three days of the Great Land Sale, 3,000 potential purchasers from the North, Kentucky, and Tennessee had awaited the opportunity to purchase Harriman land "cheerfully." Land company secretary

---

[36] Pegram, *Battling Demon Rum*, 85–108; Coker, *Liquor in the Land of the Lost Cause*, 102–117; Szymanski, *Pathways to Prohibition*, 133–134; Blocker, *Retreat from Reform*, 100–153.

[37] Advertisement, "Facts About Harriman!" *Voice*, 10 December 1891. For further discussion of Harriman, Tennessee and Prohibition Park on Staten Island, see Hamm, *Shaping the Eighteenth Amendment*, 32–33, 123, 127.

[38] E.H. Molly, "Prohibition City: An Experiment to Ascertain the Commercial Value of Sobriety," *Daily Report*, 22 April 1892. Clipping in Scrapbook,91, Box 4, Harriman, Tennessee – Miscellaneous Papers, Tennessee State Library and Archives. Nashville, TN (HTMP).

A.A. Hopkins widely circulated a description of the individuals who purchased 573 lots – almost $600,000 worth of land – as having "bore with
singular good humor the added discomforts of a protracted storm, and
the lack of everything desirable amid circumstances altogether new and
unpleasant." There was an appealing humility to Hopkins's admission
that indications of rapid improvement were few. Buyers "saw little of
present accomplishment, and were given small promise of definite things
to be done by the company on whose invitation they came."[39] Seemingly
the poor condition of the city's foundations illuminated the sterling and
plucky character of future residents.

Even a smattering of non-Prohibitionists at the first land sale were
embraced so long as they were "keen, sagacious business men who
believed business will thrive best where saloons are not, and who foresaw, as with prophetic vision, the kind of a community which must
follow where no trade comes in competition with the liquor traffic."
A.A. Hopkins asserted that such cooperation between Prohibition Party
advocates and other temperate individuals was "a splendid testimony to
the effect of Prohibition influence"; their presence was thought to show
that Harriman had already become a beacon for attracting new people
to the party.[40] Together, the families of skilled laborers, clerks, managers, factory employees, and independent businessmen had "bought"
the East Tennessee Land Company (ETLC) vision, seeing in the muddy
mess around them something beautiful.

For months in advance of the sale, advertisements for Harriman lots
had appeared in Prohibitionist publications as well as the *Methodist
Advocate*, *New England Home*, and the *Apostolic Guide*. Harriman
would mean "Prohibition and Plenty."[41] Visionaries proclaimed that
Harriman would be different from most communities, wherein even the
most virtuous citizens were unable to extricate themselves from investment in the alcohol industry because the revenue acquired through liquor
licensing was distributed to all citizens in the form of tax relief. Indiana's
Patriot Phalanx explained that "there is no doubt that high license retards

---

[39] Hopkins characterizes various leaders in "A.A. Hopkins on the Business Side of Prohibition," *Voice*, 13 March 1890. See also Walter T. Pulliam, *Harriman: The Town
that Temperance Built* (N.p.: n.p., 1978), 27. "Harriman is Widely Known," *Citizen*,
2 September 1903, says that it was 574 lots. On a third calculation of 574 lots sold
to men from 15 states, see East Tennessee Land Company, *Two Years in Harriman
Tennessee* (New York: South Publishing Company, 1892), 9, 12.

[40] "A.A. Hopkins on the Business Side of Prohibition," *Voice*, 13 March 1890.

[41] Advertisement, "Bottomed on Prohibition and Plenty," *Voice*, 31 October 1889.

the Prohibition movement by its bribery to tax-payers," and 1888 presidential candidate Clinton B. Fisk had decried how "the high license craze retards us greatly, and wherever a State adopts it – as in Pennsylvania – the increased revenue from the infamous business will blind the eyes of taxpayers making prohibition the more difficult to obtain."[42]

Harriman's homeowners, in contrast, promised through ETLC-issued deeds to abstain from the sale, consumption, and storage of alcohol on the site of their property or else forfeit their land.[43] Property taxes financed law enforcement, social relations demanded residents' commitment, and the ambitious desire to live virtuously bound community residents in a network of mutual obligations. A special anti-liquor charter incorporated the city of Harriman under the Tennessee legislature, and the state's Four-Mile Law provided further protection.[44] Prohibition would be "rooted in the very soil on which the city is built."[45]

Insofar as it was about maintaining prohibition in a small geographic location, Prohibitionists' city-building strategy bore similarities to the local option strategy partisans had long rejected. Although often overlooked by contemporary critics because they lacked the flash of state amendment campaigns and were most successful in rural areas, local option campaigns were in fact the principal technique of church groups and grassroots anti-liquor organizations. By 1906, there would be local option laws in thirty states, and more than half of America's counties would ban saloons (if not necessarily sales or drinking).[46] The key difference between what Prohibitionists and other anti-liquor advocates were

---

[42] "By This Sign We Conquer," *Lever*, 21 July 1887, reprinted from *Patriot Phalanx*.

[43] East Tennessee Land Company, *One Year of Harriman, Tennessee: Established by the East Tennessee Land Company, February 26, 1890* (New York: South Publishing Company, 1891), 50: "Section 1 of article IX of the Company's by-laws reads thus: – Every contract, deed or other conveyance or lease of real estate by the Company shall contain a proviso forbidding the use of the property, or any building thereon, for the purpose of making, storing or selling intoxicating beverages as such." Later, deeds would be used to protect other sorts of properties from use as sites for liquor consumption and sale. For example, in 1909 the owner of a milk and ice cream company in Indiana incorporated a condition that if the purchaser made or sold intoxicating liquors in the establishment, the company would revert back to the seller. See S.M. Thompson, "Newspaper Proposition," *Patriot Phalanx*, 10 June 1909.

[44] Zadel Barnes Gustafson, "Founded in Honor and Enterprise," *Voice*, 23 April 1891. The Four-Mile Law banned saloons within four miles of any Tennessee schoolhouse. Anti-liquor reformers joined with educational reformers to scatter schoolhouses all over the state.

[45] Advertisement, "Facts About Harriman!" *(Nashville) Issue*, 17 December 1891. Clipping in Scrapbook page 66, Box 4, HTMR.

[46] Pegram, *Battling Demon Rum*, 111.

doing was that Harriman's prohibition was connected to title deeds and therefore promised some degree of permanence, whereas the no license standing provided through local option was only as secure as the next election. For Prohibitionists local option was a poor option because it required energy and resources to maintain no license status while offering only very limited protection from the problem of drunken neighbors. Legal prohibition functioning at the municipal level was always "too local," as exemplified by the occasional binges by Harriman residents in the nearby wet towns of Kingstown, Rockwood, and Oakdale.[47] Local option amplified the "local" problem by also being "too optional."

In Tennessee, the Prohibition Party's hostility to local option was made still more assertive because local option law's validity under the state constitution was questionable. Tennessee's governor had vetoed a local option law in 1873 on the grounds that it involved a delegation of legislative power.[48] Tennessee was not entirely unique in this matter. In California, local option had been declared unconstitutional in 1874 because it assumed that local authorities possessed powers that were not expressly conferred by their charters. Dry advocates would hesitate to expend resources on local option campaigns for almost two decades, even after a new state constitution was written in 1879.[49] The Michigan Supreme Court likewise invalidated local option law in 1887, disregarding the rulings of high courts in Massachusetts, New Jersey, Maryland, Kentucky, Connecticut, Pennsylvania, and Minnesota, which had sanctioned local option measures.[50]

For all of these reasons, an investment in Harriman home ownership conveyed remarkable commitment to the unique elements of Prohibitionist ideology. For those who could not move, however, other means to exercise political conscience abounded. *Voice* readers were urged: "All who wish to aid in creating a town of the best class, where legitimate industries may have entire sway, are invited to cooperate." An advertisement noted three specific ways that Prohibitionists could be part of the

[47] "Banish the Saloons," *Harriman Advance*, 9 March 1893.
[48] Coker, *Liquor in the Land of the Lost Cause*, 65; Isaac, *Prohibition in Politics*, 9. Szymanski notes that by 1890 state courts had "abandoned their efforts to prevent the state legislatures from referring the liquor question to local communities for resolution," but as Richard Hamm notes, radical prohibitionists such as those in the Prohibition Party were not always attuned to developments in jurists' legal culture, or at least they seemed to suffer from lag; Szymanski, *Pathways to Prohibition*, 21, and Hamm, *Shaping the Eighteenth Amendment*.
[49] Ostrander, *Prohibition Movement in California*, 69–71.
[50] Szymanski, *Pathways to Prohibition*, 86 and 107.

Harriman project: "by location at Harriman, where the E.T.L.C. Co. has yet several thousand fine residence and business lots, for sale at moderate prices, or by advising others to locate there, or by subscribing at once for some of the remaining and last half million dollars of the Company's capital stock."[51] Prohibition Party members were particularly encouraged to follow the example of "several well-known Prohibitionists beside those numbered in the Company's Directorship" by becoming stockholders in the ETLC.[52] The money generated from stock sales would fund internal improvements, which would increase the value of company assets in property and, hence, the value of the stock.

Tellingly, this rich vision of what Harriman would be and do was crafted very quickly, almost immediately after the 1888 campaign in which cranks had ruled the Prohibition Party, and the party's electoral performance had been fairly disappointing. Opponents to the cranks were Harriman's leading element and included Frederick Gates, the Prohibition Party's 1883 candidate for New York secretary of state, chair of the 1884 executive committee of New York, and state manager for the St. John presidential campaign. Described by contemporaries as "the millionaire farmer of Frankfort, an effeminate looking man with almond eyes and a carroty beard," Gates' organizational abilities were widely appreciated and so his endorsement of a city-building scheme was taken seriously.[53] It was he who had urged fellow partisans to "give the ladies a chance" to help in the path-breaking 1884 campaign.

Additional party leaders quickly joined Gates, chartering the ETLC in 1889, just a year before construction would begin. These enterprising Prohibitionists included Clinton B. Fisk, the assistant commissioner of the Freedman's Bureau of Kentucky and Tennessee, founder of Fisk University, and 1888 Prohibition Party presidential candidate. A.A. Hopkins, Ferdinand Schumacher, James B. Hobbs, William Silverwood, Isaac K. Funk, and A.W. Wagnalls were also company directors. The latter are perhaps best known as founders of the Funk and Wagnalls textbook company, which began as a publisher of prohibition and family periodicals. Funk and Wagnalls also edited and published the *Voice*, the Prohibition Party's national periodical and a key conduit for spreading the news about Harriman.[54] A.A. Hopkins was a New York newspaper editor and

---

[51] Advertisement, "Prohibition in Title Deeds," *Voice*, 13 March 1890.

[52] Advertisement, "Down in Tennessee," *Voice*, 7 November 1889.

[53] "Characters at Syracuse," unknown publication from Buffalo, New York, 13 September 1885. Clipping in Scrapbook 1885, GBHP. I think that this strange statement was meant to be complimentary, although I do not see how.

[54] For an obituary, see "Isaac Kaufman Funk," *American Advance*, 13 April 1912.

a member of the national executive committee. Ferdinand Schumacher was "The Oatmeal King" of Ohio and also the 1883 Prohibition Party candidate for governor of that state. James B. Hobbs served as secretary of the national committee, and William Silverwood was prominent in Prohibition Party politics at the state level. Hobbs was also a former president of the Chicago Board of Trade. Without control of the national committee but unwilling to leave their party, these Prohibitionist leaders found an innovative way to be boosters and recruiters.

Still, the speed with which Harriman moved from idea to actual city bespeaks not only a well-organized party faction but also the long roots of city building as an American tradition. In particular, Harriman's creation occurred against the backdrop of a broader, century-old movement among ambitious capitalists who purchased land in the American South or West with the intent to quickly sell it at a profit and often with the intent to sell the construction of residences on it or to unearth natural resources.[55] The distinct opportunities offered by relocation to the South had been celebrated by enterprising Northern "carpetbaggers" since the Civil War, as well as by boosters for the New South.[56] Harriman's founders believed that the Cumberland gap location would

[55] On the early history of land development and land companies in the east, see Alan Taylor, *Liberty Men and Great Proprietors: The Revolutionary Settlement on the Maine Frontier, 1760–1820* (Chapel Hill: University of North Carolina Press, 1990); Charles E. Brooks, *Frontier Settlement and Market Revolution: The Holland Land Purchase* (Ithaca: Cornell University Press, 1996). A more general history of land speculation is included in John W. Reps, *The Making of Urban America: A History of City Planning in the United States* (Princeton: Princeton University Press, 1965), 349–381. On the poor popular reputation of land speculators, see Susan E. Gray, "Local Speculator as Confidence Man: Mumford Eldred, Jr., and the Michigan Land Rush," *Journal of the Early Republic* 10 (Autumn 1990): 383–406. On the persistence of land speculators' poor reputation and the historiography of land speculation, see Robert Swierenga, "Land Speculation and its Impact on American Economic Growth and Welfare: A Historiographical Review," *Western Historical Quarterly* 8 (July 1977): 283–302.

[56] On carpetbaggers, see Richard Nelson Current, *Those Terrible Carpetbaggers* (New York: Oxford University Press, 1988); James Keith Houge, *Uncivil War: Five New Orleans Street Battles and the Rise and Fall of Radical Reconstruction* (Baton Rouge: Louisiana State University Press, 2006); Lawrence N. Powell, *New Masters: Northern Planters during the Civil War and Reconstruction* (New Haven: Yale University Press, 1980). On boosterism and the New South in American imagination, see Lacy K. Ford, "Rednecks and Merchants: Economic Development and Social Tensions in the South Carolina Upcountry, 1865–1900," *Journal of American History* 71 (September 1984): 294–318; C. Vann Woodward, *Origins of the New South, 1877–1913* (1951; repr. Louisiana State University Press, 1971); Dana F. White and Victor A. Kramer, eds., *Olmstead South: Old South Critic / New South Planner* (Westport, CT: Greenwood Press, 1979); David R. Goldfield, "The Urban South: A Regional Framework," *American Historical Review* 86 (December 1981): 1009–1034; Arthur Meier Schlesinger, "The

ward off any potentially troubling associations with boom and bust while capitalizing upon widespread enthusiasms. The area possessed extraordinary natural resources, especially in mining but also in lumber, and a sober population of workers could fully exploit these resources. A nearby railroad would provide local industry and agriculture with distribution, at the same time providing a way for local merchants to obtain commodities.[57]

The idea of being part of the New South was undoubtedly appealing for Free Soil-nostalgic Prohibitionists. It was romantic to reenact the sort of solutions provided by the New England Emigrant Aid Company, which had helped found Lawrence and Manhattan during the era of Bloody Kansas. Enhancing the mystique for Prohibitionists, Harriman was built on land formerly occupied by a plantation. Wisely, partisans refrained from expressing such sentiments to Southern neighbors.[58]

As for the use of deeds to assure the perpetuation of prohibition, regardless of the character of future generations who might settle there, there were also previous examples on which Prohibitionists could draw. In the party press, Prohibitionists referenced Cattaraugus, New York; Baldwin, Kansas; Greeley, Colorado; Colorado Springs, Colorado; Pullman, Illinois; Palo Alto, California; Hermosa Beach, California; Asbury Park, New Jersey; Oeres, California; Osage City, Kansas; Pasadena, California; Wankena and Winchester, California; and Ontario, California. Contemporary to Harriman's development, temperance advocates settled in Demorest, Georgia, and Newhall and Madera, California.[59] Lawrence,

New South," in *The Rise of the City, 1878–1898* (1933; repr. Columbus: Ohio State University Press, 1999), 1–22.

[57] On the relationship between transportation, industrial manufacturing, and population composition and growth, see Peter G. Goheen, "Industrialization and the Growth of Cities in Nineteenth-Century America," and Roger F. Riefler, "Nineteenth-Century Urbanization Patterns in the United States" in *Urbanization and the Growth of Cities*, ed. Neil Larry Shumsky, vol. 1 (New York: Garland Publishing, Inc., 1996), 45–76; William Cronon, *Nature's Metropolis: Chicago and the Great West* (New York: W.W. Norton, 1991); Michael F. Sheehan, "Land Speculation in Southern California," *American Journal of Economics and Sociology* 42 (1982): 197–209; Reps, *Making of Urban America*, 382–413.

[58] On the party's general decision to downplay antislavery emphasis from the 1880s onward, see Szymanski, *Pathways to Prohibition*, 133.

[59] Most of these temperance communities' identities are clearly demonstrated as such, but a few references are rather obscure and are therefore better described in this footnote for easier location by future scholars. Baldwin, Kansas, was founded in 1857 and is referenced in "Pioneer Prohibition Town," *Patriot Phalanx*, 20 October 1910, reprinted from *American Issue*. Madera, California, is referenced in an advertisement in *Lever*, 26 March 1891. It was intriguingly named the John Brown Colony by its land company

Kansas and Vineland, New Jersey also had dry origins, albeit created through alternative legal strategies.[60] Most of these towns were viable,

agents. Hopkins Tract was the original, pre-expansion boundary of Palo Alto, which was itself founded as something of an annex to Stanford University. Timothy Hopkins (no clear relation to A.A. Hopkins) was a family friend of Leland Stanford, who requested that Hopkins place a no liquor requirement into the deeds of land purchasers despite his own interest in the wine industry. As a result, the deeds "stated that if the property owner, his heirs or his assigns 'shall at any time manufacture or sell, to be used as a beverage, any intoxicating liquor, or permit the same to be done on the premises thereby occupied, this deed shall be void and the premises revert to and become the absolute property of the devisor'"; Kathleen Donnelly, "The Quiet '20s," Palo Alto Online, http://www.paloaltoonline.com/news_features/centennial/1920A.php (accessed on 15 May 2007). In addition, some individuals established similar deed-based prohibition territories in Osage City, Kansas. The *Topeka Daily Capital*, 29 November 1883, noted a transaction wherein lands were sold with the condition that "intoxicating liquors should never be sold on the premises" and that "this condition was named in the deed of conveyance as part of the consideration; and that further condition as written out in the deed, that in case the condition should ever be broken by the purchaser or any one claiming under him, the property should revert to the seller or his heirs or assigns." Demorest, Georgia, was named after the treasurer of the Prohibition Bureau and a significant party donor; William Jennings Demorest was a close friend of Horace Waters, for whom he served as pallbearer in 1893. The land company's board of directors included Prohibitionist editor M.V.B. Bennett, and party Prohibitionist Frank B. Sibley was the company secretary. See Advertisement, "Demorest: The New Temperance Manufacturing City of the South," *New Era*, 6 December 1889. Advertisements for Newhall appeared in *Lever*, 9 January 1889. These advertisements included John P. St. John on the board of directors. Letterhead from a letter from Jesse Yarnell to T.C. Richmond suggests the existence of a St. John subdivision of the Rancho San Francisco in Newhall, California; 10 February 1892, TCRC. Wankena and Winchester, California, were founded by the Tulare Improvement Company and promoted by Nebraska Prohibitionist J.G. Miller. Miller named several Winchester streets after temperance luminaries including Finch, Willard, and George Haddock; "California Abroad: Elder Miller in California," *Weekly Censor*, 8 March 1888. The date of origin of Lyons, Nebraska, as a deed-based community is unclear, and so it is not included within the main text. For information on Lyons, see *Patriot Phalanx*, 14 January 1904, which details an unsuccessful challenge to the deed requirements by property purchasers. Nappanee, Indiana; Hoopeston, Illinois; and Waycross, Georgia, have similarly hard-to-determine dates of origin and might not have used deeds to ensure dry integrity. More information is available on these communities in "Prosperity Smiles on No-Saloon Town," *Patriot Phalanx*, 13 July 1905. Perhaps most intriguing was the community of Jireh, Wyoming, which likely developed in emulation of Harriman, Tennessee. Jireh was a deed-based dry community with a college committed to temperance education, see J.R. Cortner, "A Town That Can Never Have a Saloon," *Patriot Phalanx*, 15 September 1910. There is also a reference to Baldwin, Kansas, as the "original prohibition town" in "Pioneer Prohibition Town," *Patriot Phalanx*, 20 October 1910. Greeley, Colorado, has been more thoroughly discussed in historical literature; Kathleen A. Brosnan, *Uniting Mountain and Plain: Cities, Law, and Environmental Change along the Front Range* (Albuquerque: University of New Mexico Press, 2002), 73–74.

[60] Ocean City, New Jersey was also founded as a dry community, but I have had difficulty learning if its prohibition policy was deed based or through another form. I did not

and many thrived. Some evidence suggests that party members might have created, or at least visited, deed-based dry cities in Southern California as early as 1887; a Michigan journalist hyperbolized that "nearly every new town started in southern California has a prohibitory clause in the deed."[61] Los Angeles's *Weekly Censor* had reported the existence of about twenty such towns by 1888, some with streets named for party chair John B. Finch, WCTU president Frances Willard, and temperance martyr George Haddock.[62] A Colorado delegate to the 1888 national executive committee meeting had affirmed for the board that many Colorado towns had prohibition clauses in their deeds.[63] With great conviction, the ETLC assured investors that their "business policy in town building [was] not experimental" because of these precedents.[64]

Nonetheless, as a partisan project, the stakes of this enterprise were undeniably different. Some partisans had persistent fears that Harriman might irretrievably damage public opinion of the Prohibition Party if it failed.[65] Even the party's national executive committee,which included several of the Harriman project's investors, had issued an officially neutral response to an inquirer who requested information about the viability of the project in 1889. A subcommittee explained that Harriman was "a matter upon which it has no jurisdiction and desires to express no option" and further commented that "this Committee does not in any way favor the use of the Prohibition Party to advance the interests of any business project and depreciates the use of names of leading Prohibitionists

include this precedent in the text of the chapter because I have found no Prohibition Party references to it. A series of temperance towns are identified in Ray Hutchison, "Capitalism, Religion, and Reform: The Social History of Temperance in Harvey, Illinois," in *Drinking: Behavior and Belief in Modern History*, eds. Susanna Barrows and Robin Room (Berkeley: University of California Press, 1991), 185–188. On Lawrence and Topeka's deed-based strategies, see Bader, *Prohibition in Kansas*, 16. There is a brief allusion to deed-based settlements in Iowa in Burren R. Sherman, "Constitutional Prohibition in Iowa," *North American Review*, December 1882.

[61] Untitled, *Center*, 8 December 1887. See also J.G. Miller, "California Abroad: Elder Miller in California," *Weekly Censor*, 8 March 1888, reprinted from the *New Republic*; Miller was in the process of establishing several deed-based dry towns. Overall, 1887 was an epic year in the Los Angeles land boom. More dry advocates moved into Southern California with each passing year; Ostrander, *Prohibition Movement in California*, v, 69 and 72.

[62] J.G. Miller, "California Abroad: Elder Miller in California," *Weekly Censor*, 8 March 1888, reprinted from *New Republic*. Miller was a Prohibitionist from Nebraska who worked as a land agent for Rice & Simmonds. Haddock was a law enforcement officer killed in the process of upholding anti-liquor laws.

[63] Mr. Spragire in National Executive Committee Minutes,1 June 1888, TPP.

[64] ETLC, *One Year in Harriman, Tennessee*, 52.

[65] For example, "Bothered by the Land Company," *Voice*, 14 November 1889.

as such for such purposes."[66] Even the *Voice*, when pressed, classified Harriman as "a private business enterprise" and asserted that "the Prohibition Party has nothing whatever to do with it" so as to accommodate critics who want to insulate the party's reputation from the project's potential failure.[67]

One key anxiety was the lingering belief that city building was not a reputable practice for a political party. The Prohibition Party's founders had always taken pride in their conformity to major parties' rituals. They held conventions, nominated candidates, and distributed ballots just like their Democratic and Republican counterparts. Much as the incorporation of women members had raised unsettling questions about departure from precedent, so too did the party's newest engagement in an enterprise also practiced by free love advocates, communitarians, and religious outsiders.[68]

Over time, the ETLC made life in Harriman more comfortable to please residents and to make the city into a better showcase for critics doubting the sagacity of party commitment to such an extraordinary project. In response to those critics who worried that there would be no tax base to raise funds for infrastructure, the ETLC donated large lots for schools, government buildings, parks, and a WCTU temple. Clinton B. Fisk "promised a furnace, and pledged his personal word for its erection."[69] The ETLC even hired an architect to design the Grand Hotel of Harriman.[70] Between 1890 and 1893, the land company did many of the things that citizens might expect from a tax-funded local government, hoping to meet the concerns of residents and the national party while also increasing the value of remaining unsold lots.[71] The ETLC

expended in street improvements over $50,000; had established an electric plant and temporary water works; had begun the erection of a large and elegant hotel, and had contributed largely to the completion of another, begun by private parties;

[66] Minutes of the National Executive Committee, 8 November 1889, TPP. Italics included in the minutes.

[67] "Bothered by the Land Company," *Voice*, 14 November 1889.

[68] On American communes, see Paul S. Boyer, ed., *America's Communal Utopias* (Chapel Hill: University of North Carolina Press, 1997); Robert S. Fogarty, *All Things New: American Communes and Utopian Movements, 1860–1914* (Chicago: University of Chicago Press, 1990); Edward K. Spann, *Brotherly Tomorrows: Movements for a Cooperative Society in America, 1820–1920* (New York: Columbia University Press, 1989); Reps, *Making of Urban America*, 439–474.

[69] ETLC, *One Year in Harriman, Tennessee*, 26.

[70] Pulliam, *Harriman*, 24.

[71] This type of activity was consistent with the strategy of many nineteenth-century land companies; Reps, *Making of Urban America*, 349–413.

had erected a public school building at a cost of more than $6,000, and established a graded school system at its own expense; had erected an exposition building, used for some months to accommodate all public meetings; had made liberal donations of land for railway purposes along the line of the E.T., V. & G. Ry.; had contributed lots for the building of churches of all denominations, and of a hall for W.C.T.U. and Y.M.C.A. purposes.[72]

The East Tennessee Land Company vowed that Harriman would be like Colorado Springs, where the Colorado Springs Land Company had ful-filled its promise to build schools, churches, parks, and hotels.[73]

The ETLC also fought boom and bust by recruiting industry through newspaper advertisements offering "a suitable site, for a plant, to any reliable and desirable manufacturing concern locating at Harriman."[74] To bring industries more systemically, the ETLC organized the Harri-man Manufacturing Company (HMC) as "the chief promoter of indus-tries at Harriman."[75] The officers and board of directors were very similar to those of the ETLC. Ferdinand Schumacher, A.A. Hopkins, Frederick Gates, and A.W. Wagnalls served on both boards of direc-tors. Non-Prohibitionist John Hopewell, Jr., served as president, allow-ing him to "objectively" endorse the project while also communicating the party's ongoing desire to bring more anti-liquor advocates into its fold.

Combining the idea of economic planning with hearty capitalism, the HMC recruited businesses that could work cooperatively with each other, supplying each other's needs for raw and finished materials "so that all shall work as one concern for their own interest, the interest of the town, and the consequent greater success of the parent company."[76] In exchange for creating this hospitable economic environment, the HMC wanted a share of the profits from these businesses. The land company could also profit from manufacturers' presence in Harriman because it would increase the desirability of residential lots among workers and hence the value of its own stock. Adapting the partisan rationale for nationwide prohibition, advocates of Harriman agreed that any community would necessarily be more affluent when earnings were not lost in the saloon. Workers would spend beer money on consumer goods, which would be produced and supplied locally.

[72]   *City Directory of Harriman* (n.p.: G.M. Connelly, 1892), 28.
[73]   Reps, *Making of Urban America*, 403–404.
[74]   ETLC, *One Year in Harriman, Tennessee*, 53.
[75]   ETLC, *Two Years in Harriman, Tennessee*, 52.
[76]   ETLC, *Two Years in Harriman, Tennessee*, 64.

An aggressive ETLC campaign urged Prohibition Party members to bring national conventions to the city and to thereby fully embrace Harriman as a partisan investment. Noting that "Harriman is an *object lesson which must be made known to the world*," land company representatives asserted that "nothing will so thoroughly and effectively direct the eyes of the nation to this accomplished fact of successful Prohibition as the National Convention meeting at Harriman!"[77] ETLC representatives even went so far as to secure an entire page of the *Voice* in December 1891 to make the case for Harriman as the site of the national convention in the following year. They claimed that

Harriman, as a city, has achieved the very goal, aim and end for which the Party exists.... As such a place, then, it is befitting and proper that the Prohibition Party, with such a great cause, assembles to nominate candidates and formulate its declaration for principles by which it will enter and conduct the great Presidential campaign in the fourth centennial year of the discovery of this continent.[78]

A national convention in Harriman would institutionalize the city's status as the center of the party. Indeed, ETLC representatives used the pursuit of the national convention seat as an opportunity to define Harriman as "Home for Prohibitionists."[79]

Some of the partisan critics who remained hesitant about the Harriman project also resisted proposals to hold the 1892 national convention in Harriman. Delegates to the selection committee believed that it would be unwise to choose Harriman because it would appear that the party was directly supporting a "private enterprise."[80] In so doing, they attempted to insulate the party from the Harriman project once again. The *Harriman Advance* angrily retaliated with a response the *Voice* described as "impugning the motives of the National Prohibition Committee," even suggesting that "the choice indicates the Committee's preference for saloon associations."[81] When the 1892 convention later took place in St. Louis, nearly 300 convention delegates and other partisans took a special train to Harriman to examine the city. Several of these visitors

[77] Advertisement, "Facts about Harriman," *Voice*, 10 December 1891. Italics are author's. See also, "Facts about Harriman!" *Issue*, 17 December 1891, in Scrapbook page 66, Box 4, HTMR.

[78] Advertisement, "Facts About Harriman," *Voice*, 10 December 1891.

[79] Advertisement, "Facts About Harriman," *Voice*, 10 December 1891.

[80] "St. Louis Gets It," *Michigan Messenger*, 25 December 1891. Clipping in Scrapbook, 1, Box 4, HTMR. The Tennessee Prohibition convention was held in Harriman in 1904 without similar complaints; "Nashville Connection," *Citizen*, 25 May 1904.

[81] Untitled, *Voice*, 7 January 1892.

wrote favorable accounts of Harriman to communicate the city's value
to a national group of readers.[82]

Relishing converts of all types, some members of the Prohibitionist
press also reported instances of Democratic and Republican visitors beg-
ging to be forgiven for past oversights. The *Voice* asserted that "even
the Democrats and Republicans... become enthusiastic for Harriman as
a Prohibition city... some feel contrite and humbly ask to be admitted
to the party on probation!"[83] The *Harriman Advance* continued: "We
have never intimated that Democrats and Republicans, as such, were
not wanted here. We have hoped they would come; just as the church
invites the attendance of sinners. We have believed it would politically
and otherwise do them good."[84]

Active in the state since 1883 and formally supported by the Tennessee Temperance Alliance and state WCTU since 1888, Prohibitionists had both the time and alliances to educate themselves about Tennessee's partisan culture before Harriman's founding.[85] Harriman's new
residents must have been aware of their Southern-born neighbors' ongoing debates about the value of a minor party alternative to the Democratic
Party. Many Tennesseans perceived the Populist and Prohibition parties –
which in Tennessee had platforms closely resembling each other – as little
more than wedges for the African-American electorate. The selection of
Clinton B. Fisk, with his Union army and Freedman's Bureau connections, as the Prohibitionist candidate in 1888 likely reinforced the idea
that minor parties challenging the Democratic Party conspired to subvert white supremacy.[86] It was this assumption that Georgia's Sam Small
sought to undermine when urging that "it is not the Prohibition party

---

[82] "A Trip to Harriman," clipping in Scrapbook, 122, Box 4, HTMR; "Happy Harriman,"
Patrol, 22 July 1892, clipping in Scrapbook, page 124, Box 4, HTMR. Advertisement,
Souvenir from the National Prohibition Convention, Cincinnati, 29–30 June 1892, inside
cover, Folder: 1892, GBHP. This advertisement takes up the entire inside cover of the
official program.

[83] Advertisement, "Facts About Harriman!," *Voice*, 10 December 1891, clipping in Scrapbook, 70, Box 4, HTMR.

[84] "For Harriman," *Harriman (Tennessee) Advance*, 9 February 1893. Belligerent
Democrats and Republicans were less welcome; "No More Harriman for Him," *Harriman Advance*, 2 March 1893.

[85] Isaac, *Prohibition and Politics*, 55, 61–62.

[86] Fisk polled significantly behind the Prohibition Party's candidate for Tennessee's governor in 1888. Distinctions between Populist and Prohibitionist agendas were sometimes
difficult to discern. In 1890, for example, the Tennessee Prohibition Party's platform
was "designed to appeal to the discontented farm element"; Isaac, *Prohibition and Politics*, 64. Likewise, Tennessee's Populist platform of 1898 called for prohibition; Isaac,
Prohibition and Politics, 77.

that seeks to rule the South with the negro, but it is the liquor end of the Democratic party that, in its desperation, is using the negro to rule the South in the interest of whisky, debauchery, and drunken Democracy."[87]

The debate about partisanship and white supremacy was a subtext that also permeated Southern Methodists' perspectives on anti-liquor legislation. Some Tennessee Methodists were open to a departure from the Democratic Party on the grounds that it might liberate them from complicity in the liquor traffic.[88] However, Democratic Southern Methodists cited a decades-old principle, developed in the context of abolitionism, that their church must be nonpolitical. This position did not preclude voting but encouraged resistance to any distraction from the pursuit of spiritual purity. The WCTU, the Prohibition Party, and even temperance fraternities might be scolded for promoting temperance zeal at the cost of faithful worship. Southern Methodists' debates came to a head when outspoken dry advocate, former Democrat, and Confederate veteran David C. Kelley left his pastorate in 1890 to run for Tennessee governor on the Prohibition Party ticket. Thinkers who held to the spirituality doctrine claimed that Kelley had sullied the ministry, although they might have been just as fretful that he threatened Democratic hegemony.[89] The tense debate among Southern Methodists would continue until the collapse of the Populist Party and gradual diminishment of the Prohibitionist Party made it unlikely that Democrats, and thus white supremacy, would be overturned.

To generalize, Prohibitionists tended to view the South's Republican Party as nonexistent. They saw a vacuum where a new second party might thrive. White Southerners were at least as likely to view their political situation as one wherein pro-racial equality Republicans were sneakily covert, masked as Prohibitionists or Populists. Throughout the South, deliberation about the value of a minor party would only subside with the definitive exclusion of African-American voters through both law and violence.

Against this backdrop, Harriman's settlers attempted to establish the kind of community in which they saw their political ideals manifest in everyday life. Were they not prohibition minded, founding residents might have just as easily selected lots in the neighboring new town of

[87] "Woolly Head and Horny Heels: What Politicians Will Do to Beat the Prohibitionists When it Comes to Office-Seeking," *Center*, 21 June 1888.

[88] Coker, *Liquor in the Land of the Lost Cause*, 106–117. On protest against Democratic factionalism in the face of prohibition, see Isaac, *Prohibition and Politics*, 46.

[89] In the 1892 election, the Prohibition Party's candidate for governor polled less than half of Kelly's vote. Isaac, *Prohibition and Politics*, 67 and 69.

Cardiff, which had no strict liquor regulations but similar geographic and industrial attractions. Cardiff's land company had also drawn thousands of potential purchasers from all over the country to its first land sale in April 1890. And like Harriman, Cardiff contained banks, construction and lumber businesses, industry, hotels, an exposition building, and an iron and coal company. Cardiff had a railroad station.[90] Yet Harriman's residents seemingly preferred the distinctive way of life that the ETLC promised, as best indicated by the rapid establishment of two local parties (both favoring prohibition), temperance reading circles, and local branches of the WCTU and Prohibition Party within Harriman's first few months. Residents did not wind up in a prohibition city by accident.

Prohibitionists' ideological dedication would help sustain the migrants, many of whom found that rural Tennessee was not yet the utopian Harriman that party planners envisioned. It was dirty, undeveloped, and uninteresting. Early photos of Roane Street – the main street of Harriman – show pigs wandering aimlessly through the mud.[91] Migrants were often from Northern cities, so the difference was particularly startling. Moreover, building Harriman took a long time; laborers and owners resided in nearby "Shacktown" while homes and businesses were gradually constructed. About two dozen dilapidated-looking wooden buildings framed the single intersection that residents jokingly dubbed Broadway and Wall Street.[92] Despite steady construction beginning in 1890, Harriman of 1893 lacked sidewalks on main roads. These same main streets were ungraded and hence tended to flood on a regular basis.[93] There were still no fire bells and no bridges. There was no industrial furnace because Fisk, who had promised its construction, passed away.[94] What Harriman did have was a lot of mud and rising unemployment.[95]

---

[90] Jack Shelley and Jere Hall, eds., *Valley of Challenge and Change: The History of Roane County, Tennessee, 1860–1900* (Kingston, TN: Roane County Heritage Commission, 1986), 63–65.

[91] For example, Shelley and Hall, eds., *Valley of Challenge and Change*, 72; Pulliam, *Harriman*, 91.

[92] See photos in Pulliam, *Harriman*, 10, 14–15.

[93] "Board of Aldermen," *Harriman Advance*, 12 January 1893; "Harriman's Objections," *Harriman Advance*, 9 February 1893.

[94] "Local Lines," *Harriman Advance*, 16 March 1893; "The Supervisors," *Harriman Advance*, 9 March 1893; "Chattanooga, Harriman and Northern R.R.," *Harriman Advance*, 2 March 1893.

[95] "Local Lines," *Harriman Advance*, 2 March 1893; "What Harriman Wants," *Harriman Advance*, 30 March 1893; Isham Benefiel, Untitled, *Harriman Advance*, 13 April 1893.

It was little wonder that some frustrated Harriman residents felt that "the whole business was a failure, and that Harriman was dead" and left the community in its first few years.[96] However, steadily increasing and then plateauing population statistics suggest that most of Harriman's pioneer land purchasers dug in and stuck it out. They were invested in the project; the *Voice* noted that "the Company and the citizens have generally acted in concert in the erection of buildings. It is fair to say that the E.T.L. Co. and the Harriman M'f'g Co. represent half the improvements and the citizens the other half."[97]

Harriman's most dedicated proponents quickly adapted their once exuberant expectations to actual conditions. Local papers modestly conceded that the city's success was mitigated by "the difficulties Harriman has encountered" while assuring readers that the city looked favorable "in the light of comparison" to Southern boomtowns like neighboring Cardiff, which was struggling even more than Harriman.[98] An 1892 article in a Methodist publication similarly conceded Harriman's rural and half-built appearance while suggesting that the virtue of the community compensated for its lack of comforts. A visitor to Harriman might "not find the Utopia he has longed for [but] he will find, as the writer did, a city of happy homes, of industrious and hospitable people."[99]

Self-interest would keep Harriman dry throughout this trying time. Harriman's property derived its market value not only from its geographic attributes but also from its place within a community of like-minded residents living under prohibition; residents would continually reaffirm their belief that citizen virtue was "something real and valuable to base its growth on."[100] They repeated the refrain that a society where no one spent money on liquor would have more capital to dedicate to the development of industry and the purchase of consumer goods, leading to a healthier local economy and higher property values. Ideological

[96] "Those 'Objections,'" *Harriman Advance*, 9 February 1893. See also "No More Harriman for Him," *Harriman Advance*, 2 March 93.

[97] Zadel Barnes Gustafson, "Founded in Honor and Enterprise," *Voice*, 23 April 1891.

[98] "Three Years Old!" *Harriman Advance*, 2 March 1893; "Impressions of Harriman," *United States Investor*, January 1892, clipping in Scrapbook, 61, Box 4, HTMR.

[99] "Happy Harriman: Celebration for Pioneer's Day in the Young City," *(Atlanta, Georgia) Methodist Advocate*, 1 April 1892. Clipping in Scrapbook, page 19, Box 4, HTMR. On the similar literary techniques used to boost Wichita, Kansas, see Julie Dagenais, "Newspaper Language as an Active Agent in the Building of a Frontier Town," *American Speech* 42 (May 1967): 114–121.

[100] "Harriman," *(Knoxville) Sentinel*, 9 April 1892, clipping in Scrapbook, 64, Box 4, HTMR.

continuity with the city's dry founding principles would be further assured
by self-interest because, if Harriman residents ever revoked their dry policy, the town would lose more in financial subsidies from disappointed
partisan Prohibitionist stockholders than it could ever hope to gain in tax
revenue.[101] Partisans had concluded that "Harriman must remain solid
for Prohibition, or Harriman fails."[102]

Without having affluence as an immediate alternative and desirous
to ward off financial ruin, Harriman residents agreed that they would
lead their party – and inspire partisan financial support for their experiment – by modeling perseverance. Whatever "existence and success"
were achieved would be attributed to the "good work and great faith
of her Pioneers" and their financial allies.[103] Including stockholders
within the cadre of participants, Harriman residents praised stockholders'
"remarkable record of devotion" to Harriman "under circumstances that
would test the loyalty and the generosity of [other] men."[104] Speaking
for other Harriman residents, local writer W.C. Damon suggested that
"Harriman feels the burden of financial depression, in common with the
whole country, yet, in spite of all these things, Harriman moves right
on."[105]

When intemperance among construction workers and rebellious residents annoyed Harriman's Prohibitionists, they used violations of dry
policy as an opportunity to reassert the permanent community's commitment to the elimination of such behavior. Harriman property owners
expelled drinkers from the community, even though doing so ensured
that building construction and industrial improvement would take longer
to complete. They even asked visiting laborers to sign total abstinence
pledges, concluding that "a man who can't stay sober in Hariman [sic]
should be loaded upon the first outgoing train."[106]

Other infractions arising from traditionally difficult sectors of the
economy were likewise combated. The February 19, 1891, minutes of
the Harriman WCTU understatedly suggested how women residents
responded to a pharmacist distributing alcoholic "medicine": "suggested
and favored that we have only a short meeting, the time to be taken up

[101] "Harriman's Objections," *Harriman Advance*, 2 February 1893.
[102] "For Harriman," *Harriman Advance*, 9 February 1893.
[103] "Three Years Old!" *Harriman Advance*, 2 March 93. See also, "Harriman's Objections," *Harriman Advance*, 2 February 1893.
[104] "The Marvelous Million," *Harriman Advance*, 2 February 1893.
[105] W.C. Damon, "The Southland's Star of Hope," *Voice*, 18 August 1892.
[106] Pulliam, *Harriman*, 91–92; "Local Lines," *Harriman Advance*, 16 March 1893.

in calling on our druggist Dr. Willis."[107] Willis likely received a visit that included the women's occupation of his store and prayers offered on his behalf until he ceased vending spirits, a ritual held with the threat of another Women's Crusade behind it. When an antagonistic local resident sued for the right to receive packages of liquor sent through the mail, the Harriman city council offered to pay all fines and expenses for the defendant shipping company.[108] Similarly, a "'wildcat' who tried to sell whiskey near the Byrd ferry" was brought before the locally elected judge, fined, and condemned in the local paper's columns.[109]

In no instance was partisans' loyalty to the Harriman experiment more evident than when they continued funding the ETLC in the midst of its evident instability. Understatedly describing the depth of local economic downturn in the years following early optimism, the *Harriman Advance* noted that "the Harriman Manufacturing Company...has not been so active in the past year as it desired to be."[110] Both "businessmen and citizens" were "laboring under...financial embarrassment."[111] Seven years later, the *Harriman Advance* would less subtly describe how "the time of liquidation came" and "many were pinched, oh, so cruelly, and saw their savings go glimmering." Moreover, "one after another, firms and factories went to smash and were closed out, until the prospect looked black as midnight. Many, who could go, left."[112] Even champion booster A.A. Hopkins would later concede that he had felt that "some of us mortgaged our future that Harriman might be saved for a future of its own.... That losses came to any others has been a long regret to me."[113] Desperate, the land company appealed to "every friend of Harriman" to "put shoulder to the wheel, and lift once more," relieving the ETLC of some of its largest financial debts through the sale of more stock in the company.[114]

Some determined Prohibitionists did indeed rally to the ETLC's 1893 Million Dollar Plan, a last-ditch effort to pay off pressing debts with the sale of more company stock. The *Harriman Advance* posed a series

---

[107] Woman's Christian Temperance Union, Woman's Christian Temperance Union – Minute Book, notation for 19 February 1891, Folder 4, Box 2, HTMR.

[108] Pulliam, *Harriman*, 92.

[109] "Local Lines," *Harriman Advance*, 16 March 1893.

[110] "Harriman's Prospects and Opportunities," *Harriman Advance*, 9 March 1893.

[111] Isham Benefiel, Untitled, *Harriman Advance*, 13 April 1893.

[112] "Retrospective," *Harriman Advance*, 1 March 1900.

[113] A.A. Hopkins, "Letter from A.A. Hopkins," *Harriman (Tennessee) Record*, 1 June 1916.

[114] "Harriman's Prospects and Opportunities," *Harriman Advance*, 9 March 1893.

of rhetorical questions to remind Prohibitionists of their previous commitment to building a community wherein everyday lives exemplified political values:

What class of people furnish the vast sum of money which has been pledged for Harriman's assistance this year? The Prohibitionists, beyond any question. Why do they furnish it? Not simply to protect some prior investment of their own. Their chief purpose is to protect an industrial experiment here, based on a principle which they cherish and for which they are willing to sacrifice.[115]

Continuing to insist that Harriman was a solid financial investment, the ETLC increasingly reminded Prohibitionists of the broader partisan meanings of Harriman's success. Three years after the town's founding, the *Harriman Advance* urged readers:

let us not forget the many hundreds, who have not seen Harriman, to whom, not less than to the good work and great faith of her Pioneers, Harriman's existence and success are due. They are scattered over many states, but their money and prayers have centered here. They have been co-builders, silent partners, from the start.[116]

In return, these 3,000 investors obligated Harriman's residents "to maintain the policy on which Harriman was based, in the full and complete letter and spirit thereof": prohibition.[117]

Prohibitionists were also investing elsewhere. The showcase cities of Prohibition Park on Staten Island and Harvey, Illinois, as well as the lower-profile communities of Irona, Texas; Haddon Heights, New Jersey; and Allendale, Montana, all dramatically suggest Prohibitionists' growing and persistent enthusiasm for city building as a party strategy. Prohibition Park was Harriman's first imitator, much like Harriman but with less risk and more overt partisan boosterism. Prohibition Park's land company capitalized on trends in suburbanization by emphasizing the lots' proximity to New York City; the National Prohibition Park Company (NPPC) even advertised its spaces as "New York City Lots."[118]

---

[115] "Harriman's Objections," *Harriman Advance*, 2 February 1893.

[116] "Three Years Old," *Harriman Advance*, 2 March 93.

[117] "Three Years Old," *Harriman Advance*, 2 March 93. "Harriman's Prospectus and Opportunities," *Harriman Advance*, 9 March 1893, estimated that "non-resident investors in Harriman number 3,000, at least." This might have been a booster-style exaggeration, but in the absence of company bankruptcy records it is impossible to confirm or deny.

[118] National Prohibition Park Company, "Valuable for Home Seekers" (N.p.: n.p., 1897), 44, Folder: National Prohibition Park, Box 5, GBHP; Advertisement, "A Great Opportunity for Home-Seekers," *Voice*, 28 March 1895.

"The Park," noted the *Voice*, "is designed to be a summer home for people who wish to spend their vacation in some pleasant neighborhood near the sea, and yet be near New York City."[119] New York Prohibition Party newspaper the *True Reform* recorded the carefree leisure activities that were readily available, giving special emphasis to the "Cold Water Cyclers," a group of bicycle hobbyists.[120] Whereas the ETLC had asked purchasers to completely uproot their lives, and in the case of many Northern urbanites, reconfigure their lifestyles, the NPPC appealed to customers who searched for a less abrupt transformation. In commuting distance from New York, Prohibition Park residents could have their cake and eat it too, possessing both isolation from and proximity to familiar sources of amusement and work.

Already known as the site of Prohibition Party retreats, conventions, and workshops, the new town of Prohibition Park reinforced and publicized its partisanship in various ways. The streets evoked partisan identity because they were named after party leaders like Fisk and Willard as well as dry states like Maine. The relocation of the National Lecture Bureau to Prohibition Park in October 1891 demonstrated the national committee's support for this project, further blurring the lines between party and private enterprise.[121] The National Lecture Bureau was a professional staff of party members who served as campaign speakers, rallying and organizing would-be Prohibitionists into clubs. Its membership significantly overlapped with the leadership of the national committee. To locate the National Lecture Bureau within Prohibition Park was thus to suggest this new community's importance for future party development. The national committee's subtle increase in support between Harriman and Prohibition Park suggests that many partisans were more enthusiastic about this work after Harriman had demonstrated that city building was not a completely foolhardy venture.

Of course, some doubts would always remain. For example, in 1891 *Voice* editor Isaac K. Funk responded to a critic who charged that Prohibition Park was a speculation scheme that was "using . . . the name and prestige of the Prohibition Party for the purpose of advancing private interests." He defended the project by asserting that the board of trustees

---

[119] "The Prohibition Chautauqua," *Voice*, 2 April 1891.

[120] C.H. Mead, "Prohibition Park," *(New York) True Reform*, 17 June 1897. For an obituary on C. Henry Mead, see Frank J. Sibley, "The Farewell," *American Advance*, 17 May 1913.

[121] "Moving to Prohibition Park," *Voice*, 1 October 1891.

intended "to make it a park of service to the National Prohibition cause and party" and defensively suggested that "if you do not like what others are doing, go to work and carry out a better plan."[122]

If advertisements for the cities in which editor Funk had a direct investment – Harriman and Prohibition Park – were prominently placed within the *Voice*'s weekly columns, those for Harvey, Illinois, were also boldly featured, albeit generally on another page, beginning in late 1890. Harvey was "founded, built up, and populated by Prohibitionists."[123] Turlington W. Harvey, a Chicago Prohibitionist who had made his fortune in lumber and banking, founded the city in 1890 as a Chicago suburb. He controlled the Harvey Land Company, a means of selling residential lots, in conjunction with a board of directors including F.H. Revel, a Boston publisher of religious books and periodicals, and Christian evangelist Dwight L. Moody. Nearby, J.P. Bishop, chair of the Cook County Prohibition Committee, was director of a land company south of the initial Harvey Land Company lots.[124]

Walter Thomas Mills, the fervent narrow gauger who had been booed at the 1889 national conference for his anti-suffrage plank proposal, directed the Walter Thomas Mills Company, offering land just east of the Harvey Land Company lots.[125] It was a testament to their shared commitment to city-building strategy that Mills and the Chicago-based *Lever*'s

---

[122] I.K. Funk, "A Personal Card," *Voice*, 11 June 1891.

[123] "Prohibition Harvey in Danger," *Voice*, 22 August 1895. On the history of Harvey, see Joseph C. Biggot, "Harvey, Illinois," in *Encyclopedia of Chicago*, eds. James R. Grossman, Ann Durkin Keating, and Janice L. Reiff (Chicago: University of Chicago Press, 2004), 374; Hutchison, "Capitalism, Religion, and Reform," 184–216. Harvey was also advertised in the *Christian Advocate*, and an editor from the *Christian Herald* endorsed the project; Advertisement, *Christian Advocate*, 31 March 1892.

[124] Ray Hutchison describes Turlington Harvey as a pioneer in the concept of railroad lumbering who closed his mill on the Sabbath, served as president of the YMCA several times in the 1870s, and would eventually serve as vice president of Dwight L. Moody's Chicago Evangelical Society; "Capitalism, Religion, and Reform," 188. On Bishop, see Hutchison, "Capitalism, Religion, and Reform," 193. Regarding the founding capitalists in Harvey's land companies, Hutchison notes that this was generally a case of absentee owning, unlike Harriman; "Capitalism, Religion, and Reform," 201.

[125] Walter Thomas Mills is a particularly intriguing figure in Prohibition Party history. A supporter of women's suffrage but a member of the faction that favored excluding this issue from the party's national platform, Mills and the *Lever* – a pro-suffrage-plank paper – frequently debated with either enthusiasm or spite. Previous to the events described, Mills published a book through the Funk and Wagnalls publishing firm and also co-edited a magazine with A.J. Jutkins. After passing through Socialist ranks, Mills concluded his political career with the Non-Partisan League.

editorial staff temporarily set aside their volatile dispute over the women's suffrage plank to jointly support the Harvey venture. The *Lever* good-naturedly praised Mills as a man who "is not a stranger to our readers" because "he has done good work for our party."[126] Mills was characterized by a fellow Prohibitionist as "a man of honest intentions, good ability in many ways, immense enthusiasm and confidence – but almost wholly without caution or conservatism," a prophetic observation.[127]

To further bolster the community's Prohibition Party credentials, Harvey's land companies secured endorsements from nationally known Prohibitionist orators Mary T. Lathrop and George Hall and attorney Helen Gougar, as well as the *Lever's* advertising manager, Willard M. Wood.[128] As in Prohibition Park, city streets were named after prominent Prohibitionists, including Gougar, Lathrop, and Frances Willard. Gougar and Lathrop were also trustees of the Woman's Chicago and Harvey Land Company.[129] A.J. Jutkins and Mary Woodbridge were early lot owners and also permitted their names to be used in advertisements.[130]

Balancing realism with hype, the land companies attempted to develop Harvey as a manufacturing center as well as a "Magic City." To assure success, they promised that

> every deed says if the purchaser puts up a building that shall be used for a saloon or immoral purpose or permits any intoxicating drinks to be manufactured, sold, or given away on the premises, or permits any gambling house, or house of prostitution, the property is to revert to original owners as fully and completely as if the deed had never been made, and this without any compensation or forfeiture to the offending purchaser of the lot.[131]

By 1891, Harvey's founders would assure *Voice* readers that Harvey was "no longer an experiment, but a phenomenal success."[132] Within nine

---

[126] "Chicago Enterprise," *Lever*, 22 December 1892.

[127] H.H. Curtis to T.C. Richmond, 24 November 1892, TCRC. Mills was only four feet, six inches tall, and his opponents in the Prohibition Party had the rude habit of ridiculing his height at every opportunity.

[128] Advertisement, "The Time, The Place, The Opportunity," *Voice*, 4 June 1891. According to historian Roger Storms's notes, Gougar wrote the law for municipal suffrage in Kansas; Untitled notes, Folder: Storms, Roger Clair – Historical Research, Roger Storms Papers, Bentley Historical Library, Ann Arbor, Michigan.

[129] Advertisement, "Prohibition Park – A Wonderful Success," *Voice*, 6 October 1892; Advertisement, "Woman's Chicago and Harvey Land Co.," *Voice*, 30 June 1892.

[130] Advertisement, "One Hundred Cottage Lots," *Lever*, 26 January 1893.

[131] Advertisement, "No Saloons. No Gambling. No Prostitution," *Voice*, 12 February 1891.

[132] Advertisement, "Harvey, the Temperance, Manufacturing Center," *Voice*, 11 June 1891.

months, the community claimed a population of 2,500; by 1892, it had a population of 4,000.[133] Families moved to Harvey not only from Chicago but also from several neighboring states on the basis of their desire to live in a community that was dry and that could also provide secure and desirable work opportunities. In an 1893 advertisement, the Mills optimistically assured *Lever* readers that Harvey "will be the Prohibition Park of the Mississippi Valley."[134] Modest successes like those of Harriman, Prohibition Park, and Harvey seemed quite satisfying in the context of looming electoral defeat.

* * *

The process of city building might have been a mere side note had it not developed in the context of diminishing hopes for electoral victory. Prohibitionists had once widely assumed that their party's rise to major party status would occur at the same rapid pace that the Republican Party had developed, and their twenty-fifth anniversary was thus a bittersweet occasion. It was increasingly difficult to explain the party's continued existence and individuals' loyalty to it in terms that had public resonance and appeal. Each election after 1884 marked "no considerable advance in our voting strength." With great spirit, the national executive committee argued that "this fact, instead of tending to lessen our zeal and decrease our activity, ought to awaken us to renewed energy and spur us to more vigorous action."[135]

T.C. Richmond, a sometimes business partner of Walter Thomas Mills, led an investigation into how this "renewed energy" should be directed to avoid an outcome that "certainly cannot be called success, if we do not call it failure"? Richmond went on to speculate that

unless some change is made, unless some new plan of work is adopted, unless we get more in touch with the masses who are as honestly opposed to the saloon system as we are, unless we . . . adapt ourselves and our work to the changed and constantly changing social and political conditions of the country, the Prohibition movement will soon be a thing of the past.

As a result, "the Prohibition Party will cease not only to inspire fear in its enemies, but to command the respect of those who were once its

---

[133] Advertisement, "The Village of Harvey," *Voice*, 9 July 1891; Advertisement, "Harvey," *Lever*, 11 February 1892.

[134] Advertisement, "One Hundred Cottage Lots," *Lever*, 26 January 1893.

[135] Prohibition National Executive Committee, "No Compromise," *Voice*, 20 December 1894.

friends and supporters."[136] The Prohibition Party needed not only to encourage fellow temperance advocates into party ranks but to stay alive in the meantime.

The mood of the party in the mid-1890s was not like the enthusiastic embrace of being cranks in 1888, but more of a pessimistic resignation. Writing T.C. Richmond about his recent *Voice* article, national committee member Eugene W. Chafin declared that "I don't believe we will poll seventy five per cent of our vote next year under the present management. I mean of the men who have usually voted with us." About national chair Samuel Dickie, Chafin concluded that the chair's lack of leadership had been "magnificently exhibited from the day he was elected."[137] C.K. Perrine of the Michigan State Prohibition Committee wrote to Richmond that "I have just read your recent article in *The Voice* and wish to say Amen!"[138]

Many Prohibitionists acknowledged that they no longer expected victory any time soon; "I was not surprised at the smallness of the vote," noted a Rhode Island Prohibitionist about a local election. "I foresaw that apathy and indifference would undoubtedly keep many of our people from the polls."[139] Joshua Levering, who would soon receive the 1896 presidential nomination, ruefully declared that "the party has been in the field long enough to have become stronger and have had better success. . . . It is a good time for plain talking and looking conditions in the face."[140] Former candidate for Ohio governor and national committee member Gideon T. Stewart declared to the National Conference of Reformers that the party's history was a "history of errors" and that it had "utterly failed to accomplish" its goals.[141] Challenging the familiar metaphor that compared the party's vote tally to the ebb and flow the ocean, V.G. Farnham of Harriman, Tennessee, declared that the party had already reached its "high-water mark."[142]

A lapse of faith in the party method encouraged some Prohibitionists to rebuild alliances. Los Angeles County's Prohibition Party adopted the

---

[136] T.C. Richmond, "Strong Appeal for Change," *Voice*, 17 January 1895.

[137] E.W. Chafin to T.C. Richmond, 19 January 1895, TCRC.

[138] C.K. Perrine to T.C. Richmond, 22 January 1895, TCRC.

[139] James A. Williams, "What to do Next," *Voice*, 22 November 1894. See a similar description in "Up and At Them, Boys," *Lever*, 5 March 1896.

[140] Eli F. Ritter, "The Party's Needs," *Voice*, 6 December 1894.

[141] G.T. Stewart, "The Reform of a Political Reform Party," (N.p.: n.p., 1896), 1–2, GBHP. This text is reprinted from an address to the National Conference of Reformers held at Pittsburg, 12–14 March 1896.

[142] V.G. Farnham, "Mr. Richmond's Letter," *Voice*, 18 April 1895.

Council for the Suppression of the Saloon's plans as its own, strengthening the institutional basis for what would become a local branch of the Anti-Saloon League in the process.[143] In Tennessee, James A. Tate advised cooperation with a non-Prohibitionist temperance orator's plan to pursue diverse anti-liquor laws including local option and a pledge to only run candidates when both major parties refused to support such modest legislation. Prohibitionists accepted this proposal and agreed to refrain from nominating candidates at the 1894 Tennessee State convention. As doctrinally pure Prohibitionists might well have predicted, however, the 1894 plan produced no new anti-liquor legislation and probably undermined the party's organization; Tennessee Prohibitionists would nominate candidates of their own in 1896 and would refrain from participation in the statewide Local Option League that was founded in the same year.[144]

For Prohibitionists who would become party leaders in the ensuing decades, this potentially depressing dialogue, the public airing of desperation, and the counterproductive nature of regulatory schemes opened the possibility of shifting more support to the party's innovative political strategies. They speculated that perhaps "many of the triumphs that our party is to achieve do not depend upon its size."[145] This impetus to innovation created by the frank acknowledgment of the party's electoral failures also intensified already existing tensions between Prohibitionists who favored a broader or more narrow platform.[146] Wisconsin's *Elkhorn Blade* commented on an anticipated crisis in party organization in 1895, noting that "a great many prohibitionists, who do not deny a feeling of discouragement at the slow growth of the party, are thinking and saying, 'What next?' Some are saying 'broaden out,' while others believe that it is the 'broadening out' which has been done which has kept our ranks so thin."[147] If the problem was simply that other temperate Protestants did not want to switch parties, then there was not much Prohibitionists could do about it. However, if the problem was the Prohibition Party's agenda, then that agenda could be reshaped.

It was a discussion about Prohibition cities that most dynamically captured partisans' imaginations about the future aspirations and agenda of

---

[143] Ostrander, *Prohibition Movement in California*, 90.
[144] Isaac, *Prohibition and Politics*, 69–71.
[145] "The Triumphs of the Prohibition Party," *Voice*, 22 November 1894. See also I.K. Funk, "Mighty Advance," *Voice*, 12 September 1895.
[146] Blocker, *Retreat from Reform*, 69–77.
[147] "What Next!" *Elkhorn (Wisconsin) Blade*, 29 January 1895.

the Prohibition Party. Harriman's reports most inspired self-proclaimed narrow gaugers, who saw in them evidence supporting their argument that ideological purity might limit the rapid growth but that it ensured that there would be more opportunities to succeed in the future. These Prohibitionists planned to weather the storm by holding fast to their distinct identity. As articulated by this very stubborn section of Prohibitionists, neither fusion – the Populists' downfall – nor nonpartisan measures would tempt their party because their political agenda was framed around a conviction that, as Christians, they were bound to act with absolute moral consistency.[148] In the effort to guard their souls, Prohibitionists such as national chair Samuel Dickie vowed to "be so clearly and so honestly committed to Prohibition, to its enactment into law and to the law's vigorous enforcement, that [they would] deliberately prefer defeat with Prohibition to victory without it."[149] Such a condition could, Prohibitionists' critics noted, be easily arranged. In the meantime, however, there could be none of the lubricating compromises that facilitated fusion between parties.

The consistency with which people involved in Prohibition cities organized on the narrow side of the broad-narrow platform debate suggests that they might have encouraged the use of their communities as a symbolic site for debating the goals and purpose of the party. Zenas W. Bliss of Prohibition Park articulated his narrow gauge preferences in the *Voice*, stating that "Is it not true that every argument made by a Prohibition orator or writer in favor of some issue other than that of Prohibition divides forces within the party and keeps out workers whom we need?"[150] A year later, Bliss would conclude that "my soul is weary with the advocates of this, that, and the other divisive issue, who are continually discouraging the hearts of the faithful, and scaring would-be Prohibitionists from our door."[151] Isham Benetiel of Harriman suggested that "there is but one thing we are all agreed upon, and that is the prohibition of the liquor traffic." He urged fellow partisans: "Do not adopt foolish policies on other questions."[152] The *Harriman Advance*'s Wilber Colvin proposed

---

[148] Untitled, *Independent*, 6 October 1898; "The November Elections," *Independent*, 3 November 1898. See also "Personals," *Zion's Herald*, 13 November 1901.

[149] Samuel Dickie, "Dickie's Opinion," *Lever*, 4 December 1890. On the debate within the party, see Blocker, *Retreat from Reform*, 100–109.

[150] Zenas W. Bliss, "Stick to Prohibition Alone," *Voice*, 21 March 1895.

[151] Zenas W. Bliss, "For the Good of the Party," *Voice*, 6 February 1896.

[152] Isham Benetiel, "He Wants a Prohibition Platform," *Lever*, 26 March 1896.

a single-issue platform for the national convention's consideration – a prospect that had been hissed by a party convention and ridiculed by the *Lever* only a few years earlier – and asserted that "the Prohibition Party will never carry anything until it divests itself of all dividing issues except the sole one of the overthrow of the rum business."[153] Nettie C. Fernald of Prohibition Park also agreed with the single-issue platform. She was willing to set aside her ardent suffragist principles for the time being because she felt confident that she could "trust the party that woman helps in the hour of battle, not to be ungrateful nor unjust to her in the hour of victory."[154]

Prohibition city support for the narrow-gauge position was similarly evident among the community founders. James B. Hobbs, an ETLC trustee, sought to undermine the "dangerous tendency of prominent prohibition leaders such as John P. St. John to side track the party with fads and unimportant side issues."[155] A.A. Hopkins, ETLC secretary, agreed that "the fewer kin our dominant issue has, the sooner will it be recognized as dominant, the more surely will it dominate."[156] William T. Wardwell, who served as a prominent lawyer for Standard Oil as well as being an ETLC trustee, was well-known for his single-issue preferences. Some rivals such as former publisher M.V.B. Bennett attributed Wardwell's reluctance to make a stand on financial issues to be a direct result of his occupation and employer.[157] James Tate criticized platforms that "take position on entirely too many questions" and noted that such a platform could "divide the Prohibition strength of the country."[158] These party leaders were joined by William P.F. Ferguson, A.A. Stevens, Samuel

[153] Wilber Colvin, "First Destroy the Rum Traffic," *Voice*, 2 April 1896. See also Wilber Colvin, Untitled, *Voice*, 18 June 1896; "Others Heard From," *Voice*, 2 April 1896; Wilber Colvin, "First Destroy the Rum Traffic," *Voice*, 2 April 1896.

[154] Nettie C. Fernald, "Woman's Part in the Campaign," *Voice*, 23 July 1896. For an earlier example of the logic that a party moral about liquor would be consistently moral on other matters, see Walter Thomas Mills, "Foraker's Forum Fallacies," *Weekly Censor*, 10 November 1887. Perhaps Nettie C. Fernald was related to James C. Fernald, of the same city, who also routinely wrote letters to and articles for party newspapers.

[155] James B. Hobbs, "St. John's Platform," *Lever*, 26 March 1896.

[156] A.A. Hopkins, "Future Policy of the Party," *Voice*, 16 January 1896.

[157] M.V.B. Bennett, "Broad Gage or Single Issue?" *Voice*, 20 February 1896. A former Democrat, Wardwell actively supported several charities, including a Red Cross hospital and the Water Street Mission in New York City.

[158] James Tate, "Others Heard From," *Voice*, 2 April 1896. See also, "Want No Divisive Issue," *Lever*, 7 May 1896.

Dickie, Isaac K. Funk, J.B. Cranfill, John G. Woolley, Joshua Levering, and Hale Johnson.[159]

Historian Jack Blocker has interpreted support for the single-issue or dominant-issue platform as an expression of an always nagging but increasingly urgent push to capture the support of fellow Protestants and the support of church institutions. Only a few Prohibitionists had considered ditching the mainstream denominations to create distinctive "Prohibition churches," and most Prohibitionists remained active in Protestant congregations, still hoping to bring their peers into the party.[160] It was in pursuit of more Protestant constituents, for example, that A.A. Hopkins asserted that divisive issues such as currency, labor, and government ownership of utilities – issues that were routinely excluded from conversation at religious conventions – should be eliminated from Prohibition Party discussions as well. Disagreement provided church members with excuses to delay voting Prohibition. A dominant-issue platform would offend no one.[161]

Prohibitionists who supported the single-issue or dominant-issue platform also suggested special subscription prices for the *Voice* to members of the clergy. The state parties in Massachusetts, Illinois, and Tennessee created specialized campaigns directed at church voters. Undoubtedly the decade's spike in emphasis on recruiting from the Protestant churches was lent additional urgency by the fact that radical voters, including well-known partisans like Walter Thomas Mills and Thomas W. Organ, were finding homes within the Populist and Socialist parties, leaving as the only options suicidal fusion with Populists or a pursuit of the elusive Protestant constituency that would of necessity be less radical on economic issues. Blocker has summarized that "not the hope of success but the pressure of Populism, operating on the lever of prohibitionist failure, caused the prohibition movement's shift to the right" in terms of its de-radicalizing agenda.[162]

Even without a leftward turn, there was still room for bold ideas among the narrow-gauge contingent. The new and terrifying specter of ballot exclusion had propelled vague discontent with electoral failure into a full-fledged movement. Narrow-gauge Prohibitionists fused their fears

[159] Blocker, *Retreat from Reform*, 110–111, 115.
[160] Blocker, *Retreat from Reform*, 85–87.
[161] Blocker, *Retreat from Reform*, 74–75, 82.
[162] Blocker, *Retreat from Reform*, 119–121.

about the problems inherent to broad party platforms to their trepidations about the potential liabilities of a political system in which voters had only two platforms from which to choose. Arguing generally against the type of platforms formulated by Democrats and Republicans, narrow-gauge Prohibitionists noted that the breadth of the platforms made these ballots inefficient and often confusing tools for assessing public mandates. A vote for a dry-leaning candidate could just as easily be interpreted as a vote for his position on the tariff, race relations, or a boundary dispute.[163]

To explain why the Prohibition Party must be different from the Democrats or Republicans, these narrow-gauge thinkers provided specific examples of the liabilities of inconsistency within the other parties:

Here is a voter who says "I am a democrat." Can you tell by that declaration what his political principles are? Is he for free silver or for gold? He may be either and yet be a democrat. Here is another who says, "I am a republican." You ask him how he stands of the financial issue. If he lives in an eastern state he will tell you he believes in the gold standard. But if he lives west of the Missouri river he will probably say he believes in the free coinage of silver.

In comparison, Prohibitionists argued that their stance was clear: "Still another says 'I am a prohibitionist.' You don't have to ask him where he stands. You know his political status, his position on a great moral issue. He stands for the overthrow of the liquor traffic in state and nation. And you cannot find a prohibitionist who holds any other views on this important subject."[164]

Without a narrow, minor-party choice to serve as a safety valve for the inherent problems of the Democratic and Republican platform styles, the ability of voters to express themselves to policy makers was severely compromised.[165] Prohibitionists argued that in a political party system

[163] For examples, see "A Remedy for Political Corruption," *Citizen*, 14 June 1894; Untitled, *Voice*, 24 October 1895; Frank H. Arnold, "Why I Am a Prohibitionist," *Citizen*, 4 November 1903; "Prohibition as a Cure," *Voice*, 3 May 1894; Untitled, *Voice*, 6 June 1895; Untitled, *Voice*, 24 October 1895.

[164] "What Are You?" *Lever*, 3 September 1896.

[165] The citizens organizing pressure groups similarly critiqued the two-party system for decoupling legislative policies and voters' preferences. See Elisabeth S. Clemens, *People's Lobby*, 42. These citizens, however, located this problem less in the broad nature of party platforms and more in the alliances of special interests that constituted the party. They emphasized the lack of citizens' power more than the inability of policy makers to discern citizens' intent. Richard L. McCormick suggests that "elections in the United States seldom offered referenda on clear policy choices, and rarely did officials enter office and put through comprehensive programs based on pre-election pledges," in any case; *Party Period and Public Policy*, 15.

dominated by major parties with broad platforms, the single-issue minor party platform was a better, more efficient way for voters to express both their sentiment and the degree of their support for a particular reform. In other words, policy makers would know both what this voter wanted and how much the voter wanted it. Other Americans might also have been frustrated by the un-nuanced type of communication a typical ballot offered. For example, some voters marked their ballots with not one X by the chosen candidate but a series of Xs, as though to convey passionate sentiments that the structure of the ballot was otherwise incapable of recording. If campaigns could not be about the election of particular candidates, perhaps in the age of close elections they could nonetheless determine what issue would be the critical focus of the next campaign. Prohibition Park resident James C. Fernald explained this new interpretation of a Prohibition vote's significance: "Now what is the very utmost and greatest thing Prohibitionists can do in the campaign of 1896? We can not elect a President or a Congress. What can we do? What are we in battle for? We can force Prohibition to the front as a living issue that must and shall count in American politics."[166] Prohibitionists increasingly believed that their party institutions would preserve citizens' abilities to express themselves and to assure the continual injection of new ideas into the national political agenda, regardless of electoral success.

Prohibitionists' ingenuity is perhaps best illuminated when compared to the Populist leaders who failed to prevent institutional collapse. The question of fusing with the Democratic Party in the 1896 presidential election created irreconcilable factions within the Populist Party. Some Populists expected their party to cooperate with a major party they viewed as sufficiently reformed, whereas others wanted to preserve Populists' distinct character and organization. Anti-fusionists optimistically posited that if they could only maintain their institutions, it would ultimately facilitate a Populist renaissance in the next generation.[167] They argued that their policy ambitions – particularly moral revivalism and the elevation of producers – were not fulfilled and remained relevant concerns.[168] When most other policy ambitions were co-opted by the Democrats, however, it became difficult for Populists to justify their party's existence. Under

---

[166] James C. Fernald, "One Plank: Two Spikes," *Voice*, 14 May 1896.
[167] Peter J. Argersinger, *Populism and Politics: William Alfred Peffer and the People's Party* (Lexington: University Press of Kentucky, 1974), 292–294.
[168] These categories of the People's Party legacy are laid out by Michael Kazin in *The Populist Persuasion: An American History* (New York: Basic Books, 1995), 3.

fusionist influence, local and state parties were increasingly reluctant to nominate straight party tickets.[169]

At the same time, Populists were greatly alarmed that new anti-fusionist legislation meant that their decision to nominate the same presidential candidate as the Democrats made their party legally extinct in several states; the Populists would need to petition to secure ballot representation if they wanted to nominate candidates in future elections.[170] In the end, Populists in most states fused with the Democratic Party and thereby mortgaged the organization that might have made future claims on behalf of farmers and political reformers in exchange for the promise of some immediate gains. Benjamin Fay Mills, a popular evangelist, would summarize that the Populist Party had "sold its birthright for a mess of pottage."[171] By endorsing Democratic candidate William Jennings Bryan in the 1896 presidential election, Populists set in motion a series of events that would virtually ensure their disappearance.

Prohibitionists, in turn, were becoming strong advocates for the election reforms once proposed by Populists, including direct legislation, initiative and referendum, proportional representation, and the preferential ballot. Whereas there were only a scattering of cries for these electoral reforms in the early 1890s, by 1894 they were a regular, even weekly, feature in most Prohibition Party publications and showed few signs of abetting. The rapidity with which these cries for electoral reform became universally accepted within the party, moreover, suggested the degree to which Prohibitionists wanted to upset the status quo. Prohibitionists increasingly expressed a sense of liberation from traditional party rituals and looked toward new ways of making politics accessible to citizens.

There is a reason why the Prohibition Party became the longest-living minor party in American history, even if it was never the most successful and even if its access to state ballots declined. In terms of its purpose, the Prohibition Party reconfigured itself to resist political monopolies, or rather a duopoly, without losing any of its anti-liquor fervor. When Prohibitionists could not win a right to appear on ballots, some state and county party organizations encouraged voters to withhold their

---

[169] Lawrence Goodwyn, *The Populist Moment: A Short History of the Agrarian Revolt in America* (New York: Oxford University Press, 1978) includes a pithy description of the fusionist crisis (230–263) and describes the ensuing "deterioration of third party organization" (285).

[170] Argersinger, *Structure, Process, and Party*, 57. See also Argersinger, "'A Place on the Ballot,'" 287–306.

[171] Benjamin Fay Mills, "The New Party," *(Boston) Arena*, January 1899.

participation from the electoral process rather than become complicit in their party's exclusion. In Stockton, California, the city committee recommended "that prohibitionists abstain from voting at the coming city election" given the absence of a Prohibition Party ticket in the field.[172] By 1904, national Prohibitionist newspaper the *Citizen*'s editorial staff would similarly assert that "if our opinion has any weight Prohibitionists will NOT vote in the state election" because a vote for either major party candidate would "give assent to the continuance of present conditions" in Tennessee.[173] Many Prohibitionists grudgingly accepted non-voting as political activism until a better, proactive partisan policy could be developed and thus affirmed a "protest party" identity.

Narrow gaugers' strategy did meet some resistance. Most notably, the broad gaugers used their influence to place Oliver W. Stewart, a future national committee chair, in the position of permanent chair of the 1896 national convention. When a dominant-issue platform was nonetheless passed by the convention, R.S. Thompson, editor of the longtime party periodical *New Era*, secured the floor and asked broad-gauge delegates to meet separately. He was accompanied by a cadre of important leaders including Helen M. Gougar, John P. St. John, and I.O. Pickering, a Civil War veteran who was St. John's former law partner and whose son worked for Funk and Wagnalls.[174] These committed broad-gauge advocates organized as the National Party, formulated a platform, and nominated their own candidates.[175] Gougar would rather bitterly assert that "I left the Prohibition Party when it spit in my face for the crime of being born a woman," a reference to the party's weakening suffrage plank.[176] St. John would simply summarize that "it is time we quit slobbering over the church."[177]

---

[172] Prohibition City Committee of Stockton, California, "Disgusted Prohibitionists," *Lever*, 16 July 1891.

[173] "The Tennessee Situation," *Citizen*, 12 October 1904. See also General Secretary Baer, "Why He Votes Prohibition," *Chicago Defender*, 21 April 1898. For a reader's disagreement with this trend, see "Don't Neglect the Primaries," *Voice*, 26 April 1894.

[174] Testimony as to Pickering's character can be found in Affidavit of William S. Speer, 21 April 1921, File of Isaac O. Pickering, Civil War and Later Pension Records, National Archives in Washington DC. St. John left his law practice in 1882; Blocker, *Retreat from Reform*, 78.

[175] Blocker, *Retreat from Reform*, 115.

[176] Helen Gougar quoted in "Mrs. Gougar as a Critic," *Voice*, 25 June 1896. See also "Mrs. Gougar's Testimony Rebutted," *Voice*, 9 July 1896. Gougar had expressed impatience with the national party since at least 1892; E.J. Wheeler to T.C. Richmond, 7 April 1892, TCRC.

[177] Quoted within Blocker, *Retreat from Reform*, 112.

Broad gaugers had left the party apparatus to the narrow-gauge faction that favored political innovation. It was thus very appropriate that the Prohibition Party's 1896 official ratification of the national convention's nominees for president and vice president took place at Prohibition Park. Both literally and figuratively, the party had been brought to the narrow-gauge idea. At the ratification ceremony, partisans examined past political experiments like the Park for ideas about what political innovations might be most appropriate for their stream-lined party to pursue in the coming decades. Isaac K. Funk confidently spoke to his fellow Prohibitionists: "'I wish to congratulate you that we still have a Prohibition Party.... Such a split as we had at Pittsburg does us good.'"[178] Across the country in Harvey, Illinois, only four people showed up for a National Party meeting.[179]

In some ways, narrow gaugers had come full circle to where the cranks had been a decade before. They declared that "party building is not our work" and that "it matters little what our vote may be" – statements that would have been shocking to the party's founders.[180] No longer believing that electoral victory was imminent, and therefore no longer desperate to retain every vote within its own ranks, party leadership had simply expunged those who wanted to make the Prohibitionists conform to the image of a major party with a broad platform. They explained how the new party was stronger: "It is no longer a divided party" because "it has cut loose forever from those issues which in the past hampered and divided it."[181] A narrow gauger from Prohibition Park agreed that "our weakness has always been that some other issue has preoccupied and distracted the public mind from Prohibition."[182] National chair Samuel Dickie enthusiastically noted that "for the last five years the prohibition party has not been in as hopeful and harmonious a condition as it is today."[183] The Prohibition Party's single-issue focus on prohibition cost the party votes, rather than attracting them, yet most remaining Prohibitionists were strongly committed to this strategy because it helped maintain the distinctiveness of their organization.

[178] "The Campaign Gloriously Begun," *Voice*, 9 July 1896.
[179] Untitled, *Voice*, 16 July 1896.
[180] D.C. Babcock, "Our Business to Elect an Issue," *Voice*, 16 July 1896; "The Present Outlook," *Lever*, 12 November 1896.
[181] "The Present Outlook," *Lever*, 12 November 1896.
[182] James C. Fernald, "No More Side-Track," *Voice*, 2 July 1896. Fernald was still active with the party through at least 1905; "In a Big Blizzard!" *Kansas City Leader*, 12 January 1905. The *Kansas City Leader* was edited by Charles E. Stokes, who was also the state chair.
[183] Samuel Dickie, "Chairman Dickie Interviewed," *Lever*, 4 June 1896.

A narrow platform, its advocates argued, would make the Prohibition Party into a streamlined organization with a clear agenda and clear boundaries of membership, and this would preserve organization during a period of Democratic and Republican attacks on minor parties. Prohibitionists suggested that it was acceptable if "the Prohibition Party emerges from the campaign with a vote probably somewhat diminished" so long as it had "an organization unimpaired, with purpose unshaken."[184] It was not a problem to lose offices if it had none to lose, "so why should we feel disappointed?" so long as "the Prohibition Party has not lost its integrity."[185] Joshua Levering, a prominent Baptist who was the party's 1896 candidate for president, concluded that Prohibitionists were "diminished apparently in numbers, but otherwise stronger, more compact, and in better shape for genuine work than ever before."[186] Dramatically departing from the founders' vision of a party aspiring to assume power by winning elected offices, narrow-gauge Prohibitionists declared that "the strongest party is not always numerically largest."[187]

Fortunately, the same ballot regulations that handicapped the Prohibition Party's attempts to place candidates on new, government-printed ballots also worked for the benefit of the party when these regulations restricted the rival National Party from ballots. Unable to get petitions assembled in a timely manner, and without a past record of voting from which to qualify, the National Party was restricted from the ballot in most localities. Immediately after the split, Prohibitionists worked to ensure that "our rights to a place on the official ballot will be carefully guarded and secured" and to thereby prevent the Nationalists from appropriating credit for past Prohibitionist voting percentages.[188] The government's new role as a ballot gatekeeper also authorized it to resolve factional rivalry, extinguishing one or the other group. Like the regular and National factions of the Prohibition Party, two factions of New York's Socialist Party sought to file candidates in 1896. For them, the situation was made even more complicated because both wanted their nominations to appear under the party's name and emblem. Eventually one faction gained an injunction against the other.[189]

[184] "Eyes Front!" *Voice*, 5 November 1896.
[185] "The Victories of the Prohibition Party," *Voice*, 12 November 1896.
[186] "The Next Wisest Thing to Do," *Voice*, 31 December 1896.
[187] Henry B. Brown, "An After-Election Address," *Voice*, 12 November 1896.
[188] "The Party is All Right," *Lever*, 11 June 1896.
[189] Henry Kuhn and Olive M. Johnson, *The Socialist Labor Party During Four Decades, 1890–1930* (Brooklyn: New York Labor News, 1969), 49, 66.

Although narrow gaugers clearly established their cohort's superiority within the Prohibition Party, their ensuing weak and lack-luster campaign in 1896 nonetheless reflected a decline in national prestige. The party received only 130,000 votes, approximately 0.9 percent of the national vote; this was a substantial drop from the party's 270,000 votes in the 1892 national election.[190]

Partisans in local communities had been confused by the turn of events; in most localities, it was hard enough to create one ticket without worrying about raising a competing ticket as well. In Eau Clair, Wisconsin, for example, the county chair of the Prohibition Party had noted that while "the Prohibs here are all loyal to the old party" and "the Nationals are not in it," it was nonetheless the case that "I don't think that the split will amount to much and we are all wearing Levering buttons" for lack of a National Party candidate.[191] Many Prohibitionists did not even know that the split had occurred; the broad-narrow tension that had dominated the discussion of national leaders had less meaning for widely scattered supporters who simply wanted people to stop drinking.[192]

The National Party suffered from further internal divisions; at least some National partisans returned to the Prohibition Party soon after the split.[193] As a condition of their return, they accepted and legitimized the narrow platform as the party's overriding policy. As for the holdouts, their new home in the National Party would be destabilized by fusion with the Union Reform Party in 1900, which would in turn dissolve by 1901.

* * *

There was a dramatic shift in party ambitions after 1896, but arguably the most important legacy of the narrow-broad split would be legitimization of the unconventional political tactics with which the narrow gaugers had advanced their agenda. An interest in such tactics would persist even as the Prohibition cities faced ongoing challenges.

In 1893, Walter Thomas Mills announced to investors that the Harvey World's Fair Hotel had burned to the ground.[194] By 1895 the Harvey

---

[190] On the 1896 campaign and election, see Blocker, *Retreat from Reform*, 116–121.
[191] "Prohibition News," *Elkhorn Blade*, 7 July 1896.
[192] John Woolley, "Woolley to the Rank and File," *Voice*, 1 October 1896.
[193] "Good News from Michigan," *Voice*, 1 October 1896; "Leave the Nationals," *Lever*, 1 October 1896; A.G. Wolfenbarger, "Wolfenbarger Gives His Reasons," *Voice*, 10 September 1896. Returners trickled back over the course of a decade. For example, Untitled, *Patriot Phalanx*, 28 July 1904.
[194] Circular letter from Walter Thomas Mills to Friend (T.C. Richmond), 10 January 1893, TCRC.

Land Company had changed hands several times, and there were indications that the newest head of the association did not intend to reclaim property from prohibition violators.[195] Blocked by a non-Prohibitionist mayor who had been elected on a fusion ticket, Harvey's Prohibitionists were initially unable to obtain a vote to create local option.[196]

However, the city remained a hotbed for the politics of everyday and family life. Prohibitionist women began to reenact the Women's Crusade; this time about seventy women, under the leadership of *Harvey Citizen* editor Lucy Page Gaston, went a step further by tearing down any saloons that dared to open on the border of town.[197] Appealing to the Cook County superior court, Harvey's more restrained Prohibitionists eventually won a case that validated the legitimacy of their title deeds.[198] Gaston then sued several individuals who attempted to open liquor-selling establishments.[199] Various rulings supported and challenged previous decisions, and the official legal status of the deeds was deeply contested throughout the 1890s by Prohibitionist residents, a national audience of financial and partisan supporters, and these groups' rivals in Harvey.[200] Prohibitionists proudly publicized this struggle.

Not quite discretely enough, Walter Thomas Mills would continue pursuing profit among another clientele of idealists. On becoming a Socialist in the late 1890s – he would help found the American Socialist Party in 1901 – Mills entered into a series of ventures resembling the Harvey misfire. He not infrequently angered other Socialists, one of whom accused

---

195 "Prohibition Harvey in Danger," *Voice*, 22 August 1895.
196 "Harvey Citizens Not Permitted to Vote on License," *Voice*, 5 September 1895; "As the World Goes," *Voice*, 26 September 1895.
197 "Harvey Gives Up to Rum," *Lever*, 8 August 1895; "Women's Crusade in Harvey," *Lever*, 29 August 1895.
198 "Forever a Prohibition City," *Voice*, 28 November 1895.
199 "To Test Harvey's Deeds," *Lever*, 24 October 1895; "Bound Not to Have Them," *Lever*, 5 December 1895; "Object to Saloons in Harvey," *Lever*, 26 December 1895. Gaston had previously solved the problem of a saloon immediately east of the land association property by annexing the property to Harvey; Hutchison, "Capitalism, Religion, and Reform," 202. Lucy Page Gaston later became a prominent leader of the national anti-cigarette campaign. See Keller, *Regulating a New Society*, 115. Keller notes that Gaston's appearance strongly resembled Abraham Lincoln's, perhaps not the most flattering praise. It seems likely that Lucy Page Gaston was related to Edward Page Gaston, also of Harvey, who often gave addresses on Christian citizenship and was an officer of the National Christian Citizenship League; "Christian Citizenship," *Lever*, 7 May 1896.
200 "Harvey's Fight Against Saloons," *Lever*, 30 January 1896; "Victory for Harvey," *Lever*, 2 April 1896; "No More Saloons for Harvey," *Voice*, 2 April 1896. For a description of these events, also see Hutchison, "Capitalism, Religion, and Reform," 202–203.

him of setting up fraudulent colony schemes in Michigan, at "Comrade Yates' farm," and in Kansas City, as well as several fraudulent cooperative schooling ventures.[201] A whiff of not just ambition but dishonesty would plague Mills' post-Harvey enterprises. Even in 1893, bitter stockholders in the Harvey Hotel complained that Mills had invested with money from the Mutual Home Improvement Company, and they felt entitled to a share of the insurance settlement that was not forthcoming. At least one angry stockholder declared that he would vote with the Republicans in the future.[202]

Harriman continued to face challenges throughout the decade, including the ETLC's bankruptcy in 1893, a tornado that pillaged the downtown area in 1896, and a smallpox epidemic that struck Roane County in 1900.[203] Even John St. John lost hope and tried to sell his property in 1899.[204] Lawsuits plagued the ETCL's founders, whose business practices the courts mocked and condemned.[205] Later Prohibitionists, recalling this embarrassment, would dismiss as "schemes" the attempts "for colonizing Prohibitionists in Georgia and at Harriman, Tenn., and Harvey, Ill. and others like."[206] Such remembering left the impression that the ETLC was a pitiable failure, even as Harriman's residents optimistically struggled onward.

Encouraging incidents were not hard to find. In 1903, national secretary James Tate moved to Harriman to become chair of Tennessee's party committee and assume the chancellorship of American University. Tate built upon the *Harriman Advance*'s legacy by founding the *Citizen* as a new national organ. Prohibitionists nationwide continued to recognize

---

[201] Thomas J. Moran, "Walter Thomas Mills – His Record," from the *(Seattle) Socialist*, 2 November 1907, reprinted at http://www.marxisthistory.org/history/usa/parties/spusa/1907/1102-morgan-walterthomasmills.pdf (accessed 1 June 2012). On Mill's University in Pembroke Township, Illinois, see the *Illinois Steward*, http://web.extension.illinois.edu/illinoissteward/openarticle.cfm?ArticleID=442 (accessed 1 June 2012).

[202] J.E. (Illegible) to T.C. Richmond, 14 November 1893, TCRC.

[203] Pulliam, *Harriman*, 111; Untitled, *(Kingston) East Tennessean*, 29 December 1900. Harriman was also hit hard by the influenza epidemic in 1918, which left its funeral homes too full to accommodate all the corpses, and by the Big Flood of 1929 that immediately preceded the national depression.

[204] John St. John to I.K. Funk, 20 April 1899, John P. St. John Collection Letter Press Book 1889 (#4), JSJC.

[205] For some particularly rich examples, see Central Trust Co. of New York v. East Tennessee Land Co. (1895); Central Trust Co. of New York v. East Tennessee Land Com. et al.; Schumacher et al. v. Same (1902); East Tennessee Land Company v. Joseph R. Leeson, Same v. John Hopewell, Jr. (1903, 1904).

[206] Jasper S. Hughes, "Our Coming Conference," *Patriot Phalanx*, 27 December 1912.

Harriman as an exciting partisan experiment because of its affiliation with the *Citizen* and the paper's cohort of supporters, including national committee chair Oliver W. Stewart, Frank Wheeler, and former chair and future Albion College president Samuel Dickie.[207] Between 1903 and 1905, Stewart frequently visited Harriman on speaking tours and used his position to provide the *Citizen* with contracts for national campaign materials. The paper's editorial staff also developed Harriman's role in partisan politics by running A.A. Hopkins's feature on life "Outside the Sanctum." The very title of this travel series suggested to readers that Harriman was the sacred center of prohibition ideals and everything else was literally and figuratively peripheral.

Word of Harriman continued to permeate other party periodicals into the new century. Indiana's *Patriot Phalanx* would describe Harriman as a proud city of 4,500 people and with "brighter prospects than for some years" in 1904. Citizens protected the dry standing of their town by forming a Prohibition Alliance to stamp out violations, including the sale of "'medicine,' which it soon became evident was being used as a beverage."[208] Whereas nearby Cardiff disintegrated, Harriman's citizens prepared to embrace the statewide prohibition that would come to Tennessee in 1909.[209]

Overall, Prohibitionists' continuing investment in Harriman and other Prohibition cities expressed their desire to become "at once 'the bane and antidote' of partyism": capable of protecting the integrity of the American party system by doing politics in a dramatically different style.[210] A cynical political observer might well note that there were few other options. The combined impact of decades of electoral defeat and new electoral regulations that removed minor parties from the ballot created too many hardships for Prohibitionists in many states to maintain conventional campaigns. Whereas a conservative, dominant-issue platform was the most practical option for constituency building, party leadership

---

[207] On Samuel Dickie, see A.A. Stevens, "Samuel Dickie: An Appreciative Tribute from one of the Able Leader's Comrades," *New Voice*, 18 April 1901.

[208] Untitled, *Patriot Phalanx*, 14 January 1904. On the same page of the newspaper where this article appears, there is also a second article entitled "Sustains Reversion Clause in Deed" that describes a ruling by Nebraska's supreme court to uphold title deeds, demanding the reversion of property to the original owner if liquor is sold on site. This ruling also ordered that if the original owner was deceased, the heirs could inherit the property.

[209] Shelley and Hall, eds., *Valley of Challenge and Change*, 65.

[210] John Woolley, "Woolley Speaks for the Party," *Voice*, 11 June 1896.

had simultaneously committed the party to an innovative political style in which elections were not necessarily the main focus.

And whatever became of Harriman? It persists as a lively community of 6,350 citizens. Now with less industry, it nonetheless includes a carefully preserved downtown area and historic residential district. A local monument to "The Town that Temperance Built" reminds residents of their community's original purpose. The first liquor store opened in 1993.

6

Strenuous Bodies

In 1900 Henry Metcalf, the Prohibitionist vice-presidential candidate, gave a rather stilted speech. About the recent national convention, Metcalf summarized that "it was a body of men and women, every one of them was a devotee of the strenuous life imbued with a degree of strenuosity such as the somewhat theatrical herald of that order of merit never dreamed of." Metcalf used the word "strenuous" nine more times to describe his partisan peers. They were "strenuous for righteousness, however unpopular, strenuous for duty at what ever cost. Strenuous for humanity toward all of God's children, of whatever race or clime. Strenuous to defend brother man against tyranny, under whatever guise. Strenuous for the protection of wives and children against those machinations of greed that convert husbands and fathers into brutes."[1]

Metcalf's emphasis on being strenuous must first be understood as an attempt to capture reflected glory at a moment when the party had few other avenues for drawing notice. Vice President Theodore Roosevelt had recently delivered an address entitled "The Strenuous Life," which had introduced a new phrase into the vernacular because it expressed widespread hopes and anxieties. In contrast, the general public was becoming indifferent to the Prohibition Party. Prohibitionists' falling profile emerged as a substantial problem in the wake of the 1896 election, wherein party realignment triggered a decline in interparty competition between Democrats and Republicans.[2] The observations of one

---

[1] "Told of His Nomination," *New York Tribune*, 26 July 1900.
[2] Republican hold on the American North was largely uncontested after 1896, as was Democratic control of the South. According to Richard L. McCormick, less than a third

Congregationalist contributor about conditions in New Hampshire were echoed around the country: "While power was nearly evenly divided between the leading parties . . . the Prohibition vote was not to be lightly regarded; but it is now a question whether the dominant party cannot get along without the friends of temperance and do what it may please with the law."[3] Prohibitionists would come to ponder the comparative advantages of being hated, as they had been in 1884, rather than simply ignored. An ignored party could not build a constituency, nor could it effectively protest.

In the late 1890s and first years of the twentieth century, Prohibitionists remained on the margins of political respectability, with only a tenuous hold on electoral participation, and were frequently overlooked as participants in wider public debates. They tried to maintain their relevancy just as several transformations in the political environment further undermined them. Prohibitionists would need to simultaneously react to the apparently diminished power of the anti-liquor movement they claimed to spearhead, the backlash against women in politics, and the development of new educational and advertising styles. Of greatest importance for party leaders was the matter of how to ensure partisans' commitment even when severed – or perhaps liberated – from the responsibilities of governance.

Prohibitionists reacted to changes not of their own making, seizing on the language and ideal of *strenuousness* to define theirs as a vigorous partisan community that demanded consideration. They proved most successful when using strenuous discourse to raise awareness about abstaining, an accomplishment deftly achieved through the coordination of dry consumers to solicit total abstainer life insurance policies. Such policies publicized the health consequences of alcohol consumption and conveyed an impression that abstainers were the most strenuous citizens. Other attempts to define a strenuous political femininity and reclaim the vitality of spectacular politics were certainly ambitious, if at

---

of Americans lived in states where elections were closely contested; *Party Period and Public Policy*, 177. American citizens' indifference to the Prohibition Party might be interpreted as part of a trend of mounting indifference to partisan politics, as highlighted in McGerr, *Decline of Popular Politics*. On the importance of unstable political alignments for catalyzing anti-liquor advocacy, see Szymanski, *Pathways to Prohibition*. Whereas the Anti-Saloon League would eventually become adept at exploiting factionalization within parties, the Prohibition Party – as a partisan outsider – would not; Szymanski, *Pathways to Prohibition*, 143, 146.

[3] E.B., "Prohibition in the State," *(Boston, MA) Congregationalist*, 1 June 1899.

times clumsily executed. The nascent tensions between men and women, and between grass roots and national leadership, that these endeavors revealed would profoundly shape the party's experience in the coming century.

* * *

In 1898 delegates to the International Temperance Congress held at Prohibition Park, Staten Island, boldly resolved "to bring the leading life insurance companies to acknowledge publicly, what they admit privately, that total abstainers are at least twenty per cent. safer risks than moderate drinkers, and then to take the further logical step to grant these total abstainers the benefit of their abstemious habits in lower insurance."[4] Just two years later, Prohibition Party leaders such as Samuel Dickie, Henry Faxon, Joshua Levering, Silas C. Swallow, and Isaac K. Funk united with Populist William Peffer, Anti-Saloon League president Hiram Price, and other ministers and reformers to petition the Equitable Life Assurance Society of the United States to create a special class of insurance for abstainers.[5] Still divided on matters of political strategy, a diverse group of anti-liquor leaders recognized their common interest in lower costs.

The Equitable had been the world's largest insurance company since 1886, and the creation of a temperance class by this company in 1900 might not only reward abstainers but inspire large numbers of Americans to purer habits.[6] The Security Mutual Life Insurance Company and the Security Trust and Life Insurance Company quickly followed the Equitable's lead.[7] Thus even though there was not a dramatic increase in the number of companies offering dry life insurance – there were at least 5 to 10 providers offering dry life insurance at any point between 1890 and 1905, from among the 100 or so industrial life insurance companies and several hundred fraternal and assessment providers – temperance advocates could be gratified by a significant increase in the size and status of

---

[4] "Lines of Temperance Work," *Friends' Intelligencer*, 14 May 1898.

[5] "Temperance and Life Insurance," *New Voice*, 11 August 1904. Henry Faxon also belonged to the Anti-Saloon League, working with Howard Hyde Russell in 1896–1897 to hire detectives for enforcing liquor laws in Massachusetts; Hamm, *Shaping the Eighteenth Amendment*, 147.

[6] On the Equitable's growth, see Morton Keller, *The Life Insurance Enterprise, 1855–1910: A Study in the Limits of Corporate Power* (Cambridge: The Belknap Press of Harvard University Press, 1963), 16–17; R. Carlyle Buley, *The Equitable Life Assurance Society* (New York: Appleton-Century-Crofts, 1959).

[7] "Stamp the Fake to Death," *New Voice*, 16 October 1902; Advertisement, *New Voice*, 26 November 1903; "Temperance and Life Insurance," *New Voice*, 11 August 1904.

the companies offering such insurance.[8] Industrial insurance companies'
new level of attention to dry clients emerged just as assessment-based
insurance, which assessed living policy holders at the time of a fraternal
brother or fellow client's death, was stumbling under the weight of too
many claims and too few young members.[9]

Moreover, a relationship with corporate America was extremely
important for the anti-liquor movement because it bestowed some prestige during a period of seeming decline. State amendment campaigns
ended in defeat and eventually petered out. Even in Kansas, wherein state
prohibition remained the law, there was a general laxity of enforcement
at both the state and local levels that one historian has described as a
"headlong retreat."[10] Local option successes suggested the movement's
strength but remained relatively underreported, leaving an impression of
"apparent futility." The anti-liquor movement was unable to capture the
distaste for saloons articulated by Americans in numerous editorials and
at revivals.[11]

It was nonetheless surprising that dry advocates chose to focus on,
of all commodities, life insurance. Just a few years before, the directors and 5,327 clients of the Total Abstinence Life Association (TALA)
had been devastated by bankruptcy because their company had overin-
vested in East Tennessee Land Company bonds.[12] Land company secretary A.A. Hopkins had spent much of 1893 asking TALA directors to stall

---

[8] Creating a comprehensive list of these providers is very difficult, but in the course of my
research through industry encyclopedias, industry yearbooks, and the Prohibition press,
the following companies and societies definitely met the criteria of being dry companies
or having a dry department at some point in their history: Eagle Life and Health Insurance Company, American Temperance Life Insurance Company, Temperance Mutual
Benefit Association, Sons of Temperance National Mutual Relief Society, National Temperance Relief Union, Royal Templars of Temperance, Temperance Benevolent Association, American Temperance Life Insurance Association of New York, Portland Temperance Reform Club, Total Abstinence Life Association, Mutual Reserve Fund, Young
Men's Protestant Temperance and Benevolent Society, American Union Life Insurance
Company, Catholic Temperance and Benefit Association, Temperance and General Life
Assurance Company, Security Mutual Life Insurance Company, Security Trust and Life
Insurance Company, The Equitable, Standard Life Insurance Company of America, and
National Temperance Life. Fraternal insurance was not without prestige related to the
ideals of self-sufficiency joined to mutualism, but industrial insurance's prestige was
related to ostensible mastery of the marketplace.

[9] David T. Beito, *From Mutual Aid to the Welfare State: Fraternal Societies and Social
Services, 1890–1967* (Chapel Hill: University of North Carolina Press, 2000), 131–136.

[10] Bader, *Prohibition in Kansas*, 118.

[11] Pegram, *Battling Demon Rum*, 109–111.

[12] "Want a New Company," *Chicago Daily Tribune*, 17 August 1893.

repayment, only to have both companies drown in the process.[13] Although non-Prohibitionists held the top positions, Prohibitionist executive board members A.J. Jutkins, Walter Thomas Mills, and T.C. Richmond – each involved with various land enterprises – had perhaps been too eager in promoting the ETLC as an investment.[14] Other Prohibitionist executive board members such as editor J.A. Van Fleet, national chair Samuel Dickie, Good Templar organizer John Sobieski, orator George W. Bain, and national party secretary Samuel D. Hastings certainly shared in the responsibility. At stake in these enterprises was "the good name of Prohibition," for if the party's leadership came to be viewed as self-serving and corrupt, the entire movement could be dismissed.[15]

Jonathan Willis, a Prohibitionist voter and client, lost faith in the party when the Total Abstinence Life Association took his money. Claiming to have purchased a policy from the TALA rather than some other company because he thought the Prohibition Party leaders serving as directors were the "salt of the earth," Willis announced his disenchantment.

Now if I had put my money in the hands of the saloon men or any such characters I would not have been surprised at such doings. However I find that the difference between the saloon men and those who have so much to say against them are not much difference.... Now my faith is to be shook up by finding out that we did not know the hearts of such men as we had been ... voting for.

Willis concluded that

now I will wait and see if said good (?) men are going to send me back my money, or will they be like all the rest of mankind: dishonest. If I get my money all well and good. But I will not lose it and keep quiet. If I lose it I shall never vote a Prohib. ticket again.[16]

---

[13] A.A. Hopkins to T.C. Richmond, 23 August 1893, TCRC.

[14] "Insurance News," *Chicago Daily Tribune*, 11 April 1893. Advertisements for the ETLC and TALA sometimes appeared side by side in the party press. For example, see *Voice*, 16 October 1890. TALA president William Singleton also served as a reference for the Women's Land Syndicate of South Waukegan, Illinois, a position he shared with Prohibitionist Jason Hobbs, Esther Pugh (treasurer of the national WCTU), and Caroline Byell (secretary of the national WCTU). Previous to the Total Abstinence Life Association, the New York Accident Insurance Company (president: Clinton Fisk) had also appealed to Prohibitionists in national party papers, albeit without offering a particular program for dry clients. See an advertisement in the *Voice*, 4 July 1889. Fisk seems to have been rather promiscuous in his endorsements, recommending to readers an emulsion for weight gain before moving on to join the Harriman boosters in 1890; Advertisement, *Voice*, 30 January 1890.

[15] A.A. Hopkins to T.C. Richmond, 23 August 1893, TCRC.

[16] Jonathan G. Willis to T.C. Richmond, 24 November 1892, TCRC.

Willis was angry and promised vengeance, but other clients faced tragedy. As TALA was spiraling downward, E.P Huntington was on his deathbed. His pastor wrote to TALA director T.C. Richmond to express alarm that Huntington's policy had just been canceled. Huntington was a party newspaper editor and might well have broadcast news of his abandonment had he been able, but he was nonetheless denied any coverage.[17]

Quite unlike the Total Abstinence Life Association, the life insurance companies offering total abstinence insurance in the new century rarely emphasized any common moral or political ground with their potential policy holders. To modern thinkers, this might seem like a missed opportunity. No fear of alienating drinking customers could come into play when the advertising copy appeared in dry newspapers such as the *Voice*, the National Temperance Society's *National Advocate*, or Methodist-targeted publications. And it is not as though the tactic of appealing to group identity was unprecedented; consider the significant role that appeals to racial pride played in how African-American assessment-based life insurance companies marketed to their clients.[18] In contrast, the new Equitable advertisements that started appearing in the *Voice* after the company's total abstinence policy premiered did not even publicize that a total abstainer policy existed. At no point did the most solicitous companies – American Temperance Life Insurance Association, the Mutual Reserve Fund, the Security Mutual Life Insurance Company, the Security Trust and Life Insurance Company, and the Equitable – claim that their managers were universally dry or that they favored legal prohibition.[19]

There are two likely reasons for life insurance companies' reluctance to engage in fiery pro-prohibition rhetoric. First, companies offering total abstinence policies sought to convey their conformity with the overall marketing and investment strategies of their industry. As befitting companies offering products to cover a lifetime, life insurance companies tended to emphasize the long-term point of view over the routine upheavals of election cycles in their marketing materials.

[17] T.J. Snodgras to T.C. Richmond, 6 October 1893, TCRC; William Singleton to T.C. Richmond, 11 October 1893, TCRC.

[18] Robert C. Puth, "Supreme Life: The History of a Negro Life Insurance Company, 1919–1962," *Business History Review* 43 (Spring 1969): 4–6; C(arter) G. Woodson, "Insurance Business Among Negroes," *Journal of Negro History* 14 (April 1929): 202–226; Walter B. Weare, *Black Business in the New South: A Social History of the North Carolina Mutual Life Insurance Company* (1973; repr. Durham, NC: Duke University Press, 1993); Beito, *From Mutual Aid to the Welfare State*, 36–42.

[19] On the drinking habits of ATLIA staff, see "American Temperance Life Insurance Association," *Insurance Times*, May 1903.

Second, companies adding total abstinence departments generally found themselves modifying procedures that had more or less been in place for decades. Few of the companies established since the 1840s had been willing to grant policies to individuals perceived as drunkards, and some penalized moderate drinkers. This was less from a conviction that alcohol was intrinsically dangerous than from the fact that one's drinking habits indicated a series of other potential problems, including death through accidents, brawling, and capital punishment.[20] From the business principle of refusing to grant policies to drunkards, the creation of total abstinence policies was a small step. Fundamentally, there were no path-breaking marketing pitches because the product itself was not radically new, at least from insurance companies' points of view.

If *Voice* readers bought dry life insurance policies – and the decade-long runs of these advertisements both before and after the Equitable's policy invention suggests that at least some did – they were hardly dupes. Prohibitionists were at least in part responding to a change wherein health and vitality had emerged as the hallmarks of good citizenship. In "The Strenuous Life" Roosevelt condemned "ignoble ease" and urged American men to develop "those virile qualities necessary to win in the stern strife of actual life." Roosevelt's immediate objective was to commit Americans to advancing imperialism in Puerto Rico, Cuba, the West Indies, and the Philippines, with an eye to other interests. However, because physical health ensured power, Americans must prepare themselves for battle. To a great extent the strenuous life became equated with an ability to be forceful, as is intriguingly suggested by a 1902 *Washington Post* advertisement for a patent medicine relieving constipation. Publicized under

[20] "A Misleading Statement," *Christian Advocate*, 7 February 1889. For example, see "The Science of Health: Alcohol and Longevity," *Phrenological Journal and Science of Health*, August 1896. Such a policy of discriminating against imbibers was also the norm in England among the Lancashire and Yorkshire Accident Insurance Company, the Accident Insurance Company, the British Empire Mutual Insurance Company, and the Emperor Life Assurance Company; "Alcohol and Death-Rates," *Medical and Surgical Reporter*, 6 February 1892, reprinted from the *British Medical Journal*; "Temperance and Longevity," *Scientific American*, 8 December 1883, reprinted from the *Lancet*. See also Sharon Ann Murphy, *Investing in Life: Insurance in Antebellum America* (Baltimore, MD: Johns Hopkins University Press, 2010), 55–56. On fraternal orders' refusal of membership and its life insurance benefits to drunkards and sometimes anyone affiliated with the liquor trade, see Beito, *From Mutual Aid to the Welfare State*, 9, 35, 45. The *National Freeman* also pointed to the irony that at least one Kentucky-based insurance company would insure whiskey as a commodity, but considered it a poor investment to grant a fire insurance policy to the consumer himself; Untitled, *National Freeman*, May 1881.

the title "The Strenuous Life," the advertisement described straining at the toilet with humorous effect.[21]

Without ever abandoning moral arguments, the temperance movement gradually shifted emphasis to alcohol's health-depleting consequences.[22] The WCTU's Department of Scientific Temperance Instruction (STI) and the Scientific Temperance Association, for example, began on a small scale in 1880 and triumphed by 1901, when every state required scientific temperance instruction.[23] Department head Mary Hunt claimed that it had become a "misconception" to think of temperance as a "moral question" instead of a "scientific" matter.[24] This was perhaps an overstatement, for the moral argument remained quite vibrant and the health argument had been reputable since Benjamin Rush's treatise in 1805, but Hunt's claim nonetheless illustrates the exuberance with which anti-liquor reformers embraced a scientific rationale.[25]

The most important idea introduced by STI was that total abstainers were healthier than drinkers because alcohol was a poison. As with other poisons, discussion of moderate consumption was preposterous.[26] So profound was the effect of alcohol on the human body, anti-liquor advocates argued, that it was theoretically possible that one parent's drunkenness at the time of conception could damage the quality of offspring, and childhood tippling could lead to "retarded growths and imperfections of development."[27] Only a lifetime of abstaining could counterbalance such

---

[21] "The Strenuous Life," *Washington Post*, 24 September 1902.

[22] For example, see Bader, *Prohibition in Kansas*, 161.

[23] Ruth Clifford Engs, "Scientific Temperance Federation," in *Alcohol and Temperance in Modern History: An International Encyclopedia*, eds. Jack S. Blocker, Jr., David M. Fahey, and Ian R. Tyrrell, vol. 2 (Santa Barbara, CA: ABC-Clio, 2003), 545–546. On the history of Scientific Temperance Education, see Jonathan Zimmerman, *Distilling Democracy: Alcohol Education in America's Public Schools, 1880–1925* (Lawrence: University Press of Kansas, 1999). Prohibitionists involved with STI included Amanda Way and Fanny Rastall.

[24] Mary Hunt, "A Moral or Scientific Question?" *New Voice*, 5 May 1904.

[25] Benjamin Rush, "The Effect of Ardent Spirits Upon Man" (1805). Rush was a physician and had signed the Declaration of Independence. For a history of alcohol regulation as a movement to protect public health, see Mark Lawrence Schrad, "The First Social Policy: Alcohol Control and Modernity in Policy Studies," *Journal of Policy History* 19:4 (2007): 428–458.

[26] "Temperance and Life Insurance," *New Voice*, 11 August 1904, reprinted from Thomas Whittaker, "Alcohol Beverages and Longevity," *Contemporary Review*, March 1904. See also Monroe, ed., *Journal of the General Conference of the Methodist Episcopal Church . . . 1888*, 457.

[27] On recapitulation and Lamarkian theories of evolution, see Carl Degler, *In Search of Human Nature: The Decline and Revival of Darwinism in American Social Thought* (New York: Oxford University Press, 1991), 4–47. See also T.D. Crothers, "How Does the Moderate Use of Alcohol Affect Longevity?" *New Voice*, 11 August 1904; this was

a congenital inheritance, and thus lengthen the term of life. Moreover, argued STI textbooks and pamphlets, "moderation" was merely an intermediate status on the way to what modern people would call *alcoholism*; it was a question of where one was located on the path, not in what direction it went. Such arguments resonated well across many regions. In the American South, evangelicals increasingly argued that "there was no middle ground between the teetotaler and the drunkard" and that no one had the ability to drink "responsibly."[28]

STI advocates and Southern evangelicals thereby challenged the widely held idea that some consumption made moderate drinkers the most vigorous class, healthier (and presumably longer living) than either drunkards or total abstainers. Most nineteenth-century Americans who defined themselves as moderate drinkers owned medicines with high alcohol content or consumed a daily dram for the sake of health as well as sociability. As individuals and in religious contexts, American Jews, for example, sometimes asserted that their moderate and sacramental consumption – and relatively low rates of drunkenness – demonstrated that the substance itself was not inherently harmful and that "American Jews could serve as a model of the rational, self-mastered citizen." *Life* magazine would agree and further suggested that Jews' consistent but sparing use of alcohol probably explained their good digestion.[29] Such ideas were popularly reinforced by brewery advertisements describing beer as a food, a tonic, and a digestive aid.[30] A prestigious national study group, the Committee of Fifty, kept alive the notion that moderate drinking was not inherently dangerous and recommended modification of STI curriculum.[31]

Unfortunately, the critical eye that dry advocates used when evaluating the claims of brewers was missing when they examined their new corporate partner. As a whole Prohibitionists did not challenge the life insurance industry's customary stance that it stood for the protection of widows and orphans and was as philanthropic as it was profitable; life insurance corporations claimed to be more about redistribution than

---

originally a paper read before the Association of Medical Directors of Life Insurance Companies. See also Richard Fidler, "Health, Heredity, and Physical Culture," originally presented before the YMCA, reprinted in *Patriot Phalanx*, 7 March 1901. These ideas persisted for decades; "How Alcohol Effects the Generations," *National Enquirer*, 8 November 1917.

[28] Coker, *Liquor in the Land of the Lost Cause*, 39.

[29] Marni Davis, "'No Whisky Amazons in the Tents of Israel': American Jews and the Gilded Age Temperance Movement," *American Jewish History* 94 (September 2008): 155, 151.

[30] For examples, see Isaac, *Prohibition and Politics*, 134.

[31] Bordin, *Woman and Temperance*, 137; Bader, *Prohibition in Kansas*, 100.

capital accumulation.[32] Prohibitionists' deliberate blindness or naivety about the purpose of life insurance companies seems to have existed at least until New York's Armstrong Investigation issued its 1905 report, a document that would implicate the Equitable and other life insurance companies in unsavory banking practices and the widespread bribery of Republican office holders.[33]

However, before judging the anti-liquor movement too harshly, one should consider the extent to which life insurance companies could provide a service that dry reformers could not provide for themselves. For all of anti-liquor advocates' bravado, abstainers' critics could note that there had been no persuasive, highly publicized, large-scale study comparing the health consequences of moderate consumption and abstinence. Instead, throughout the 1890s and 1900s, the most commonly cited statistical basis for insurance discrimination against moderate drinkers was a single data set produced by a British company: the United Kingdom Temperance and General Provident Institution of London. The company insisted that clients in their temperance section lived as much as 20 percent longer than moderate drinkers, a claim that was repeated by the American press for at least a decade and a half.[34] This source was relentlessly cited despite the fact that American insurance companies had not relied on British actuary tables for decades; the British had a lower life expectancy, and so the statistics were not generally accepted as interchangeable.[35]

---

[32] On the evolution from commodity production to capitalism and the role of capital accumulation in this process, see Richard Schneirov, "Thoughts on Periodizing the Gilded Age: Capital Accumulation, Society, and Politics, 1873–1898," *Journal of the Gilded Age and Progressive Era* 5 (June 2006): 189–224. On how the life insurance industry customarily explained its business and its purpose, see Viviana A. Rotman Zelizer, *Morals and Markets: The Development of Life Insurance in the United States* (New York: Columbia University Press, 1979); Murphy, *Investing in Life*; Keller, *Life Insurance Enterprise.*

[33] On Americans' recognition that corporations were corrupt, and that they corrupted politics in turn, see McCormick, "The Discovery that Business Corrupts Politics," 247–274. McCormick dates this transformation as occurring between 1904 and 1908.

[34] "Temperance Notes," *Friends' Review,* 9 May 1889; "Alcohol and Death Rates," *(Philadelphia) Medical and Surgical Reporter,* 6 February 1892; "The Science of Health: Alcohol and Longevity," *Phrenological Journal and Science of Health,* August 1896; "Temperance and Life Insurance," *New Voice,* 11 August 1904; T.D. Crothers, "How Far Does the Moderate Use of Alcohol Affect Longevity," *New Voice,* 11 August 1904; "Total Abstinence and Longevity," *Watchman,* 18 August 1904; "Total Abstinence and Life Insurance," *(Philadelphia) The Friend: A Religious and Literary Journal,* 6 May 1905.

[35] Keller, *Life Insurance Enterprise,* 60. On the deficit of precise actuarial data, see also Weare, *Black Business in the New South,* 15, 68, and 85.

In the 1880s and 1890s the anti-liquor movement had substituted carefully selected anecdotes conveyed in fiction and journalism for objective data. Magazine and newspaper articles routinely suggested that a drunkard could be spotted not only by his trail of morally irresponsible acts but also by how he walked uncertainly, burped and urinated without control, and then languidly passed out. A drunkard's body was defined by a loss of volition; his swerving form was evidence of an invasion of the drinker's body and will.[36] The drunkard was, above all, predictably yet spontaneously suicidal. Even someone as apparently vigorous as Thomas Kennay, a lifeguard who had rescued many from drowning, would contemplate a preposterous death by jumping down a manhole after a two-day drinking spree.[37] When anecdote was insufficient to make their point, anti-liquor advocates tended to assert that alcohol's disabling effects were well documented by "science," only rarely explaining which "scientific" authorities were being referenced. Idaho Methodists, for example, resolved in 1892 that "science, experience, and the Bible" all advised total abstaining, without further elaboration.[38]

In acknowledging that life insurance companies were the best authorities to determine whether or not moderate drinking was perilous, the anti-liquor movement merely modified the tactics of other reformers. They switched the expertise of social scientists for that of capitalists.[39] In the willingness of life insurance companies to sell to total abstainers at a discount, even before actuarial charts could be revised, Prohibitionists and other temperance advocates found the reputable expertise the party and other dry advocates had been missing. Presidential candidate Silas C. Swallow would declare in the *North American Review* that the fact that "many life-insurance companies make a special premium for abstainers" proved that alcohol's problematic nature had become widely accepted.[40] In 1904, a *New Voice* multipage spread and ancillary articles praised the total abstinence life insurance idea.[41]

---

[36] Parsons, *Manhood Lost*, 18–52.

[37] "Of Course," *Voice*, 16 July 1891.

[38] H.K. Hines, ed., *Official Journal of the Ninth Session of the Idaho Annual Conference of the Methodist Episcopal Church Held at Payette, Idaho, August 11th to 15th, 1892* (Portland, OR: James A. Hines, 1892), 25.

[39] On the history of social science expertise, see Thomas Haskell, *The Emergence of Professional Social Science: The American Social Science Association and the Nineteenth-Century Crisis of Authority* (Urbana: University of Illinois Press, 1977).

[40] Silas Swallow, "Prohibition – Why?" *North American Review*, October 1904. See also Silas Swallow, "If a Prohibitionist Were President," *Leslie's Monthly Magazine*, November 1904.

[41] *New Voice*, "Temperance and Life Insurance," 11 August 1904.

Anti-liquor advocates might have found ways to discount the evidence of life insurance actuaries if the gradually emerging data had not supported their policy agenda. This was not the case, however. The anti-liquor argument against moderate drinking was "robbed of its thunder by the dispassionate figures of the actuary," but Prohibitionists were generally supportive of actuaries' conclusions. After reading the summaries of actuarial reports included in Associated Press materials, partisan Prohibitionists probably resented the implication that the new evidence was important because it was "free from the prejudice which stultifies most of the Prohibition literature." They nonetheless concluded that

the actuaries' figures and the [Associated Press] conclusions that accompany this disparagement are the strongest proof of the correctness of the Prohibitionist's argument that could possibly be asked for. These newly arrived at conclusions of the insurance statistician are the most remarkable fact as to the relation of the moderate drinker to longevity and the expectation of life yet brought to light.[42]

To hear Prohibitionists tell of it, actuaries had confirmed that abstainers were the most strenuous of all citizens.

* * *

Turn-of-the-century Americans came to view "physical strength and strength of character as the same thing" and shared a rising conviction that "the body did not *contain* the man, expressing the man within; now, that body *was* the man."[43] As interpreted by historian Gail Bederman, these assumptions greatly influenced the interpretive path favored by Roosevelt's audience. "The Strenuous Life" initially "preached the virtues

---

[42] "Insurance Deserts the Tippler," *New Voice*, 20 December 1904.

[43] E. Anthony Rotundo, *American Manhood: Transformations in Masculinity from the Revolution to the Modern Era* (New York: Basic Books, 1993), 223; Michael S. Kimmel, *Manhood in America A Cultural History*. 2nd ed. (1998; New York: Oxford University Press, 2006), 86, italics are author's. In *Rehabilitating Bodies*, Lisa A. Long suggests that 1885 to 1905 was an extraordinarily prolific period for literature reflecting upon "corporeal instabilities" as a means of producing and reproducing gender and racial identities; *Rehabilitating Bodies: Health, History, and the American Civil War* (Philadelphia: University of Pennsylvania Press, 2003), 21–22. Causes for this transformation included perceived threats from non-Protestant immigration, women's rights, and the ascendency of large corporations (and ebbing of the self-made man). On the connections between physical and political strength, see also Jeanne Petit, "Breeders, Workers, and Mothers: Gender and the Congressional Literacy Test Debate, 1896–1897," *Journal of the Gilded Age and Progressive Era* 3 (January 2004): 35–58. Robyn Muncy describes the extent to which manhood was still viewed as contingent on economic independence in "Trust-busting and White Manhood in America, 1898–1914," *American Studies* 38 (Fall 1997):

of military preparedness and imperialism, but contemporaries understood it as a speech about manhood."[44] Such ideas could be blended
with a variety of moral messages, the common thread being a conviction that men needed to recapture public life from "mollycoddles" and
women.[45]

The rise of so-called Muscular Christianity, a religious movement
imported from England in the 1860s that flourished in the early 1900s,
was premised on the idea that masculine physical prowess could be
harnessed to Christian service.[46] Jesus's image was reclaimed from the
domain of timid, feminine churchgoers; Jesus was depicted as a brawny
craftsman capable of intellectual and physical triumphs. As best embodied by athlete-turned-preacher Billy Sunday, religious experience called
men to civic action.[47] The connection between Muscular Christianity,
temperance, and the strenuous life was made explicit by local religious
leaders such as Reverend J.J. Axtell of Royal Oak, Michigan, whose
adventures in "fighting the devil with his own weapons" included one
case of knocking a saloon keeper in the jaw. The *Chicago Daily Tribune*
reported that Axtell might inspire other religious reformers to similarly
"assume what Governor Roosevelt so happily calls a more 'strenuous
life.'"[48]

The consequences of a man's nonconformity to the strenuous life
mystique could hardly be overemphasized. As summarized by historian

21–42. For an additional example about American men's anxieties about declining physical weakness and manhood, see Stephen H. Norwood, "The Student as Strikebreaker:
College Youth and the Crisis of Masculinity in the Early Twentieth Century," *Journal
of Social History* 28 (Winter 1994): 331–349. Fears that there was a pervasive crisis in
masculinity were expressed not only by Roosevelt but also through increased mass participation in ostensibly masculinity-building activities such as body-building, hunting,
and boxing.

44 Bederman, *Manliness and Civilization*, 193.

45 On the meaning of "mollycoddles," see Kevin Murphy, *Political Manhood: Red Bloods,
Mollycoddles, and the Politics of Progressive Era Reform* (New York: Columbia University Press, 2008).

46 Kimmel, *Manhood in America*, 117–118. On Muscular Christianity, see Clifford Putney, *Muscular Christianity: Manhood and Sports in Protestant America, 1880–1920*
(Cambridge, MA: Harvard University Press, 2001); Neal Garnham, "Both Praying And
Playing: 'Muscular Christianity' and the YMCA in North-east County Durham," *Journal
of Social History* 35 (Winter 2001): 397–407.

47 On Billy Sunday, see Margaret Bendroth, "Why Women Loved Billy Sunday: Urban
Revivalism and Popular Entertainment in Early Twentieth-Century American Culture,"
Religion and American Culture: A Journal of Interpretation 14 (Summer 2004): 251–
271.

48 "Muscular Christianity," *Chicago Daily Tribune*, 14 December 1899.

204 The Politics of Prohibition

Kevin Murphy, "the strenuous model" of manhood was being used "to marginalize the careers and projects of political actors successfully stigmatized as weak and effeminate," a process facilitated by the assumption that physical weakness was a sign of homosexuality.[49] Prohibitionists had reason to worry that they would be excluded from even a small "protest group" role in setting the nation's political agenda if they appeared to compromise other men's masculinity and possess none of their own. They had always battled the liquor industry's portrayal of prohibition as an attack on masculine prerogatives and had likewise fought against the major party politicians who questioned the manhood of independent voters, but now partisan Prohibitionists had to worry that they might be portrayed as sickly or lethargic, physically and therefore ethically unfit.[50] There would prove more than a whisper of such ideas in the comments of Wisconsin's Anti-Saloon League superintendent T.M. Hare, who scoffed at "extreme and visionary" anti-liquor crusaders for being "long-haired, wild-eyed, squeaky-voiced cranks."[51]

Early twentieth-century Prohibitionists argued that abstainers had anticipated the strenuous life by promoting good health. Their attempts to re-brand themselves as strenuous were nonetheless complicated by the most innovative aspect of their party culture: the inclusion of women as full party members. The strenuous life ideal emphasized masculine rigor, whereas Prohibitionists were rather dependent on and dedicated to the women in their ranks. What might a strenuous life for women look like? Should vigorous women be more like men? Or should they practice a parallel sort of feminized vigor? Roosevelt's speech on "The Strenuous Life" only went so far as to chastise women afraid to become mothers, and Muscular Christianity's supporters tended to combine the endorsement of physicality with a dose of hypermasculinity.[52]

Still assuaging the conflicts raised by suffrage plank debates, Prohibitionists probably would have preferred to delay investigation into the possibility of strenuous womanhood. However, an unanticipated media sensation – Carry Nation and her famous battle ax – forced the issue. In the first years of the twentieth century, Nation initiated a far more destructive version of the direct action protests favored by Women's Crusaders in the 1870s and a more prolonged and publicized version of the

---

49 Murphy, *Political Manhood*, 3.
50 See, for example, Kimmel, *Manhood in America*, 92; Bader, *Prohibition in Kansas*, 94. On the association of independent voting and questionable masculinity, see McGerr, *Decline of Popular Politics*, 14.
51 *Wisconsin Issue*, December 1905, quoted within Blocker, *Retreat from Reform*, 208.
52 Putney, *Muscular Christianity*, 149.

attacks on saloons propagated by women in the 1850s. Nation smashed illegal saloons to bits.[53]

To no one was Nation more often compared than John Brown, himself a rather complicated historical figure.[54] And like Brown, Nation had little interest in the sanctity of private property, a tendency her enemies viewed as anarchist and anticapitalist.[55] However, at least equally important is how Nation's activities catalyzed anxieties about gender roles and civic life. Nation's supporters defended her by insisting on her gentle character. In an article entitled "A John Brown Raid," the *Backbone* described Nation as "about sixty years of age, educated, refined and motherly."[56] She was a "poor, old, gray-headed grandmother."[57] Supporters denied the worst of Nation's offenses, asserting, for example, that "most and probably all of the newspaper gossip about her slapping a sheriff's face and talking to Gov. Stanley in an unwomanly fashion is mere newspaper rot."[58]

Other presses took a different view, claiming that Nation was physically intimidating because she was nearly 6 feet tall and 180 pounds. She was from the turbulent west, and she engaged in physical violence; Nation could be either dismissed or praised as having strenuous, masculine features.[59] The question of Nation's gendered character lent itself to moral controversy; Nation accepted payment for lectures and even starred in a play based on her life and thereby left herself vulnerable to charges of insincerely exploiting the anti-liquor movement for profit.[60] The defense

---

[53] These saloons were illegal under state prohibition, but nonetheless probably paid federal taxes, with the saloon operators viewing the tax as a form of license; Hamm, *Shaping the Eighteenth Amendment*, 2. On the campaigns in the 1850s, see Szymanski, *Pathways to Prohibition*, 83.

[54] For example, "A John Brown Raid," *Backbone*, January 1901; "'Marching On' in Kansas," *New Voice*, 10 January 1901; "The Real Situation," *Patriot Phalanx*, 28 February 1901. John Brown was a frequent reference point in the *Voice's* articles and advertisements. For example, Advertisement for *John Brown and his Friends*, *Voice*, 4 October 1894. See also Fran Grace, *Carry A. Nation: Retelling the Life* (Bloomington: Indiana University Press, 2001), 159–160.

[55] Blocker, *Retreat from Reform*, 137.

[56] "A John Brown Raid," *Backbone*, January 1901.

[57] "'Marching On' in Kansas," *New Voice*, 10 January 1901.

[58] "Hatchet Crusade," *Backbone*, February 1901. The theme of misrepresentation also appears in "Mrs. Nation Denies," *New Voice*, 19 September 1901; "Mrs. Nation in Nebraska," *New Voice*, 2 January 1902; "Saloons Fear Mrs. Nation," *New Voice*, 3 April 1902.

[59] Nation's actual height is a matter of controversy. Recent biographer Fran Grace suggests that Nation was just over five feet; *Carry A. Nation*, 223.

[60] For example, "Mrs. Nation Visits Indianapolis," *Patriot Phalanx*, 4 April 1901. The narrative of Nation's life was made potent on the basis how little she wanted to depart

of Nation got more complicated in late 1901, when her legal separation
from her husband called for closer scrutiny of her character. Thomas
Edison's short film *Why Mr. Nation Wants a Divorce*, for example,
included an unflattering portrait of Carry Nation as a mother who
deserted her family to pursue a career.[61] In 1903, it was widely reported
that Nation had to be physically removed from the White House when
she attempted to visit President Roosevelt; Nation was eventually arrested
after shouting from the Senate's balcony.[62] As other women drew on
Nation's example, the matter of Nation's propriety became still more
important. Most notably, Myra McHenry of Wichita smashed saloons
for two decades and sometimes did so while dressed as a man.[63]

Some Prohibitionists enthusiastically embraced Nation for her use of
violence. In Los Angeles, the California Prohibition party convention
mentioned Nation "in almost every speech and song," and Nation's sister
was in attendance. National chair Oliver W. Stewart even declared that
"it is a wonder there isn't an army of women with hatchets instead of
one."[64] A few national WCTU leaders such as Eliza Stewart and Mary
Hunt supported Nation on the record, as did a great proportion of the
organization's membership.[65] More clearly than Prohibitionists had ever
done, Nation publicized that the problem of enforcement was distinct
from that of legislation. If she appeared to overstep, then it was because
the context for her actions was exceptional. The *Backbone* noted that
"our conflict with the saloon is war and we condone many things in war
which we will not excuse under other circumstances."[66]

---

from conventional living. Thus supporters would claim that "she has no ambition to
be famous" to defend her honor; "The Real Situation," *Patriot Phalanx*, 28 February
1901.

[61] Previously the ostensible support of Nation's husband had been cited as a factor con-
tributing to her respectability; "'Marching On' in Kansas," *New Voice*, 10 January 1901;
"Driving Mrs. Nation Insane," *New Voice*, 9 May 1901. Edison's film is referenced in
Grace, *Carry A. Nation*, 161.

[62] "Carry-ing Conseter-nation," *Backbone*, December 1903; "Calls to See President," *Citizen*, 9 December 1903.

[63] Grace, *Carry A. Nation*, 200–201; Bader, *Prohibition in Kansas*, 157. McHenry was
from Wichita, divorced from her husband after twenty-eight years of marriage. On
Nation's other imitators, see also "Vertebrae," *Backbone*, October 1902; "Mrs. Nation's
Raid Spreads," *New Voice*, 7 February 1901; "Mrs. Nation's New Disciple," *Patriot
Phalanx*, 26 February 1903; "Driven to Desperation," *Patriot Phalanx*, 14 February
1901, reprinted from *Auburn (Indiana) Daily Courier*; "The Hatchet in Indiana," *Patriot
Phalanx*, 28 February 1901; "It is War," *Backbone*, December 1901; "Renewed War in
Kansas," *New Voice*, 16 May 1901.

[64] "Prohibition the Slogan," *Los Angeles Times*, 19 March 1901.

[65] Grace, *Carry A. Nation*, 213.

[66] "It is War," *Backbone*, December 1901.

The *Backbone* supported Nation, but while asserting that she acted within legal bounds, the paper also conceded that "the wisdom of Mrs. Nation's course is another matter, upon which good citizens will differ."[67] Incidents of Prohibitionists attempting to distance themselves from Nation abound. When Nation came to Berkeley, California, the WCTU refrained from sending a delegation to meet her, leading Nation to proclaim to the *San Francisco Chronicle* that "'no wonder you have saloons...when you have such a conservative Women's [sic] Christian Temperance Union among you.'"[68] Likewise, Illinois Prohibitionists were "panic stricken" when some anti-prohibitionists sent Nation an "invitation" to visit the state's Prohibition convention, and Nation accepted. The chair sent Nation a telegram to dissuade her from coming, to no avail.[69]

Prohibitionist Frank W. Emerson, a Kansas pastor and editor who would be the party's candidate for governor in 1902, most clearly articulated the gendered stakes of women's violence for Prohibitionist men. He emphasized that "the world needs men" who would "fight against the wrongs and abuse," even while voicing apprehensions about women's increasing aggressiveness.[70] Emerson was a featured speaker when 3,000 men gathered at a Topeka mass meeting, deliberately scheduled while Nation's speaking tour visited Iowa and Illinois, for the purpose of recapturing the movement from women. Historian Robert Smith Bader has described how "open joints in the capital city brought embarrassment enough to the temperance enthusiasts, but having women take the lead in doing something about them was intolerable."[71] Emerson did eventually join Nation on at least one Topeka rampage, although there is no record to suggest if the experience affirmed or settled his concerns.[72]

Conservative Prohibitionists were never able to shake the disconcerting possibility that Nation's actions were, as historian Jack Blocker has noted, "the all-too-obvious product of [Prohibitionists'] own teachings." Her hatchet "raised the specter of prohibitionists all over the country taking up the attack on the saloons without assistance from the party which claimed

---

[67] "Mrs. Nation," *Backbone*, February 1901. On ensuing debates, see also Bader, *Prohibition in Kansas*, 148.

[68] "Mrs. Nation Not a Welcome Guest," *San Francisco Chronicle*, 4 March 1903.

[69] "Illinois 'Drys' Victims of Joke," *Chicago Daily Tribune* 2 July 1902; "Illinois State Prohibitionists Meet," *Patriot Phalanx*, 10 July 1902.

[70] F. W. Emerson, "The Preacher and His Church in Politics," quoted in Bader, *Prohibition in Kansas*, 143.

[71] Bader, *Prohibition in Kansas*, 144.

[72] Grace, *Carry A. Nation*, 169–171.

to constitute the vanguard for the war on the saloon." Prohibitionists did
not stop being fraternity members, parents, activists, and neighbors just
because they were partisan. And how significant were the differences
between what Nation did and what the women Crusaders had done,
in terms of using direct action strategies? Tied up with the question of
whether or not Prohibitionists should endorse Nation were questions
about the party's political strategy and respectability; these were the two
elements of their record regarding which Prohibitionists had traditionally
felt themselves the most perfect. Nation "disturbed their equilibrium."[73]
If only the strenuous should participate in politics, then what was the
proper course for women? To become manlike, or to leave the party
behind? Most Americans would say the latter, but the presence of women
already in the party certainly complicated the matter for Prohibitionists.

For her part, Nation seemed content to work as a one-woman show,
mostly eschewing association with organized temperance, and only selectively referencing her WCTU affiliation. However, she reached out to Prohibitionists on several occasions. Nation's personal letterhead declared
that "Republican and Democratic votes mean the same thing – licensed
saloons," a statement that some Prohibitionists took as an endorsement
of their party.[74] "All this agitation," concluded the *Patriot Phalanx*, "has
created a strong undercurrent toward the Prohibition party."[75] In 1904,
Nation's plans for a girls' training school in Topeka proposed a board
of directors consisting only of Prohibitionist women, although the plans
were never fulfilled.[76] In 1905, Nation attended the Woman's Prohibition
Club of America's first convention; the party press described her as one
of the "prominent Prohibition Leaders" in attendance."[77]

When responding to the Nation phenomenon, Prohibitionists took
some cues from the larger public dialogue about whether women could

---

[73] Blocker, *Retreat from Reform*, 136.
[74] "The Carry Nation Home," *New Voice*, 19 May 1904. Likewise, Nation attempted to
cast both a "Republican kind of villain" and a "Democratic villain" in her play; "Carrie
Nation is Going on Stage," *Citizen*, 7 October 1903. She also appeared in the temperance
classic *Ten Nights in a Barroom*; "Mrs. Nation on the Stage," *Citizen*, 25 November
1903.
[75] "The Past and Future," *Patriot Phalanx*, 2 January 1902. See also "Mrs. Nation Gets a
Hearing," *New Voice*, 16 July 1903.
[76] Grace, *Carry A. Nation*, 212; Bader, *Prohibition in Kansas*, 148. Nation supported the
Associated Charities of Kansas City in their attempt to build a home for "drunkards'
wives"; "Carrie Nation is Going on Stage," *Citizen*, 7 October 1903.
[77] "Women Plan for Work," *Kansas City Leader*, 29 June 1905. The convention was also
called the Woman's National Prohibition Council.

be strenuous. Kate Upson Clark described in the *Los Angeles Times* the "strenuous life-crushing burdens of the well-to-do city man's wife."[78] Likewise, the makers of Warner's Safe Cure" suggested that "The Strenuous Life" was "more wearing on women than on men."[79] Blanche Bates, a popular actress, showed that she "does not exactly believe in the 'strenuous life' but she is a warm advocate of muscular femininity" by decking an overly persistent suitor blocking her path.[80] What these accounts often had in common was an assumption that the strenuous life was something that women engaged, rather than something that they embodied. "It is unfair as well as unjust" noted the *Cincinnati Commercial Gazette*, "to a young woman to send her forth manacled by ignorance to take part in the strenuous life confronting every man and woman of to-day."[81]

More close to home, advocates of Muscular Christianity struggled to define the features of a "Muscular Woman." There were gestures toward making women and girls more physically active through the YWCA, but more often Protestant women's place in the strenuous life was to act as helpers for men during these men's quests for physical improvement.[82] Prohibitionists were attentive to mainstream and Christian influences but never really resolved the matter of whether women could be strenuous, a process made more puzzling given that they had been early adopters of the term *New Woman*. In 1895, *Voice* publishers had attempted to build interest for Frances Willard's book entitled *How to Win* by posing the question of "What is a 'New Woman'?" and suggesting that Willard provided an answer.[83] The *Voice* attempted to capture the term for the WCTU, applying it to this organization's members in general.[84]

[78] "The Times' Answers by Experts: A Puzzle Explained: A Housewife's Answer," *Los Angeles Times*, 25 August 1902. Clark would marry George Creel.

[79] "The Strenuous Life," *New York Tribune*, 22 May 1900.

[80] "Can Use Her Fists," *Los Angeles Times*, 15 May 1901.

[81] "College Girls as Wives," *Cincinnati Commercial Gazette*, 1 May 1901. This article was also reprinted in the *Pittsburgh Post-Gazette*. On the rare occasions that women were not only subjected to the strenuous life but leading it, the popular press emphasized the disreputability of such actions. For example, when teacher Frances Caspari was arrested for running a Ponzi scheme, the *Los Angeles Times* described hers as a strenuous life. Her own attorney declared that she was insane. See "She Got Rich Quickly, But Goes to Jail: The 'Strenuous Life' of Frances Caspari," *Los Angeles Times*, 8 February 1901.

[82] Putney, *Muscular Christianity*, 144–161.

[83] Advertisement, *Voice*, 26 September 1895.

[84] "The 'New Woman,'" *Voice*, 10 October 1895. See also "The New Woman," *Voice*, 16 July 1896.

Educated and refined, the New Woman might be praised for her endeavors to limit child labor, purify milk supplies, end prostitution, create foster homes, and dispose of garbage because such reforms did not necessarily encroach on the masculine domains of formal politics and economy. If the New Woman entered the paid work force, it was generally in new "pink-collar" pursuits or female segregated arenas rather than in the course of usurping men's occupations. Although there were many nuances to the New Woman – some unflattering – she and her cohort were perceived as something more than previous generations of women without necessarily being perceived as a lesser version of modern men.[85] And yet the term New Woman does not appear with great frequency in Prohibitionists' discussions of Carry Nation and strenuous femininity.

Such an oversight bespoke a pervasive if hard-to-quantify pulling back from women members and from women's distinct interests. After Willard's 1898 death, the WCTU began drifting away from the party, and the party was less than attentive. The WCTU would set aside its official endorsement of the Prohibition Party in 1901 and begin sending a delegate to the Anti-Saloon League's governing committee.[86] Even the decision to organize as consumers of life insurance policies rather than some other commodity suggested the Prohibition Party's new attitude toward women; in an age wherein consumerism was becoming part of wives' dominion, life insurance was primarily purchased by male breadwinners, and so the emphasis on life insurance asserted a particular world view in which husbands acted and wives were protected. In the quest to invent strenuous femininity, Prohibitionists got lost along the way and eventually gave up.

* * *

An evolution in campaign style accompanied the rise of the strenuous life, bringing men's bodies under still greater scrutiny. Whereas presidential candidates had once been expected to merely support their party's platforms – and indeed would have been viewed as dishonest if they had accepted a nomination based on a platform they disparaged – a new generation of "hustling candidates" directly communed with voters,

---

[85] On the New Woman archetype, see Martha H. Patterson, *Beyond the Gibson Girl: Reimagining the American New Woman, 1895–1915* (Urbana: University of Illinois Press, 2005); Jean V. Matthews, *The Rise of the New Woman: The Women's Movement in America, 1875–1930* (Chicago: Ivan R. Dee, 2003).

[86] Hamm, *Shaping the Eighteenth Amendment*, 135.

presenting themselves as the origin and embodiment of the national party's impulses and agendas.[87]

During the 1900 campaign, Vice President Roosevelt's drive remained the gold standard against which all other candidates would be measured. The *Chicago Tribune* described its surprise that Roosevelt's "voice and physique have been able to stand the merciless wear and tear that have recently been put upon them." "None but a man of remarkable physical endurance could have stood it as long as he has without respite," the editors concluded.[88] Not immune to social pressures, the Prohibition Party arranged for a special train to tour the country from September to November 1900, carrying the presidential and vice-presidential candidates, national chair, and various orators.[89] Candidate John G. Woolley delivered an estimated 450 to 500 speeches to showcase his endurance as well as his message.[90] If the Democrats had put forth any candidate other than William Jennings Bryan, whom the *Chicago Tribune* described as "a phenomenon in endurance, even in the eyes of the medical profession," they would have found themselves completely out-manned by Roosevelt.[91] However, it was Bryan who had initiated the "whistle-stop" campaign style during his 1896 campaign. Opponent William McKinley had at that time conceded that "I might just as well put up a trapeze on my front lawn and compete with some professional athlete as go out speaking against Bryan."[92]

The irony is that even as campaigns became a physical fitness test for candidates, voters were relegated to the sidelines by a new politics of publicity and education. Liberal reformers were largely responsible for purging parades, bands, bonfires, and other spectacles that they believed encouraged voters to blindly support the same party's candidates in every election. Such frivolities, Goo-Goos asserted, facilitated

[87] John F. Reynolds, *The Demise of the American Convention System, 1880–1911* (New York: Cambridge University Press, 2006), 62–104. On the preceding pattern of aloof candidates, see McGerr, *Decline of Popular Politics,* 35–37.

[88] "The Strain of Campaigning," *Chicago Tribune,* 7 October 1900.

[89] "Across the Continent," *Backbone,* August 1900.

[90] "Prohibition on Wheels," *Backbone,* October 1900; "A Notable Campaign Tour," *Backbone,* November 1900.

[91] "Trails Left by Candidates," *Chicago Tribune,* 14 October 1900.

[92] Bascom M. Timmons, *Portrait of an American: Charles G. Dawes* (New York, 1953), 56, found within Michael Taylor, "The Bicycle Boom and the Bicycle Bloc: Cycling and Politics in the 1890s," *Indiana Magazine of History* 104 (September 2008): 218. Presidential candidates would learn the electoral liabilities of not touring and the physical ailments derived from doing so; McGerr, *Decline of Popular Politics,* 172–173, 174.

politicians' nepotism and patronage.[93] Named for their pursuit of "good government," influential Goo-Goos encouraged citizens to read the newspaper and pamphlets and to vote independently. Local Republican and Democratic strategists, in turn, changed their goal from getting party regulars to the polls to courting swing voters; Get Out the Vote campaigns focused almost exclusively on the middle class.[94] Goo-Goos' educational campaigns, moreover, tended to refine and amplify changes that were inextricable from cities' evolving geography. Cramped conditions were not conducive to large meetings in public venues – marketplaces, public buildings, parade routes – where issues could be and had been deliberated.[95] Among Democrats and Republicans, party membership provided fewer and fewer opportunities and incentives to mingle across lines of race and class. Voters became less the agents of political change than the environment in which politicians tested their mettle, and there was an ensuing decline in mass participation.

For Prohibitionists, it was the sharp contrast between candidate and voter levels of activity that was so worrying. Many Prohibitionists had been schooled in deliberative democracy by participating in temperance fraternities and other civic associations and had continued to practice these techniques in their party conventions.[96] What kind of democracy was it that demanded contact between candidates and voters but not among the electorate? Whether it was organic or planned, Prohibitionists in New York and other municipalities confronted the demise of deliberation, and the declining prestige of this ideal, by adapting strenuous life doctrine. They transformed Roosevelt's critique of individual laxity into a critique of the lackluster body politic – that is, the broad civil society within which partisan politics is situated.

Prohibitionists found that picnics, parades, banquets and weddings – spectacular and social politics – could be more than pleasant reprieves from organizational politics; they were seamlessly integrated with the

[93] On the role of spectacle in nineteenth-century popular politics, see McGerr, *Popular Politics*, 3–41. Major parties also continued some of these practices, but they were often viewed as old-timey novelties, without much ideological content; McGerr, *Decline of Popular Politics*, 145–151.

[94] McGerr, *Decline of Popular Politics*, 184–210; Liette Gidlow, *The Big Vote: Gender, Consumer Culture, and the Politics of Exclusion, 1890s–1920s* (Baltimore, MD: Johns Hopkins University Press, 2004).

[95] Ryan, *Civic Wars*, 309. On the preceding decades' "dance of accommodation between candidate and people, between rich men and poor men," see McGerr, *Decline of Popular Politics*, 30–33.

[96] On the role of civic associations, including the Sons of Temperance, in training Americans for governance, see Skocpol, *Diminished Democracy*, 105–106.

politics. "A very enjoyable Prohibition banquet" held in Missouri was praised when it enrolled several new members in the party.[97] When the Young People's Prohibition League of Brooklyn took a trolley ride to Brighton Beach, its route passed under a large Prohibition banner that the organization had hung across a busy street.[98] An evening social in Indianapolis included literary readings, recitations, dialogues, and songs.[99] Even the small town of Hitterdhal, Minnesota, reported that it had a strange combination of resources at its disposal: "a Prohibition choir, has a Prohibition brass band, publishes a local Prohibition paper, owns a band wagon, a stand for singers and speakers, a merry-go-round."[100] In Clay County, Indiana, Prohibitionists held their 1902 nominating convention during a picnic.[101] And Fourth of July picnics that featured orators, singers, and drum corps were routine.

Even without the renewal of classic nineteenth-century practices such as torchlight parades – which Prohibitionists had only infrequently used, because of both their small numbers and fear of retribution – Prohibitionists in these communities found ways to be visible to other citizens. In this sense they were similar to the Populists, who throughout the late 1890s engaged in "ceremony and display, demonstrations of the collective strength of the people" by forming parades, glee clubs, and bands wherever their numbers were sufficiently concentrated. Earlier Americans had engaged in rallies and other public events to offer "visible endorsement of the people" to major party candidates; Prohibitionists and Populists performed these same techniques at the beginning of a new century to demonstrate the withholding of such support.[102]

Of course, if the goal of Prohibitionists' tactics was to restore their role in political debate, especially by creating events that independent-minded or mainstream newspapers might cover, they were not entirely successful. As one measure, Prohibitionists were referenced by the *New York Times* in seventy-seven articles in 1886 (the year of highest state returns), seventy-nine times in 1892, thirty-eight times in 1896, and thirty-one times in 1900. They then experienced a sharp drop to thirteen times in

---

[97] "Prohibitionists Banquet in Missouri," *New Voice*, 11 April 1901. National party leaders began to attend local banquets with greater frequency. For example, see Carrie Lee Carter-Stokes, "More Banquets," *Kansas City Leader*, 18 May 1905.

[98] "Y.P.P.L. News," *New Voice*, 5 September 1901.

[99] "A Social Evening," *Patriot Phalanx*, 20 March 1902.

[100] "Progress as Reported from Thirty-Four States and Territories by *New Voice* Special Correspondence," *New Voice*, 13 August 1903.

[101] "To Nominate at a Picnic," *Patriot Phalanx*, 5 June 1902.

[102] McGerr, *Decline of Popular Politics*, 5, 216–217.

1904. Most of these few articles reviewed state conventions or provided the candidates' names; the *Times* did not review picnics and seldom-quoted from oratory performance. The *New York Tribune* mentioned the party thirty-three times in 1886, twenty-seven times in 1892, twenty-eight times in 1896, and twenty-one times in 1900, and then dramatically dropped to nine times in 1904. Likewise, The *Chicago Tribune*, a bit slow to recognize the party in any capacity, featured the Prohibition Party nine times in 1886, fifty times in 1892, twenty-nine times in 1896, fifteen times in 1900, and eighteen times in 1904. In many instances, articles referencing the Prohibition Party were derogatory, either because they mocked the party as the epitome of something preposterous or because they featured interviews with people denying that they were Prohibitionist. In a few precious cases, journalists presented Prohibitionists' words verbatim.

A revival of social and spectacular politics – strenuous politics – did nevertheless aid the Prohibitionists in other ways. Just as such tactics had done for the major parties in previous decades, the Prohibitionists' concerts and picnics particularly appealed to young voters.[103] In the recruitment of young members, the *New Voice* advised that would-be organizers consider that a young man "lives and moves and has his being in an atmosphere of comradeship." Therefore, an older member should never "insinuate yourself as a general overseer or a disciplinary chaperon" but instead allow the natural process of friendship to develop, bonding younger members to the reform in the process.[104] The politicization of friendship was on display when, for example, each of the four young men in a Prohibitionist quartet "had friends who would come out to hear the quartette, so our circle was widened."[105] The ensuing social life could be vigorous enough that the *Patriot Phalanx* felt bound to remind partisans that meeting should be "not only entertaining, but thoroughly educational."[106]

Partisan community life partially explains the party's low rates of leadership loss. Prohibition Party state chairs, for example, had an annual turnover rate of only 22.5 percent between 1899 and 1904.[107] Community life also explains the otherwise irrational commitment of rank-and-file partisans to a party mired in decades of electoral failure. To illustrate,

---

[103] On young men in nineteenth-century spectacular politics, see McGerr, *Decline of Popular Politics*, 40.

[104] "Winning Young Men," *New Voice*, 16 July 1903.

[105] Frank H. Hadley, "Best Methods of Work," *Patriot Phalanx*, 8 January 1903.

[106] Untitled, *Patriot Phalanx*, 8 January 1903.

[107] On the low rates of turnover among Prohibition Party state chairs, see Blocker, *Retreat from Reform*, 161.

consider the example of Manhattan's George B. Hillard.[108] Hillard was important enough to be recorded in the party press but not so important that his name was never misspelled.[109] He served terms as a member of the county committee of and Prohibition Park's athletic association. He was a delegate to the state convention, and served on the New York County Prohibition Executive Committee and numerous banquet committees. He ordered campaign buttons and obtained parade permits and, on one occasion, seems to have paid the party's gas bill. There is a hint in the scrawled instruction to Hillard that "don't fail, please, to have Mr. Wardwell over in time," that Hillard was occasionally the reliable man assigned to be the keeper of party luminaries.[110]

For Hillard, membership in the Prohibition Party was meaningful enough that he or his descendants deposited a copious collection of programs, circular letters, memos, pamphlets, and ephemera spanning the 1880s to 1910s at two different New York area archives, both preserving an invaluable record of the partisan community's rich texture and testimony of his own devotion. A scrapbook exclusively containing clippings on Prohibition Party events and nominations suggests that Hillard carefully combed the daily press. His activities, moreover, brought him into close contact with other Prohibitionists on a routine basis. In 1900, Hillard attended a series of meetings at Sing Sing Heights run by the party's Literary and Lecture Bureau, a mass meeting on Fulton Street, Henry Metcalf's notification meeting at Carnegie Hall, an informal conference with party chair Oliver W. Stewart, summer meetings held by National Prohibition Park's University Temple, and a state committee meeting. He received tickets to William T. Wardwell's ratification rally at the Brooklyn Historical Society, was invited to sit on the platform during a mass meeting at Cooper Union, and helped watch the polls during the November election. He occasionally joined the Central Prohibition

---

[108] "Editorial," *Backbone*, April 1904.

[109] For a comic variety of misspelling examples, see the National Temperance Society's printed invitation, Folder: National Temperance Society, Box 5, GBHC. Hillard handwrote an *H* over the *B*, perhaps a bit miffed by the oversight. Also, Letter from Clarence E. Pitts to George H. Hibbard, 20 June 1904, Folder: 1904 – Corresp & Ms. Material, Box 3, GBHC; "The Banquet to Dr. Swallow," *New Voice*, 24 April 1902 identifies Hillard as "Hiller." How relieved Hillard must have been when identified correctly, as was the case when he was recognized as the president of New York City's Prohibition club in the 13th district; "Preparing for Action," *New Voice*, 19 January 1888.

[110] Handwritten message on back of invitation from Mr. and Mrs. I.K. Funk to a parlor meeting, Folder F, Box 5, GBHC. See a similar request for Hillard's services on the handwritten postcard from A.M.C. Barton to Hillard, 12 April 1904, Folder: North Side Prohibition Workers' Club, Box 5, GBHC.

Workers' Club's activities, attended Elizabeth, New Jersey's Clinton B. Fisk Prohibition Club banquet, and chaperoned Young People's Prohibition League events. He almost certainly attended John McKee's annual St. Patrick's Day rally, which took place at the Brooklyn leader's home.[111]

Of course, Prohibitionists did adopt some features of the ascendant educational style. Their numbers were scattered around the country, making newspapers, pamphlets, and campaign textbooks necessities, and they were constantly having to explain their party principles to potential recruits unfamiliar with party doctrine.[112] And to credit the Prohibition Party with reclaiming the vitality of political interaction is not to deny that money was a consideration in formulating the party's unfolding strategy. For example, New Yorkers' decision to hold "home meetings" or "parlor meetings" rather than renting space was likely driven by financial necessity. At the same time, this practice of home meetings also resonated with the party's values, validating the role of women and domesticity. The number of such meetings was probably quite great, especially in Hillard's New York. For example, the Young People's Prohibition League of Harlem planned over fifty home meetings in 1901.[113]

Home meetings could take the form of simple receptions or might include a program with music and discussion on a predetermined topic.[114] The Yorkville and Harlem Club president, Mrs. C.H. Simmons, elegantly described the character of one such meeting:

[L]et your memory unfold itself and turn backward a year to the parlor meeting in December, when we gathered at the home of our president. Outside it was bitterly cold, but inside warm and cheerful. The bright decorations of our national colors,

---

111 On McKee's annual party, see "Prohibition Personals," *Citizen*, 9 March 1904. Hillard and McKee corresponded frequently, and the correspondence references visits and conversations.

112 Michael McGerr explains that "trying to spread new ideas, third parties naturally relied on pamphlets and literature. But the third parties . . . did not pursue a liberal politics of education. Their political style was based firmly on the tradition of spectacular partisanship, which enfolded literature within the emotional display of communal ritual." McGerr even suggests that Prohibitionists exemplified this trend; *Decline of Popular Politics*, 215. For an example of how Pasadena, California Prohibitionists financed an enormous billboard, see Untitled, *Patriot Phalanx*, 3 March 1904.

113 "Y.P.P.L. Notes," *New Voice*, 1 August 1901.

114 "New Year's Reception by Harlem Y.P.P.L.," *New Voice*, 10 January 1901; "Y.P.P.L. Parlor Meetings," *New Voice*, 19 December 1901; "Y.P.P.L. Events," *New Voice*, 9 January 1902; "New York's Battle Lines," *New Voice*, 6 March 1902; "Under the White Banner," *New Voice*, 18 September 1902; "News of State Work," *Patriot Phalanx*, 31 July 1902; "A Prohibition Red-Letter Week," *New Voice*, 7 April 1904; "Social Week," *New Voice*, 28 June 1904.

mingling with holly and mistletoe and the prettily trimmed tree gave us almost our first glimpse of Christmas cheer. The meeting was a success, both from a social and a financial standpoint, and each one carried away not only a pleasant memory of the meeting, but some little token from the tree.

Simmons went on to describe similar meetings at other homes throughout the winter and spring. About an April meeting, she wrote "here were parlors, hallways and even stairs crowded" with happy Prohibitionists.[115] Homes might be crowded, but they nonetheless offered a warmth that one imagines was lacking from the Prohibition Rally and Banquet arranged to celebrate the grand opening of the Stephen Merritt Burial and Cremation Company's new headquarters.[116] Although this, too, built up partisan community and held back lethargy.

This was a generation of Prohibitionists that would literally as well as figuratively reproduce itself – and thereby reaffirm the virility of its body – through intimacy. One of the reasons that home meetings were so praised was in part because "a social atmosphere is a necessary factor," and the presence of women helped with "creating and maintaining" this ambiance.[117] The marriage of 1892 presidential candidate John T. Bidwell and Chico, California WCTU president Annie E.K. Bidwell, had been fairly low profile, but in the 1900s the partisan press highlighted the marriage of Prohibitionist Noah J. Wright and Clara Parrish, the national secretary of the Young Women's Christian Temperance Union.[118] D. Leigh Colvin wedded Mamie White of Indianapolis, who was an award-winning party orator.[119] C.W. Dorsett and his wife were both law school graduates who opened a catering firm in Minneapolis before C.W. Dorsett was nominated for Minnesota governor.[120] Husband-and-wife singers

---

[115] Clipping entitled "Yorkville and Harlem Club," Scrapbook page 22, Folder: 1899, Box 2, GBHP.

[116] Postcard invitation, Folder: Merritt, Stephen, Box 5, GBHC. Stephen Merritt was also a minister and publisher of the *(New York) Living Issue*.

[117] One of the Young Men of the League, "The Young Women of the Y.P.P.L.," *New Voice*, 4 September 1902.

[118] "The Wright-Parrish Wedding," *New Voice*, 7 November 1901.

[119] "Swallow and Carroll," *Backbone*, July 1904. White would gain a place on the IPA's National Executive Committee as a vice president later in the same year. For biographical information on David Leigh Colvin, see a note alongside David Leigh Colvin, "Party Power and Influence in American Politics," *American Advance*, 28 June 1913. Colvin would also serve as secretary of the National Legislative Conference, an organization supporting the Eighteenth Amendment.

[120] A *Backbone* article describing the couple noted Mrs. Dorsett's support for women's suffrage, but did not include her first name; "C.W. Dorsett," *Backbone*, September 1904.

were always popular, and some couples co-hosted home meetings.[121] By the turn of the century, the *Voice* was reporting that the adult children of Prohibitionist couples were beginning to advocate for the party.

Overall, the Prohibition Party of the 1890s and early 1900s was in the midst of a generational shift in leadership from founders such as James Black and John Russell, and mid-era leaders such as Samuel Hastings and John B. Finch, to new national leaders including Harry Warner, Virgil Hinshaw, and D. Leigh Colvin.[122] Minnesota's *Backbone* heartily rejoiced that "our ticket is made up of men who have hardly reached the meridian of life" and men who "represent the younger element of the party," and in Ohio, "a trio of stalwart youngsters of the ranks – three interesting chaps" were leading the party.[123] In 1902, the *New Voice* would report with some relief that "it is not true that there are no young men in the Prohibition party. There are many of them... from the National Chairman down" and that "the men who are leading the Prohibition movement are young men."[124] The thirty-five-year-old national chair, Oliver W. Stewart, would agree, concluding that "this is the age of young people."[125]

---

[121] For example, Mr. and Mrs. Arthur J. McColl were popular Prohibition singers and speakers in Iowa, and Mr. and Mrs. Horace Simmons went on a national tour in 1904; "The McColls," *New Voice*, 4 September 1902; "The Simmonses," *New Voice*, 26 May 1904.

[122] This is not to say that older leaders abandoned the movement. See, for example, John Russell, "Father Russell Not Alarmed," *Voice*, 16 April 1896; John Russell, "Nature of the Issue," *Backbone*, February 1900; John Russell, "Why Through a Party?" *Vindicator*, 17 November 1911; a description of John Russell presenting the national convention gavel in "Prohibitionists Launch Presidential Campaign," *American Advance*, 20 July 1912. On Hasting's death, a representative of the Young People's Prohibition League would give a literary "salute from the Young Guard of the Prohibition cause to one of the Old Guard as he passes on"; "Passing of 'Father' Hastings," *New Voice*, 2 April 1903. Hastings had embodied the diverse interests of his cadre, not only serving as party secretary but also with the Sons of Temperance, American Board of Commissioners for Foreign Missions, and as a trustee of the Rockford Female Seminary. Recruiting young people to the temperance cause had been a difficulty for the movement for decades, as perhaps most winningly described by Ostrander's discussion of the Good Templars' debates about whether or not to permit dancing at lodge functions in the 1860s; *Prohibition Movement in California*, 25.

[123] "Young Men to the Front!" *Backbone*, August 1902; "Ohio's Young Blood at the Helm," *New Voice*, 1 January 1903. See also "About the Convention," *Patriot Phalanx*, 13 March 1902.

[124] "Wanted: The Young Men," *New Voice*, 22 May 1902. See also "Young Men in American Politics," *New Voice*, 9 April 1903; "'Where Rolls Oregon,'" *Citizen*, 9 March 1904.

[125] "Greetings from Leaders," *Patriot Phalanx*, 24 July 1902.

Younger leaders, in turn, sought to cultivate the next generation through the Intercollegiate Prohibition Association (IPA), operating in some form in 1890, officially founded in 1892 as a co-educational organization, revitalized in 1899–1900, and legally chartered in 1901.[126] As early as 1893, student organizations at 146 universities held oratorical contests, petitioned their institutions for coursework on temperance topics, suggested books for their libraries, and lobbied to eliminate alcohol at university banquets. Prohibitionists were quick to point out that the IPA was surpassed only by the Young Men's and Young Women's Christian Associations in total membership among college students.[127]

None of this – the social calendar, the home meetings, the marriages and families – was new in practice for either the Prohibition Party or other parties, but the backdrop of major parties' shift to educational politics meant that Prohibitionists highlighted what was lost when citizens did not interact politically. As Prohibitionists emphasized what made their party different from Democrats and Republicans, in turn, they came to focus less on doctrinaire consistency and more on supporting local efforts; it was in local politics that the party's distinct culture stood out most clearly. "Let the Prohibition party be rational as well as strenuous," argued the *New Voice* editorial staff in 1904, concluding that such a shift acknowledged that "we have arrived at the era of the rank and file."[128]

Letting the rank and file lead would, to no small extent, be complicated by the fact that it required a suspension of doctrines that had guided national party leaders for decades. Local parties had often diverged from national leaders' instruction to remain aloof from nonpartisan and inter-partisan politics; the supposedly serious doctrinal divisions inhibiting cooperation between the Prohibition Party, the Anti-Saloon League (ASL), and other groups at the national level bore less relevance at the local level, wherein partisans were sensitive to the smallness of their number. In some instances, national leaders retaliated against local leaders whom they perceived as challengers to their authority.[129] Local partisans had nevertheless made connections across party lines when they could

---

[126] "Collegians Incorporate," *New Voice*, 10 January 1902; Blocker, *Retreat from Reform*, 128.

[127] Lisa Andersen, "Intercollegiate Prohibition Association (IPA)," *Alcohol and Temperance in Modern History*, 316–317; Harry S. Warner, *An Evolution of the Understanding of the Problem of Alcohol: A History of College Idealism* (Boston: Christopher Publishing House, 1966); "Work of the Colleges," *New Voice*, 8 January 1903.

[128] "Party Reorganization," *New Voice*, 1 December 1904.

[129] William P.F. Ferguson, "The Rule of Party Life and Power," *Vindicator*, 17 November 1911.

improve their neighborhoods, and they shared religious and fraternal associations with other anti-liquor advocates. Local Prohibitionists had often voiced apprehension about alienating friendly ASL workers and questioned whether there was a significant difference in party and ASL tactics.[130]

Coalitions between Prohibitionists and temperance advocates were once illicit but were now discussed and applauded by the party press in previously unimaginable ways. Most of what historians know about the nonpartisan work performed by earlier Prohibitionists comes from the reports of nonpartisan periodicals; the Prohibition Party had not extensively or regularly discussed how many in its ranks participated in nonpartisan campaigns. In the new century, however, the *New Voice* estimated that nine-tenths of the work put forward to advance local option laws came from Prohibitionists and claimed that this had been the case for the past twenty years.[131] Prohibitionists in Tennessee likewise took pride in having been "chiefly responsible" for the extension of that state's Four-Mile Law.[132] A rank-and-file Prohibitionist from Gallatin, Missouri crowed that "we nominated a splendid non-partisan city ticket in a large and enthusiastic mass meeting" and proudly concluded that "but for our little band of Prohibitionists nothing would have been done. The whole moral welfare of the country rests upon the shoulders of Prohibitionists."[133] The secretary of Texas's Prohibition Party noted that while, "strictly speaking, there is no such thing in Texas as party work in local option elections," it was nonetheless

a fact that perhaps 50 per cent of the workers, committees, etc, in local option campaigns are party Prohibitionists; that far more than that proportion of the speakers and lecturers vote the party ticket; and party voters contribute more to local option funds, according to their numerical strength, than do temperance Democrats or Republicans. But all this work is done by our people without the party name.[134]

Some Prohibitionists found that the relationships created between nonpartisan and Prohibition Party organizations energized party work.

[130] For example, "The League's Pretensions," *New Voice*, 8 August 1901.
[131] "The New Voice and Local Option," *New Voice*, 11 September 1902. See also "For a New York Campaign," *New Voice*, 9 October 1902; "A Michigan County's Work," *New Voice*, 1 August 1901; "Captured the League," *New Voice*, 5 September 1901.
[132] "Confidence in Tennessee," *New Voice*, 4 September 1902.
[133] S.S.H., Untitled, *Kansas City Leader*, 31 March 1904.
[134] P.F. Paige, "The Concrete Facts of Practical Politics," *New Voice*, 16 July 1903. See also, "Honor to Whom Honor," *Citizen*, 28 October 1903.

Greencastle, Indiana's Prohibitionists praised the Democratic lawyer leading their local campaign.[135] Prohibitionists in California joined "Sunday
closing schemes, law enforcement leagues, election of good men, etc . . ."
when they doubted their ability to win victory through a local ticket.[136]
Historian Jack Blocker has tabulated that between 1898 and 1901, several
Prohibitionists served as members of the ASL's state and national committees. One former and two future Prohibition Party presidential candidates attended ASL conventions, as did national chair Samuel Dickie.
Six Prohibitionists served on the ASL Board of Directors.[137] Blocker has
demonstrated that "party leaders in California, Nebraska, and New York
accepted leadership positions in the leagues of their states. In Mississippi,
Ohio, Wisconsin, Oregon, and Illinois, cooperation between party and
League went forward on a more or less official basis" throughout most of
1902–1903.[138] Prohibitionists "almost to a man" had entered the ASL-
led no-license campaign of 1904 in Los Angeles County, despite misgivings that it permitted wholesale and retail liquor businesses.[139] Archival
evidence provides little information about Prohibitionists' financial contributions to the ASL and other nonpartisan campaigns, but partisans
clearly provided labor and votes.[140] In Kansas, the nonpartisan Kansas
State Temperance Union and the state Prohibition Party had a better
relationship with each other than the state party possessed within its own
ranks, which were dissolving into "debilitating personality clashes and
internecine warfare."[141]

In the course of explaining why he would support the Illinois' Anti-
Saloon League's local option bill in 1903, party chair and state legislator
Oliver W. Stewart was caught between opposition to nonpartisan legislation as a matter of doctrinaire consistency and the alliances with
nonpartisanship carved out at the local level. He asserted that

I intended to support the bill because I felt it to be a move in the right direction. I
explained that it was not a Prohibition party measure, that we of the Prohibition

---

[135] A.F. Riley, "Remonstrance Effort at Greencastle," *Patriot Phalanx*, 31 July 1902.
[136] A.B. Taynton, Letter to the editor, "The Trouble with Robinson," *New Voice*, 9 July
1903.
[137] Blocker, *Retreat from Reform*, 141.
[138] Blocker, *Retreat from Reform*, 176.
[139] Ostrander, *Prohibition Movement in California*, 95.
[140] Blocker, *Retreat from Reform*, 141.
[141] Bader, *Prohibition in Kansas*, 158. This was a change from the mid-1880s, when the
Times had advised "every prohibitionist to keep his money out of the hands of the
Kansas Temperance Union, unless you wish to contribute directly to the Republican
State Campaign fund"; Untitled, *Times*, 16 April 1885.

party would never accept it as a finality. I also asserted that so far as our party is concerned, if I consulted that alone, I would hope for the defeat of the bill.[142]

This was a rather conflicted message, and Stewart's election as a vice president of the Illinois Anti-Saloon League did little to clarify the matter.[143]

The shift in focus from doctrine to activism had made local politics more important than ever, bringing about some concessions from national leaders. These concessions, in turn, revealed that here had been at least some dissonance between local and national visions all along. Earlier comments, such as one partisan's 1895 declaration that if the national committee would not arrange for conferences of Prohibitionists, Populists, and Socialists, then the state chairs should do so, now seemed prescient.[144]

The ways in which Prohibitionists engaged in social and spectacular politics provides one explanation for why the party both survived and grew ever more irrelevant. On the one hand, local Prohibition parties' active social agendas put them at risk for appearing amateurish when Democrats and Republicans moved toward an educational style of communication with voters. On the other hand, a commitment to interactive politics made party membership enjoyable and amplified the otherwise scarce benefits of party loyalty.

* * *

Prohibitionists conceded that they were unlikely to become a governing party but creatively reacted to transformations in the political landscape that might have stifled their protests. Their strategies took up Roosevelt's emphasis on bodily vigor and manhood and further suggested that political bodies needed to be engaged as actively as physical ones. Prohibitionists entered the twentieth century advocating deliberative democracy as their foremost interest. This gave them a perspective distinct from liquor retailers arguing for individual rights and Anti-Saloon League organizers urging local determination.[145]

---

[142] Oliver W. Stewart, "Representative Stewart Supports Local Option Bill as Prohibition Step in Right Direction," *New Voice*, 12 March 1903. See also Oliver Stewart, "Why Prohibitionists are Undiscouraged," *Outlook*, 11 April 1903.

[143] Blocker, *Retreat from Reform*, 185.

[144] E.B. Howard to T.C. Richmond, 20 April 1895, TCRC. For another example of state and county leaders considering a gathering that would circumvent national leadership, see "A National Council: Shall We Have It?" *National Prohibitionist*, 3 March 1910.

[145] On radical prohibitionists' rejection of individual rights discourse, see Hamm, *Shaping the Eighteenth Amendment*, 43.

Prohibitionists' allegiance to the ideal of a strenuous body politic also explains, at least in part, some partisans' harsh responses to progressive reformers' apparently common sense proposals. Prohibitionists lent no systematic support and often downright resisted when reformers sought to purify the convention system of nominating candidates by pledging delegates to support particular candidates or candidates to support particular positions.[146] Public opinion, a few pathbreaking Prohibitionists would argue, could only be created and revealed in the context of deliberative exchanges among people of diverse levels of influence and intellect. Some Prohibitionists had long suspected that pledging delegates and candidates carried undemocratic implications because it undermined the interactive aspect of politics. Rather, every delegate should "regard his instructions as what lawyers would call *ultra vires*" because "we can not see how any delegate would feel that he could honorably enter a convention for deliberation when he himself is shut against all argument." "It is presumed that delegates go...to deliberate, to speak their own mind, and to hear what others from the various sections of the country have to say," claimed the *Voice*.[147] The *New Voice* could assert as late as 1904 that it would "trust the convention to make its selection" for a national candidate, rather than anticipating a convention wherein the conclusion was already determined.[148] Even the program was left unsettled, given that "no one has any authority to prepare a program for the national convention" because "the convention controls its own time and conducts its affairs in its own way."[149]

The implications of a growing obsession with deliberative exchange – and not simply voting – as the most important component of democracy would become clearer in the following decades. It would fundamentally shape Prohibitionists' response to the biggest campaign in American temperance history: the push for a national amendment.

---

[146] For a rare counterexample wherein Prohibitionists questioned candidates about particular issues in advance of their election, see "Prohibition Party Tactics," *New Voice*, 30 July 1903.
[147] "Will Delegates Be Free?" *Voice*, 21 May 1896. See also "Mistaken Zeal," *Voice*, 3 September 1885.
[148] "Miles," *New Voice*, 2 June 1904.
[149] "Program Suggestions," *New Voice*, 9 June 1904.

PART III

PARTISANSHIP, POLICY, AND PROTEST VOTES

7

Opposing the Prohibition Amendment

In 1913, leading Prohibitionists irritated other anti-liquor advocates and confused much of the party's rank and file with a very provocative gesture: They refused to endorse the national prohibition amendment campaign. To many, the seemingly bizarre decision to withhold resources from a constitutional crusade merely indicated that Prohibitionists were petty individuals who did not want to contribute to an anti-liquor movement they no longer led. Anti-Saloon League (ASL) national superintendent Purley Baker would pointedly assert that "as we enter the final charge in this century-old war there are two things that no individual or organization can practice and hold an honorable place in the history of the struggle: One is the childish complaint that any are not having due credit for what is done, and the other is the narrow policy of non-cooperation."[1] This condescending reprimand undoubtedly expressed some truth about how the Prohibition Party felt toward the rival organization that had succeeded it as the movement leader. However, Prohibitionists' position can be better understood with consideration of how, for party doctrinaires, the amendment's campaign embodied a dangerous attempt to rationalize governance at the expense of democracy.

Prohibitionists' opposition to the amendment campaign was, first and foremost, rooted in their anxieties about the reification of Democratic and Republican dominance over the party system. A reform that many progressives viewed as a great accomplishment – the ascendency of direct

[1] The speech given by Purley Baker was reprinted in P.A. Baker, "Report of the General Superintendent of the Anti-Saloon League of America," *(Westerville, Ohio) American Patriot*, December 1913.

primary elections in the early twentieth century – struck Prohibitionists as
the capstone procedure in an undemocratic legal trend. Rigorous requirements for appearance on primary ballots and the ensuing abolition of
nominating conventions left many minor parties ineligible to nominate
candidates. Although minor parties might continue to emerge, the threshold for their formation was getting higher and the likelihood of actually
displacing a major party was getting lower. Even Prohibitionists' indignant turn toward innovative political activities such as concentration and
pledge campaigns, as well as the aggressive use of lawsuits and direct
action, could promise only survival, not success. Given Democrats' and
Republicans' historical tendencies to dodge the liquor issue and minor
parties' continued marginalization within the party system, Prohibitionists claimed that an amendment campaign would be a futile drain on
anti-liquor movement resources.

Prohibitionists' conviction that an amendment campaign was unlikely
to be successful was eventually superseded by the fear that such a
campaign would actually succeed. An amendment promoted by pressure groups such as the Anti-Saloon League would undermine authority
embedded within the party system, Prohibitionists argued. Dependent on
Democrats and Republicans to introduce legislation, nonpartisan groups
were unlikely to win except by means that, according to Prohibitionist
doctrinaires, circumvented the people's will. Not for Prohibitionists was
any argument that the supermajorities required by the amendment process
would assure that amendments reflected broad public consensus; Prohibitionists emphasized the process's least democratic elements. Namely, the
ASL-led amendment campaign was advanced without any referendum
from the people, was ratified by office holders whose elections preceded
the emergence of the amendment as a political issue, and was enacted
at a speed outpacing opportunities for civic deliberation. Prohibitionists
certainly had many unsavory things to say about individual Anti-Saloon
League leaders;their conflicts were rooted not only in personal slights but
in substantial critiques of nonpartisan groups' institutional limitations.
Prohibitionists came to fear their marginalization within the party system and the party system's simultaneous marginalization as a governing
institution in equal measure.

The arguably undemocratic nature of the prohibition amendment
struck Prohibitionists as a counterproductive. Even if such an amendment
could be passed, they argued, it would be impossible to enforce because
neither the people nor the office holders would take responsibility for
it. After 1919, Prohibitionists would have the opportunity to test their

hypothesis that an Eighteenth Amendment would discredit the cause without drying up the country. Drawing on a political vision that elevated the idea of everyday politics ordered through political parties, Prohibitionists would attempt to inscribe these values onto the new institutions that were rapidly reconfiguring American politics, generally without accomplishing very much. Ironically, the ideas they espoused would register most firmly with organizations advocating the amendment's repeal.

* * *

Prohibitionists had a short-lived period of harmony with other twentieth-century reformers, all groups agreeing that the party system did not sufficiently manifest the electorate's desires; the goal of the secret ballot was not yet fulfilled.[2] Nevertheless, Prohibitionists and progressives found themselves becoming rivals when reformers' strategies for enhancing the democratic integrity of the Democratic and Republican parties accommodated – and even bolstered – these parties' dominance over party politics for the foreseeable future. It was the development of direct primary elections that most refined Prohibitionists' and progressives' animosity toward each other.

Progressive reformers hoped that direct primary elections could combat an increased concentration of power within the major parties that left Democratic and Republican conventions vulnerable to hijacking attempts by corporate monopolists and capitalist barons. Malevolent forces might bully delegates at nominating conventions into doing their will, hence leaving the voter with no satisfactory candidates from which to choose. Charles Evans Hughes was elected New York's governor in 1906 after he led the Armstrong investigation, exposing the life insurance industry's corruption. He suggested that moneyed interests "are ever at work stealthily and persistently endeavoring to pervert the government to the service of their own ends." Hughes then affirmed that "all that is worst in our public life finds its readiest means of access to power through

---

[2] On the good government movement, see McGerr, *Decline of Popular Politics*, 62–65; Sproat, *"The Best Men,"* 243–271; Kornbluh, *Why America Stopped Voting*, 122–137. For an example of how early twentieth-century political theorists looked at parties with both favor and suspicion, see Andrew C. McLaughlin, *The Courts, The Constitution, and the Parties* (Chicago: University of Chicago Press, 1912). And, of course, none of this is meant to convey that manifesting the electorate's desires was the only purpose imagined for the party system. The distribution of jobs, projects, and money also remained important and were perhaps the critical function of parties as defined by many of the politicians themselves.

the control of the nominating machinery of parties," wherein backroom deals could have unsavory consequences for the general public.[3] The first binding, direct primary election laws were enacted in Florida and Minnesota in 1901. These reforms were of such apparently obvious value that almost all states enacted direct primary election laws within two decades.

Prohibitionists briefly joined in the support for direct primary elections because the selection of candidates by mass democracy, rather than by party elites and "the interests," might eliminate spoils, theoretically removing a powerful incentive for voters to cast exclusively Democrat or Republican ballots.[4] The party spoke in the economic language endemic to its era, condemning the "liquor trust" at every opportunity, and doing so despite many indications that no such unified entity existed.[5] In some cases, the Prohibition Party's support for primary laws remained intact because the rigorous timelines forced more professional organization on too often lethargic and haphazard local parties, and the standards for ballot qualification were essentially symbolic. In New York, Prohibitionists continued to hold conventions for candidate selection and then needed a fairly small number of enrolled Prohibitionists – about 3 percent of total enrolled partisans – to sign a petition ratifying these nominations.[6]

Overall, however, the Prohibition Party's position reversed when it became clear that lawmakers in most states embedded regulations into primary election laws that completely abolished the convention system for nominating candidates, even for minor parties. Without a significant vote in the previous election, a minor party could not qualify to participate in direct primary elections, and yet without access to nominating

---

[3] Charles Evans Hughes, quoted in Richard L. McCormick, "The Discovery that Business Corrupts Politics," 267.

[4] "The Legislature," *Backbone*, April 1901; "A Chance Offered for the People to Rule," *Patriot Phalanx*, 21 July 1904. For examples of resurging enthusiasm, see J. Raymond Schmidt, "Evil System of Party Caucus," *Patriot Phalanx*, 17 March 1911; "The Presidential Candidate," *Vindicator*, 1 March 1912.

[5] On the idea of a liquor trust, see Hamm, *Shaping the Eighteenth Amendment*, 44–48, 100–101. Hamm also notes that Howard Hyde Russell initially envisioned the Ohio Anti-Saloon League as a "temperance trust" (131). Contemporaries in the liquor industry were likely underorganized. For example, see the concerns registered in Percy Andreae, *Plan of Organization, at the Convention of the United States Brewers Association, at Atlantic City, on October 3rd, 1913* (N.p.: n.p, 1913). For an analysis of how Progressive reformers used similar antimonopoly discourse in describing prostitution traffic, see Mara L. Keire, "The Vice Trust: A Reinterpretation of the White Slavery Scare in the United States, 1907–1917," *Journal of Social History* 35:1 (Autumn 2001): 5–41.

[6] "Duty of Enrolled Prohibitionists," *Backbone*, 28 August 1913; "Petitions Furnished," *Backbone*, 24 June 1914; "The Prohibition Ticket," *Backbone*, 8 July 1914.

conventions these parties' only means to determine official nominees was to circulate petitions among vast numbers of voters. Minnesota's Prohibitionists, for example, were horrified to find that not only major parties but also minor parties would be subject to primary election laws. These laws required that parties polling less than 10 percent of the previous vote nominate candidates by petition, rather than by convention.[7] In Ohio and Kansas – states with a large dry element – Prohibitionists reported their difficult struggle to circulate the petitions required for their party to regain a place on the ballot.[8] Problems persisted in West Virginia and Oklahoma.[9] The Illinois party's 16,000 votes in 1912 were insufficient to retain its place on the ballot; in 1915, the Chicago party feared that partisans would be "disfranchised" if petitions received too few signatures.[10]

As a result of such procedural requirements, the advantage gap between major parties and minor parties was widened and institutionalized; Democrats and Republicans received government financing for the selection of their nominees via the ballot box, whereas minor parties were required to take on additional expenses. "Petty requirements," Oregon Prohibitionists concluded, would "make the work of Prohibitionists in a number of counties quite difficult."[11] Progressives' reforms had destabilized the problematic domination of parties by elites but also exacerbated the exclusion of minor parties and, hence, institutionalized Democrats' and Republicans' dominance.

For Prohibitionists in Minnesota, primary laws had become an "outrageous burden of expense which an old-party Legislature has put upon the minor parties in order to secure a place upon the ballot." This legislation

---

[7] "A Fight for the Party's Rights," *Backbone*, May 1902. See also "Primaries and Petitions," *(Minneapolis, Minnesota) Public Weal*, June 1906. On a similar situation in Michigan, see "Importance of Legal Details," *Vindicator*, 15 March 1912.

[8] "Ohio Working Hard for Official Ballot Place," *Backbone*, 3 August 1912; Prescott Gillilan, "Insistent Call for a More Just Nomination Law," *Patriot Phalanx*, 27 September 1918; "Kansas, Partially Disfranchised, Fights On," *American Advance*, 2 November 1912.

[9] Finley C. Hendrickson, "To Crush Political Liberty," *Patriot Phalanx*, 10 March 1916; "Outrange Against American Citizenship," *Patriot Phalanx*, 7 April 1916; "Oklahoma Also Tries Disfranchising Plan," *Patriot Phalanx*, 7 April 1916; "To Choke Off Minor Parties," *Patriot Phalanx*, 14 April 1916.

[10] Robert H. Patton, "Stand by Our Flag," *American Advance*, 7 December 1912. Patton conjectured that it might be easier to nominate by petition than it would be to get enough signatures to guarantee the party a place on the primary election ballots. If true, for whatever reason, this would make the Illinois case rather unique. On Chicago, see "Chicago's Petition," *Prohibition Journal*, 25 February 1915.

[11] "Is it Old Party Trickery?" *New Voice*, 9 January 1902.

"has made it practically impossible for the latter to nominate complete county and legislative tickets without so impoverishing their treasuries as to prevent an active campaign to elect the ticket named."[12] In Michigan, the state chair urged all Prohibitionists to support their primary ticket because "a party that does not poll for its primary ticket 15 percent of its vote for secretary of state at the election . . . will lose its place on the official ballot at the November election." He urged Prohibitionists to focus "your resentment at this palpable effort to compel you to vote a license party ticket or be disenfranchised."[13] Prohibitionists began to fantasize that someday Republicans would be in the awkward position Prohibitionists now occupied. California's Prohibition Party struggled to rally around the idea that "it won't be many years before Republicans will be going around with petitions asking the privilege of being permitted to go on the official ballot," but this bravado rang false.[14]

Demonstrations of building public enthusiasm for the anti-liquor movement lent poignancy to Prohibitionists' frustrating experiences with primary election laws and ballot exclusion. As the ASL rose to prominence by leading grassroots temperance organizations in local and county option campaigns, Prohibitionists were left conflicted. On the one hand, local option successes demonstrated the exciting existence of an untapped constituency. Some Prohibitionists compromised their earlier pronouncements against gradualist reforms, hoping that individuals participating in local option campaigns could eventually be corralled into the party. And sometimes the ASL did support Prohibitionist candidates, as was the case in the brewery and distillery town of Peoria, Illinois, in 1903.[15] "So far as we can learn," the *New Voice* noted in 1904, "in every case where a party Prohibition nominee was successful at the recent election, the campaign was conducted in hearty cooperation with the Anti-Saloon League of kindred interests."[16]

---

[12] "The Legislative Plan," *Public Weal*, 15 July 1906. Minnesota continued to have problems as the cost of placing nominations on the ballot rapidly increased. George F. Wells, editor of the *Public Weal*, wrote the *Patriot Phalanx* to explain that "when we have not nominated a complete state and electoral ticket it has been for the reason that the Minnesota law has compelled us to put up $50 for each name on such tickets . . . by the time we had raised a fund . . . we had largely exhausted our resources and had nothing left for a campaign" in "Explains the Situation," *Patriot Phalanx*, 6 February 1908.

[13] P.F. Paige (Michigan chair), "Vital for Michigan," *Vindicator*, 15 March 1912.

[14] "It's Coming," *(Los Angeles) California Voice*, 29 May 1902.

[15] Thomas R. Pegram, "The Dry Machine: The Formation of the Anti-Saloon League of Illinois," *Illinois Historical Journal* 83 (Autumn 1990): 183.

[16] "Hens and Chickens," *New Voice*, 1 December 1904.

However, close coordination with the ASL could be problematic for a reason that previous generations of doctrinaire Prohibitionists had anticipated: The ASL siphoned many anti-liquor advocates away from party activism. Advocates such as T.C. Richmond and Lutheran minister T.K. Thorvildsen would desert the party for the Anti-Saloon League by the turn of the century. Thorvildsen had declared that "I am through with the Prohibition Party" after refusing his election as a delegate to the Wisconsin convention, and there is no telling how many rank-and-file Prohibitionists followed this lead.[17] Most shocking was the departure of John G. Woolley, the party's 1900 presidential candidate. Woolley was a featured speaker at the 1904 Anti-Saloon League convention and temporarily transformed the *New Voice* into a general temperance periodical.[18]

Historians have suggested that the ASL held greater appeal than the Prohibition Party because it warded off interdenominational jealousy and because it was unlikely to create factions within any faith group.[19] Declining Prohibition Party returns in states with significant county and local option campaigns – Ohio, Indiana, Illinois, Kentucky, and Oregon – support these historians' contentions that potential Prohibitionists had been seduced away by the ASL.[20] However, many of the states where the Prohibition Party's returns not only declined but truly bottomed out – Alabama, Montana, New Hampshire, Rhode Island, Vermont, and Wyoming – were states wherein local option campaigns were more sporadic, suggesting that factors other than ASL-led local option successes were also at play. Most likely, the trickle of Prohibitionists and prospective Prohibitionists into ASL campaigns amplified the already existent ballot exclusion problem, combining to stall and impede party progress where growth might otherwise have been anticipated.

Reexamining recent procedural reforms, progressives and other good government advocates gradually came to share Prohibitionists' conclusion that secret ballots and primary elections were inadequate to the massive task of purifying party politics. Troublingly, government-printed ballots seemed to compound problems wrought by the abolition of the convention system; government printing required that nominations be

---

[17] T.K. Thorvildsen to T.C. Richmond, 25 August 1898, TCRC.
[18] Blocker, *Retreat from Reform*, 185.
[19] Ostrander, *Prohibition Movement in California*, 89; Szymanski, *Pathways to Prohibition*, 49–50.
[20] The connection between successful county and local option campaigns and declining Prohibition Party votes is made by D. Leigh Colvin in *Prohibition in the United States*, 341.

finalized by a certain date in advance of the election, and major parties generally held their primary elections immediately before this date. The combined effect undermined the ability of citizens to organize the nomination of alternative candidates if they did not prefer their parties' nominees. Neither minor parties nor factional candidates were routinely available options for voters.[21] In response, some frustrated political reformers devoted increasing attention to developing administrative agencies as a means of circumventing party politics altogether.[22]

In the pages of the *North American Review*, for example, Republican Senator Elihu Root attempted to explain the various strands of thought behind early twentieth-century Americans' interest in reshaping political institutions. The Nobel Peace Prize recipient concluded that many emerging reforms – "direct nominations, party enrollments [voter registration], instructions to delegates, Presidential-preference primaries, independent nominations" – were about helping citizens shape their parties and challenge the authority of bosses within them. The conduct of parties had historically been outside the scope of government regulation, and only with the newer developments in election law had government really come to recognize parties as organizations with which it had an intimate connection, even a dependency. Root eventually dismissed this group of movements for being "movements not toward something definite, but away from something definite."[23]

Far more significant to Root was a second cluster of challenges to traditional forms of government, including the initiative, the compulsory referendum, the recall, and the popular review of judicial decisions on

---

[21] State parties continued to split – with one faction bolting – into the 1890s, but the practice declined in terms of national political campaigns. For further examples and comments on the scale of bolting practices, see Richard Franklin Bensel, *The Political Economy of American Industrialization, 1877–1900* (New York: Cambridge University Press, 2000), 101–111.

[22] On the split character of reform during this period – the cultivation of mass democracy alongside the elevation of expert opinion – see Shudson, *The Good Citizen*, 166–167; Walter Dean Burnham, "The System of 1896: An Analysis" in Paul Kleppner et al., *The Evolution of American Electoral Systems* (Westport, CT: Greenwood Press, 1981), 166–169; Kornbluh, *Why America Stopped Voting*, 128–130, 138–160; Samuel P. Hays, "The Politics of Reform in Municipal Government in the Progressive Era," in *Bosses and Reformers: Urban Politics in America, 1880–1920*, eds. Blaine A. Brownell and Warren E. Stickle (Boston: Houghton Mifflin Company, 1973), 155–156. Nancy Cohen attributes this split character to the persistent authority and changing meanings of liberal ideology in *Reconstruction of American Liberalism*, 217–256. On the growth of the administrative state, see Skowronek, *Building a New American State*.

[23] Elihu Root, "Experiments in Government and the Essentials of the Constitution – I," *North American Review*, July 1913.

constitutional questions.[24] These reforms were important, but also problematic; Root argued that they replaced a relatively efficient government process with an unwieldy one, and with little hope that it would consistently produce better government policies. Root implicitly lent support to a third alternative: the administrative state. Administrative agencies run by experts could make decisions in the peoples' interests while being buffered from corrupt political parties and the capricious whims of mass democracy. Even at the state and municipal levels, such practices were becoming key features of progressive reform. In New York, Governor Charles Evans Hughes subtly removed controversial economic questions from legislative agendas, instead transferring authority to administrative agencies such as the Public Service Commission.[25]

The significance of the ensuing debate between progressives, who sought to skirt partisan corruption, and the Prohibition Party, which continually advocated party system reform, lay in an incredibly important question: Was it more important that government embody the people's interests, or that it embody the people's intent? To protect the people's interests, many progressives argued, there were times when the most vital responsibilities of government should be removed from the influence of the parties for which people voted. In such a populous nation confronted by such complicated problems, perhaps it was simply unfeasible to hold government accountable to popular opinion while expecting it to run with the efficiency of a corporate enterprise.[26] These progressives argued that only experts and specialists could possibly understand the knotty matters of a nation wherein so many issues were interconnected.

Progressives who advocated government by administrative agencies de-emphasized the importance of citizen deliberation, instead advocating

---

[24] Elihu Root, "Experiments in Government and the Essentials of the Constitution – I," *The North American Review*, July 1913.

[25] McCormick, *Party Period and Public Policy*, 305–306.

[26] On Americans' struggle to understand the complicated and interconnected nature of early twentieth-century society, see Haskell, *Emergence of Professional Social Sciences*; Morton Keller, *Affairs of State*, 534; Wiebe, *Search for Order*. For the Anti-Saloon League's related argument that democratic government is insufficiently prepared to regulate a complex political economy, see the preface of Peter H. Odegard's 1928 study of the Anti-Saloon League. Odegard notes that "in a Greek city state or in a New England town the determination of the collective will upon a particular problem will occasion no great difficulty. But direct democracy falls down in the face of increasing numbers."; *Pressure Politics: The Story of the Anti-Saloon League* (New York: Columbia University Press, 1928), vii.

objective expertise. In contrast, Prohibitionists' political philosophy was preoccupied with deliberation. This obsession sometimes led the party in directions that appeared contradictory. For example, Prohibitionists were perfectly willing to circumvent state legislatures by using the initiative and referendum if they believed such legislatures had been "bought" by the liquor traffic. On the other hand, they also argued that local option remained a subversion of legislative authority, expressing great respect for representative governance. For Prohibitionists, the fact that deliberation occurred – either in the legislature or among the masses – was more important than where it occurred. It was as an apparent decline of deliberation in the broad public sphere came to twin the declining opportunities for Congressional deliberation that Prohibitionists began casting themselves as deliberation's great defenders.[27]

Deliberation had already yielded fruits that seemed promising to partisan Prohibitionists. They argued that the people knew their own interests perfectly well – that they might draw on scientific and expert knowledge but could make their own reasonable judgment. The people's desire to eliminate the liquor industry, for example, could be measured by their church membership, by the resolutions of church meetings, by citizens' votes in support of local option, and by their support for state amendments. Alabama, Georgia, Mississippi, and North Carolina all became dry in 1907 and 1908.[28] With such success behind them, anti-liquor activists might selectively ignore the stall in their progress during the five following years. Prohibitionists argued that "the great majority of voters are unalterably opposed" to the trade in liquor, "that the great mass of American citizens – are convinced that alcohol is dangerous," and that "a very large number of the people – I think more than a majority – are opposed to the liquor traffic."[29] According to Prohibitionists, citizens had consulted with ministers, scientists, and social workers and had been persuaded by the information presented.

---

[27] On the decline of congressional debate and the critical role played by the Reed rules in the House, see Peter H. Argersinger, "No Rights on This Floor: Third Parties and the Institutionalization of Congress," *Journal of Interdisciplinary History* 22 (Spring 1992): 655–690. Prohibitionists might be said to have carried the torch lit by Populist critics.

[28] Hamm, *Shaping the Eighteenth Amendment*, 135.

[29] "The Minnesota Legislative Plan," *Public Weal*, 1 August 1906. See also Charles R. Jones, "The 'Good Man' Theory, or the Prohibition Ticket – Which?" *Patriot Phalanx*, 14 April 1910; "While We Wait," *Vindicator*, 27 June 1913; "For Open Discussion," *Vindicator*, 4 July 1913; "The 'No' Vote," *Vindicator*, 10 November 1911.

Prohibitionists did not naively assert that the people were infinitely wise. However, they did argue that people's foolishness could be mitigated if more parties competed for their votes because such competition would uplift the general discourse of politics. As conditions stood, the two parties dominating the party system had origins in a now dead issue – slavery – that had rendered them unprepared to engage a new, radical, and moral issue like prohibition. Because there had never been an agreement within either the Democratic and Republican parties' ranks about whether prohibition should be promoted or opposed and because the prohibition question would subsume all others once introduced, wary Democratic or Republican leaders refused to take a stand.

In turn, the problem with major party leaders' reluctance to discuss prohibition was that it inevitably undermined political expression by citizens, who could not ratify an idea until it was introduced by a party platform. Democrats and Republicans, Prohibitionists asserted once again, "have wholly ceased to be political parties in any proper sense of that term. They are a unit upon the perpetuation of the drink traffic and practically a unit in the policy of allowing the 'interests' to prey upon the people."[30] The dominance of these parties over the party system had discredited an otherwise appropriate means of ensuring democratic government. As an alternative, experimenting with strategies such as the conditional pledge and concentration campaigns helped Prohibitionists challenge the cultural and institutional artifices upholding Democratic-Republican control. These techniques also illuminated the untapped deliberative, and hence democratic, capacity of the party system itself.

The conditional pledge was a signed promise that committed an individual to vote with the Prohibition Party only if enough other people also pledged to guarantee electoral victory, or at least a great impact. The first such campaign might have been proposed in 1890, but the Prohibitionists' first lively conditional pledge campaign was in 1903 in a single county in Pennsylvania, and Prohibitionists continued to return to the idea of a pledge throughout the early twentieth century.[31] In 1908, Indiana's Prohibition Party initiated the first truly well-organized plan to collect pledges, arguing that "there is nothing underhanded or secret about this vote pledging" and that it was merely an attempt to collect

[30] "The Political Parties," *Vindicator*, 5 April 1912.
[31] "Gigantic Plan to Secure Three Million Pledges to Vote the Prohibition Ticket in 1912," *Clean Politics*, 24 November 1910.

on the promises of those individuals who argued that "'If I believed you could win I would vote with you.'"[32] A small national pledge campaign emerged in the same year.[33] Party newspapers seemed enamored with the idea that collecting pledges would let women members indirectly control and vicariously cast votes before they had suffrage.[34]

In 1910, *Clean Politics*, a party newspaper with a national circulation, sponsored the first enthusiastic national conditional pledge campaign sponsored. By this point, Prohibitionists had grown far more sophisticated and ambitious. They argued that "if political parties are divided in 1912 and every indication would lead one to think they will be, and the Socialists continue to grow, three million votes might elect a President. That is just why the three million mark is set."[35] Indeed, Socialists would consistently spur Prohibitionists to new ventures, their strength peaking between 1910 and 1912 with the election of dozens of mayors.[36] Some Prohibitionists boldly challenged themselves to gather an enrollment of seven million pledges.[37] In their excitement, Prohibitionists embraced the conditional pledge as a "sensational new method" despite over a decade of use.[38]

---

[32] "A Fair Fight," *Patriot Phalanx*, 11 June 1908. See also "State Conference Commends New Plan," *Patriot Phalanx*, 9 December 1910; W.L. Overholser, "'You Can't Win,'" *Patriot Phalanx*, 23 December 1910.

[33] "A Serious Situation Faces the Committee," *Patriot Phalanx*, 8 October 1908; "Commends Venango Plan," *Patriot Phalanx*, 10 December 1908.

[34] "Women Can Vote Twice," *National Prohibitionist*, 30 January 1908; "For Three Million Votes," *Patriot Phalanx*, 1 December 1910; "The Three Million Pledge," *Patriot Phalanx*, 23 December 1910.

[35] "Gigantic Plan to Secure Three Million Pledges to Vote the Prohibition Ticket in 1912," *Clean Politics*, 24 November 1910. Also see "The Three Million Pledge," *Patriot Phalanx*, 23 December 1910; "Voters Ready to Sign," *Patriot Phalanx*, 3 February 1911; "The Three Million League," *Patriot Phalanx*, 22 September 1911.

[36] McCormick, *Party Period and Public Policy*, 177. For an example of Prohibitionists attempting to recruit Socialists, see Alex Gustafson, "Prohibition, or Socialism, Which First?" *American Advance*, 20 April 1912. Socialists had even been welcomed in Harriman, where they were given a respectful hearing; "That Speech at Park," *Citizen*, 9 September 1903. I have only found one reference to the National Woman's Party in Prohibition papers: F.S.H., "How Suffrage Won," *Patriot Phalanx*, 18 January 1918.

[37] "National Meeting for Indianapolis," *Patriot Phalanx*, 15 November 1912; Walter S. Haynes, "A Detailed Seven Million Plan," *Vindicator*, 20 December 1912. For five million as the magic number, see "The Things that were Settled at the Conference," *American Advance*, 8 February 1913. On the problems with coordinating this campaign under primary laws, see V.G. Hinshaw, "The 'Five Million Voters' Enrollment' Plan," *American Advance*, 22 February 1913.

[38] C.E. Newlin, "Don't Hold Out Hopes," *Patriot Phalanx*, 13 December 1912. The Prohibition Party's attraction to the pledge idea might have had origins in the importance

In addition to the conditional pledge, Prohibitionists struggled to renew the integrity of the party system through concentration campaigns. Gaining popularity after brief tests in Minnesota and Indiana in 1902, these campaigns were organized with the idea that Prohibitionists should "mass the forces of the party in favorable states or districts for the purpose of actually electing a large number of public officials."[39] Prohibitionists would raise funds nationally and then direct these funds into a few carefully chosen districts. In some ways, this replicated the strategy developed in Harriman, wherein partisans brought public attention to a small success rather than scattering resources around the country.

Pleased by the results of concentration campaigns, Prohibitionists believed that they had "won victories in places by methods of concentration when it seemed to be well nigh impossible."[40] The party was victorious in districts in California and Illinois, electing several state representatives. Minnesota chair W.G. Calderwood urged Prohibitionists to "show our ability at practical politics by refusing to waste time or effort seeking things that would be of no use to us," instead dedicating party resources to areas where work was most likely to bear fruit.[41] Prohibitionists again used the Socialists as a reference point, arguing that

of pledging in early- and mid-nineteenth century temperance reform; various temperance fraternities and the Father Matthew movement had asked individuals to pledge to personally abstain from alcohol. The conditional pledge campaign also evolved from earlier movements that had asked voters for a promise regardless of the actions of fellow voters; the non-conditional pledge had essentially been voter registration before there were primary elections that would make a registration procedure necessary. In an unexpected validation of a once very controversial man and plan, the *Patriot Phalanx* also reminded readers of another set of roots for the current strategy. Walter Thomas Mills, of anti-suffrage plank and Harvey, Illinois fame, had argued for a united effort of one million voters' pledges at the 1889 meeting, an idea that had been quickly snuffed out as part of a greater controversy. See "For Three Million Voters," *Patriot Phalanx*, 1 December 1910. Mills' plan had been adamantly rejected by the editorial staff of the *New Era* on the grounds that it conceded that it was otherwise acceptable for a man to vote against his principles.

[39] "The Great National Conference," *Vindicator*, 24 January 1913. See also "The Man for the Hour," *Vindicator*, 7 June 1912. See J. Hohman, "Concentration," *Vindicator*, 3 January 1913; Charles R. Jones, "National Chairman Jones' Bulletin," *Clean Politics*, 26 August 1909. There is some evidence of encouragement to focus on campaigns in "close states" or "pivotal states" as early as 1888; National Executive Committee Minutes, 1 June 1888, TPP.

[40] At the 1913 national convention, E.L.G. Hohenthal presented a paper entitled "Concentration" that was later published in *Vindicator*, 24 January 1913.

[41] W.G. Calderwood, "A Change in Policy," *Patriot Phalanx*, 29 December 1904. For an early indictment of Calderwood's character by prominent Prohibitionists, see "Calderwood Again," *Lever*, 7 October 1885.

"the value of the election of Victor Berger to Congress by the Socialist party [in 1910] has been almost beyond estimate to that organization. Our plans and resources have been spread over such a wide territory that their application has been too inefficient to secure results."[42] The Prohibition Party eventually established a national Concentration Committee, led by Calderwood. In 1914, concentration campaigns were built behind Eugene W. Chafin's campaign for an Arizona senate seat, and Oregon's George Cleaver, Pennsylvania's William P.F. Ferguson, and California's Charles H. Randall for their respective state legislatures.[43]

Regardless of their pride in a few notable electoral successes, twentieth-century ballot restrictions nonetheless ensured that more and more Prohibitionists were precluded from participating in the ritual that widely defined *party* as such: voting. In state after state, Prohibitionist men who had previously expressed their partisanship through voting rituals and campaign celebrations now found that these opportunities were endangered or even eliminated. The party was not completely stifled – votes were cast in forty of the forty-five states in 1904, albeit with only five votes in Florida, and embarrassing triple-digit votes in ten other states – but it was also readily observable that the party's ballot qualification status was dropping. Scattered evidence suggests that although the party appeared on thirty-nine of the forty-seven official state ballots in 1890, it appeared on only twenty-eight of the forty-eight states by 1908.[44]

---

[42] "The Election of Congressmen," *American Advance*, 1 February 1913.

[43] Prohibitionists experienced the ancillary advantages of having someone in office obligated to them. For example, the Southern Californian widow of Prohibitionist Thomas W. Organ must have been grateful when Randall intervened on her behalf to expedite her portion of the Organ pension, which her husband had received for Civil War service; Commissioner G.M. Saltzgaber to Hon. C.H. Randall, 13 October 1919, File of Thomas W. Organ, Civil War and Later Pensions, National Archives in Washington D.C.

[44] The statistics on party returns are far more precise and reliable than those recording on what official state ballots the Prohibition Party actually appeared. Regarding the number of states for which the Prohibition Party received returns in 1908, see William D.P. Bliss, ed., *The New Encyclopedia of Social Reform* (New York: Funk & Wagnalls Company, 1908), 974, for the claim of thirty-nine states. Funk and Wagnalls were members of the Prohibition party, in addition to being publishing giants. Svend Petersen identifies forty states as receiving Prohibition party returns; *A Statistical History of the American Presidential Elections* (New York: Ungar, 1963). Roger C. Storms, a Prohibitionist who wrote his party's history, records that the 1908 presidential and vice-presidential candidates campaigned in twenty-eight states, and the current Prohibition party historical society asserts that the party appeared on twenty-eight official state ballots in 1908; *Partisan Prophets: A History of the Prohibition Party* (Denver: National Prohibition Foundation, Inc., 1972), 32. See also http://prohibitionists.org/History/votes/votes.html (accessed January 2011).

No doubt this was especially mortifying in the context of liquor advocates' tendency to taunt anti-liquor men for being effeminate; Prohibitionist men made good efforts to be in step with the strenuous life, but not being able to vote their party preference was a woman-like deficiency.

Unable to do much more than fume about the ASL threat, some Prohibitionists framed their strategies for the party's future around the ballot restriction problem. Prohibitionists in an optimistic state of mind emphasized how ballot reforms might provide their party with a strategic advantage. National chair Charles Jones rallied his fellow partisans with the hope that, as Americans grew dissatisfied with Democrats and Republicans, they would have no choice but to become Prohibitionists because "it is almost impossible to organize a new political party. The state laws are so strict that the names of candidates can with difficulty be got upon the tickets at all."[45] Merely surviving long enough might someday translate into victory.

Conformity with direct primary election laws, however, severed lingering notions that the Prohibition Party had a special commitment to women members. Because direct primary laws' terminology specified that only voters could nominate party candidates, women were legally excluded from the nomination process for the first time. Women could not serve as delegates when there were no conventions and could not sign petitions when they were not recognized by the government as voters. This impulse insidiously shaped the Prohibition Party's political culture. Even in informal primaries run by Prohibition Party newspapers, it was now only "every Prohibition voter (including women in those states where women are voters)" who was "entitled to vote"; women in non-suffrage states – in other words, most women – were not so invited.[46] The new condition of primary election laws and the persistent reality of women's disenfranchisement encouraged Prohibitionists to adjust the nature of their once inclusive political style. The substantive authority women had once been granted was now lacking, their voices and experiences marginalized.

It was the combination of two seemingly inverse strategic responses to exclusion from ballots – Prohibitionists' attempt to protect their party's right to participate in elections and the resolution to boldly experiment with innovative partisan strategies circumventing elections – that

---

[45] "Prohibition Party: Has it a Future," *Patriot Phalanx*, 16 September 1909. On this same point, see Oliver Stewart, "The Prohibition Party – A Restatement," *National Enquirer*, 8 March 1917.
[46] "Voters, Prepare Your Ballots!" *Vindicator*, 22 March 1912.

institutionalized the gradual devaluing of women's membership that had been in progress since 1884. This was first apparent when the party created, publicized, and funded Young Men's Prohibition Clubs at unprecedented levels. These clubs were intended to attract new voters, but they also unambiguously privileged the recruitment of men over the recruitment of women. After all, only men were eligible to sign the petitions required to get the party on the official ballot.

Some women responded by urging greater support for Woman's Prohibition Leagues, first founded in 1894, but these clubs functioned less as a training ground for new members than as auxiliaries. As described by the *Voice*, the Woman's Prohibition League in New York "usually met on the same evening in separate rooms [from the party meeting], a social following the transaction of business in each organization."[47] The national WCTU had requested that the Prohibition Party discontinue the separate Woman's Prohibition Leagues as early as 1895, seeing the other organization as a rival that undermined not only the WCTU's turf but women's status in the party.[48]

Embracing the Woman's Prohibition League's successor, the Woman's Prohibition Club (WPC) of America, as a superior alternative to the WCTU *because* of its dependency, and hence challenging women's existing authority within the Prohibition Party, one male Prohibitionist asserted that "I always considered the WCTU deficient as a help to Prohibition and especially to the Prohibition party. It is entirely too indefinite.... Now let them resolve to join bodily the Prohibition council and become an annex to the Prohibition party, the same as the Women's Republican club is an annex to that party."[49] In retort, a proud WCTU Prohibitionist responded that "if to 'help' means ... to get up teas and sell aprons to turn money into the pockets of the members of the Prohibition party – why, the WCTU is too busy with larger things." Moreover, the Prohibitionist woman "does not need to be an 'annex' to anything.... It takes more than Prohibition speeches and 'campaigns' to make votes."[50]

[47] "The Women Help," *Voice*, 25 October 1894.

[48] WCTU petition within Minutes of the National Committee, 11 December 1895, TPP.

[49] Fred Meyer, "The Woman's Club," *New Voice*, 20 July 1905. For a less aggressive version of the same argument, see "Woman's Prohibition Club of America," *Kansas City Leader*, 5 January 1905; "Woman's Prohibition Club," *National Prohibitionist*, 16 April 1908. Women sometimes perpetuated the idea that deference was preferable. For example, Prohibition State Executive Committee of Minnesota, 21 August 1905, Volume 1 – Minutes, PSECM.

[50] Margaret B. Platt, "Woman's Club," *New Voice*, 17 August 1905. Madison, Wisconsin and the state of Pennsylvania each had a – perhaps connected – Woman's Prohibition

For all the appeal of access to party politics, women had autonomous organizations and need not accept a subordinated place.

By the twentieth century, WCTU members were downright peeved about the loss of women's status in the party. Elizabeth Stanley reminded fellow partisans that "some of our women are county chairmen of the Prohibition party" and would therefore resist being "run off in a little squad by ourselves." She described Indiana's WCTU members as feeling "dumped."[51] Once resigned to being "run off," women such as WCTU lecturer Cora E. Seberry wrote to the Prohibition Party's national president that the WCTU "has been more true to your Party than it has ever been to us" and that she would therefore "put all the time and money of my command into my own organization" rather than help the party any further.[52] After 1905, even the WPC would have little party support; the national committee offered no financial help to the organization and noted that "we do not feel justified in encouraging the Club to anticipate such an appropriation" in the future.[53] Even as some chose to organize separately, many women Prohibitionists resented that their inclusion in party life was limited and secondary, a reality expressed in party directives such as "clubs must be organized, designed to reach especially the young men – and clubs for women as well."[54]

At the same time, Prohibitionist men eagerly adapted women's direct action and petitioning techniques to influence policy through non-electoral means. For example, the influence of women who used their bodies to make saloons into unusable spaces was apparent in Prohibitionists' 1905 campaign urging anti-liquor advocates to write President Theodore Roosevelt with their complaints about the liquor traffic. They planned to flood the president's mail boxes so that "it would require two weeks' solid work for ten clerks to merely file these letters away" and "should an attempt be made to answer these letters, it would require one hundred clerks working one hundred days to accomplish the task."[55]

Party Club in the early 1910s. In 1914 yet another national organization for women Prohibitionists, called the Woman's National Prohibition Federation, was founded.

[51] Elizabeth Stanley, "Women's Work for Prohibition," *Patriot Phalanx*, 14 July 1904.

[52] Cora E. Seberry to Charles Jones, 12 February 1908, Folder: Correspondence 1894–1907, CJP.

[53] Minutes of the Executive Committee, 6 January 1905, TPP. There were some efforts by the WPC state organizations to continue requesting money from state parties. For example, "Woman's Prohibition Club," *National Prohibitionist*, 2 January 1908.

[54] Daniel A. Poling, "An Expert Diagnosis and a Prescription to Match," *American Advance*, 11 January 1913.

[55] "Write to the President," *New Voice*, 19 October 1905. See also "About Jones," *New Voice*, 23 November 1905.

Prohibitionists illuminated how exuberant political expression could challenge bureaucracy.

The best examples of how Prohibitionist men appropriated women's political style were from the party's heightened enthusiasm for pressing lawsuits, once the favored technique of women with civil damage claims. Early experiments included lawsuits related to the enforcement of state amendments, epitomized by the Prohibition Party's decision to provide legal support when *Mugler v. Kansas* was argued before the Supreme Court in 1887.[56] In 1889, the *Voice* encouraged male Prohibitionists to "get lawyers to volunteer their help and begin suits." *Voice* editors reminded Prohibitionists to "not heed the talk that this is not the work of a political party" – certainly the prevalent opinion of the time – because "any blow that cripples the saloon is your work."[57] Taking such sentiments to heart, wealthy Prohibitionist William Jennings Demorest attempted to rally dry forces behind lawsuits calling the constitutionality of license into question.[58]

With some experimental lawsuits under their belts and pressure mounting from discriminatory election laws, Prohibitionists pushed back with lawsuits directly challenging the legitimacy of various ballot reforms, now using a women's strategy to protect men's prerogative of electoral participation. In Minnesota in 1906 the Prohibition Party sued the Secretary of State to regain its place on the ballot and, in a rare instance of good fortune, the court ruled in the party's favor.[59] It was far more common to lose lawsuits, no matter how poignantly they illuminated the undemocratic implications of new laws meant to purify politics. For example, a Minnesota Prohibitionist candidate unsuccessfully sued in district court and then state supreme court to overturn legislation requiring all candidates to pay $10 for a place on the ballot and to hence subsidize the costs associated with protecting voters from harassment.[60] In Indiana, Prohibitionists were likewise disturbed by how government officials interpreted the state's Corrupt Practice Act of 1912 to exclude Prohibition Party

---

[56] Hamm, *Shaping the Eighteenth Amendment*, 52–53.
[57] "Forward!" *Voice*, 28 November 1889. Prohibitionist men had a longer history of turning over information about saloons to local prosecutors. For example, see Bader, *Prohibition in Kansas*, 66.
[58] A.A. Hopkins to T.C. Richmond, 10 November 1893, TCRC.
[59] "We Won!" *Public Weal*, June 1906; Prohibition Executive Committee of Minnesota Minutes, 23 April 1906, Volume 1 – Minutes, PSECM.
[60] Prohibition Executive Committee of Minnesota Minutes, 2 July 1906, Volume 2 – Minutes, PSECM; "Prohibitionists Must Pay," *Public Weal*, 1 August 1906.

candidates for failing to file statements detailing their campaign expenses. This was despite the fact that they had accrued none. Prohibitionists again turned to lawsuits to clarify the law's terms.[61] Lost opportunities to participate in elections because of new election laws were both irksome and inspiring.

Men who saw themselves as disenfranchised in the wake of new ballot laws that excluded minor parties from elections had co-opted women's traditional strategies for engaging in politics. They did so without soliciting responses from women to this trend, or even providing a statement that the party was self-aware of what was occurring. It seems likely that male Prohibitionists could not openly credit women Prohibitionists without undermining their own embattled manhood. However, the consequences of appropriation and noncrediting had great importance because, with men engaging in direct action and pressing lawsuits, the party no longer required women's active participation. For historians, the irony is that Prohibitionist women's displacement occurred against the backdrop of Republicans' and Democrats' decision to organize auxiliaries of women sympathetic to their parties. Prohibitionist women's standing declined, and the gap between what the Prohibition Party offered women and what the other parties offered women shrunk dramatically. For Prohibitionist women, the gradual increase in suffrage states was therefore bittersweet because their opportunity to make a vote that conveyed their political position was contracting; they were no longer esteemed party policy makers and their party was largely excluded from ballots.

Of concern to all Prohibitionists, procedural impediments to minor party development signaled the beginning of a century of Democratic-Republican dominance over the party system. This is not to say that there would be no more minor party challenges, but that these challenges would not result in the kind of success that Republicans had once had, and that the threshold for organization and, above all, maintenance and substantial growth of a new political party would require a virtually prohibitive amount of personal and financial resources from people who had the least of both. From this perspective, the fact that minor party candidates received over 30 percent of the vote in the 1912 campaign was far less significant than the Progressive Party's quick collapse and the Socialists' inability to capitalize on promising returns.[62]

---

[61] "Candidates Failed to Comply with Law," *Patriot Phalanx*, 30 August 1912.

[62] Previous scholars have attributed the decline and stagnation of the Socialist Party to a rising standard of living, the appeal of Woodrow Wilson, World War I patriotism

A 1913 internal debate made explicit the Prohibition Party's consideration of how much more they should attempt to reform the party system before abandoning it. This discussion was propelled by the claims of Oliver W. Stewart, a controversial former national chair, who used the columns of the most influential Prohibition Party newspaper to boldly argue that "representative government by the party method has failed" because of "the refusal of political parties to keep their pledges and of the servants of the people in legislative hall, on the bench, and in executive position to do, not simply as they were bidden, but as they have promised to do."

Stewart observed that Americans were beginning "to seek for some method by which [they] may exercise a more direct control of the representatives elected through [their] agency." They would look for a new method that would "assure efficiency, with a quick flow of power from the people to the representative and the accountability from the representative to the people." Noted Stewart, "the overwhelming failure of the party method has caused millions to lose their old time loyalty of allegiance to party, and distrust has compelled the individual to seek for some method by which he may exercise a more direct control of the representatives elected through its agency."[63] Could this be the end of the party system?

and suppression of dissent, factionalism, and Eugene Debs's refusal to run in 1916. See Garlin Burbank, *When Farmers Voted Red: The Gospel of Socialism in the Oklahoma Countryside, 1910–1924* (Westport, Conn.: Greenwood Press, 1976), 108–32; Anthony Esposito, *The Ideology of the Socialist Party of America, 1901–1917* (New York: Garland, 1997); Ira Kipnis, *The American Socialist Movement, 1897–1912* (New York: Columbia University Press, 1968); Sally M. Miller, *Victor Berger and the Promise of Constructive Socialism, 1910–1920* (Westport, Conn.: Greenwood Press, 1973); Robert J. Fitrakis, *The Idea of Democratic Socialism in America and the Decline of the Socialist Party* (New York: Garland, 1993). Scholars of the Progressive Party have explained its decline in terms of the absence of a compelling and unifying program, the party's dependency on Theodore Roosevelt as its candidate, and the absence of local-level party organization. See Harold L. Ickes, "Who Killed the Progressive Party?" *American Historical Review* 46 (January 1941): 306–37; Amos Pinchot, *History of the Progressive Party, 1912–1916* (1958; Westport, Conn., 1978); Sidney Milkis, *Theodore Roosevelt, the Progressive Party, and the Transformation of American Democracy* (Lawrence: University of Kansas Press, 2009), 260–68. On the 1912 election, see James Chase, *1912: Wilson, Roosevelt, Taft, and Debs – the Election That Changed the Country* (New York: Simon & Schuster, 2004).

63 Oliver W. Stewart, "Changing Views of Government," *Vindicator*, 14 February 1913. Stewart had been removed from party chairmanship on the basis of quite possibly true complaints about embezzlement. See, for example, Samuel Dickie, "Dickie Calls it 'Loot,'" *Kansas City Leader*, 24 November 1904. A measure of his extraordinary unpopularity with some members of the party is preserved in the correspondence of John P. St. John, Scrapbook 7, Box: 3, JSJP.

Stewart touched a nerve among fellow partisans who quickly disavowed any such movement within the party to undermine the party system, either with direct democracy and recall – as Stewart seemed to propose – or with the administrative agencies progressive reformers advocated. The *Vindicator's* editorial staff argued that deeming the entire system a failure was going too far and that blame should be limited to the individual parties running this system and to the citizens who continued to support these parties.[64] The associate editor, Orrin H. Graham, chastised Stewart by urging that "such a variety and uniformity of mistaken and ill-considered ideas has not lately appeared in a public address." He was most offended by what he interpreted as Stewart's claim that "political parties prevent the people of this country from ruling it," arguing that "very much the contrary is the case." Graham concluded that "because the American people have cut themselves with the axe through their own folly is no evidence that it is not a good axe. . . . Because they have successfully voted everything wrong by the party method is proof . . . that they can effectually vote everything right by the party method if they will."[65]

William A. Brubaker had been the 1911 candidate for mayor of Chicago before becoming Michigan's state chair. He added that "when [Stewart] speaks of the failure of the party method of government, I think he falls into error. It is true, as every intelligent man knows, that the party method has failed to give the people good government, but the cause of that will be found elsewhere. It has always given them as good government as they demanded."[66] W.G. Calderwood agreed that "no man ever secured a political result excepting through the Party method . . . we need the people and the people need the Party."[67] Here was the limit of the Prohibition Party's willingness to explore new ways of organizing democracy: The party system should and would remain intact.

In immediate terms, Prohibitionists' critique of Democrats, Republicans, and ballot laws expressed their desire for continued relevance in American politics, even as their political world was rapidly changing. Party members hoped to maintain leadership opportunities, participate in a meaningful moral reform, and socialize as a community. And the new strategies they developed offered a solution – however fragile – that kept the constituency together at a time when there were fewer and fewer candidates for whom Prohibitionists could vote, and thus the ritual of

[64] "Mr. Stewart's Address," *Vindicator*, 11 February 1913.
[65] Orrin H. Graham, "Graham vs. Stewart," *Vindicator*, 28 February 1913.
[66] William A. Brubaker, "Stewart's Conference Address," *Vindicator*, 14 March 1913.
[67] W.G. Calderwood quoted in "Calderwood Grapples A.S.L.; Friendly Debate Ensues," *American Advance*, 17 February 1912.

voting could not keep them united. Simultaneously a new problem emerged: Prohibitionists worried about the weakening of their party's resolve and the spiking movement of Prohibitionists into close alliance with other anti-liquor groups and even the major parties.[68]

* * *

It was the grand scale of the Anti-Saloon League (ASL) that made it imperative for Prohibitionists to respond when the ASL initiated an amendment campaign in 1913. This nonpartisan pressure group's popularity had increased rapidly after its founding in 1893, and by 1905 it could easily claim to be the largest national anti-liquor association.[69] Although the ASL did not reveal the number of Americans contributing to its funds, its national periodical had a circulation of about 4.7 million in 1912, as compared to the 200,000 votes cast for the Prohibition Party's 1912 presidential candidate.[70] For Prohibitionists who had already weathered the National League's attempts to woo away the party's base, this newest anti-liquor group fused together new and old problems. Not only did ASL strategy amplify the limitations of the Democratic and Republican parties while simultaneously eroding national faith in the party system, but now this rival was promoting a constitutional amendment that was deeply flawed. At its most generous, the Prohibition Party press would hopefully suggest that "considering the distance the Anti-Saloon League has already come," the rival organization might soon fight "not only for National Prohibition, but Prohibition with a party in power committed to that policy."[71]

Leading Prohibitionists had consistently argued that any political strategy that did not start with transforming the party system could not possibly create a dry America. First, there was the problem of getting Congress

---

[68] "The Prohibition Party," *Patriot Phalanx*, 28 June 1912; W.G. Calderwood, "Calderwood on County Option," *Vindicator*, 2 February 1912; "Mr. Smith's Criticisms," *Vindicator*, 1 March 1912; J. Burritt Smith, "Non-Partisan Poison," *Vindicator*, 1 March 1912; William Frost Crispin, "Stand By the Party," *Vindicator*, 5 April 1912. As an intriguing side note, J. Burritt Smith was T.C. Richmond's law partner in Madison, Wisconsin, at the same time that they both held state-level offices in the Prohibition Party. His obituary appears in "A Brief Sketch of Mr. Smith's Life," *Prohibition Journal*, 7 January 1915, reprinted from *Madison Democrat*.

[69] Blocker, *Retreat from Reform*, 199.

[70] Ernest Cherrington, "Twenty Eventful Years," Anti-Saloon League Web site: http://www.westervillelibrary.org/AntiSaloon/resources/twenty_eventful_years.html (accessed 16 April 2007), 9.

[71] "The Columbus Conference," *Backbone*, 27 November 1913.

to pass an amendment. They warned that "no Congress has sat in Washington since the Civil War at the hands of which it would be reasonable to expect the submission of a constitutional amendment prohibiting the liquor traffic."[72] Democrats' and Republicans' control of Congress and the refusal of these parties to publicly declare a position for the electorate to vote for or against meant that Congress lacked appropriate authority: "A Republican or a Democrat, elected on a party platform declaring for the high license policy, or by its silence endorsing the existing policy of government, could not honestly favor Prohibition" because doing so would require him to move far beyond the mandate that voters and his party had given him.[73] As condescendingly as possible, New York's *Backbone* explained that "there is not a Prohibitionist in America who does not believe that a Prohibition amendment to the Federal Constitution is an iridescent dream. Any man who believes to the contrary is a subject for a writ de lunatic inquirendo."[74]

Drawing on a decade of using pressure tactics to persuade state legislators, the ASL argued that no mandate through a platform would be necessary to persuade federal legislators. It was not party affiliation and party caucus that most influenced the actions of elected officials, but rather each office holder's fear of losing the next election. Thus, legislators only needed to be convinced that their seats would be in danger if they opposed a national amendment. The ASL declared that "we believe the time is fully ripe for the launching of a campaign for national Prohibition – not by any party, or parties, but by the people," that is, by nonpartisan means.[75] Prohibitionists indignantly inquired, "How can the people act in a political matter without organization as a political party? The very nature of our government, the very character of political action... posits the impossibility of effective accomplishment without political organization."[76]

The Prohibition Party argued that pressure groups pretended to be an alternative to government through party politics when really

---

[72] The Vindicator's Editor, "Throw Wide the Gates," *Vindicator*, 9 May 1913. See also "The Really Short and Easy Way," *Vindicator*, 19 December 1913; Anonymous New York Businessman, "The Ravings of a 'Nut,'" *Vindicator*, 4 September 1914.

[73] John A. Shields, "The 'Good Man' Theory," *Vindicator*, 20 November 1914. See also Sumner W. Haynes, "Prohibition Amendment: An Address at the Indiana State Prohibition Conference," *Vindicator*, 15 August 1913.

[74] "Prohibition Bill Introduced in Senate," *Backbone*, 13 January 1916.

[75] The board of trustees of the Anti-Saloon League of America quoted in "The League's Program," *Vindicator*, 30 May 1913.

[76] "The League's Program," *Vindicator*, 30 May 1913.

they redirected the energies of reformers back into the same dominant parties that eroded the party system's democratic character. Prohibitionists asserted that "it is the business of the Anti-Saloon League to keep alive the Republican and Democratic parties."[77] Prohibitionists dismissed the ASL as "another attempt to solve the liquor problem, while leaving the liquor sellers and their allies in charge of the machinery of government."[78] Because the ASL could not get anything that the major parties did not choose to provide, there was no reason to expect that a national amendment could ever actually get through Congress until these major parties were replaced.

The pan-temperance unity created through actions such as life-insurance ventures proved fleeting, and debates between Prohibitionists and nonpartisan ASL leaders came to a head at religious conferences. The ASL won skirmishes at conference after conference because it did not present itself as an alternative to church-led activism; unlike in the Prohibition Party, the churches had formal (if superficial) control over the ASL organization through denominational representatives on the governing board.[79] Throughout the 1890s, Prohibitionists such as Silas C. Swallow and James B. Hobbs had served as delegates to Methodist Episcopal Church conferences, and James Black, J.G. Evans, A.B. Leonard, and Samuel Dickie had held various positions on the conference's Permanent Committee on Temperance and Prohibition, including that of chair. It was frustrating to Prohibitionists that their standing as delegates did not translate into support for the Prohibition Party, doing little to stop the tide of church resolutions implicitly or explicitly shunning party organization as an alternative to the ASL.

The extent to which Prohibitionists were censored when they sought to bring their churches into the party fold became especially clear in 1900 when Samuel Dickie served as chair of the Methodists' Temperance and Prohibition Committee. Dickie caused no small amount of controversy when he accused President William McKinley, a Republican and Methodist, of being implicated in the nonenforcement of statutes eliminating liquor sales at army canteens. In particular, Dickie's report referred to the "puerile and absurd construction placed upon the Anti-Canteen

---

[77] "Non-Partisan Fallacy," *Clean Politics*, 5 August 1909. Peter H. Odegard, a contemporary and historian of the ASL, dismissed such accusations as "amusing." See *Pressure Politics*, 81.

[78] John Hipp (secretary Colorado committee), "The Correspondent," *Vindicator*, 12 September 1913.

[79] Blocker, *Retreat from Reform*, 166.

law, so called" and suggested that the convention was "pained and disappointed" by the president's lack of support for the law. The ultimate result was extensive debate, a minority report substituted for the report of the Dickie-led faction, and the addition of an explicit resolution by the General Conference that "the foregoing resolution" on withholding support from political parties committed to license "must not be considered as in the interest of any political party."[80]

There was a similar trend of shunning Prohibitionists and praising the ASL at state and regional religious conferences. In 1900, the New York East Conference of the Methodist Episcopal Church commended "the work that is being done by the Loyal Legion, the Woman's Christian Temperance Union, the Connecticut Temperance Union, the Law and Order League of Connecticut, and the Anti-Saloon League," leaving the Prohibition Party out of the list.[81] By 1904, the same conference's Temperance Committee would more boldly proclaim that "we urge that temperance activities be removed as far as possible from the domain of political partisanship. We have little or nothing to expect from that quarter."[82] In Idaho, Methodists could be assured that "our preachers are all prohibitionists of the reasonable sort" because they chose to join "their energies with those of co-operating ministers and anti-saloon agents."[83] Connecticut Baptists appropriated the ASL's motto when resolving that "the saloon must go!"[84] If Prohibitionists were going to oppose the ASL, they would be very much alone.

Although the party had viewed the Anti-Saloon League with "serene but respectful indifference" in the 1890s, many Prohibitionists would come to view it as an "evil power."[85] Prohibitionist leaders asserted that

[80] David S. Monroe, ed., *Journal of the General Conference of the Methodist Episcopal Church Held in Chicago, Illinois, May 2–29, 1900* (New York: Eaton & Mains, 1900), 311–312, 314–315. See also "Debate on the Temperance Report," *Zion's Herald*, 6 June 1900. This law limited soldiers' access to liquor.

[81] Calvin B. Ford and Nathan Hubbell, eds., *Minutes of the New York East Conference of 1900* (New York: Press of Eaton and Mains, 1900).

[82] *Minutes of the New York East Conference of 1904* (New York: Hodgetts and C.E. Barto, 1904), 103.

[83] *Official Journal of the Idaho Annual Conference of the Methodist Episcopal Church, Twenty-Fifth Session Held at Weiser, Idaho, August 20–23, 1908* (Boise, ID: Capital News Job Room, 1908), 31.

[84] P.S. Evans and C.A. Piddock, eds., *Seventy-Eighth Annual Report of the Connecticut Baptist Convention, and the Eighty-Second Annual Report of the Connectiut Baptist Educational Society* (Hartford, CT: Press of the Smith-Linsley Company, 1901), 60.

[85] J.J. Ashenhurst, "The Anti-Saloon League," *Backbone*, April 1898; E.P. Fisher, "Why License Parties are Popular," *Patriot Phalanx*, 3 January 1913.

the ASL conspired to deny Prohibitionist speakers access to churches where they wanted to lecture, refused to endorse most Prohibition Party candidates, and siphoned resources from temperance advocates that might otherwise be used in Prohibition Party campaigns. Frances Beauchamp, national committee secretary, explained in a private letter to party chair Charles Jones that "the League seems to have exercised a spell over the preachers. They are afraid to call their souls their own, – I mean the preachers, not the League. I don't know whether the League possesses any such article or not." She concluded that "did I once say I hate them, I certainly have no reason to change my mind."[86] National committee member W.G. Calderwood dryly asserted that "I am constrained by temperament, training, and some bitter experiences not to be swept from my feet by enthusiasm" in response to the Anti-Saloon League's new proposal for an amendment.[87] Still less restrained, Indiana attorney Sumner W. Haynes concluded that "there [sic] 'omni-partisan' movements make me sick."[88]

The wave of nonpartisan local option, law enforcement, and state amendment campaigns that developed in the 1900s and 1910s, largely led by the ASL and its state affiliates, revealed that the only thing more consistent than Prohibitionists' doctrinaire rejection of nonpartisan campaigns was the participation of individual Prohibitionists within them. Even when the party seemed to unite against the ASL, such as when the Los Angeles County party ran a candidate against an ASL-endorsed supervisor in 1909, the party's voters split between the two candidates. Historian Gilman Ostrander summarized that the California Prohibition Party "found its own leadership divided again and again over the issue of fighting or supporting the League" and parted ways by 1911.[89] James B. Cranfill served in Texas' state prohibition campaign in 1911 by writing supportive articles in newspapers.[90] West Virginia's Ratification Federation included the state Prohibition Party as well as the usual suspects when it achieved state prohibition through referendum in 1912.[91] Colorado's

[86] Frances Beauchamp to Charles Jones, 3 March 1914, Folder: Correspondence, 1909–1942, CJP. Beauchamp had been elected the Kentucky party's chair in 1911.

[87] W.G. Calderwood, "The A.S.L. Convention," *Vindicator*, 21 November 1913.

[88] S.W. Haynes, "Haynes Expresses Himself," *Patriot Phalanx*, 24 November 1911. Haynes was born in 1855, was admitted to the bar in 1879, served as a Presbyterian church elder and five-time delegate to the Prohibition Party national convention, and was a 1908 Indiana gubernatorial candidate; "Who Is Haynes," *Patriot Phalanx*, 5 May 1916.

[89] Ostrander, *Prohibition Movement in California*, 95, 121–122.

[90] Ivy, *No Saloon in this Valley*, 109.

[91] Szymanski, *Pathways to Prohibition*, 158.

unsuccessful state amendment campaign included Prohibitionists in 1912, although partisans turned to a promoter endorsed by the national party to guide their 1914 campaign for "government" rather than "lifeless law."[92]

Many rank-and-file Prohibitionists remained of "two minds...as regards constitutional Prohibition," both for and against the ASL-led campaign.[93] Even given the tension between organizations, the party's decision to withhold support from the ASL national amendment campaign did not come easily. On one level, the resolution to refrain was rooted in the problem of the Prohibition Party's own constituency building and maintenance. National leaders were unable to assure themselves that there was a way "to avoid having the sentiment and interest which we create stampeded into non-partisan campaigns."[94] They so argued even as, very grudgingly, they acknowledged that Prohibitionists were not always prepared to offer voters an alternative. The ASL seized on a report of how in Pittsburg, for example, the county Prohibition Party nominated candidates from the major parties to "fill out" their nominations, all the while declaring that they were "standing strictly for Prohibition and against allowing themselves to be swallowed by the old parties."[95]

Doctrinaire Prohibitionists wanted to protect their party out of self-interest but also because their party embodied a vision and ideal of democracy that was losing traction – one that prioritized personal relationships and deliberation, dedication to a significant cause, and routine participation in a local party. At the highest levels of the Prohibition Party, national conventions with hundreds of delegates continued to insist on line-by-line discussion of party platforms prior to ratifying them. This was long after the practice had subsided in the Democratic and Republican national conventions, if such debate had ever been more than an artifice. For Prohibitionists, the loss of party would mean the end of a rewarding way of doing politics and defining democracy; Prohibitionists identified their party as "without question the most democratic organization in political annals."[96] Abandoning the Prohibition Party would

---

[92] "Is this Cooperation," *Prohibition Journal*, 7 May 1914.

[93] "Patience," *Vindicator*, 21 November 1913. This split was largely expressed in a division in the editorial stances of party periodicals. The *Vindicator* and the *Patriot Phalanx* sometimes offered tepid, conditional support for the amendment, whereas the *Prohibition Journal* and the *Campaigner*, which mainly circulated in Wisconsin and Iowa, spoke for party orthodoxy.

[94] "The Present Problem," *Vindicator*, 2 May 1913.

[95] "Party Prohibs Endorse Old Party Drys," *American Issue*, April 1914.

[96] "The Progressive Prohibition League," *American Advance*, 16 December 1911.

seemingly convey consent to a form of politics wherein select groups of experts managed the electorate.

The ASL's organizational style – a set of characteristics that this pressure group shared with new corporate businesses – included the widespread use of professional organizers, paid lobbyists, and a full-time staff to coordinate its expanding network.[97] Historian Richard Hamm has summarized that "where the Prohibition party and WCTU were democratic and open, the league was bureaucratic and secretive."[98] ASL supporters participated by donating money and promising votes rather than by debating and setting policy. Prohibitionists noted this important difference, suggesting that at an ASL conference "the 'delegates' are only spectators. The government is not democratic, of the people; it is not even republican, or representative. The directors are the sole legislative, judicial and executive arm of the government of the organization." Thus, the delegates' "only function was to be entertained."[99]

The Anti-Saloon League gracefully sidestepped the question of whether its internal procedures were democratic by adamantly defending the democratic value of its overall strategy. After all, the ASL was trying to create situations wherein the people could vote for legislation. The organization supported the initiative and referendum in Washington state, for example, and often emphasized that government should be by "the people" and not by parties.[100] And its primary tactic was to focus public opinion on legislators so that they would enact desired legislation and then to ensure its enforcement through the use of the court system. The ASL's approach to law enforcement emphasized that "the league must work to make public sentiment for enforcement" and should not "relieve public, regular officers of their job but rather 'stimulate' them to act."[101]

---

97 On the ASL's internal organization, see Odegard, *Pressure Politics*, 9–17; Kerr, *Organized for Prohibition*, 116–122. On the professionalism of special interest groups generally, see Skocpol, *Diminished Democracy*.

98 Hamm, *Shaping the Eighteenth Amendment*, 130.

99 "Anti-Saloon League Convention," *Minnesota Patriot*, November 1913. See also "Brubaker on Union," *Vindicator*, 28 November 1913; "Non-Partisanism Fallacies," *Clean Politics*, 5 August 1909; "League or Party? Question of Method," *Patriot Phalanx*, 14 April 1910. Jack Blocker memorably described the ASL's internal culture as "elitist, manipulative, and, ultimately, antidemocratic," thereby lending credibility to Prohibitionists' own assessment; *Retreat from Reform*, 154.

100 Clark, *The Dry Years*, 102; "Calderwood Grapples A.S.L.; Friendly Debate Ensues," *American Advance*, 17 February 1912.

101 Hamm, *Shaping the Eighteenth Amendment*, 143.

Such interpretations, of course, might be reconsidered in the light of the ASL's reluctance to introduce prohibitory legislation for a mass vote when the organization was unsure of victory, or even an impressive turnout. For example, throughout the 1910s California's ASL debated incessantly about whether or not to endorse an initiative that the state's Prohibition Party advanced. The initiative would have prohibited the manufacture, sale, distribution, or gift of liquor, but the ASL often refused to endorse the measure for fear that the inevitable failure would make the movement a laughingstock.[102] A similar situation emerged in Missouri.[103] In other instances, ASL leaders advocated prohibition obtained through the judiciary rather than through representative assemblies.[104] And in terms of law enforcement, state ASLs often provided private citizens with information about how to hire detectives and advance private prosecutions, a process on the verge of vigilantism. Seven state leagues retained attorneys.[105]

An amendment that appeared to bypass mass approval, Prohibitionists claimed, would be impossible to enforce and would thereby discredit the cause. They urged that if, by some chance, "we now pass an amendment prohibiting the manufacture and sale of alcoholic drinks and put that law into the hands of a party that is too cowardly to dare, to indifferent to care, and too subservient to assert itself, the old cry that Prohibition does not prohibit will have truth enough in it to damn the measure when passed."[106] They declared that "we do not want any more constitutional amendments, or other Prohibition laws, until we have adequate provision for their enforcement."[107] And they expressed their apprehension that such lack of enforcement might eventually discredit the authority of all law.[108] It would be "a source of infinite corruption and" and "a condition bordering upon anarchy."[109]

---

[102] Ostrander, *Prohibition Movement in California*, 121–123. On the ASL's eventual change in position, see Ostrander, *Prohibition Movement in California*, 134. Untitled, *Prohibition Journal*, 21 January 1914. See also Szymanski, *Pathways to Prohibition*, 176, and on Illinois, 180–181. For a counterexample in Maryland in 1908, wherein the ASL introduced a local option bill for the purpose of focusing debate rather than passing, see Pegram, "Temperance Politics and Regional Political Culture," 85.

[103] Blocker, *Retreat from Reform*, 216.

[104] Hamm, *Shaping the Eighteenth Amendment*, 139.

[105] Hamm, *Shaping the Eighteenth Amendment*, 144–145.

[106] "The Federal Amendment," *Minnesota Patriot*, September 1913.

[107] "Repudiation or Growth?" *Vindicator*, 7 November 1913. See also William C. Dean, "Hardest Battle Yet to Come," *Vindicator*, 12 December 1913; Eugene W. Chafin, *Government by Administration* (Chicago: n.p., ca. 1912).

[108] "The Amendment Scheme," *Vindicator*, 25 July 1913.

[109] William P.F. Ferguson, "'Bring up the Regiment,'" *Vindicator*, 31 October 1913.

Recalling Reconstruction, Prohibitionists suggested that the amendment "will be found absolutely insufficient unless it is in the hands of a party definitely committed to the prohibition policy. No man thinks that the 14th and 15th amendments to the constitution of the United States were adequate of themselves to insure liberty to the slave. It took a party committed to that policy."[110] Whereas the ASL might taunt Prohibitionists who "had been yelling for national Prohibition all their lives" and then "appeared with their hammer to knock that very proposal," doctrinaire partisans affirmed that a "middle-of-the-road Prohibitionist" must "look askance on the constitutional amendment proposition" because "a prohibition law, either statutory or constitutional, does not destroy the liquor traffic" unless accompanied by an administration pledged to enforce it.[111] George Grant, a member of the *Vindicator*'s editorial staff, expressed his concern that the amendment campaign would suffocate the Prohibition Party and that then "the whole fight would have to be fought over again, without, so far as I can see, the slightest advantage from the adoption of the amendment."[112] Even if a constitutional amendment were passed, anti-liquor advocates would still need a party that favored prohibition to do this work. Essentially, the amendment was "national option" that projected on the entire country the already established problems of local option.[113]

Debates among party members regarding the amendment persisted throughout the years from 1913 to 1917. In a particularly heated example, the former state chair of California took that state's chief party publication to task for overtly supporting the national amendment campaign. The current state chair then defended the state organ by arguing that the former chair failed to consider that "had the Prohibitionists of California opposed or been the least indifferent in support of the Prohibition amendment, we should simply have been wiped off the map and lost our standing as a recognized party of the state," evoking ongoing fears about the repercussions of ballot qualification standards. "For Prohibitionists to oppose or be indifferent in an amendment campaign cannot be satisfactorily explained to the average voter," he claimed. What was most important was that the state party's coffers were receiving unprecedented

---

[110] "The Federal Amendment," *Minnesota Patriot*, September 1913. See also W.G. Calderwood, "Prohibition as a Political Platform," *Vindicator*, 18 October 1912.

[111] Untitled, *Prohibition Journal*, 11 December 1913, reprinted from *American Issue*; "The Real Need," *Prohibition Journal*, 8 January 1914.

[112] George Grant, "The 'Final' Step," *Vindicator*, 11 July 1913.

[113] "National Option On Us," *Prohibition Journal*, 1 October 1914.

donations, and many more voters had registered for the party in Los Angeles County.[114] The Ninth Congressional District of Los Angeles even elected Charles H. Randall to congress on the Prohibition Party ticket. With the national party having endorsed the idea of a national amendment in several party platforms, rank-and-file constituents often viewed any insistence that such an amendment be conditional on the party's rise to power to be an arbitrary distinction, or else a logical fallacy.[115] Not only in California, but also in Oregon, Pennsylvania, and New York, the state parties departed from national policy by pursuing the amendment enthusiastically or uniting behind "independent" pro-amendment candidates.[116] Individual national leaders, including A.A. Hopkins, also voiced their support.[117]

Prohibitionists who opposed the ASL and its amendment campaign as an undemocratic experiment advanced by an undemocratic organization were appalled to find that many enthusiastic Prohibitionist speakers had joined the Flying Squadron. This group of traveling lecturers from several parties asked voters to publicly promise to not vote for any party that did not explicitly support a national prohibition amendment in its platform.[118] Intriguingly, the party's amendment advocates in the Flying Squadron shared a critical ideological assumption with anti-amendment Prohibitionists: Democratic and Republican leadership would never permit the national amendment to pass through Congress. The Prohibitionists working within the Flying Squadron argued that because neither Republicans nor Democrats would accept a pro-amendment platform, their program would necessarily commit many new people to vote for

[114] "Party and Constitutional Amendments," *Patriot Phalanx*, 15 May 1914. On the California party's occasionally renegade activities, see "Is California All Right?" *Prohibition Journal*, 5 March 1914.

[115] "Should Party Support the Amendment Plan?" *Patriot Phalanx*, 20 November 1914; Robert H. Patton, "Shall the Constitution of the United States Be Amended for Prohibition? How and When!" *(Indianapolis, Indiana) National Enquirer*, 22 December 1915.

[116] "Lost in Oregon," *Prohibition Journal*, 10 September 1914; "A Disintegrating Doctrine," *Prohibition Journal*, 5 November 1914; "Off the Track," *National Enquirer*, 5 March 1914.

[117] A.A. Hopkins, "Dr. Hopkins Writes a Letter," *Prohibition Journal*, 10 September 1914.

[118] For more information on the Flying Squadron, see Colvin, *Prohibition in the United States*, 411–412. For an example of concern that this organization was a subterfuge for destroying the party, see "The 'Flying Squadron,'" *Prohibition Journal*, 8 January 1914. Eugene Chafin left the organization in 1915, ostensibly because he felt censored from suggesting that the constitutional amendment could not be successful; "The Partisan Nature of the Question Cannot Be Suppressed," *Campaigner*, September 1915. The *National Enquirer*'s J. Frank Hanley remained in the Flying Squadron's ranks.

the Prohibition Party. On these terms, it was lukewarmly supported by Indianapolis' *Patriot Phalanx*, one of the most widely read and influential Prohibitionist papers. About the idea of a formal union with the ASL, the same paper would jump to remind readers that the question of method was "not a quibble. It is the real problem."[119]

Anti-amendment Prohibitionists thus took up a second tactic, reminding their ranks that the kind of permanency a national prohibition amendment offered made it almost as undesirable as its undemocratic origins in the ASL and its nonpartisan character. They drew on years of experience combating a liquor industry that had mastered ways to circumvent local option laws and state prohibition amendments through legal loopholes. W.G. Calderwood explained to fellow partisans that "it is many times harder to amend the Constitution than it is to enact a statute."[120] Anti-amendment Prohibitionists argued that the problem with an amendment was that it could never promise anything more valuable than simple legislation but would be incredibly difficult to modify; an amendment campaign was an unnecessarily complicated process for securing an undesirable goal. "Why," asked attorney Sumner W. Haynes, "should we hurry to write into the constitution a thing that is not now unconstitutional?"[121]

Whereas Prohibitionists largely assumed that the failure of state amendments to be enforced suggested that a national amendment would also fare poorly, the Anti-Saloon League's movement proposed that a national amendment would be better enforced than state amendments.

[119] Editor's response, "What About Methods?" *Patriot Phalanx*, 24 April 1914. The *Prohibition Journal* would give pro-Flying Squadron Prohibitionists a hearing, but its editorial policy remained very much opposed to the idea. For example, see "Party Loyalty," *Prohibition Journal*, 5 February 1914. The question of whether or not it was ethical to lend support for the purposes of demonstrating the failure of other prohibition strategies was the subject of frequent party debate.

[120] W. G. Calderwood, "The League and the Party," *Vindicator*, 13 March 1914. The discussion regarding the respective merits of constitutional and statuary prohibition is a frequent item in the records of the Minnesota committee that Calderwood chaired. For an example, see George F. Wells to George B. Stafford, 10 December 1915, Folder: Minutes / Financial Records – October 4–December 15, 1915, PSECM.

[121] Sumner W. Haynes, "Too Much Hurry May Spoil It All," *Patriot Phalanx*, 11 July 1913. See also "Mr. Sizer's Position," *Prohibition Journal*, 25 February 1914; J.L. Sizer, "Mr. Sizer Recants," *Prohibition Journal*, 25 February 1914; "The Amendment Delusion," *Prohibition Journal*, 14 May 1914; David L. Dobson, "Defends Constitution," *Prohibition Journal*, 4 June 1914; Eugene Chafin, "Extract From Mr. Chafin's Latest Address," *Prohibition Journal*, 18 March 1915; Untitled, *Patriot Phalanx*, 12 January 1917.

Such optimism was manifest in the amendment's eventual language – language that was largely written under the guidance of the ASL – which would demand both state and federal enforcement. Theoretically, double enforcement would ensure twice the enforcement. Leading up to the national amendment, the Oklahoma ASL supported national prohibition because it would "remove the burden of the difficulty of enforcing the Prohibition law from the states that have already enacted Prohibition laws."[122] Moreover, Anti-Saloon League leaders agreed that the Constitution held unsurpassed cultural and political authority and that harnessing prohibition to this kind of authority would secure the permanency of the reform. Oddly, the Anti-Saloon League did not really respond to Prohibitionists' insistence that a federal statute might be a better way to ensure national prohibition.

The debate between the Prohibition Party and the ASL about the likelihood of a Democratic and Republican Congress to pass an amendment, and the desirability of an amendment in comparison to a national statute, was cut short by the extraordinary momentum of the ASL's campaign. By late 1915, Prohibitionists searched for a position adaptable to this new circumstance.

The party increasingly argued that the best way to protect the integrity of anti-liquor reform during the impending time of its federal trial would be to anticipate the liquor industry's arguments and insidious strategies as much as possible. The Prohibitionists' goal was not always to refute the liquor industry's claims but to study these claims as a way to prune the traffic's ability to undermine enforcement. For example, Prohibitionists listened attentively when the National Model License League (NMLL) argued that prohibition never prohibited under any state constitution. The NMLL blamed the Anti-Saloon League for this situation, arguing that the ASL had systematically pushed forward legislation that contained no requirements to prevent liquor from being shipped into dry areas. As a by-product of the ASL's focus on restricting the sale of liquor, legislation rarely contained any restrictions on consumption or private stills. This was worrying to the NMLL for different reasons than it would be Prohibitionists; the NMLL argued that most state constitutional amendments merely drove legitimate businessmen from the industry – legitimate businessmen who could be used to regulate the trade and keep it clean

---

[122] "Oklahoma for National Prohibition," *American Issue*, June 1914, reprinted from *McAlester (Oklahoma) News-Capital*. See also A.C. Bane, "Why National Prohibition?" *American Issue*, 20 March 1915.

of vice. They claimed that under state amendments liquor consumption was not curtailed, but simply became less supervised.[123] Americans should care because unlicensed liquor products were more often adulterated, and unlicensed sale was connected to gambling and prostitution.

Prohibitionists were unlikely to pity any saloon keeper pushed out of business because their party had never viewed the liquor seller's work as legitimate. However, they agreed with the National Model License League that a carelessly phrased amendment posed serious problems. Building on their earlier claims that prohibition was already constitutional, Prohibitionists first rehashed their contention that "if we have a Constitution that allows us to prohibit the liquor traffic entirely, prior to its amendment, and we then add an Amendment specifying certain limitations as to what part or portion of the traffic shall be prohibited thereafter, the implication will be that every other part and portion, with all its collateral cunning, is sanctioned." This would create a new problem – namely, that "if we ever wish to get rid of the traffic entirely, as we surely will and do, we may find that the option we had has been taken away by Constitutional Amendment and that it will take another Amendment to restore our rights."[124]

Prohibitionists conceded that "every member of the Prohibition Party will accept with gratitude an opportunity to vote for honest prohibition of intoxicating beverages" while insisting that this would only be the case "if you use the words prohibition of beverages." They urged the ASL to

simply say nothing about liquor for medical, mechanical and (un)sacramental purposes. Liquor so used are not beverages. . . . Of course we may be dull and impractical, and fanatical: but what do 'you-uns' mean? What is constitutional law? Should it not express finality of judgment? If experiments are yet needful, is it not simpler to enact statutory measures, subject to easier revision and correction? When we know what we want, and when we have strength to demand what we want, is time enough to ask for national constitutional amendments. But now let us go after the best legislation we can get; but let us ask for nothing known to be ineffective.[125]

In asking for a national amendment, the ASL had adopted a critical component of the Prohibition Party's absolutist stance, implicitly arguing that state and local prohibition would always result in some violation. The ASL simultaneously diverged from Prohibitionists when it deliberately

[123] J.M Gilmore, "Does Prohibition Prohibit?" *North American Review*, March 1915.
[124] George W. Norman, "Prohibition Party the Only Place for Sincere Prohibitionists," *Patriot Phalanx*, 9 June 1916.
[125] "That National Constitutional Amendment," *Patriot Phalanx*, 30 June 1916.

argued for an amendment that focused on the sale of alcoholic beverages rather than their consumption. If consuming alcohol was a moral problem, posed Prohibitionists, then why did the ASL deliberately avoid directly engaging this problem?

The language in the first section of the amendment proposed by the ASL and supported by a 1915 committee with "representatives of all the leading temperance organizations of the United States," excluding the Prohibition Party, was as follows:

Section 1. The sale, manufacture for sale, transportation for sale and importation for sale of intoxicating liquors for beverage purposes in the United States and all territory subject to the jurisdiction thereof and exportation thereof are hereby prohibited.[126]

Historians have generally assumed that Congress constructed the amendment to prohibit selling but not consuming simply so that federal investigators could find witnesses to prosecute cases. The ASL's decision to focus on sale, rather than consumption, was also consistent with its strategy for building a coalition among the broadest possible group of opponents to the liquor traffic. The ASL was not prepared to use the law to demand total abstinence because its leaders did not believe that a total abstinence amendment could be passed, but they wanted something.[127] Some Prohibitionists suggested that it was dishonest to request only a part of that reform which they most wanted, and this timidity would create more problems than the amendment was worth.

With the amendment looking more and more likely, a few Prohibitionists returned to a Flying Squadron-type argument that poor enforcement might be the final, critical push needed to persuade Americans to elect a party that would enforce anti-liquor legislation. Other partisans vehemently squashed these suggestions. The *National Prohibitionist* editor, William P.F. Ferguson, expressed skepticism about the tendency of some national party leaders to lend assistance to campaigns for the amendment, even on limited terms. He asked,

When we appear as the champions of a nonpartisan campaign, anywhere, is it not at least assisting in educating the people to the idea that the Prohibition party is not needed? In theory, the failure of the people to secure real Prohibition by state action ought to lead them toward the support of a political party that will

---

[126] "Committee Statement on History, Wording, and Scope of Resolution for National Prohibition as Introduced in Congress," *American Issue*, 25 December 1915.

[127] Kerr, *Organized for Prohibition*, 196–197 and 209–210; "Conference Decides Hobson Resolution to Remain Unchanged," *American Issue*, 24 July 1915.

give them national Prohibition. In practice, it never has. A Prohibition state is a state where it is hard to get voters to vote for the Prohibition Party.[128]

Other Prohibitionists agreed. They resolved that

we recognize that the work of building a Prohibition party now involves enormous difficulties, but we insist that it is easier to do it now than it by any possibility can be when to every argument that exists against it now, there shall be added the popular impression that the whole question has been settled by the adoption of a constitutional amendment.[129]

In 1916, internal spats between two factions of the Prohibition Party, factions whose rivalry was principally about personal dislike for each other and only loosely about ideological division, resulted in a fragmented party agenda at the very moment when coherence was most required. The two factions compromised by choosing Virgil Hinshaw, who was not involved with either faction, as the new national chair.

Hinshaw's selection, however, bore unexpected fruit. Hinshaw attempted to adapt the party to its new political circumstances by drawing it into a closer relationship with the ASL.[130] Likewise, the party's presidential and vice-presidential candidates in 1916 – also selected because they were aligned with neither faction – were men with little previous experience with the party and hence little grounding in party doctrine. J. Frank Hanley, the presidential nominee, was a former Republican governor of Indiana and Ira Landrith, the vice-presidential nominee, was better known as the chair of the Tennessee YMCA, an early leader of Tennessee's Anti-Saloon League, and a contributor to the Flying Squadron and *Cumberland Presbyterian*.[131] Party historian D. Leigh Colvin, who was an active party member during this era, defined the ensuing campaign as being "chiefly upon the principle of prohibition

---

[128] William P. F. Ferguson, "Some Important Questions," *Vindicator*, 17 November 1916.
[129] "Now or Later," *Vindicator*, 25 February 1916.
[130] This position was perhaps most encouraged by the *National Enquirer*, a party paper whose editorial staff included former chair Oliver W. Stewart. Under Hinshaw's influence, the Prohibition Party was included under the umbrella of a new "National party," founded in October 1917. Prohibitionist Ira Landrith was named national chair of the National Party. See "New 'National' Party Organized at Chicago," *National Enquirer*, 11 October 1917; "Amalgamated," *Campaigner*, October 1917.
[131] Landrith's switch to the Prohibition Party seems to have evolved in the wake of his 1908 threats to the Democratic Party that he would scratch all "indecent" candidates even if there was nothing left; Isaac, *Prohibition and Politics*, 145. On Landrith's conversion to the Prohibition Party, see "Ira Landrith Becomes a Party Prohibitionist," *Patriot Phalanx*, 30 June 1916.

rather than upon the distinctively party argument" because the candidates, who were the principal speakers at most events, knew more about prohibition than they did about the Prohibition Party.[132]

The reaction against the party's drift into a moderate position under its new leaders was pronounced and angry. Those who had traditionally been policy setters complained in the press and at conventions that the national committee "appear[ed] almost wholly to have lost the distinction between the aim and object of the Prohibition party, as a party, and the general nonpartisan Prohibition movement."[133] They challenged, "let us insist that every committee of the party confine itself strictly to party work, spend the energies of its workers and the funds committed to it for party work and for party work alone. Let us tolerate no talk about 'a' Prohibition party from our party's official leadership."[134] They pondered how "a few individuals of us scold about it and a few brave editors (mighty few), have warned against it, but the great voting millions of moral people, with honest desires to get rid of liquor, have never heard that they are merely being worked on a schedule that is permeated to the core with compromise."[135] The national amendment campaign was "one of the most deceptive and delusive non-partisan propositions that has yet been put up to the temperance people of the nation."[136]

The compromises that threatened party integrity were part of an attempt to protect party ranks, which were continually depleted with each passing election; once hearty Prohibitionists drifted into the Democratic and Republican parties. Individuals outside the Prohibition Party concluded that the "downfall of the Prohibition party" – its shrinking returns, scattered organization, and disappearance from ballots – was intimately connected to the success of prohibition. The *New York Times* suggested that "every new victory for Prohibition drives another nail in the coffin of the Prohibition Party."[137]

In a long editorial, former national chair Oliver W. Stewart conceded that it would be most consistent to insist on the election of Prohibition Party candidates in advance of the amendment's ratification and to thereby ensure enforcement. He noted that some partisan leaders "fought the (amendment) proposition, exposing what they alleged were

---

[132] Colvin, *Prohibition in the United States*, 424.
[133] "The Facts," *Vindicator*, 24 November 1916.
[134] The Vindicator's Editor, "Suggested Party Policy," *Vindicator*, 15 December 1916.
[135] G.K. Hubbard, "The Dodging of a Vital Issue," *Vindicator*, 15 December 1916.
[136] "Getting Nowhere," *Prohibition Journal*, 28 May 1914.
[137] "A Party in the Sere and Yellow Leaf," *New York Times*, 11 July 1916.

its fallacies, and pronounced it a waste of effort." However, the amendment was ultimately seductive to "Prohibitionists of the rank and file,
whose unerring instinct told them what to do." Local partisans "turned
aside from the Party organization...and gave their aid to other organizations. Some of them continued voting the ticket, but many ceased doing
even that." It was most likely that "such voters of the Party go joyfully
forward to help get national constitutional prohibition, waving adieu
to the Party as they go." State parties, caught between national party
doctrine and local enthusiasm for the amendment, "hesitated, vacillated
and did nothing."[138] Current national chair Virgil Hinshaw pointed to a
few states that were exceptions to the vacillating majority. In California,
Oregon, Arizona, Missouri, Ohio, Iowa, and Minnesota, Prohibitionist
leaders in the state parties had invited other dry leaders to join them in
forming dry federations and state alliances.[139]

* * *

Congress passed the national prohibition amendment in December 1917,
showing bipartisan support in excess of the two-thirds majority required
in both the House and Senate. This event completely undermined Prohibitionists' assumption that Republican and Democratic congressmen
would not act unless elected on a prohibitionist platform.

The extent to which legislators believed they were expressing their constituents' preferences was of extraordinary interest for contemporaries
and remains a matter of scholarly debate. Votes on local option and
referendum statutes, regular contact with local dry organizations and
liquor industry representatives, and correspondence with individual citizens would have enlightened even the dullest representatives.[140]

---

[138] Oliver Stewart, "Has the Prohibition Party a Future?" *National Enquirer*, 4 January
1917. See also Elcharles A. DeVore, "An Unselfish Program," *Patriot Phalanx*, 9 August
1918; Robert H. Patton, "Patton Says it is Not Disloyal," *Patriot Phalanx*, 6 September
1918; "Mr. Hanley and the Pennsylvania Campaign," *Patriot Phalanx*, 8 November 1918.

[139] Virgil Hinshaw, "Hinshaw Delivers and Interesting Prohibition Address at Lexington,"
National Enquirer, 11 January 1917; "Hinshaw Gets in Fight," *National Enquirer*,
20 September 1917; "Union of Forces in Minnesota," *National Enquirer*, 11 October
1917.

[140] Hamm, *Shaping the Eighteenth Amendment*, 204–205; Szymanski, *Pathways to Prohibition*, 196. Christopher M. Loomis notes that historian Peter Odegard attributed
to the ASL the strategy of educational work, including a large amount of pamphlets
and newspapers published for the purpose of creating public opinion that could then
be used to pressure politicians in the form of citizens' correspondence; "The Politics of
Uncertainty: Lobbyists and Propaganda in Early Twentieth-Century America," *Journal*

Then again a voter might support regulation or even prohibition without preferring a constitutional amendment. Concerns about miscommunication between voters and policy makers were amplified by the possibility that pressure groups like the ASL could invent public opinion as well as harness it. Beginning in the 1910s and gaining momentum throughout the 1930s, the new scale of lobbyists' propaganda endeavors called into question "whether citizens could obtain reliable information about their interests" and thus "cast doubt on the ordinary citizen's capacity to participate in democratic politics."[141] Incentives for attentiveness to the ASL included good publicity in the ASL press, advice, documentation, and assistance with reelection.[142]

The role of professional lobbyists in bringing about the amendment was given particular significance by the nature of the federal law, which would more completely imbue the body with political meaning. Thus, ensuing debates between Prohibitionists, the ASL, and anti-prohibitionists over the amendment's enactment and enforcement demonstrated the extraordinary malleability of democratic intellectual traditions. These debates questioned the legitimacy of government organization wherein political parties shared responsibility for creating government with pressure groups. Was such a government, Americans wondered, still a democracy? Might it be more democratic, or at least better government?

The first round of debate emerged out of the wartime moment in which prohibition was enacted. To conserve grain supplies, Congress passed a temporary wartime prohibition measure in April 1917 and the Fuel Control Act in August 1917. John M. Olin, a Prohibition Party national committee member from Wisconsin, had written the Senate to argue that an amendment to the Food Control Bill subverted the process of democratic review. He argued that "the bill...is not an honest one, or at least is not being advocated honestly." Olin asserted that it would be

---

of *Policy History* 21 (2009): 199. Blocker likewise notes that "while submission and ratification indicate the ability of the League to manipulate legislators," especially when combined with the state referenda results, "they do not necessarily reflect a popular majority in favor of prohibition"; *Retreat from Reform*, 235. The nature of the state referenda ranged from modest anti-saloon laws to laws banning consumption, and because many of these states had smaller populations, the victories within these states did not necessarily suggest a national movement toward prohibition. In comparison, Richard L. McCormick claims that legislators during the party period "knew their constituents well," whether or not this actually translated into policy making that would assist them; *Party Period and Public Policy*, 4.

[141] Loomis, "The Politics of Uncertainty," 189, 190.
[142] Hamm, *Shaping the Eighteenth Amendment*, 205.

far better if "prohibition should stand upon its own merits" as an issue for discussion and debate.[143] Prohibitionists thereby joined with other critics who accused the ASL of having unfairly exploited congressional patriotism and legislators' reluctance to oppose any wartime measure. With the transition from wartime statutes to an amendment, the prohibition issue became supercharged. Was it just to pass such afar-reaching law while so many young soldiers were stationed abroad? These soldiers were not necessarily aware of the amendment's rapid progress nor were they in a situation where communication with policy makers was particularly easy.[144] Despite years of public consideration, legal historian Richard Hamm has described the congressional debates leading to the amendment as "sporadic and brief" because "the emergency surrounding war mobilization precluded long debate on the prohibition amendment."[145]

The extent to which speedy congressional approval had been unanticipated can perhaps best be measured by the extent to which opponents remained disorganized and relatively complacent, totally unprepared for an anti-ratification campaign.[146] Opposition mostly expressed itself through liquor industry or hotel owners' organizations, whose representativeness of the general population was highly questionable; the ASL could far more persuasively argue that it embodied public opinion because, as nonconsumers and non-sellers, their lobbyists' actions could not be dismissed as self-interested. No anti-prohibition civic groups that distinguished themselves from the liquor industry would organize until the advent of the Association Against the Prohibition Amendment (AAPA) in November 1918, mere months before the amendment was enacted. And this group of businessmen and former military personnel would remain unincorporated until December 1920.

Responding to critics, the ASL defined theirs as an endeavor to "bring the question of National prohibition *directly before the people* of the Nation by adopting a joint resolution submitting a prohibitory Constitutional amendment to the legislatures of the several States."[147] Only after

---

[143] John M. Olin quoted in "Congress: Prohibition," *Outlook,* 25 July 1917.

[144] A nice synopsis of these concerns is included within Hamm, *Shaping the Eighteenth Amendment,* 227–255.

[145] Hamm, *Shaping the Eighteenth Amendment,* 240.

[146] Hamm, *Shaping the Eighteenth Amendment,* 241; David E. Kyvig, *Repealing National Prohibition* (Chicago: University of Chicago Press, 1979), 36–52; Kerr, *Organized for Prohibition,* 160–184.

[147] Harold T. Pulsifer, "The Anti-Saloon League Convention," *Outlook,* 21 July 1915. Italics mine. See also "Resolutions Adopted by the National Convention at Atlantic

receiving a two-thirds majority vote in both the House of Representatives and the Senate might an amendment move toward ratification, a process wherein three-fourths of the states must approve it. Congress instructed the states as to whether state legislatures or state conventions would be the required method and had specified state legislatures for the Eighteenth Amendment.[148]

However, the ratification process is not incontrovertibly left to "the people," even if it requires a supermajority of three-fourths of representative assemblies' support.[149] For the ASL, which was deeply invested in the idea of achieving a policy, it was not necessarily a problem if most citizens never actually voted on the amendment. In the past, the ASL had preferred to pursue legislation through Ohio's state assembly rather than through popular votes.[150] In New York the ASL had likewise protested when timid politicians and liquor industry advocates suggested that state legislatures should propose popular referendums regarding the federal amendment. This objection was raised despite the fact that an indirect public referendum had some precedent; in Tennessee and Florida, state legislatures were not permitted to ratify a federal amendment until after an election at which candidates could be asked their positions on the amendment.[151] And, moreover, the ASL's New York superintendent,

City," *American Issue*, 24 July 1915; "Advice to U.S. Senators and Congressmen," *American Issue*, 16 October 1915.

[148] If two-thirds of the states' legislatures propose a constitutional convention, the ensuing amendment might also be sent to the various states for ratification. However, this has not happened once in American history.

[149] Clement E. Vose notes that "debate between wets and drys became a dispute over electoral systems." See Vose, "Repeal as a Political Achievement," in *Law, Alcohol, and Order: Perspectives on National Prohibition*, ed. David E. Kyvig (Westport, CT: Greenwood Press, 1985), 101.

[150] Odegard, *Pressure Politics*, 121–122. Rural counties – long believed to hold the driest sentiment – were disproportionately represented in the legislature in comparison to their total population.

[151] "Legislatures and the People's Will," *New York Times*, 29 December 1917. This problem arose a second time when, in November 1917, Ohio voters both narrowly approved a statewide prohibition law and overwhelmingly adopted a state constitutional amendment reserving the right to review general assembly actions on the potential ratification of any federal amendments. When the Ohio General Assembly ratified the national amendment in January 1919, the legality of this ratification became a subject of debate. The Anti-Saloon League sent representatives to assist with the resulting legal case, arguing that ratification requirements were unconstitutional. The Supreme Court eventually ruled in *Hawke v. Smith* that referendums on the actions of state legislatures in the case of amendments were not protected or permitted by the constitution. For further description of this sequence of events, see Kyvig, *Repealing National Prohibition*, 14–16.

William Anderson, had only a year before challenged the United States Brewers' Association, taunting them by arguing that "the way to save the saloons, if, as the brewers claim, the people really want them, is to submit the question to a vote, so that the people can put the seal of their approval upon the liquor traffic."[152] Detractors, including Prohibitionists, would emphasize and exploit the matter of citizens' lack of direct vote on the Eighteenth Amendment in the course of making anti-amendment appeals.[153] In many ways the amendment was democratically enacted – and certainly legally enacted – but Prohibitionists valued wide deliberation followed by the direct vote as the gold standard of democratic expression.

The Anti-Saloon League was somewhat handcuffed by their own claim to have been "forcing Congress to obey orders by putting the fear of retirement in the breasts of politicians" when claiming democratic ground.[154] Anti-prohibitionists, who were admittedly prejudiced on the matter, concluded that ASL strategy was therefore the work of a bully pushing legislators into supporting an amendment that their constituents did not necessarily favor.[155] The ASL's tendency to bring petitions at congressional hearings was hardly the same as agreeing to a national referendum. And a referendum was made especially desirable by the fact that there was so much wet sentiment. COD shipments into legally dry states suggested many Americans' disinterest in alcohol restriction.[156]

A few outlying Prohibitionists urged that "we never considered that the liquor question should be submitted to a vote of the people, as that implies the right of a majority to do wrong," bucking the direct democracy trend.[157] Others argued that it was still possible to turn the ratification process into an authentic gauge of public sentiment. By removing people who were hostile to prohibition from office, citizens would indirectly convey that they wanted the amendment. Still, doctrinaire Prohibitionists concluded that the people possessed too few real opportunities to express

---

[152] William H. Anderson, "For a Vote on Prohibition," *New York Times*, 1 March 1916.

[153] "Review of States: On National Constitutional Prohibition," *Minnesota Patriot*, 4th Quarter 1917; Sumner W. Haynes, "Constitutional Amendment," *Patriot Phalanx*, 25 February 1916.

[154] Odegard, *Pressure Politics*, 129.

[155] Richard F. Hamm, "Short Euphorias Followed by Long Hangovers," in *Unintended Consequences of Constitutional Amendment*, ed. David E. Kyvig (Athens: University of Georgia Press, 2000), 183. On correlations and divergences between legislators and constituents in state constitutional campaigns, see Ivy, *No Saloon in this Valley*, 47.

[156] Hamm, *Shaping the Eighteenth Amendment*, 179.

[157] "There Will be a 'Referendum' Anyway in 1918," *Campaigner*, June 1917.

themselves on the ratification issue because problems with the party system had gone unresolved. All elections, those immediately before a ratification legislature or otherwise, obscured the voice of the people because they confined citizens to voting for only one of two parties, neither of which had declared an official position on the amendment issue. Prohibitionists suggested that only the election of Prohibition Party candidates would fully affirm that Americans wanted an amendment because the Prohibition Party was the only one to offer citizens an opportunity to unequivocally express for what issue they offered support and the degree of their support. And even here the amendment process potentially inhibited the exercise of public will. As the *Patriot Phalanx* would point out to its readers, a legally enacted amendment might still represent "rule of the minority" if ratified by "36 states with 46 million against 12 states representing 56 million population."[158]

Previously, Prohibitionists had mobilized around the idea that Democratic and Republican legislators *would not* pass the amendment; now they increasingly argued that these elected leaders *should not* have done so. Setting aside the matter of personal communication with constituents, Prohibitionists insisted that it was a breach of contract between the voter and the legislator when the legislator acted on an issue for which he had no clear mandate via the party's platform. And most state legislators acting on prohibition were elected previous to the passage of the amendment by Congress, on the basis of party platforms that did not explicitly take a stand on the prohibition issue.

For decades Democrats and Republicans had conspired to keep the prohibition issue out of politics and now, Prohibitionists asserted, major party politicians had acted without sufficient consultation with the people. The extraordinarily rapid rate at which the national amendment was ratified, moreover, compounded the problem. Prohibitionists argued that the only remaining way that the people could assert themselves was by setting aside their hesitation about platforms and systematically voting for pro-ratification or anti-ratification candidates for the state legislatures, regardless of their party affiliation. However, here even tepid democracy was subverted, claimed Prohibitionists, because the state legislatures were voting in favor of ratification before an election could award or remove any elected officials from their seats. Where was the opportunity for democratic review of this radical and far-reaching reform?

[158] "The Senate and the Constitutional Amendment," *Patriot Phalanx*, 10 August 1917.

On January 16, 1919, Nebraska became the thirty-sixth state to ratify the national amendment, ensuring its enactment; all states except for Connecticut and Rhode Island would eventually ratify. Some Prohibitionists could not contain their joy that their cause was finally acknowledged in such a spectacular way. One Rhode Island Prohibitionist noted that "Prohibition has not come as we Prohibitionists had hoped or expected, still victory has arrived, and that most suddenly. For this we are profoundly thankful."[159] Perhaps, considered other Prohibitionists, the party had sold its birthright – a rich tradition of valuing process more than outcome, and enforcement more than legislation – too quickly. William P.F. Ferguson offered a final gloomy summary of the past year's trajectory. In a letter to the *Patriot Phalanx*'s editor, Ferguson wrote:

I don't want to throw a coolness on your "meeting," but I can't pitch any victory song in the key in which some folks are singing it. I am fairly well gratified that the American people have concluded to adopt prohibition, but I am not at all enthusiastic about the method by which they have reached it, nor specially optimistic about the future.

Ferguson explained that "in my way of thinking, it does make a lot of difference whether a thing is done in the right way or in the wrong way." To this end,

the thing we have been fighting for since the days of Farwell Hall has not been accomplished. The politicians and the line-of-least-resistance people have sidestepped the real issue. The worst thing about it is, that, even if the prohibition reform comes to pass by this means, that which is the great end of any reform movement, as Wendell Phillips taught us, the renovation of government, has not come to pass.

The purpose of the party was not simply to enact a law, but to fundamentally change government so that its institutions resonated with democratic ideals. In contrast, "the prohibition movement [that] should have ground to powder the whisky parties and the whisky politicians" had instead "lifted a lot of them onto pedestals."[160] Later recalling this moment, party historian D. Leigh Colvin would similarly describe how "a great moral principle was implanted in the Constitution, but there was but little betterment in the quality of our politics."[161]

---

[159] Frederick T. Jencks, "Sudden Victory," *Patriot Phalanx*, 24 January 1919.
[160] William P.F. Ferguson, "Thinks 'Twas Done Wrong," *Patriot Phalanx*, 24 January 1919.
[161] Colvin, *Prohibition in the United States*, 400. Pierre S. du Pont, *A Business Man's View of Prohibition* (Washington, DC: Association Against the Prohibition Amendment, 1930?

Only after the Eighteenth Amendment was already enacted did individuals from outside the liquor industry begin a systematic plan to counteract the enthusiasm of the Anti-Saloon League-led movement.[162] One explanation for delay is that statewide campaigns had not only energized dry forces, but had, in the course of gradually eliminating saloons, undermined a key location wherein drinking Americans might have come together to coordinate political action.[163] This explanation might also suggest why it was that prominent citizens who generally had not frequented saloons even when legal who now organized the Association Against the Prohibition Amendment (AAPA), the Women's Organization for National Prohibition Reform (WONPR), and the Voluntary Committee of Lawyers. These were national organizations built on the traditions of the Constitutional Liberty League of Massachusetts, the Moderation League in New York, and the Moderation League of Ohio.[164] They coordinated a still broader support network drawn from bar associations, medical societies, veterans, and organized labor.

From the beginning, anti-prohibitionists drew more heavily from the Prohibition Party's argument than they did from those of liquor industry organizations, albeit without explicitly crediting Prohibitionists. After the enactment of the Eighteenth Amendment, Elihu Root would serve as one of the attorneys in the *National Prohibition* cases, a 1920 legal challenge to the amendment's constitutionality. Root, defending a New Jersey brewer, argued that the substantive portion of the prohibition amendment was a direct act of legislation, whereas the Constitution was otherwise about the powers or organization of government. This was fundamentally a restatement of Prohibitionists' explanation for why their party supported a prohibition statute but not a prohibition amendment.

Root fused this technical argument to a broader problem that Prohibitionists had also illuminated when he argued for the fundamental,

---

[162] Kyvig, *Repealing National Prohibition*, 5.

[163] Michael Lewis, "Access to Saloons, Wet Voter Turnout, and Statewide Prohibition Referenda, 1907–1919," *Social Science History* 32 (Fall 2008): 373–404.

[164] Executive Committee of the Board of Directors for the Association Against the Prohibition Amendment, "Report to the Directors, Members, and Friends of the Association Against the Prohibition Amendment," (N.p: n.p., 1928), 7. For organizational histories, see Kenneth D. Rose, *American Women and the Repeal of Prohibition* (New York: New York University Press, 1996); David E. Kyvig, "Women Against Prohibition," *American Quarterly* 28 (1976): 465–482; Catherine Murdock, *Domesticating Drink: Women, Men, and Alcohol in America, 1870–1940* (Baltimore: Johns Hopkins University Press, 1998), 134–158; Fletcher Dobyns, *The Amazing Story of Repeal: An Exposé of the Power of Propaganda* (Chicago: Willet, Clark & Company, 1940).

undemocratic injustice whereby a minority could perpetually prevent repeal of the amendment simply because a law happened to be enacted through the Constitution rather than settled through regular legislative means. To pass a law by harnessing it to the Constitution, Root argued, was simply undemocratic. On June 7, 1920, Root and the other attorneys attempting to overturn the Eighteenth Amendment lost by a unanimous Supreme Court decision.[165]

Repealists then argued that the lack of democratic integrity behind the amendment's enactment could lead to massive discrediting of law itself; believing that the majority had not ruled, otherwise obedient citizens would be reluctant to grant the amendment's credibility. An undemocratic government, minister and professor Robert Ellis Thompson argued, "may put millions of people into an attitude of opposition to law in general."[166] James Wadsworth, Jr., a Republican senator from New York, agreed that public discontent about prohibition would lead to "widespread contempt of law and of the Constitution itself."[167] The membership pledge signed by all women joining the WONPR made explicit the connection between prohibition and anarchy; a new member declared that "I believe that National Prohibition has incited crime, and increased lawlessness, hypocrisy and corruption."[168] From his seat on the finance committee of General Motors' executive board, John J. Raskob concluded that "if the Prohibition Amendment and laws at present on our books...are resulting in a lack of respect for law in our institutions, it is but a short step to such a lack of respect for property rights as to result in bolshevism."[169] At stake, in other words, was the integrity of law and civil society.

[165] For further summary of these events, see Kyvig, *Repealing National Prohibition*, 17–19. This argument would be repeated by Fabian Franklin, a former editor of the Independent, in *What Prohibition Has Done to America* (New York: Harcourt, Brace & Company, 1922).

[166] Robert Ellis Thompson, "The Drawbacks to Prohibition," *Irish World and American Industrial Liberator*, 15 February 1919.

[167] James Wadsworth, Jr., "Public Contentment," speech at dinner in his honor, New York City, 20 February 1920, quoted in David E. Kyvig, *Repealing National Prohibition*, 76.

[168] Quoted in "Statement Made by Mrs. Courtlandt Nicoll at the Meeting of the New York County Advisory Council at the Plaza Hotel," 12 June 1929, WONPR Papers. Cited in Rose, *American Women and the Repeal of Prohibition*, 86.

[169] John J. Raskob to R.N. Holsaple, 14 November 1928, Raskob Papers, Eleutherian Mills Historical Library, Wilmington, Delaware, quoted in David E. Kyvig, *Repealing National Prohibition*, 84. Rascob was a member of the AAPA. For a counterexample of Americans expressing concern that repeal would convey disrespect for law, see Lisa G. Materson, "African American Women, Prohibition, and the 1928 Presidential

Organized anti-prohibitionists also borrowed heavily from Prohibitionists' argument that the method of enacting prohibition was the fundamental problem.[170] Pierre du Pont, speaking under the auspices of the AAPA, claimed that prohibition signaled that "we have carelessly fallen into a habit of allowing ourselves to be ruled by a minority of a strong determination, so that our laws no longer have the consent of the governed." As such, "we have accepted methods that are not American." Du Pont continued, noting that "the people of the United States, or a majority of them, never authorized laws intended to prevent altogether the use of intoxicating liquor."[171] General Ransom H. Gillett, a World War I veteran and former Republican New York assemblyman, provoked an audience during a debate by asking, "Does anybody in this audience ever remember having had an opportunity [to vote] on whether you wanted that [amendment] ratified or not? I don't recall that it was ever submitted to the vote of the people as to whether or not we should ratify it."[172] Gillett repeatedly asserted that his opposition to the prohibition amendment was not about liquor – he conceded the dangers of alcohol consumption – but fundamentally about rule by the people.

The AAPA, WONPR, and Voluntary Committee were pressure groups made up of elite Americans, but they also possessed a democratic element at the core of their stated agenda.[173] Most intriguingly, the Voluntary Committee created a new vision for how democracy could be restored within the amendment process, arguing that an amendment to repeal the Eighteenth Amendment should be ratified through special conventions

---

Election," *Journal of Women's History* 21 (Spring 2009): 63–86. Materson argues that African-American women's organizations expressed concern that repealing prohibition would lay the groundwork for repeal of the Thirteenth, Fourteenth, and Fifteenth amendments.

[170] Hamm, "Short Euphorias Followed by Long Hangovers," 183. Hamm suggests that amendment opponents initially favored arguments attacking the amendment on grounds of its content – particularly the expansion of federal authority – but increasingly focused on the problem of the amendment's adoption. See also Vose, "Repeal as a Political Achievement," 100–114.

[171] Pierre S. du Pont, *A Business Man's View of Prohibition* (Washington, DC: Association Against the Prohibition Amendment, 1930?), 3–4.

[172] Ransom H. Gillett in "Repeal of the Prohibition Amendment," *Reference Shelf* (July 1923), 23. Gillett was invited to the debate on the basis of his leadership in the AAPA.

[173] On the modeling of the AAPA on the ASL, see Kyvig, *Repealing Prohibition*, 46. See also Hamm, "Short Euphorias Followed by Long Hangovers," 183; Odegard, *Pressure Politics*, viii.

of the states.[174] This bold statement of democratic method drew on the liquor industry's early argument that a popular referendum had been required, but had not actually been taken, to ratify the amendment in twenty-two of the thirty-six states whose legislatures had approved it.[175] It also built on the recent strategy of repealing "state Volstead Acts"; several state legislatures held referendums on whether or not their state enforcement acts should be repealed.[176]

The AAPA considered the speech of William Borah – an Idaho Republican and one of the Senate's most conspicuously independent thinkers – to be suggestive of ideal democratic process. Borah urged the superiority of state conventions for the consideration of whether or not the Eighteenth Amendment should be repealed, arguing that voters had not necessarily known that this issue would arise before the elections of state legislators who would ratify the prohibition amendment and that they had therefore not necessarily voted for candidates with whom they agreed on the question. In contrast, state conventions wherein delegates were selected by the people as their representatives on this one particular issue would be "the only method whereby popular expression on this proposition...could be had."[177]

As suggested by repealists, the state convention idea fused traditional and new ideals regarding political organization and democracy. On one hand, it was about a nineteenth-century model of democratic gatherings. State conventions had been used during the original ratification of the Constitution, and their revival had been suggested by Abraham Lincoln in his first inaugural address. Lincoln had argued that if an amendment on the slavery issue was to be created it ought to be worked out through the convention method because "it allows amendments to originate with

---

[174] Hamm, *Shaping the Eighteenth Amendment*, 270.

[175] On Prohibitionists' observation of this strategy, see "Victory!" *Minnesota Patriot*, 1st Quarter 1919; "Referendum is Illegal," *Campaigner*, February 1919; "Wets Could Only Win Delay by Referendum," *Campaigner*, March 1919.

[176] Executive Committee of the Board of Directors for the Association Against the Prohibition Amendment, "Annual Report to the Directors, Members and Friends of the Association Against the Prohibition Amendment," (N.p.: n.p., 1929), 9–14; Executive Committee of the Board of Directors for the Association Against the Prohibition Amendment, "Annual Report to the Directors, Members and Friends of the Association Against the Prohibition Amendment" (N.p.: n.p., 1931), 8–12.

[177] Senator Borat quoted in Association Against the Prohibition Amendment, "Annual Report of the President of the Association Against the Prohibition Amendment for the year 1932" (Washington, DC: Association Against the Prohibition Amendment, 1932), 14–15.

the people themselves, instead of only permitting them to take, or reject, propositions, originated by others, not especially chosen for the purpose, and which might not be precisely such, as they would wish to either accept or refuse."[178] On the other hand, the state convention idea was about equal suffrage and direct democracy. Delegates would serve as the embodiment of their constituencies, instructed by their constituencies.

Indeed, the Twenty-First Amendment, repealing the Eighteenth, would be the first to require the use of state conventions for its ratification. Special conventions were not intended to be deliberative bodies and thus resoundingly abandoning the Prohibitionists' vision of democratic exchange. The Prohibition Party's legacy would neither be about policy nor deliberative democracy. These conventions did nonetheless preserve the idea of delegates' responsibility to vote the position that they ran and to clearly articulate their position in advance.[179] The Prohibition Party had successfully infused some idea of representatives' accountability into the new century's political norms, if not with precisely the desired features.

* * *

In the twentieth century, Prohibitionists were simultaneously confronted with new ballot laws that made it more difficult to build a constituency, the ascendancy of nonpartisan pressure groups claiming that partisanship was not necessary, and the advent of administrative agencies run by appointed rather than elected officials. These conditions ensured that minor parties' marginalization and the party system's devolving prestige were interconnected stories. And given this context, the decision of Prohibitionist doctrinaires to refrain from the amendment campaign should be understood as an expression of concern about the state of American democracy.

Prohibitionists were never alone in this struggle, and the actions of their minor party peers suggest the variety of potential responses. Some

---

[178] Abraham Lincoln, "First Inaugural Address," 4 March 1861, in *Abraham Lincoln, Slavery, and the Civil War: Selected Writings and Speeches*, ed. Michael P. Johnson (New York: Bedford/St. Martin's, 2001), 114.

[179] Hamm, "Short Euphorias Followed by Long Hangovers," 184. Such state conventions had initially been proposed in 1914 by Senator Mann of Illinois during debates about the Hobson resolution but had been vehemently opposed by the ASL; Odegard, *Pressure Politics*, 155.

minor parties ran candidates under the names of other parties, co-opting the ballot qualification records of major parties and other minor parties, both forcefully and by invitation. From among the minor parties that attempted to run frankly minor party-identified candidates in major party primaries (and thereby "borrow" the larger party's vote-return history and ballot qualification status), the most prominent example occurred in North Dakota.[180] Socialists victoriously ran candidates against regular Republicans in the Republican Party primary elections between 1916 and 1918, essentially causing party realignment when Republican regulars abandoned the de facto Socialist Party (which campaigned as the ballot-qualified "Republican" party) to join with Democrats. This strategy would be replicated in twelve other states.[181]

Prohibitionists' decision to withhold support from the amendment campaign was an act of resistance to the changing political conditions that disadvantaged minor parties. It also assured the Prohibition Party's perpetual status as a marginal political entity. It alienated the party from other anti-liquor organizations and confused a significant portion of the party's own constituency. It was hard to persuade temperance workers to refrain from such a compelling policy movement when continued electoral failure and financial hardship were the likely alternative.

At the core of Prohibitionists' philosophy had always been the conviction that the faith of Christian citizens living under democratic government obligated them to use the ballot to promote national moral uplift. So it was with a diligence inspired by religiosity that twentieth-century Prohibitionists sought to preserve what they believed were the political values of an earlier era – loyalty, community, and deliberation – and to inscribe these values onto new political institutions. Prohibitionists followed their consciences and urged others to do the same.

New political institutions made elections more regular and outcomes more clear, and also made government more efficient. Overall, American democracy in the twentieth century was about achieving outcomes that the people found acceptable. Prohibitionists would nonetheless argue that the changes in political institutions necessary to achieve this vision made it

---

[180] Burbank, *When Farmers Voted Red*, 118. In 1912, Progressives initially attempted to run their candidates on Republican tickets, but Republicans were eventually able to eliminate these pseudo-Republican candidates in every state but California.

[181] Fitrakis, *Idea of Democratic Socialism*, 12–13, 109; Lipset and Marks, *It Didn't Happen Here*, 56–57, 265; "Legal Obstacles to Minor Party Success," *Yale Law Journal* (June 1948): 1289–90.

more difficult for citizens to communicate what they truly wanted. These achievements the nuances of public opinion, leaving policy makers without either the means or the need to perfectly learn the people's will. For citizens holding powerful moral obligations, the institutional imperatives to conform and compromise were only tenuously accepted.

Epilogue

Most Americans expected that national prohibition would produce a more orderly society with less liquor consumption. They reasoned that government enforcement, especially combined with the expense of purchasing black market liquor smuggled from Canada, would function as a deterrent. And in the wake of the Eighteenth Amendment's enactment an initial decline in arrests for drunkenness, a drop in hospitalization for alcoholism, and even post-repeal statistics showing a decrease in taxable revenue from liquor sales all suggested that Americans had modified their consumption habits. By this measure, the Eighteenth Amendment was a success.[1]

The Anti-Saloon League was initially thrilled with this apparent validation of its strategy, only becoming humbled when high profile lawlessness emerged. Deficits in law enforcement destabilized the ASL in part because the organization had never substantially questioned whether government would enforce prohibition law once it was in place. The sheer scope of speakeasies, gin joints, nightclubs, moonshine, cocktails, and gangsterism showed that concurrent enforcement by both federal and state laws and agencies left no one truly accountable.[2] Congress underfunded federal agencies, while several states issued so-called prohibition laws that actually authorized the sale of some wines and beer. Only a small percentage of liquor sellers were arrested and prosecuted, but even this number

---

[1] Aaron and Musto, "Temperance and Prohibition in America," 164–165, quoted in Kerr, *Organized for Prohibition*, 277.

[2] On the matter of why the amendment included concurrent enforcement, see Hamm, *Shaping the Eighteenth Amendment*, especially 266–269.

overwhelmed the courts. In some cases, juries refused to convict liquor sellers out of principle. With few signs of the promised dry utopia, would-be ASL donors turned away from the organization, instead giving money to missions abroad, church facilities at home, or temperance educational endeavors.[3] The ASL's foremost historian has argued that "the league clearly was a failure after 1920."[4]

Mass disobedience to prohibition law was humiliating evidence that many Americans did not desire prohibition, but poor law enforcement did not necessarily discredit the Prohibition Party's political strategy in the same way that it discredited that of the ASL. The party's plan had never entailed getting prohibition in advance of public opinion and had always demanded that this opinion be registered through party votes.[5] Throughout the 1920s, the Prohibition Party would persevere for reasons best described by its 1920 vice-presidential candidate: "Because of the intolerable situation in relation to administration, the very function preeminently stressed by the Prohibition party throughout its history, the Prohibitionists, although badly disorganized, determined they could not do otherwise than continue the battle for prohibition administration."[6] Ongoing problems with ballot requirements would strike at the party without actually killing it; the Prohibition Party persisted even as its presence on state ballots continued to shrink from twenty-six states in 1920 to sixteen states in 1924. And there was some reason for hope. With the women's suffrage amendment's ratification in 1920, Prohibitionists selected a woman as the party's vice-presidential candidate, hoping to capitalize on a surge in women's support. Marie C. Brehm of California had been an Illinois WCTU president and state president of the Equal Suffrage Association of Illinois.

The Prohibition Party formulated a strategy rooted in its ideological traditions while still evolving in response to repealists. In a dramatic turn, the party more firmly (if still grudgingly) accepted its transformation from a constituency-building organization to a protest party. It might have superficially appeared that the party acted with continuity when its 1928 national convention nominated a candidate, William Varney, and pledged this candidate to superior law enforcement that major

---

[3] Kerr, *Organized for Prohibition*, 242–274.
[4] Kerr, *Organized for Prohibition*, 277.
[5] Jack S. Blocker Jr., "Prohibition Party (United States)," in *Alcohol and Temperance in Modern History*, 493–495.
[6] Colvin, *Prohibition in the United States*, 464.

parties would ostensibly be reluctant to provide. However, when confronted with a campaign between wet Democrat Al Smith and Republican Herbert Hoover, the party (seemingly intentionally) underfunded Varney and ran him on a platform that promised his immediate withdrawal if the party's national committee decided to endorse the Republican ticket. Varney would only appear on six states' tickets, despite the likelihood that the party could have been – even in the context of discriminatory ballot qualification standards – at least a bit more successful if it had so intended. Remarkably, even the national committee chair, D. Leigh Colvin, went on the record with his support for Hoover and against Smith. The Prohibition Party had not campaigned for the amendment, but repeal would indisputably make the idea that "prohibition doesn't prohibition" an albatross Prohibitionists could not hope to jettison in the future.

With the publication of the Wickersham Commission's report in 1931, the weaknesses of prohibition policy became the subject of popular knowledge and debate. From here, the writing was on the wall. The Eighteenth Amendment was repealed with the Twenty-First Amendment in 1933. The ASL would dwindle until its demise in 1948. The Prohibition Party, however, kept itself organized and lively. Still full of rather cantankerous people, and only on the Louisiana ballot in 2012, the party nonetheless pushes onward to the present day.

Appendix

Year	National Vote	Prohibition Vote	% of Total Vote
1872	6,463,622	5,588	0.09
1876	8,413,774	9,630	0.11
1880	9,211,264	10,364	0.11
1884	10,052,264	150,957	1.50
1888	11,377,363	250,122	2.19
1892	12,045,676	271,111	2.25
1896	13,917,359	131,285	0.94
1900	13,962,035	210,200	1.51
1904	13,558,404	259,163	1.91
1908	14,892,337	252,704	1.67
1912	15,024,576	209,644	1.40
1916	18,540,328	220,505	1.19
1920	26,724,624	189,467	0.71
1924	29,084,798	57,551	0.20
1928	36,797,607	20,106	0.05
1932	39,743,909	81,869	0.21

Sources: Donald R. Desking, Jr., Hanes Walton, Jr., and Sherman C. Puckett, *Presidential Elections, 1789–2008: County State and National Mapping of Election Data* (Ann Arbor: University of Michigan Press, 2010); Svend Petersen, *A Statistical History of the American Presidential Elections* (New York: Unger, 1963).

Bibliography

Primary Sources: Newspapers

American Advance (Chicago, IL), 1911–1913
American Issue (Westerville, OH), 1914–1916
American Patriot (Westerville, OH), 1913–1916
American Reformer (New York), 1882–1884
Backbone (New York and Utica), 1912–1916
Backbone (St. Paul, MN), 1897–1904
California Voice (Los Angeles), 1901–1902
Campaigner (Madison, WI), 1915–1919
Cardiff Herald (Tennessee), 1890
Center (Detroit, MI), 1885–1888
Citizen (Harriman, TN), 1903–1905
Clean Politics (Indianapolis, IN), 1909–1911
Delaware Signal (Ohio), 1873–1885
East Tennessean (Kingston), 1900
Elkhorn Blade (Wisconsin), 1895–1896
Harriman Record (Tennessee), 1916
Harriman Weekly Advance (Tennessee), 1893–1900
Kansas City Leader (Missouri), 1904–1905
Kansas Prohibitionist (Columbus), 1883–1884, 1886
Lever (Chicago, IL), 1881–1899
Michigan Prohibitionist (Detroit), 1884–1885
Minnesota Patriot (Minneapolis), 1913–1919
Minnesota Radical (Waseca), 1876, 1879–1880
National Enquirer (Indianapolis, IN), 1915–1917
National Freeman (Chicago, IL), 1881
National Prohibitionist (Chicago, IL), 1907–1911
New Era (Springfield, OH), 1885, 1888–1889
New Voice (Chicago, IL), 1900–1905
New York Daily Witness, 1876–1878

New York Pioneer, 1885
Our Union (Brooklyn, NY), 1877–1879
Patriot Phalanx (Indianapolis, IN), 1897–1898, 1903–1919
Peninsular Herald (Detroit, MI), 1868–1872
Prohibition Era (Cleveland, OH), 1872
Prohibition Journal (Madison, WI), 1913–1915
Public Weal (Minneapolis, MN), 1906–1908
Statesman (Chicago, IL), 1887–1888
Times (Columbus, KS), 1884–1885
True Reform (New York, New York), 1897
Vindicator (Franklin, PA), 1911–1916
Voice (New York, New York), 1884–1896
Weekly Censor (Los Angeles, CA), 1886–1889
Western Leader (Minneapolis, MN), 1894
XVI Amendment (Ness City, KS), 1885

Primary Sources: Databases of Periodicals

American Periodicals Series Online, 1740–1900
Making of America
Proquest Historical Newspapers

Primary Sources: Archival Records

Callahan, P.H. Papers. Bentley Historical Library. Ann Arbor, MI.
Civil War and Later Pension Files, Pension Records for John C. Pepper, Isaac O. Pickering, Thomas W. Organ. National Archives Building. Washington DC.
Dickie, Samuel. Scrapbook. Bentley Historical Library. Ann Arbor, MI.
Goodell, William. William Goodell Family Papers, Series I: William Goodell Papers, Special Collections and Archives. Hutchins Library, Berea College, hosted through the online portal "Slavery, Abolition, and Social Justice: 1490–2007."
Harriman, Tennessee – Miscellaneous Records. Tennessee State Library and Archives. Nashville, TN.
Hastings, Samuel D. Scrapbooks. Wisconsin Historical Society Rare Books Collection. Madison, WI.
Hillard, George B. Papers. New York Public Library Special Collections. New York, New York.
Hillard, George B. Brooklyn Prohibition Collection. Brooklyn Historical Society. Brooklyn, New York.
Jones, Charles R. Papers. Bentley Historical Library. Ann Arbor, MI.
Kansas Prohibition Scrapbooks. Kansas State Historical Library. Topeka, KS.
Papers of the Prohibition Party of Pickaway County. Ohio Historical Society. Columbus, OH.
Prohibition National Committee Records. Bentley Historical Library. Ann Arbor, MI. Joint Ohio Historical Society-Michigan Historical Collections-Woman's Christian Temperance Union microfilm edition, Temperance and Prohibition Papers.

Prohibition Party Miscellaneous Items. Kansas State Historical Library. Topeka, KS.

Prohibition State Executive Committee (Minn.) Records, 1876–1956. Minnesota Historical Society. St. Paul, MN.

Richmond, T.C. Correspondence. Wisconsin Historical Society Special Collections. Madison, WI.

St. John, John P. Collection. Kansas Historical Library. Topeka, KS.

Storms, Roger. Papers. Bentley Historical Library. Ann Arbor, MI.

Willard, Frances. Papers. Joint Ohio Historical Society-Michigan Historical Collections-Woman's Christian Temperance Union microfilm edition, Temperance and Prohibition Papers.

Woodbury, Nathan. Papers. Joint Ohio Historical Society-Michigan Historical Collections-Woman's Christian Temperance Union microfilm edition, Temperance and Prohibition Papers.

Primary Sources: Books, Directories, Election Records, and Handbooks

Arthur, T.S. *Woman to the Rescue*. Philadelphia: J.M. Stoddart, 1874.

Bede, J. Adam, Thomas J. Caton, and Oliver W. Stewart. *A Triangular Debate, Held at Hutchinson, Minnesota, Tuesday, January 14, 1902*. N.p.: B.B. Haugan, 1902.

Bliss, William D.P., ed. *The New Encyclopedia of Social Reform*. New York: Funk & Wagnalls Company, 1908.

Brain, Belle M. *Weapons for Temperance Warfare*. Chicago: United Society for Christian Society, 1897.

Calkins, Raymond. *Substitutes for the Saloon*. Boston: Houghton, Mifflin, & Co., 1901.

City Directory of Harriman. N.p.: G.M. Connelly, 1892.

Desking, Donald R., Jr., Hanes Walton, Jr., and Sherman C. Puckett. *Presidential Elections, 1789–2008: County State and National Mapping of Election Data*. Ann Arbor: University of Michigan Press, 2010.

East Tennessee Land Company. *Two Years in Harriman, Tennessee*. New York: South Publishing Company, 1892.

East Tennessee Land Company. *One Year in Harriman, Tennessee: Established by the East Tennessee Land Company, February 26, 1890*. New York: South Publishing Company, 1891.

Gordon, Ernest. *When the Brewer Had the Stranglehold*. New York: Alcohol Information Committee, 1930.

Haggard, J.W. *History of the Prohibition Party: A Ready Reference Book of Facts and Figures to Which is Added a Scrap-book Attachment*. Bloomington, IL: Lancet Print, 1888.

Jutkins, A.J. *Hand-book of Prohibition*. Chicago: Lever Printing, 1885.

Jutkins, A.J. *Hand-book of Prohibition*. Chicago: R.R. McCabe & Co., 1884.

Landis, Charles K. *The Founder's Own Story of the Founding of Vineland, New Jersey*. Vineland, NJ: Vineland Historical and Antiquarian Society, 1903.

Lewis, Dio. *Prohibition a Failure or a True Solution to the Temperance Question*. Boston: James R. Osgood and Company, 1875.

Lyon, G.H. *The Only Alternative of Success: Some Condition of Success in the Prohibition Party is Wanting. What is It?* N.p.: G.H. Lyon, 1896.

Petersen, Svend. *A Statistical History of the American Presidential Elections.* New York: Ungar, 1963.

Political Prohibitionist for 1887. New York: Funk and Wagnalls, 1887.

Political Prohibitionist for 1889. New York: Funk and Wagnalls, 1889.

Prohibition Party. *A Condensed History of the Prohibition Party: The 75 Year Struggle for National Prohibition.* Chicago: The National Prohibitionist, ca. 1944.

Register of the American Temperance University for 1897–98. Harriman, Tennessee: The Advance Steam Print, ca. 1898.

Van Norman, Louis E. ed. *An Album of Representative Prohibitionists.* New York: Funk and Wagnalls, 1895.

Vineland, N.J. Philadelphia: Sickler, 1890.

Vineland, New Jersey: Its Advantages as a Place of Residence, Health Resort, Manufacturing Center, and Farming Community. Vineland, NJ: Mayor and City Council and the Vineland Board of Trade, n.d.

Washington State Central Committee of the Prohibition Party. *Prohibition Party Campaign Text-Book for the State of Washington, 1892.* Tacoma, WA: Puget Sound Printing Company, 1892.

Wheeler, E.J. *Prohibition: The Principle, the Policy, and the Party. A Dispassionate Study of the Arguments For and Against Prohibitory Laws, and the Reasons Governing the Political Action of its Advocates.* New York: Funk and Wagnalls, imprinted as 1880 but more likely ca. 1890.

Willard, Frances Elizabeth. *Woman and Temperance, or The Work and Workers of the Woman's Christian Temperance Union.* 3rd ed. Hartford, CT: Park Publishing Co., 1883.

Willard, Frances, and Mary Livermore. *A Woman of the Century.* Buffalo, NY: Charles Wells Moulton, 1893.

Primary Sources: Pamphlets and Proceedings

American Woman Suffrage Association. *Constitution of the American Woman Suffrage Association.* Boston, 1869.

Andreae, Percy. *Plan of Organization, at the Convention of the United States Brewers Association, at Atlantic City, on October 3rd, 1913.* N.p.: n.p., 1913.

Anthony, Susan B. *Declaration of Rights of the Women of the United States by the National Woman Suffrage Association, July 4th, 1876.* N.p.: n.p., 1876.

Black, James. *Is There a Necessity for a Prohibition Party?* New York: National Temperance Society, 1876.

Black, James. *The Liquor Traffic versus Political Economy.* N.p.: n.p., ca. 1870.

Black, James. *The National Prohibition Party.* New York: National Temperance Society and Publication House, 1893.

Brooks, H.M. *Common Sense, or Why the Prohibition Party Has Failed.* Paris, IL: Beacon Company, ca. 1890.

Carrow, G.H. *"Do Not Take Temperance into Politics!"* N.p.: n.p., 1879.

Case, George L. *The Prohibition Party: Its Origin, Purpose, and Growth.* Cleveland, OH: 1889.

Cassidy, James. *The Saloon versus the Labor Union.* N.p.: n.p., 1911.

Chafin, Eugene W. *Government by Administration.* Chicago: n.p., ca. 1912.

Common Sense, or Why the Prohibition Party has Failed, also Four Speeches in Reply to Van Bennett in the Bennett-Brooks Debate on Prohibition. Paris, IL: Paris Beacon Co. Book and Job Print, ca. 1890.

Dennison, W.H. *Prize Essay: How to Interest, Instruct, and Retain Our Members.* Newcastle-on-Tyne: W.H. Dennison, 1874.

Dorchester, Daniel. *Non-Partisan Temperance Effort: Defined, Advocated, and Vindicated.* Boston: The National League (Non-Partisan and Non-Sectarian) for the Suppression of the Liquor Traffic, 1885.

Dorchester, Daniel. *Non-Partisan Temperance League.* Boston: The National League for the Suppression of the Liquor Traffic, 1885.

Dunn, James B. *The Evils of Beer Legislation.* New York: National Temperance Society and Publication House, ca. 1870.

du Pont, Pierre S. *A Business Man's View of Prohibition.* Washington, DC: Association Against the Prohibition Amendment, ca. 1930.

Executive Committee of the Board of Directors for the Association Against the Prohibition Amendment. *Report to the Directors, Members, and Friends of the Association Against the Prohibition Amendment.* Washington, DC: Association Against the Prohibition Amendment, 1928–1933.

Evans, P.S., ed. *Seventy-First Annual Report of the Connecticut Baptist Convention Held with the Central Church of Norwich, October 16th and 17th, 1894.* New Haven, CT: Hoggson & Robinson, 1894.

Evans, P.S., and C.A. Piddock, eds. *Seventy-Eighth Annual Report of the Connecticut Baptist Convention, and the Eighty-Second Annual Report of the Connecticut Baptist Educational Society.* Hartford, CT: Press of the Smith-Linsley Company, 1901.

Faust, Alfred, ed. *Minutes of the New York East Annual Conference of 1912 of the Methodist Episcopal Church.* New York: Alfred Hodgetts and C.E. Barto, 1912.

Fifty-Sixth Annual Meeting of the Connecticut Baptist Convention Held with the Second Baptist Church, Danbury, October 14th and 15th, 1879. Hartford, CT: Case, Lockwood & Brainard Company, 1879.

Ford, Calvin B., and Nathan Hubbell, eds. *Minutes of the New York East Conference of 1900.* New York: Press of Eaton and Mains, 1900.

Ford, Calvin B., and Nathan Hubbell, eds. *Minutes of the New York East Conference of 1901.* New York: Eaton and Mains, 1901.

Foster, J. Ellen. *The Republican Party and Temperance.* N.p.: n.p., 1888.

Franklin, Fabian. *What Prohibition Has Done to America.* New York: Harcourt, Brace & Company, 1922.

Graham, Henry. *Will a Prohibition Party Help the Cause of Prohibition?* Boston: The National League (Non-Partisan and Non-Sectarian) for the Suppression of the Liquor Traffic, 1885.

Griffin, Albert. *Powerless for Good, but Powerful for Evil: An Address to Third Party Prohibitionists.* New York: L.W. Lawrence, 1887.

Hines, H.K., ed. *Official Journal of the Ninth Session of the Idaho Annual Conference of the Methodist Episcopal Church Held at Payette, Idaho, August 11th to 15th, 1892.* Portland, OR: James A. Hines, 1892.

How Shall a Party Win? Chicago: Union Signal Print, 1884.

LaFollette, Robert M. *Primary Elections for the Nomination of All Candidates by Australian Ballot: Address Delivered Before Michigan University, Ann Arbor, Michigan, March 12, 1898.* N.p., ca. 1898.

Landis, Charles K. *Vineland, New Jersey, and its Attractions.* Philadelphia: n.p., 1880.

Lehmann, Frederick W. *Speech on Prohibition, Delivered by Hon. Frederick W. Lehmann of St. Louis, at the Odeon, October 22, 1910.* St. Louis, MO: Citizens Defense Committee, ca. 1901.

Livermore, Mary A. *Should Women Have a Vote on the Liquor Traffic?* N.p.: n.p., ca. 1885.

Merrill, S.M. *Outline Thoughts on Prohibition: People or Party – Which?* Cincinnati: Cranston & Stowe, 1886.

Minutes of the New York East Conference of 1903 of the Methodist Episcopal Church. New York: Eaton & Mains, 1903.

Minutes of the New York East Conference of 1904 of the Methodist Episcopal Church. New York: Alfred Hodgetts and C.E. Barto, 1904.

Minutes of the New York East Conference of 1905 of the Methodist Episcopal Church. New York: Alfred Hodgetts and C.E. Barto, 1905.

Minutes of the New York East Conference of 1906 of the Methodist Episcopal Church. New York: Alfred Hodgetts and C.E. Barto, 1906.

Minutes and Register of the Twenty-Ninth Session of the Providence Annual Conference of the Methodist Episcopal Church held at Fall River, Mass., March 24–30, 1869. Boston: Rand, Avery & Frye, 1869.

Monroe, David S., ed. *Journal of the General Conference of the Methodist Episcopal Church Held in Chicago, Illinois, May 2–29, 1900.* New York: Eaton & Mains, 1900.

Monroe, David S., ed. *Journal of the General Conference of the Methodist Episcopal Church Held in New York, May 1–31, 1888.* New York: Phillips & Hunt, 1888.

National Prohibition Reform Party: Its Candidates, Platform, Address, and Some Reasons Why it is Pre-eminently Deserving the Support of the People of the United States. Detroit: Wm. A. Scripps, Printer, 1876.

National Woman Suffrage Association. *An Appeal to the Women of the United States by the National Woman Suffrage and Educational Committee, Washington D.C.* Washington, DC: n.p., 1871.

Official Journal of the Idaho Annual Conference of the Methodist Episcopal Church, Twenty-Fifth Session Held at Weiser, Idaho, August 20–23, 1908. Boise, ID: Capital News Job Room, 1908.

Olin, John. *The Prohibition Party and Woman Suffrage: A Plea for an Honest Platform.* Madison: The Wisconsin Prohibitionist, 1888.

Organ, Thomas W. *Biographical Sketch of General Neal Dow.* New York: National Executive Committee of the Prohibition Reform Party, 1880.

Organ, Thomas W. *Exploitation Politics and Suggestive Facts.* White Plains, NY: Westchester News Press, 1910.

Pentecost, George Frederick. *Prohibition in Politics.* New York: Funk & Wagnalls, 1886.

Pierce, Isaac Newton. *Prohibition: Is it Right? How to be Obtained? Is a Party Necessary?* N.p.: n.p., 1884.

Powell, A.M. *The Results of Prohibition.* New York: National Temperance Society and Publication House, 1873.

Proceedings of the Fourth National Convention of the Prohibition Reform Party Held at Cleveland, Ohio, June 17th 1880. New York: National Committee of the Prohibition Reform Party, 1880.

Proceedings of the National Temperance Congress. N.p.: n.p., ca. 1890.

Prohibition Party in Maine: Its Platform, Its Candidates, Its Convention, Its Address to the Temperance People. Auburn: Willis S. Morse, 1880.

R.R.R.: Repent, Reform, Reorganize. N.p.: n.p., 1888.

Repeal of the Prohibition Amendment. New York: The H.W. Wilson Company, 1923.

Rush, Benjamin. *An Inquiry into the Effects of Alcohol upon the Human Body and Mind with an Account of the Means of Preventing, and of the Remedies for Curing Them.* New Brunswick, NJ: A. Blauvelt, 1805.

Russell, John. *An Adequate Remedy for a National Evil; or a Vindication of the National Prohibition Party.* Detroit: The New World Book and Job Print, 1872.

Russell, John. *Is the Prohibition Party a Feasible and Reliable Agency for Securing the Enactment and Execution of Prohibitory Laws?* N.p.: n.p., ca. 1870.

Russell, John. *The Liquor Traffic versus Political Economy.* N.p.: n.p., ca. 1870.

Russell, John. *Plea for a National Temperance Party.* Detroit: Peninsular Herald Print, ca. 1868.

Smith, Gerrit. *The Anti-Dramshop Party.* N.p.: n.p., 1871.

Stewart, Mother (Eliza Daniels). *Memories of the Crusade.* 3rd ed. Chicago: H.J. Smith & Co., 1890.

Thayer, William. *The Fruits of License.* New York: National Temperance Society and Publication House, ca. 1870.

The Third Party, As Seen by the New York Independent, the Leading Religious Journal. New York: S.W. Benedict, 1886.

Third-Party Temperance Efforts: Facts Which Should Be Thoroughly Digested. N.p.: n.p., 1886.

Waters, Horace. *A Third Party Needed.* N.p.: New York, 1882 or 1886?

White, J.S. *The Third Party.* N.p.: n.p., ca. 1884.

White, Robert. *The National Prohibition Party – A Reply to Some Criticisms.* Philadelphia: The Christian Statesman, 1884.

Williams, Albert. *The Prohibition Reform Party Speech of Hon. Albert Williams, of Ionia, Michigan, Made at Ionia, Mich., September 22, 1876.* N.p.: n.p., 1876.

Woman's Christian Temperance Union. *The Reason Why.* Chicago: Woman's Temperance Publishing Association, 1884.

Woodbury, Nathan Franklin. *The Republican Party and its Nominees, (Blaine and Logan), Opposed to Prohibition and in Favor of a Continuation of the Liquor Traffic.* N.p.: n.p., 1884.

Woodruff, George W. ed. *Journal of the General Conference of the Methodist Episcopal Church Held in Cincinnati, Ohio, May 1–28, 1880.* New York: Phillips & Hunt, 1880.

Woolley, John G. *A Hundred Years of Temperance.* Westerville, OH: American Issue Publishing Company, ca. 1908.

Woolley, John G. *The Liquor Problem to Date.* Westerville, OH: American Issue Publishing Company, ca. 1913.

Woolley, John G. *Prohibition: With the People Behind It.* Westerville, OH: American Issue Publishing Company, ca. 1912.

Woolley, John G. *The Rape of the Law.* Westerville, OH: American Issue Publishing Company, 1911.

Woolley, John G. *The Wounds of a Friend.* Westerville, OH: American Issue Publishing Company, ca. 1915.

Yarrington, J.T. *The Great Question.* Pennsylvania?: n.p., 1873.

Primary Sources: Autobiographies and Collected Letters, Speeches and Writings

Adams, Henry. *The Letters of Henry Adams.* Edited by J.C. Levenson, Ernest Samuels and Charles Vandersee. Cambridge, MA: Belknap Press of Harvard University Press, 1982.

Delavan, Edward C. *Temperance Essays, and Selections from Different Authors.* New York: National Temperance Society and Publication House, 1884.

Finch, John B. *The People versus the Liquor Traffic: Speeches of John B. Finch, Delivered in the Prohibition Campaigns of the United States and Canada.* 1883; New York: R.W.G. Lodge, 1887.

Godkin, E.L. *The Gilded Age Letters of E.L. Godkin.* Edited by William M. Armstrong. Albany: State University of New York Press, 1974.

Hay, John Milton, and William Dean Howells. *John Hay-Howells Letters: The Correspondence of John Milton Hay and William Dean Howells, 1861–1905.* Edited by George Monteiro and Brenda Murphy. Boston: Twayne Publishers, 1980.

Lincoln, Abraham. *Abraham Lincoln, Slavery, and the Civil War: Selected Writings and Speeches.* Edited by Michael P. Johnson. New York: Bedford/St. Martin's, 2001.

National Temperance Society. *Temperance Tracts.* New York: National Temperance Society, 1874.

Pulliam, Walter T. *Harriman: The Town that Temperance Built.* Harriman, TN: Pulliam, 1978.

Roosevelt, Theodore. *The Letters of Theodore Roosevelt.* Edited by Elting E. Morison. Cambridge, MA: Harvard University Press, 1951.

Stewart, Gideon T. *The Prohibition Party Against the Rum Power with its Crime Ruled Political Parties and Crime Consenting Churches, From the Public Addresses of Gideon T. Stewart.* N.p.: n.p., 1889.

Thoreau, Henry David. *Civil Disobedience: Solitude and Life Without Prejudice.* 1849; repr. Amherst, NY: Prometheus Books, 1998.
Willard, Frances Elizabeth. *Glimpses of Fifty Years: The Autobiography of an American Woman.* New York: Woman's Temperance Publication Association, 1889.

Secondary Scholarship

Abbott, Richard. *The Republican Party and the South, 1855–1877 – The First Southern Strategy.* Chapel Hill: University of North Carolina Press, 1986.
Aldrich, John H. *Why Parties?: The Origin and Transformation of Political Parties in America.* Chicago: University of Chicago Press, 1995.
Alexander, Ruth M. "'We Are Engaged as a Band of Sisters': Class and Domesticity in the Washingtonian Temperance Movement, 1840–1850." *Journal of American History* 75 (December 1988): 763–785.
Altschuler, Glenn C., and Stuart M. Blumin. *Rude Republic: Americans and Their Politics in the Nineteenth Century.* Princeton: Princeton University Press, 2000.
Anderson, Truman D., and Jere Hall, eds. *A Guidebook to Historic Places in Roane County, Tennessee.* Kingston: Roane County Heritage Commission, 1997.
Appleby, Joyce. "The Personal Roots of the First American Temperance Movement." *Proceedings of the American Philosophical Society* 141 (1997): 141–159.
Argersinger, Peter H. "No Rights on This Floor: Third Parties and the Institutionalization of Congress," *Journal of Interdisciplinary History* 22 (Spring 1992): 655–690.
Argersinger, Peter H. "'A Place on the Ballot': Fusion Politics and Antifusion Laws," *American Historical Review* 85 (April 1980): 287–306.
Argersinger, Peter H. *Populism and Politics: William Alfred Peffer and the People's Party.* Lexington: University Press of Kentucky, 1974.
Argersinger, Peter H. *Structure, Process, and Party: Essays in American Political History.* Armonk, NY: M.E. Sharpe, 1992.
Bader, Robert Smith. *Prohibition in Kansas: A History.* Lawrence: University of Kansas Press, 1986.
Baker, Jean H. *Affairs of Party: The Political Culture of Northern Democrats in the Mid-Nineteenth Century.* Ithaca: Cornell University Press, 1983.
Baker, Paula. "The Culture of Politics in the Late Nineteenth Century: Community and Political Behavior in Rural New York." *Journal of Social History* 18 (Winter 1984): 167–194.
Baker, Paula. "The Domestication of Politics: Women and American Political Society, 1780–1920." *American Historical Review* 89 (June 1984): 620–647.
Baker, Paula. *The Moral Frameworks of Public Life: Gender, Politics, and the State in Rural New York, 1870–1930.* New York: Oxford University Press, 1991.
Barrows, Susanna, and Robin Room, eds. *Drinking: Behavior and Belief in Modern History.* Berkeley: University of California Press, 1991.

Bederman, Gail. *Manliness and Civilization: A Cultural History of Gender and Race in the United States, 1880–1917*. Chicago: University of Chicago Press, 1996.

Bendroth, Margaret. "Rum, Romanism, and Evangelism: Protestants and Catholics in Late-Nineteenth-Century Boston." *Church History* 68 (September 1999): 627–647.

Bendroth, Margaret. "Why Women Loved Billy Sunday: Urban Revivalism and Popular Entertainment in Early Twentieth-Century American Culture." *Religion and American Culture: A Journal of Interpretation* 14 (Summer 2004): 251–271.

Bensel, Richard Franklin. *The American Ballot Box in the Mid-Nineteenth Century*. New York: Cambridge University Press, 2004.

Bensel, Richard Franklin. *The Political Economy of American Industrialization, 1877–1900*. New York: Cambridge University Press, 2000.

Beito, David T. *From Mutual Aid to the Welfare State: Fraternal Societies and Social Services, 1890–1967*. Chapel Hill: University of North Carolina Press, 2000.

Blake, Nelson Manfred, and Carol V.R. George, eds. *Remember the Ladies: New Perspectives on Women in American History*. Syracuse: Syracuse University Press, 1975.

Blocker, Jack S., Jr. *American Temperance Movements: Cycles of Reform*. Boston: Twayne Publishers, 1988.

Blocker, Jack S., Jr. *"Give to the Winds Thy Fears": The Women's Temperance Crusade, 1873–1874*. Westport, CT: Greenwood Press, 1985.

Blocker, Jack S., Jr. "Separate Paths: Suffragists and the Women's Temperance Crusade." *Signs* 10 (Spring 1985): 460–476.

Blocker, Jack S., Jr. *Retreat from Reform: The Prohibition Movement in the United States, 1890–1913*. Westport, CT: Greenwood Press, 1976.

Blocker, Jack S., Jr., David M. Fahey, and Ian R. Tyrrell, eds. *Alcohol and Temperance in Modern History: An International Encyclopedia*. 2 vols. Santa Barbara, CA: ABC-Clio, 2003.

Blue, Frederick J. *The Free Soilers: Third Party Politics, 1848–1854*. Urbana: University of Illinois Press, 1973.

Bluestone, Daniel M. *Constructing Chicago*. New Haven: Yale University Press, 1991.

Bordin, Ruth. *Frances Willard: A Biography*. Chapel Hill: University of North Carolina Press, 1986.

Bordin, Ruth. *Woman and Temperance: The Quest for Power and Liberty, 1873–1900*. Philadelphia: Temple University Press, 1981.

Boyer, Paul S., ed. *America's Communal Utopias*. Chapel Hill: University of North Carolina Press, 1997.

Boyer, Paul S., ed. *Urban Masses and Moral Order in America 1820–1920*. Cambridge, MA: Harvard University Press, 1978.

Broderick, Francis L. *Progressivism at Risk: Electing a President in 1912*. New York: Greenwood Press, 1989.

Brooks, Charles E. *Frontier Settlement and Market Revolution: The Holland Land Purchase*. Ithaca: Cornell University Press, 1996.

Brosnan, Kathleen A. *Uniting Mountain and Plain: Cities, Law, and Environmental Change along the Front Range.* Albuquerque: University of New Mexico Press, 2002.

Brownell, Blaine A., and Warren E. Stickle, eds. *Bosses and Reformers: Urban Politics in America, 1880–1920.* Boston: Houghton Mifflin Company, 1973.

Buhle, Mary Jo. *Women and American Socialism, 1870–1920.* Urbana: University of Illinois Press, 1981.

Buley, R. Carlyle. *The Equitable Life Assurance Society of the United States.* New York: Appleton-Century-Crofts, 1959.

Burbank, Garlin. *When Farmers Voted Red: The Gospel of Socialism in the Oklahoma Countryside, 1910–1924.* Westport, CT: Greenwood Press, 1976.

Burnham, John C. *Bad Habits: Drinking, Smoking, Taking Drugs, Gambling, Sexual Misbehavior, and Swearing in American History.* New York: New York University Press, 1993.

Burnham, John C. "New Perspectives on the Prohibition 'Experiment' of the 1920s." *Journal of Social History* 2 (Fall 1968): 51–68.

Burnham, Walter Dean and Ronald P. Formisano, Samuel P. Hays, and Richard Jensen, eds. *The Evolution of American Electoral Systems.* Westport, CT: Greenwood Press, 1981.

Burnham, Walter Dean. "Periodization Schemes and 'Party Systems.'" *Social Science History* 10 (Autumn 1986): 263–314.

Calhoun, Charles W. *Conceiving a New Republic: The Republican Party and the Southern Question, 1869–1900.* Lawrence: University Press of Kansas, 2006.

Campbell, Tracy. *Deliver the Vote: A History of Election Fraud, An American Political Tradition – 1742–2004.* New York: Carroll & Graf Publishers, 2005.

Carlson, Douglas W. "'Drinks He to His Own Undoing': Temperance Ideology in the Deep South." *Journal of the Early Republic* 18 (Winter 1998): 659–691.

Chambers, William Nisbet, and Walter Dean Burnham, eds. *The American Party Systems: Stages of Political Development.* Rev. ed. 1967; repr. New York: Oxford University Press, 1975.

Chase, James. *1912: Wilson, Roosevelt, Taft & Debs – the Election That Changed the Country.* New York: Simon & Schuster, 2004.

Chavigny, Katherine A. "American Confessions: Reformed Drunkards and the Origins of the Therapeutic Culture." PhD Dissertation, University of Chicago, 1999.

Cherny, Robert W. *American Politics in the Gilded Age, 1868–1900.* Wheeling, IL: Harlan Davidson, Inc., 1997.

Cherrington, Ernest H. *The Evolution of Prohibition in the United States of America: A Chronological History of the Liquor Problem and the Temperance Reform in the United States from the Earliest Settlements to the Consummation of National Prohibition.* Westerville, OH: American Issue Press, 1920.

Cherrington, Ernest H., ed. *Standard Encyclopedia of the Alcohol Problem.* 6 vols. Westerville, OH: American Issue Publishing Company, 1925–1930.

Clark, Norman H. *Deliver Us From Evil: An Interpretation of American Prohibition.* New York: W.W. Norton & Company, 1976.

Clark, Norman H. *The Dry Years: Prohibition and Social Change in Washington.* Seattle: University of Washington Press, 1965.

Clemens, Elizabeth S. *The People's Lobby: Organizational Repertoires and the Rise of Interest Group Politics in the United States, 1890–1925.* Chicago: University of Chicago Press, 1997.

Cohen, Nancy. *The Reconstruction of American Liberalism, 1865–1914.* Chapel Hill: University of North Carolina Press, 2002.

Coker, Joe. *Liquor in the Land of the Lost Cause: Southern White Evangelicals and the Prohibition Movement.* Lexington: University Press of Kentucky, 2007.

Colvin, D. Leigh. *Prohibition in the United States: A History of the Prohibition Party and of the Prohibition Movement.* New York: George H. Doran Company, 1926.

Conroy, David W. *In Public Houses: Drink & the Revolution of Authority in Colonial Massachusetts.* Chapel Hill, NC: University of North Carolina Press, 1995.

Conzen, Kathleen Neils. "Community Studies, Urban History, and American Local History." In *The Past Before Us: Contemporary Historical Writing in the United States,* ed. Michael Kammen. Ithaca: Cornell University Press, 1980.

Costain, Anne. "Representing Women: The Transition from Social Movement to Interest Group." *Western Political Quarterly* 34 (March 1981): 100–113.

Cronon, William. *Nature's Metropolis: Chicago and the Great West.* New York: W.W. Norton, 1991.

Current, Richard Nelson. *Those Terrible Carpetbaggers.* New York: Oxford University Press, 1988.

Dagenais, Julie. "Newspaper Language as an Active Agent in the Building of a Frontier Town." *American Speech* 42 (May 1967): 114–121.

Dannenbaum, Jed. "The Origins of Temperance Activism and Militancy Among American Women." *Journal of Social History* 15 (Winter 1981): 235–252.

Davis, Marni. "'No Whisky Amazons in the Tents of Israel': American Jews and the Gilded Age Temperance Movement." *American Jewish History* 94 (September 2008): 143–173.

Degler, Carl. *In Search of Human Nature: The Decline and Revival of Darwinism in American Social Thought.* New York: Oxford University Press, 1991.

DiSalvo, Daniel. *Engines of Change: Party Factions in American Politics, 1868–2010.* New York: Oxford University Press, 2012.

Dobyns, Fletcher. *The Amazing Story of Repeal: An Exposé of the Power of Propaganda.* Chicago: Willet, Clark & Company, 1940.

Dodd, Jill Siegel. "The Working Classes and the Temperance Movement in Antebellum Boston." *Labor History* 19 (Fall 1978): 551–531.

DuBois, Ellen. *Feminism and Suffrage: The Emergence of an Independent Women's Movement in America, 1848–1869.* Ithaca, NY: Cornell University Press, 1978.

Duis, Perry R. *The Saloon: Public Drinking in Chicago and Boston, 1880–1920.* Urbana: University of Illinois Press, 1983.

Edwards, Rebecca. *Angels in the Machinery: Gender in American Party Politics from the Civil War to the Progressive Era.* New York: Oxford University Press, 1997.

Epstein, Barbara L. *The Politics of Domesticity: Women, Evangelism and Temperance in Nineteenth-Century America.* Middletown, CT: Wesleyan University Press, 1981.

Esposito, Anthony. *The Ideology of the Socialist Party of America, 1901–1917.* New York: Garland, 1997.

Evans, Eldon Cobb. *A History of the Australian Ballot System in the United States.* Chicago: University of Chicago Press, 1917.

Fahey, David M. *Temperance and Racism: John Bull, Johnny Reb, and the Good Templars.* Lexington: University Press of Kentucky, 1996.

Fehlandt, August F. *A Century of Drink Reform in the United States.* Cincinnati: Jennings and Graham, 1904.

Filene, Peter. "An Obituary for the Progressive Movement." *American Quarterly* 22 (Spring 1970): 20–34.

Finegold, Kenneth. *Experts and Politicians: Reform Challenges to Machine Politics in New York, Cleveland, and Chicago.* Princeton: Princeton University Press, 1995.

Fink, Leon. *Workingmen's Democracy: The Knights of Labor and American Politics.* Urbana: University of Illinois Press, 1983.

Fitrakis, Robert J. *The Idea of Democratic Socialism in America and the Decline of the Socialist Party.* New York: Garland, 1993.

Fitzgerald, Michael W. *Splendid Failure: Postwar Reconstruction in the American South.* Chicago: Ivan R. Dee, 2007.

Fogarty, Robert S. *All Things New: American Communes and Utopian Movements, 1860–1914.* Chicago: University of Chicago Press, 1990.

Foner, Eric. *Reconstruction: America's Unfinished Revolution, 1863–1877.* New York: Harper & Row, 1988.

Foner, Eric, and John A. Garraty, eds. *The Reader's Companion to American History.* Boston: Houghton Mifflin Company, 1991.

Ford, Lacy K. "Rednecks and Merchants: Economic Development and Social Tensions in the South Carolina Upcountry, 1865–1900." *Journal of American History* 71 (September 1984): 294–318.

Foster, Gaines M. *Moral Reconstruction: Christian Lobbyists and the Federal Legislation of Morality, 1865–1920.* Chapel Hill: University of North Carolina Press, 2002.

Fredman, L.E. *The Australian Ballot System: The Story of an American Reform.* Lansing: Michigan State University, 1968.

Freeman, Jo. *A Room at a Time: How Women Entered Party Politics.* New York: Rowman & Littlefield Publishers, Inc., 2000.

Garnham, Neal. "Both Praying and Playing: 'Muscular Christianity' and the YMCA in North-east County Durham." *Journal of Social History* 35 (Winter 2001): 397–407.

Gerring, John. *Party Ideologies in America, 1828–1996.* New York: Cambridge University Press, 1998.

Gidlow, Liette. *The Big Vote: Gender, Consumer Culture, and the Politics of Exclusion, 1890s–1920s.* Baltimore: Johns Hopkins University Press, 2004.

Gillespie, J. David. *Politics at the Periphery: Third Parties in Two-Party America.* Columbia: University of South Carolina Press, 1993.

Gillette, William. *Retreat from Reconstruction: 1869–1879.* Baton Rouge: Louisiana State University Press, 1979.

Ginzberg, Lori D. *Elizabeth Cady Stanton: An American Life.* New York: Hill and Wang, 2009.

Ginzberg, Lori D. *Untidy Origins: A Story of Woman's Rights in Antebellum New York.* Chapel Hill: University of North Carolina Press, 2005.

Ginzberg, Lori D. *Women and the Work of Benevolence: Morality, Politics, and Class in the Nineteenth-Century United States.* New Haven: Yale University Press, 1990.

Goldfield, David R. "The Urban South: A Regional Framework." *American Historical Review* 86 (December 1981): 1009–1034.

Goodman, Paul. *Towards a Christian Republic: Antimasonry and the Great Transition in New England.* New York: Oxford University Press, 1988.

Goodwyn, Lawrence. *The Populist Moment: A Short History of the Agrarian Revolt in America.* New York: Oxford University Press, 1978.

Gordon, Linda. *Heroes of their Own Lives: The Politics and History of Family Violence.* New York: Viking Press, 1988.

Gould, Lewis L. *Grand Old Party: A History of the Republicans.* New York: Random House, 2003.

Gould, Lewis L. *Progressives and Prohibitionists: Texas Democrats in the Wilson Era.* Austin: University of Texas Press, 1973.

Grace, Fran. *Carry A. Nation: Retelling the Life.* Bloomington: Indiana University Press, 2001.

Gray, Susan E. "Local Speculator as Confidence Man: Mumford Eldred, Jr., and the Michigan Land Rush." *Journal of the Early Republic* 10 (Autumn 1990): 383–406.

Griffin, Clifford S. *Their Brothers' Keeper: Moral Stewardship in the United States, 1800–1865.* 1960; Repr. Westwood, CT: Greenwood Press, 1983.

Grossman, James R., Ann Durkin Keating, and Janice L. Reiff, eds. *Encyclopedia of Chicago.* Chicago: University of Chicago Press, 2004.

Guinn, John F. "Father Mathew's Disciples: American Catholic Support for Temperance, 1840–1920." *Church History* 65 (December 1996): 624–640.

Gusfield, Joseph R. *Symbolic Crusade: Status Politics and the American Temperance Movement.* Urbana: University of Illinois Press, 1963.

Gustafson, Melanie. *Women and the Republican Party, 1854–1924.* Urbana: University of Illinois Press, 2001.

Gustafson, Melanie, Kristie Miller, and Elisabeth Israels Perry, eds. *We Have Come to Stay: American Women and Political Parties, 1880–1960.* Albuquerque: University of New Mexico Press, 1999.

Hales, Jean Gould. "Co-Laborers in the Cause: Women in the Ante-Bellum Nativist Movement." *Civil War History* 25 (1979): 119–138.

Hamm, Richard F. *Shaping the Eighteenth Amendment: Temperance Reform, Legal Culture, and the Polity, 1880–1920.* Chapel Hill: University of North Carolina Press, 1995.

Haskell, Thomas L. *The Emergence of Professional Social Science: The American Social Science Association and Nineteenth-Century Crisis of Authority.* Urbana: University of Illinois Press, 1977.

Hild, Matthew. *Greenbackers, Knights of Labor, and Populists: Farmer-Labor Insurgency in the Late-Nineteenth-Century South*. Athens: University of Georgia Press, 2007.

Hofstadter, Richard. *The Age of Reform: From Bryan to F.D.R.* New York: Vintage Books, 1955.

Hofstadter, Richard. *The Idea of a Party System: The Rise of Legitimate Opposition in the United States, 1780–1840*. Berkeley: University of California Press, 1970.

Houge, James Keith. *Uncivil War: Five New Orleans Street Battles and the Rise and Fall of Radical Reconstruction*. Baton Rouge: Louisiana State University Press, 2006.

Ickes, Harold L. "Who Killed the Progressive Party?" *American Historical Review* 46 (January 1941): 306–337.

Isaac, Paul E. *Prohibition and Politics: Turbulent Decades in Tennessee, 1885–1920*. Knoxville: University of Tennessee Press, 1965.

Ivy, James D. *No Saloon in the Valley: The Southern Strategy of Texas Prohibitionists in the 1880s*. Waco, TX: Baylor University Press, 2003.

Kazin, Michael. *The Populist Persuasion: An American History*. New York: Basic Books, 1995.

Keire, Mara L. "Dope Fiends and Degenerates: The Gendering of Addiction in the Early Twentieth Century." *Journal of Social History* 31 (Summer 1998): 809–822.

Keire, Mara L. "The Vice Trust: A Reinterpretation of the White Slavery Scare in the United States, 1907–1917." *Journal of Social History* 35 (Autumn 2001): 5–41.

Keller, Morton. *Affairs of State: Public Life in Late Nineteenth Century America*. Cambridge, MA: The Belknap Press of Harvard University Press, 1977.

Keller, Morton. *The Life Insurance Enterprise, 1885–1910: A Study in the Limits of Corporate Power*. Cambridge, MA: Belknap Press of Harvard University Press, 1963.

Keller, Morton. *Regulating a New Society: Public Policy and Social Change in America, 1900–1933*. Cambridge, MA: Harvard University Press, 1994.

Kerr, K. Austin. *Organized for Prohibition: A New History of the Anti-Saloon League*. New Haven: Yale University Press, 1985.

Key, V.O., Jr. *Politics, Parties, and Pressure Groups*. New York: Thomas Y. Crowell Company, 1942.

Key, V.O., Jr. *Public Opinion and American Democracy*. New York: Alfred A. Knopf, 1961.

Key, V.O., Jr. "Secular Realignment and the Party System." *Journal of Politics* 21 (1959): 198–210.

Key, V.O., Jr. *Southern Politics in State and Nation*. New York: Alfred A. Knopf, 1949.

Kimmel, Michael S. *Manhood in America: A Cultural History*. 2nd ed. 1998; New York: Oxford University Press, 2006.

Kipnis, Ira. *American Socialist Movement, 1897–1912*. New York: Columbia University Press, 1968.

Kleppner, Paul. *Continuity and Change in Electoral Politics, 1893–1928.* New York: Greenwood Press, 1987.

Kleppner, Paul. *The Third Electoral System, 1853–1892.* Chapel Hill: University of North Carolina Press, 1979.

Kleppner, Paul. *Who Voted?: The Dynamics of Electoral Turnout, 1870–1980.* New York: Praeger Publishers, 1982.

Kornbluh, Mark. *Why America Stopped Voting: The Decline of Participatory Democracy and the Emergence of Modern American Politics.* New York: New York University Press, 2000.

Kraditor, Aileen S. *Means and Ends in American Abolitionism: Garrison and his Critics on Strategy and Tactics, 1834–1850.* New York: Vintage Books, 1970.

Kuhn, Henry, and Olive M. Johnson. *The Socialist Labor Party During Four Decades, 1890–1930.* Brooklyn: New York Labor News, 1969.

Kyvig, David E. *Explicit and Authentic Acts: Amending the Constitution, 1776–1995.* Lawrence: University Press of Kansas, 1996.

Kyvig, David E., ed. *Law, Alcohol, and Order: Perspectives on National Prohibition.* Westport, CT: Greenwood Press, 1985.

Kyvig, David E. *Repealing National Prohibition.* Chicago: University of Chicago Press, 1979.

Kyvig, David E., ed. *Unintended Consequences of Constitutional Amendments.* Athens: University of Georgia Press, 2000.

Kyvig, David E. "Women Against Prohibition." *American Quarterly* 28 (Autumn 1976): 465–482.

Laurie, Bruce. *Beyond Garrison: Antislavery and Social Reform.* New York: Cambridge University Press, 2005.

"Legal Barriers Confronting Third Parties: The Progressive Party in Illinois." *University of Chicago Law Review* 16 (Spring 1949): 499–523.

"Legal Obstacles to Minor Party Success," *Yale Law Journal* 57 (June 1948): 1276–1297.

Lender, Mark Edward. *Dictionary of American Temperance Biography: From Temperance Reform to Alcohol Research, the 1600s to the 1980s.* Westport, CT: Greenwood Press, 1984.

Leonard, Gerald. *The Invention of Party Politics: Federalism, Popular Sovereignty, and Constitutional Development in Jacksonian Illinois.* Chapel Hill: University of North Carolina Press, 2002.

Lewis, Michael. "Access to Saloons, Wet Voter Turnout, and Statewide Prohibition Referenda, 1907–1919." *Social Science History* 32 (Fall 2008): 373–404.

Lewis-Beck, Michael, and Peverill Squire. "The Politics of Institutional Choice: Presidential Ballot Access for Third Parties in the United States." *British Journal of Political Science* 25 (October 1995): 419–427.

Lipset, Seymour Martin and Gary Marks. *It Didn't Happen Here: Why Socialism Failed in the United States.* New York: W.W. Norton, 2000.

Long, Lisa A. *Rehabilitating Bodies: Health, History, and the American Civil War.* Philadelphia: University of Pennsylvania Press, 2003.

Loomis, Christopher M. "The Politics of Uncertainty: Lobbyists and Propaganda in Early Twentieth-Century America." *Journal of Policy* History 21 (2009): 187–213.

Maisel, L. Sandy. *Parties and Elections in America: The Electoral Process.* 2nd ed. New York: McGraw-Hill, Inc., 1993.

Marsden, George M. *Fundamentalism and American Culture: The Shaping of Twentieth-Century Evangelicalism, 1870–1925.* New York: Oxford University Press, 1980.

Marszalek, John F., and Wilson D. Miscamble, eds. *American Political History: Essays on the State of the Discipline.* Notre Dame: University of Notre Dame Press, 1997.

Materson, Lisa G. "African American Women, Prohibition, and the 1928 Presidential Election." *Journal of Women's History* 21 (Spring 2009): 63–86.

Matthews, Jean V. *The Rise of the New Woman: The Women's Movement in America, 1875–1930.* Chicago: Ivan R. Dee, 2003.

Mattson, Kevin. *Creating a Democratic Republic: The Struggle for Urban Participatory Democracy during the Progressive Era.* University Park: Pennsylvania State University Press, 1998.

Mayer, George H. *The Republican Party, 1854–1966.* 2nd ed. New York: Oxford University Press, 1967.

Mayfield, John. *Rehearsal for Republicanism: Free Soil and the Politics of Antislavery.* Port Washington, NY: Kennikat Press, 1980.

McCaffery, Peter. *When Bosses Ruled Philadelphia: The Emergence of the Republican Machine, 1867–1933.* University Park: Pennsylvania State University Press, 1993.

McCormick, Richard L. "The Discovery that Business Corrupts Politics: A Reappraisal of the Origins of Progressivism." *American Historical Review* 86 (April 1981): 247–274.

McCormick, Richard L. *The Party Period and Public Policy: American Politics from the Age of Jackson to the Progressive Era.* New York: Oxford University Press, 1986.

McGerr, Michael E. *The Decline of Popular Politics: The American North, 1865–1928.* New York: Oxford University Press, 1986.

McGerr, Michael E. "Political Style and Women's Power, 1830–1930." *Journal of American History* 77 (December 1990): 315–333.

McLaughlin, Andrew C. *The Courts, the Constitution, and Parties: Studies in Constitutional History and Politics.* Chicago: University of Chicago Press, 1912.

Merriam, Charles E. *Primary Elections: A Study of the History and Tendencies of Primary Election Legislation.* Chicago: University of Chicago Press, 1912.

Milkis, Sidney M. *Political Parties and Constitutional Government: Remaking American Politics.* Baltimore: Johns Hopkins University Press, 1999.

Milkis, Sidney M. *The President and the Parties: The Transformation of the American Party System Since the New Deal.* New York: Oxford University Press, 1993.

Milkis, Sidney M. *Theodore Roosevelt, the Progressive Party, and the Transformation of American Democracy.* Lawrence: University Press of Kansas, 2009.

Miller, Sally M. *Victor Berger and the Promise of Constructive Socialism, 1910–1920.* Westport, CT: Greenwood Press, 1973.

Mittelman, Amy. *Brewing Battles: A History of American Beer*. New York: Algora Publishing, 2008.

Muncy, Robin. *Creating a Female Dominion in American Reform, 1890–1935*. New York: Oxford University Press, 1991.

Muncy, Robin. "Trustbusting and White Manhood in America, 1898–1914," *American Studies* 38 (Fall 1997): 21–42.

Murdock, Catherine Gilbert. *Domesticating Drink: Women, Men, and Alcohol in America, 1870–1940*. Baltimore: Johns Hopkins University Press, 1998.

Murphy, Kevin. *Political Manhood: Red Bloods, Mollycoddles, and the Politics of Progressive Era Reform*. New York: Columbia University Press, 2008.

Murphy, Sharon Ann. *Investing in Life: Insurance in Antebellum America*. Baltimore, MD: Johns Hopkins University Press, 2010.

Ness, Immanuel, and James Ciment, eds. *The Encyclopedia of Third Parties in America*. Armonk, NY: Sharpe Reference, 2000.

Norwood, Stephen H. "The Student as Strikebreaker: College Youth and the Crisis of Masculinity in the Early Twentieth Century." *Journal of Social History* 28 (Winter 1994): 331–349.

Odegard, Peter H. *Pressure Politics: The Story of the Anti-Saloon League*. New York: Columbia University Press, 1928.

Ostrander, Gilman M. *The Prohibition Movement in California, 1848–1933*. Berkeley: University of California Press, 1957.

Parsons, Elaine Frantz. *Manhood Lost: Drunken Men and Redeeming Women in the Nineteenth-Century United States*. Baltimore: Johns Hopkins University Press, 2003.

Pascoe, Peggy. *Relations of Rescue: The Search for Female Moral Authority in the American West, 1874–1939*. New York: Oxford University Press, 1990.

Patterson, Martha H. *Beyond the Gibson Girl: Reimagining the American New Woman, 1895–1915*. Urbana: University of Illinois Press, 2005.

Pearson, C.C., and J. Edwin Hendricks. *Liquor and Anti-Liquor in Virginia, 1619–1919*. Durham, NC: Duke University Press, 1967.

Pegram, Thomas R. *Battling Demon Rum: The Struggle for a Dry America, 1800–1933*. Chicago: Ivan R. Dee, 1998.

Pegram, Thomas R. "The Dry Machine: The Formation of the Anti-Saloon League of Illinois." *Illinois Historical Journal* 83 (Autumn 1990): 173–186.

Pegram, Thomas R. "Temperance Politics and Regional Political Culture: The Anti-Saloon League in Maryland and the South, 1907–1915." *Journal of Southern History* 63 (February 1997): 57–90.

Perman, Michael. *The Road to Redemption: Southern Politics, 1869–1879*. Chapel Hill: University of North Carolina Press, 1984.

Petit, Jeanne. "Breeders, Workers, and Mothers: Gender and the Congressional Literacy Test Debate, 1896–1897." *Journal of the Gilded Age and Progressive Era* 3 (January 2004): 35–58.

Pierson, Michael. *Free Hearts and Free Men: Gender and American Antislavery Politics*. Chapel Hill: University of North Carolina Press, 2003.

Pinchot, Amos R.E. *History of the Progressive Party, 1912–1916*. 1958; New York: New York University Press, 1978.

Pivar, David Jay. *Purity Crusade: Sexual Morality and Social Control, 1868–1900.* Westport, CT: Greenwood Press, 1973.

Powell, Lawrence N. *New Masters: Northern Planters During the Civil War and Reconstruction.* New Haven: Yale University Press, 1980.

Puth, Robert C. "Supreme Life: The History of a Negro Life Insurance Company, 1919–1962." *Business History Review* 43 (Spring 1969): 1–20.

Putney, Clifford. *Muscular Christianity: Manhood and Sports in Protestant America, 1880–1920.* Cambridge, MA: Harvard University Press, 2001.

Reichley, James. *The Life of the Parties: A History of American Political Parties.* New York: Free Press, 1992.

Reps, John W. *The Making of Urban America: A History of City Planning in the United States.* Princeton: Princeton University Press, 1965.

Reynolds, John F. *The Demise of the American Convention System, 1880–1911.* New York: Cambridge University Press, 2006.

Richardson, Darcy G. *Others: 'Fighting Bob' La Follette and the Progressive Movement: Third-Party Politics in the 1920s.* New York: iUniverse, Inc., 2008.

Richardson, Heather Cox. *The Death of Reconstruction: Race, Labor, and Politics in the Post-Civil War North, 1865–1901.* Cambridge: Harvard University Press, 2001.

Ritter, Gretchen. *Greenbacks and Goldbugs: The Antimonopoly Tradition and the Politics of Finance in America.* New York: Cambridge University Press, 1997.

Rodgers, Daniel T. "In Search of Progressivism." *Reviews in American History* 10 (December 1982): 113–132.

Rorabaugh, William J. *The Alcoholic Republic: An American Tradition.* New York: Oxford University Press, 1979.

Rose, Kenneth D. *American Women and the Repeal of Prohibition.* New York: New York University Press, 1996.

Rosenstone, Steven J., Roy L. Behr, and Edward H. Lazarus. *Third Parties in America: Citizen Response to Major Party Failure.* 2nd ed. Princeton, NJ: Princeton University Press, 1996.

Rotundo, E. Anthony. *American Manhood: Transformations in Masculinity from the Revolution to the Modern Era.* New York: Basic Books, 1993.

Rusk, Jerrold G. "The Effect of the Australian Ballot Reform on Split Ticket Voting: 1876–1908." *American Political Science Review* 64 (December 1970): 1220–1238.

Ryan, Mary. *Civic Wars: Democracy and Public Life in the American City during the Nineteenth Century.* Berkeley: University of California Press, 1997.

Ryan, Mary. *Women in Public: Between Banners and Bullets, 1825–1880.* Baltimore: Johns Hopkins University Press, 1990.

Sanders, Elizabeth. *Roots of Reform: Farmers, Workers and the American State, 1877–1917.* Chicago: The University of Chicago Press, 1999.

Schafer, Joseph. "Prohibition in Early Wisconsin." *Wisconsin Magazine of History* 8 (March 1925): 281–299.

Schlesinger, Arthur Meier. *The Rise of the City, 1878–1898.* 1933; repr. Columbus: Ohio State University Press, 1999.

Schlesinger, Arthur M., Jr., ed. *History of U.S. Political Parties*. New York: Chelsea House Publishers, 1973.

Schneirov, Richard. "Thoughts on Periodizing the Gilded Age: Capital Accumulation, Society, and Politics, 1873–1898." *Journal of the Gilded Age and Progressive Era* 5 (June 2006): 189–224.

Schrad, Mark Lawrence. "The First Social Policy: Alcohol Control and Modernity in Policy Studies." *Journal of Policy History* 19 (2007): 428–458.

Schudson, Michael. *The Good Citizen: A History of American Civic Life*. New York: The Free Press, 1998.

Sheehan, Michael F. "Land Speculation in Southern California." *American Journal of Economics and Sociology* 42 (April 1982): 197–209.

Shelley, Jack, and Jere Hall, eds. *Valley of Challenge and Change: A History of Roane County, Tennessee, 1860–1900*. Kingston, TN: Roane County Heritage Commission, 1986.

Shumsky, Neil Larry, ed. *Urbanization and the Growth of Cities*. Vol. 1. New York: Garland Publishing, Inc., 1996.

Silbey, Joel H. *The American Political Nation, 1838–1893*. Stanford: Stanford University Press, 1991.

Silbey, Joel H. *The Partisan Imperative: The Dynamics of American Politics before the Civil War*. New York: Oxford University Press, 1985.

Silbey, Joel H. *A Respectable Minority: The Democratic Party in the Civil War Era, 1860–1868*. New York: W.W. Norton and Company, 1977.

Sinclair, Andrew. *Era of Excess: A Social History of the Prohibition Movement*. 1962; repr. New York: Harper & Row Publishers, 1964.

Sismondo, Christine. *America Walks into a Bar: A Spirited History of Taverns and Saloons, Speakeasies and Grog Shops*. New York: Oxford University Press, 2011.

Skocpol, Theda. *Diminished Democracy: From Membership to Management in American Civic Life*. Normon: University of Oklahoma Press, 2003.

Skowronek, Steven. *Building a New American State: The Expansion of National Administrative Capacities, 1877–1920*. New York: Cambridge University Press, 1992.

Spann, Edward K. *Brotherly Tomorrows: Movements for a Cooperative Society in America, 1820–1920*. New York: Columbia University Press, 1989.

Sproat, John G. *"The Best Men": Liberal Reformers in the Gilded Age*. 1968; repr. Chicago: University of Chicago Press, 1982.

Stanley, Amy Dru. *From Bondage to Contract: Wage Labor, Marriage, and the Market in the Age of Slave Emancipation*. New York: Cambridge University Press, 1998.

Stewart, James Brewer. *Holy Warriors: The Abolitionists and American Slavery*. 1976; repr. New York: Hill and Wang, 1997.

Storms, Roger. *Partisan Prophets: A History of the Prohibition Party, 1854–1972*. Denver, CO: National Prohibition Foundation, Inc., 1972.

Summers, Mark Wahlgren. *Era of Good Stealings*. New York: Oxford University Press, 1993.

Summers, Mark Wahlgren. *Party Games: Getting, Keeping, and Using Power in Gilded Age Politics*. Chapel Hill: University of North Carolina Press, 2004.

Summers, Mark Wahlgren. *Rum, Romanism, and Rebellion: The Making of a President, 1884*. Chapel Hill: University of North Carolina Press, 2000.

Sundquist, James. *Dynamics of the Party System*. Rev. ed. Washington, DC: The Brookings Institution, 1983.

Swierenga, Robert. "Land Speculation and its Impact on American Economic Growth and Welfare: A Historiographical Review." *Western Historical Quarterly* 8 (July 1977): 283–302.

Szymanski, Ann-Marie E. *Pathways to Prohibition: Radicals, Moderates, and Social Movement Outcomes*. Durham: Duke University Press, 2003.

Taylor, Alan. *Liberty Men and Great Proprietors: The Revolutionary Settlement on the Maine Frontier, 1760–1820*. Chapel Hill: University of North Carolina Press, 1990.

Taylor, Michael. "The Bicycle Boom and the Bicycle Bloc: Cycling and Politics in the 1890s." *Indiana Magazine of History* 104 (September 2008): 213–240.

Thomas, Harrison Cook. *The Return of the Democratic Party to Power in 1884*. New York: Columbia University Press, 1919.

Timberlake, James H. *Prohibition and the Progressive Movement, 1900–1920*. Cambridge: Harvard University Press, 1966.

Tyrrell, Ian. "Drink and Temperance in the Antebellum South: An Overview and Interpretation." *Journal of Southern History* 48, no. 4 (November 1982): 485–510.

Tyrrell, Ian. *Sobering Up: From Temperance to Prohibition in Antebellum America, 1800–1860*. Westport, CT: Greenwood Press, 1979.

Tyrrell, Ian. *Woman's World / Woman's Empire: The Woman's Christian Temperance Union in International Perspective, 1800–1930*. Chapel Hill: University of North Carolina Press, 1991.

Varon, Elizabeth R. "Tippecanoe and the Ladies, Too: White Women and Party Politics in Antebellum Virginia." *Journal of American History* 82 (September 1995): 494–521.

Volk, Kyle. *Moral Minorities & the Making of American Democracy* (forthcoming, Oxford University Press).

Volk, Kyle. "The Perils of 'Pure Democracy': Minority Rights, Liquor Politics, and popular Sovereignty in Antebellum America." *Journal of the Early Republic* 29 (Winter 2009): 641–679.

Volpe, Vernon L. *Forlorn Hope of Freedom: The Liberty Party in the Old Northwest, 1838–1848*. Kent, OH: Kent State University Press, 1990.

Voss-Hubbard, Mark. *Beyond Party: Cultures of Antipartisanship in Northern Politics before the Civil War*. Baltimore: Johns Hopkins University Press, 2002.

Walters, Ronald G. *American Reformers, 1815–1860*. New York: Hill and Wang, 1978.

Ware, Alan. "Anti-Partisan and Party Control of Political Reform in the United States: The Case of the Australian Ballot." *British Journal of Political Science* 30 (January 2000): 1–29.

Ware, Alan. *The American Direct Primary: Party Institutionalization and Transformation in the North*. New York: Cambridge University Press, 2002.

Warner, Harry S. *An Evolution of the Understanding of the Problem of Alcohol: A History of College Idealism*. Boston: Christopher Publishing House, 1966.

Weare, Walter B. *Black Business in the New South: A Social History of the North Carolina Mutual Life Insurance Company*. 1973; repr. Durham, NC: Duke University Press, 1993.

White, Dana F., and Victor A. Kramer, eds. *Olmstead South: Old South Critic/ New South Planner*. Westport, CT: Greenwood Press, 1979.

White, Richard. "Information, Markets, and Corruption: Transcontinental Railroads in the Gilded Age." *Journal of American History* 90 (June 2003): 19–43.

Wiebe, Robert. *The Search for Order, 1877–1920*. New York: Hill and Wang, 1967.

Woodson, C.G. "Insurance Business Among Negroes." *Journal of Negro History* 14 (April 1929): 202–226.

Woodward, C. Vann. *Origins of the New South, 1877–1913*. 1951; repr. Baton Rouge: Louisiana State University Press, 1971.

Zelizer, Viviana A. Rotman. *Morals and Markets: The Development of Life Insurance in the United States*. New York: Columbia University Press, 1979.

Zimmerman, Jonathan. *Distilling Democracy: Alcohol Education in America's Public Schools, 1880–1925*. Lawrence: University Press of Kansas, 1999.

Index

CPSIA information can be obtained at www.ICGtesting.com
Printed in the USA
LVOW08s1723010416

481764LV00001B/94/P